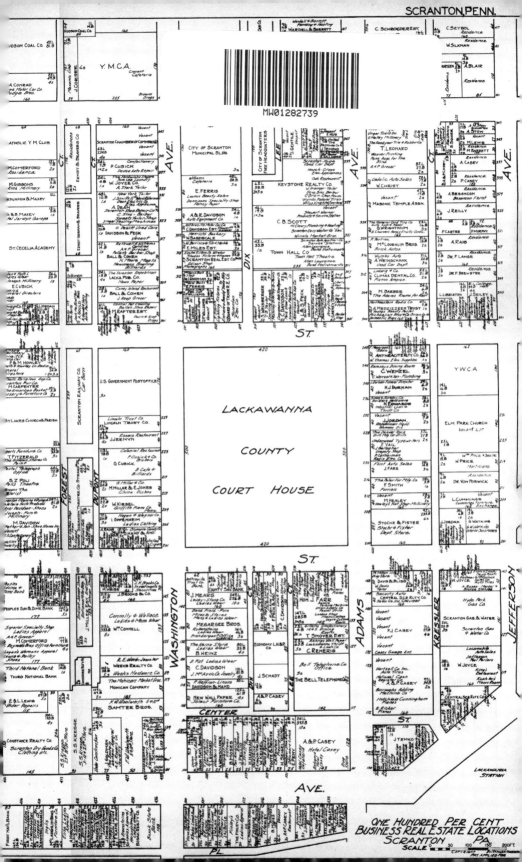

LACKAWANNA

COUNTY

COURT HOUSE

• • •

Advance Praise

Few would dispute that Jane Jacobs has changed the way generations see and experience cities. But no one before Glenna Lang has probed so fully where Jacobs herself gained that vision. In this beautifully composed, deeply researched, and fascinating twin portrait of Jacobs and her hometown of Scranton, Lang reveals how this medium-size city built on anthracite coal shaped an urban ideal that would ultimately reverberate worldwide.

> —**Lizabeth Cohen**, Harvard University; author of Bancroft
> Prize-winning *Saving America's Cities: Ed Logue and the
> Struggle to Renew Urban America in the Suburban Age*

Jane Jacobs's First City is a brilliant work of scholarship that convincingly shows how Jane Jacobs's canonical works developed in the historic, mid-sized city of Scranton. It is clearly a labor of love, of great dedication, and filled with appreciation for all of its subjects, not only Jane Butzner [Jacobs]. The overwhelmingly new material, brilliantly contextualized, will have a lasting impact.

> —**Peter Laurence**, Associate Professor of Architecture,
> Clemson University; author of *Becoming Jane Jacobs*

A fascinating and wonderfully written book that shows how Scranton played an enormous role in shaping Jane Jacobs's thinking about urban life. It reframes not only who Jacobs was, but also what Scranton was in the early 20th century.

> —**Mark Hirsch**, Senior Historian, National Museum
> of the American Indian, Smithsonian Institution

In your hands is a cornucopia of discoveries, one excavation after another, about how and what Jane Jacobs came to know about the connection between cities and the people who live in them. Here's a snapshot of five-year-old Jane in her father's open-air car, in Scranton—Jane *in a car* for goodness' sake—on the street where she grew up, or a description of teenager Jane at the top of the stairs, listening to her father with his medical colleagues in the living room below, discussing the new ideas of Dr. Freud. These were secrets until Glenna Lang dug them out. What luck!

    —**Max Allen**, Jane Jacobs's producer for the Massey Lectures on CBC
      Radio and editor of *Ideas That Matter: The Worlds of Jane Jacobs*

This book is well written and wise. I felt a nostalgic yearning for a Scranton of this era, which is the America that produced my mother's side of the family. It restores and presents Scranton in all its subdued glory with ordinary men, women, and children going about their daily business, creating, as though Muybridge had photographed it, the mosaic of Scranton life, with its resplendent color and texture, so deeply American. We need to think about what this means to us, especially at the present moment.

    —**Chandos Brown**, Professor of History and American Studies,
      College of William and Mary

Glenna Lang paints a compelling picture of Scranton's rich history and community-centered way of life, and how these molded Jane Jacobs's influential ideas and writing about cities. *Jane Jacobs's First City* illustrates Scranton as an attractive place to raise a family, make an impact in the community, and develop lifelong relationships—all of which remain true to this day, and which we continue to foster and embrace.

    —**Paige Gebhardt Cognetti**, Mayor, City of Scranton

Jane Jacobs's
First City

Jane Jacobs's
First City

• • •

*Learning from
Scranton, Pennsylvania*

GLENNA LANG

NEW VILLAGE PRESS • NEW YORK

Published in the United States by New Village Press
bookorders@newvillagepress.net
www.newvillagepress.org
New Village Press is a public-benefit, nonprofit publisher
Distributed by NYU Press

Hardcover ISBN: 978-1-61332-139-3
Paperback ISBN: 978-1-61332-138-6
EBook ISBN: 978-1-61332-140-9
EBook Institutional ISBN: 978-1-61332-141-6

Publication Date: May 2021
First Edition

Library of Congress Cataloging-in-Publication Data

Names: Lang, Glenna, author.
Title: Jane Jacobs's first city : learning from Scranton, Pennsylvania / Glenna Lang.
Description: First edition. | New York : New Village Press, 2021. | Includes bibliographical refer-
  ences and index. | Summary: "The late urbanist and author Jane Jacobs's canonical work on the
  life and planning of great cities and on city and national economies grew from social and ethical
  foundations formed in her home city, Scranton, Pennsylvania. The book is a detailed portrait of
  Jane's early life and of the city she grew up in. It shows the development of Jane's acute observational abilities from childhood through her desire in early adulthood to understand and write
  about what she saw. The seeds of her ideas developed in Scranton - once the thriving anthracite-mining capital of the world - that shared many qualities with other medium-size, industrial
  cities of the early twentieth century. It was a place of great diversity. Small businesses flourished
  and a wide variety of ethnic groups, including African Americans, lived cheek by jowl. Even
  recent immigrants could save enough to buy a house. Quality public education was cherished
  and supported by all. Opposing political parties joined forces to tackle problems, newspapers
  gathered and reported information with a sense of civic purpose and responsibility, and citizens
  worked together for the public good. The book demonstrates why, at the end of Jacobs's life,
  her thoughts and conversations increasingly turned to Scranton and the potential for cohesion
  and inclusiveness held by contemporary medium-size cities"—Provided by publisher.
Identifiers: LCCN 2020043451 (print) | LCCN 2020043452 (ebook) | ISBN 9781613321393
  (hardcover) | ISBN 9781613321386 (paperback) | ISBN 9781613321409 (ebook) |
  ISBN 9781613321416 (ebook other)
Subjects: LCSH: Jacobs, Jane, 1916–2006. | Scranton (Pa.)—History. | Women authors, American
  —20th century—Biography.
Classification: LCC F159.S4 L36 2021 (print) | LCC F159.S4 (ebook) | DDC 307.1/216092 [B]—dc23
LC record available at https://lccn.loc.gov/2020043451
LC ebook record available at https://lccn.loc.gov/2020043452

Front cover photo, top: Scranton, looking south from YMCA building, 1905–1920. Courtesy of
  Springfield College Archives and Special Collections. *Front cover photo, center:* Jane Butzner,
  c. winter 1925–1926. Estate of Jane Jacobs. *Back jacket flap photo:* Esmé von Hoffman
Illustration p. viii–ix: Panoramic View of Scranton, Pennsylvania, 1890. Courtesy of Library of
  Congress, Geography and Map Division. *Endpapers:* City of Scranton, Pennsylvania, 1929,
  central city streets, by Nathan Nirenstein, Springfield, Massachusetts. Courtesy of Susan
  Carter White Pieroth, Lackawanna County, PAGenWeb: lackawannapagenweb.com
Cover design: Lynne Elizabeth. *Interior design and composition:* Leigh McLellan Design

• • •

In memory of my guides and inspirations who were
not able to finish this journey with me

I'm telling you all this because I don't want to take it with me.
—Marie Van Bergen Mansuy (1915–2012)

Mary Catharine "Kay" Schoen Butzner (1920–2013)

Jane Butzner Henderson (1946–2016)

Gladys Engel Lang (1919–2016)

Kurt Lang (1924–2019)

• • •

Contents

LACKAWANA   RIVER.

WASHINGTON   AVE.

ROARING   BROOK.

LACKAWAN

SCRA

DRAWN BY T.M. FOWLER & JAS. B. MOYER

1 PUBLIC SCHOOLS
2 DICKSON MANF'G CO.
3 LOCOMOTIVE WORKS
4 DICKS STEEL WORKS
5 BRASS WORKS JAS. M. EVERHART, PRO
6 SCRANTON GLASS CO. WORKS
7 IRON FORGE JAS. MOFFIT & SPENCER.
8 MEARS & HAGEN HALL
9 ARMORY
10 COURT HOUSE
11 L. & B. DEPOT
12 ROLLING MILL N° 1, L.I.C. CO.
13 BLAST FURNACE

17 ROLLING MILL N° 2, & STEEL WORKS
18 DRINKER & MACHINE SHOPS
19 HAMPTON COLLIERY L. I. & C. CO.
20 D.L. & W. SHOPS
21 DIAMOND BREAKER ----- D. L. & W.
22 OXFORD BREAKER "   "
23 HAMPTON BREAKER "   "
24 CAYUGA "   "
25 MANVILLE ------ D. H. & D. L. & W.
26 O. S. JOHNSON
27 GAS WORKS
28 PROVIDENCE COAL CO. BREAKER
29 TRIPP COAL CO. 2ND OPENING

ON PENN.
90.

* * *

"My Own City"

A CURIOUS AND OBSERVANT girl named Jane Butzner was born and spent her most formative years in the anthracite coal–mining capital of the world, Scranton, Pennsylvania. In November 1934, at age eighteen, she made a beeline for New York City, began her career as a writer, met her life partner, and became the well-known Jane Jacobs, whose ideas would indelibly affect the world's thinking about cities. Her groundbreaking book, *The Death and Life of Great American Cities*, argued vividly and compellingly against the prevailing wisdom that cities had little value and were best renewed through wholesale obliteration of run-down areas and old neighborhoods. Meticulously, Jacobs analyzed the components of a city and what made cities flourish or decline. *Death and Life* has remained in print continuously since it first sent out shock waves in 1961. It has been translated into at least thirty languages. Today, we have absorbed into our thinking about cities the concepts she identified in her book. We recognize the ideas of mixed uses, density, walkability, and "eyes on the street" as fundamental to our once again thriving and desirable urban centers.[1]

To build her case, Jacobs famously described what she saw from her Greenwich Village windows as a "sidewalk ballet," a round-the-clock procession of characters going about their daily lives. Although she threaded supporting examples throughout her book from other great American cities, critics dismissed her conclusions as relying too heavily on her observations of the unconventional New York City neighborhood. Jane never specifically cited Scranton in *Death and Life*, yet the seeds of her ideas about cities originated in her years during the 1920s and 1930s in her home city in northeastern Pennsylvania. Here she witnessed and experienced the cohesion of the many types of diversity and the messy complexity of her city, and she learned the function and necessity of close-knit neighborhoods. In an era now vanishing from memory, in this medium-size city, citizens regularly participated in neighborhood as well as citywide activities, fostering a strong sense of community, social responsibility, and civic pride.

A far cry from the past-its-prime backwater depicted in the hit television show *The Office*, Scranton—when Jane was growing up there—was prosperous, attractive, and the third most populous city in Pennsylvania, trailing only Philadelphia and Pittsburgh. An early adapter of technology, Scranton took the nickname "the Electric City" because it boasted the nation's first successful electric streetcar system. Its downtown streets were lined with impressive architecture and jammed with people and vehicles. Fine stores drew crowds from the city and its region, as did institutions such as theaters, clubs, a museum, a central public reference library, schools, and colleges. By the late nineteenth century, Scranton thrived as an iron- and steel-manufacturing center supported by a network of railroads. Fueling the iron and steel furnaces—and a wealth of other industries, includ-ing the textile factories, where women worked—the hard anthracite coal that burned hot and clean constituted the basis of the city's robust economy. At the turn of the nineteenth century, when the largest steel producer left town unexpectedly, the city relied ever more heavily on its single plentiful natural resource, which it exported to industrial areas around the United States. In 1909, when Jane's parents set-tled together in the city, Scranton reigned as the premier city of the anthracite-mining region. Ninety-five percent of American anthra-cite lay under this five-hundred-square-mile swath in Pennsylvania's Wyoming-Lackawanna Valley. During their peak year of production

Coal miners, each missing a leg. Photo by Hudson Coal Company
photographer John Horgan, Jr., c. 1920–1925. Courtesy of
Pennsylvania Anthracite Heritage Museum.

in 1917, the state's anthracite miners extracted 100 million tons of
hard coal.[2]

From early childhood on, and certainly before she turned ten, Jane
developed a passion for urban life. Her attraction to the central-city
section of her hometown was so overpowering that it transformed
a trip to the dentist into an adventure. "These observations that I
made . . . in New York were not the first seeds of *The Death and Life
of Great American Cities*," Jane explained in her later years. "Actually
I was, from the time I was a very small child . . . interested in my own
city, Scranton, Pennsylvania, and I was interested especially in the
downtown. I was so interested in it that I liked it when I had a dental
appointment—and believe me it was not painless dentistry in those
days—but I liked it because I could go downtown. . . . I thought it
was fascinating. . . ."[3]

Naturally inquisitive and contemplative, young Jane closely observed her urban environment. Before she was old enough to go to school, she accompanied her parents and siblings along the blocks of various-size houses and clusters of stores. The slate sidewalks both annoyed and fascinated her. Towering coal breakers loomed in the distance, and light industry lay within a short walk from home. But the lure of downtown —with its grand railroad station, the motley shop windows "displaying individuality and imagination," and the stream of humanity in constant motion—stimulated Jane most of all. As a schoolgirl in the adjacent borough of Dunmore, Jane made friends and had classmates who reflected the area's diverse population. She explored the streets and alleys of her neighborhood and noted the small enterprises tucked in all over. In Girl Scouts, she practiced observation of nature and applied the same skills to studying the city. When she attended eighth grade and high school in central city, she reveled in her element. After graduating, Jane forswore college and apprenticed as a journalist at the city's morning newspaper, where she completely immersed herself in the myriad aspects and workings of her city.[4]

As a young reporter, Jane became increasingly aware of Scranton's anomalies and the dichotomies that coexisted in her city. Reputed for its superior public schools, the Electric City also had the most notorious and popular red-light district in the Northeast. Within walking distance from the magnificent edifices of downtown, the city was dotted with man-made hills of coal waste, visible reminders of the enormous amount of "black gold" extracted from the ground below and its heavy toll on the people who toiled there. Unlike those in any other city, Scranton's houses and other buildings regularly fell into the hollowed-out mines underlying much of the city, posing a constant, silent threat to its citizens.

Throughout her life, Jane's fundamental method of studying cities was to act as a city naturalist and observe "the immense number of parts that make up a city, and the immense diversity of those parts." She trusted her eyes and noted everything she saw. Then she mulled

Woolworth's central-city store, 317–319 Lackawanna Avenue, Scranton, 1920s. Courtesy of Norma Reese via Susan Pieroth.

over the interrelationship of the components. She came up with an unusual technique for testing her ideas and understanding her observations. Starting in childhood, partly to fend off boredom, she imagined conversing with historical figures unfamiliar with what she explained to them because they were from an earlier time. Thomas Jefferson, Ben Franklin, and eventually Cerdic the Saxon—in keeping with their particular interests and personalities—asked stimulating questions and helped Jane work through her thoughts.[5]

As an avid reader, Jane simultaneously soaked up the history of her own city. Beginning in 1840, entrepreneurs and innovators from the eastern seaboard as well as upstate New York and Pennsylvania launched a metropolis on a scantily populated site. The new settlement's iron forges, coal mines, railroads, and manufacturing proliferated at a remarkable pace. People moving westward, seeking opportunity, came to the fledgling Scranton in droves and contributed to the phenomenal rise of the city's industry and its diversifying economy. Among them, brothers C. S. (Charles Sumner) and F. W.

(Frank Winfield) Woolworth, after trying out their first variety store in Harrisburg, chose Scranton as the headquarters for their "five-and-ten-cent stores." In 1882, they opened a Woolworth's in the heart of the city and began what would become one of the largest international retail chains. Subsequently, C.S. built his French Renaissance Revival mansion in Scranton and made it his home base. Soon after Scranton's inception, immigrants from overseas began to pour in, eager to partake of the plentiful work in the mines, factories, and other businesses. The first wave of immigration brought Germans, Welsh, and Irish, while Polish, other Eastern Europeans, and Italians followed. Exceptionally large numbers of people emigrated from the anthracite-mining region of South Wales and the sulfur-mine area in Sicily. In Scranton, this assortment of people from various nations and of diverse ethnicities—both newcomers and earlier arrivals—resided close together amid industry and manufacturing.[6]

Jane's parents were among these opportunity seekers who set their sights on Scranton as a good place to start a business and raise a family. As new Scrantonians, they soon became active and engaged members of the community, participating in the abundant social, benevolent, and political organizations. Boy and Girl Scouts, religious institutions, clubs at school, and theatrical productions offered similar activities for school-age children. Scranton's intricate web of organizations and citywide events brought people together. Young and old, from all walks of life, pitched in during the city's yearly "clean-up" week and the annual Community Chest collection to help their fellow residents in need.

Compared to great metropolises like Philadelphia, the smaller city of Scranton was relatively tolerant, but it was not without discrimination, especially against African Americans and Jews. Schools and residences in close proximity constituted a polyglot population, so people of different backgrounds naturally interacted with one another. Jane and her three siblings—from a solidly middle-class family active in the Presbyterian church—went to public schools with and were taught by mainly working-class Catholics. The Butzner kids

Jane with her father in his car, backyard of Monroe Avenue house, perhaps off to tend patients, c. 1921. Estate of Jane Jacobs.

not only attended grammar school with children of miners but also continually confronted the coal breakers, where laborers sorted coal above the mines, while colliers entered and—if they were lucky— exited the shafts and tunnels below. These ominous-looking, looming structures punctuated the landscape of the city and its environs. When Jane attended school in central-city Scranton, she sat side by side with Eastern European Jewish and African American schoolmates. Her father, a physician, treated patients of varying means, including miners and immigrants who lived beyond the city limits and could not afford to pay him. On occasion, Jane accompanied her father in the car to visit them. Growing up with well-honed powers of observation in a close-grained, multicultural city helps explain why Jane would become an incisive analyst of urban life who appreciated and sympathized with the less advantaged. She was an ardent supporter of civil rights. In *Death and Life*, Jane stated in no uncertain terms, "our country's most serious social problem [is] segregation and discrimination," particularly of African Americans.[7]

To understand the roots of Jane's ideas in her childhood experiences and environment, I have sought to recover an almost-lost Scranton by reconstructing the physical and societal world in which she lived. I was extremely fortunate to discover Scrantonians who knew Jane as a youth. Conversations with young Jane's contemporaries who remembered her vividly, as well as with others who knew of her through a parent or friend, provided invaluable information and insights. A high school friend of Jane—and recent arrival from Italy—wrote an extraordinary narrative about his immigrant experience and life in the city in volume two, *Growing Up American,* of his memoir *The Education of a Reluctant Radical.* Others interviewed gave firsthand accounts of the city during this era. Jane's family members kindly allowed a rare peek into their collection of Jane's memorabilia. In discussions and writings throughout her life, Jane herself inserted elucidating anecdotes from her childhood and first city, thus leaving us her own accounts.[8]

Scranton was small enough that its daily newspapers covered innumerable details of ordinary life, including scholastic achievements, club activities, and social events— unparalleled reflections of a bygone era. Not only the city-desk reporters and women's-page writers but also the fastidious census takers, the collectors of data for city directories, the record keepers in schools, clubs, churches, City Hall, the courts, and more allowed me to assemble the pieces and get a feel for the community in which Jane came of age. Sadly, when Scranton's civic pride waned, not all city institutions preserved their records, considering them of little interest or value. But through the historical facts and documents that survived, frozen in time, without the distortion of hindsight, we come to know Jane's schoolmates and teachers, her neighbors, her church, the organizations she and her parents belonged to, her first mentors and coworkers, in addition to her own and her family's activities. These shreds of evidence reveal forgotten figures who influenced Jane and the lives of many Scrantonians. Delving into Jane's Scranton years led to unexpected discoveries—such as the considerable significance of the Girl Scouts and the African American community in Jane's life and in the city at large—some of which were previously unknown and others which contradicted family lore.

Not only the place where Jane grew up and the people with whom she came into contact but also the times in which she lived had a profound effect on this budding writer. Jane experienced Scranton between the disillusionment following the First World War and the deprivation of the Great Depression. In the intervening years, she saw enormous technological advances in communication, transportation, and machinery. The impact of new technology could be felt both at home and in the larger world, from appliances that lightened the burden of housework for women to the advent of radio broadcasting, the pervasive popularity of movies that talked, and the threefold increase in automobile ownership—and the accompanying traffic jams. In January 1920, when Jane was not quite four years old, the "Dries," whom her mother—but not her father—wholeheartedly supported, achieved their goal of nationwide prohibition of alcoholic beverages. Eight months later, after a seventy-two-year struggle, American women won the right to vote. Known as the Roaring Twenties with its "revolution in manners and morals," the decade ushered in the Prohibition work-around and requisite vice of speakeasies, which, unlike saloons, catered to men *and* women. Hemlines rose, and an ever growing number of women smoked cigarettes and, more important, entered the workforce. In 1920, for the first time, the U.S. Census tallied more people living in cities than in rural areas.[9]

Walking in Jane's footsteps of a century ago in contemporary Scranton conjures up a sense of her life and times. The buildings and the streetscapes that remain today lend clues that enable us to imagine her city of the latter 1910s through the early 1930s. The city's domestic, commercial, and civic architecture that stood at that point conveys the prevailing tastes and shows us how people lived and what they valued. From splendid structures built during Jane's day and prior to it, we see that Scranton exhibited great pride, embraced culture, valued education, and cared for its people.[10]

Early on, Jane's family, teachers, and the community recognized her talent for writing. From a young age, she also displayed great interest in history. When Jane was twenty-one, her great-aunt Hannah Breece entrusted her to shape her memoir for publication. Aunt Hannah had worked as a missionary and schoolteacher in the Alaskan wilderness for fourteen years, beginning at age forty-five, in 1904. She had kept journals and letters with accounts of her adventures, but she had failed to interest a publisher. In the 1990s, after setting aside the project for more than half a century, Jane took another look and, in her words, "got such a bang out of it, I just decided it should be published. Editing it was probably the three happiest months of my working life." To gain a better understanding of the material and fill gaps in the story, Jane, with a few family members, retraced Hannah's steps in Alaska and combed archives, where she discovered supplementary documents. "When I did the research in Alaska, I found myself wishing I had a whole extra life to live to be a historian."[11]

In *A Schoolteacher in Old Alaska*, Jane masterfully combined Hannah's writing with her memories of her great-aunt's character and what she gleaned from the archives and her visit to Alaska. Jane left us no draft of a memoir of her childhood in Scranton, but she recognized the importance of preserving a connection to what has come before. In *Cities and the Wealth of Nations*, Jane upheld the necessity of preserving the memory of how things had once been done and of the good things in a civilization before those—and the memories of those memories—disappear. She had witnessed this kind of amnesia while spending six months with her missionary aunt Martha Robison in a tiny backwoods hamlet of Appalachia, just before fulfilling her dream of moving to New York.[12]

Late in her career, Jane revealed to an interviewer, "I was always interested in cities and that is probably why I didn't just end up writing one book [on cities]." For more than forty years after the publication of *Death and Life*, with its Scranton underpinnings, Jane continued to ponder and write about what makes cities thrive or deteriorate. She examined the working components of cities, interacting spontaneously and constantly changing. "The other books since [*Death and Life*] are all in a sense sequels and outgrowths of it," Jane said. In her next two books, *The Economy of Cities* and *Cities and the Wealth of Nations*, she analyzed and expounded on the economic aspects of cities and their surrounding regions. She wrote *Systems of Survival* as a conversation on the "moral foundations of commerce and politics," a topic that no doubt presented itself in pondering the Mafia, which sank its first American roots in and around Scranton. All but *The Nature of Economies* and *The Question of Separatism* contain substantiating examples from and explicit references to Scranton. Jane's home city piqued her interest not only about cities but also about moral systems, economies, governments, and history.[13]

Neither an academic nor a professional urban planner, Jane Jacobs had the advantage of maintaining an unconfined and fresh perspective as an outsider. Although pundits positioning themselves at varying points on the political spectrum have tried to claim Jane as one of theirs, she was adamantly nonideological, a freethinker who refused to ally herself with a political party or doctrine of any sort. Her oeuvre embodied her tenets. She took a stand against large-scale, top-down plans and favored citizen participation and individualized solutions based on knowledge from local residents. She believed that urban planners should listen to and understand the needs of the neighborhood before offering their design solutions. Drawing conclusions from her own observations and commonsense analysis—a method anyone can use—Jacobs inspired people across America and the world to look at cities and their economies with a fresh eye. "Downtown is for people," she proclaimed, and cities should never be subordinate to cars. People should "get out and walk" and, in this way, get to know their cities. She extolled mom-and-pop stores and other small businesses interspersed in neighborhoods, which fostered community, as opposed to oversize chain stores and shopping malls. Jacobs supported filling in unused spaces and rehabilitating, rather than demolishing, old buildings. Always courageous and never afraid to speak up for what she believed, Jane—even as a child—took action when she thought it necessary.[14]

Jane had been born into Scranton's economic heyday. She was a child during two of its most crippling strikes and afterward watched the city's coal-centered economy sputter and, in the mid-1920s, begin its long descent as the nation turned toward other fuels. Scranton's depression, in essence, started before other parts of the country plummeted into the Great Depression. Living through the great crash and Depression heightened Jane's interest in the economy. The smaller scale of her city made it a veritable laboratory for studying the forces and factors of production, trade, services, capital, and labor.

Jane grew attached to each of the three cities—Scranton, New York, and Toronto—in which she lived consecutively for substantial numbers of years and to her primary abode in each. Manifesting her fondness for her childhood home in Scranton, Jane dedicated her very first and least-known book, *Constitutional Chaff*, "To 1712 Monroe Avenue." Columbia University Press published this reputable work about the rejected proposals of the Constitution's authors in 1941, when its author, then known as Jane Butzner, was twenty-five, single, and a six-year resident of New York. Twenty years later, Jane dedicated *Death and Life* "TO NEW YORK CITY, where I came to seek my fortune and found it by finding" her husband and three children. In 1992, at age seventy-six, she paid tribute in *Systems of Survival* to all three of her longtime homes. Its inscription read "To 1712 Monroe Avenue, 555 Hudson Street, and 69 Albany Avenue." Only in *Death and Life* did the dedication have a direct connection to the book's subject.

Even after she moved to New York, in 1934, and Toronto, in 1968, world-renowned author Jane Jacobs held on to her connection with Scranton. At first she returned to visit her mother and brothers, then to try to save her city economically and architecturally, next—for sentimental reasons—to attend her fiftieth high school reunion, and finally as a way station and touchstone following family funerals. In 1996, after her husband's burial in her family's plot near Bloomsburg, Pennsylvania, Jane proposed that a group of relatives detour to Scranton so that she could show them the city. She toured them through the downtown, pointing out what was left of the city's grandeur, and stopping in front of her unchanged childhood home. Particularly in her ninth decade, Jane thought about and often spoke of her hometown to those who looked to her for wisdom and fresh insights on urban matters. When author and social critic James Howard Kunstler traveled to Toronto to converse with Jane in 2000 for an article he planned to write about her in *Metropolis* magazine, he was somewhat exasperated. "I was planning to write a book on some doomer-ish themes such as peak oil, climate change, and other converging catastrophes of the day, and I thought Jane might shed some light on these things. But she kept on deflecting my questions," he complained. "All she wanted to talk about was growing up in Scranton, Pennsylvania."[15]

In her final years, I believe, Jane, the unfettered and iconoclastic thinker, now internationally hailed, was reexamining her Scranton roots and the ties that bound her to her first city. She understood the worth of smaller, gritty cities and lessons we might take from them and from the shared values of the people in the time and place in which she had grown up. Ultimately, this book presents a dual portrait of Jane Jacobs and her city of Scranton. It considers the importance of not only great but also medium-size cities, an issue that seemed to loom ever larger in Jane Jacobs's mind toward the end of her life, when her ruminations returned to the vibrant, diverse, empathic community at a human scale that had first nurtured her and her ideas.

SCRANTON, PA.   Washington Ave.

2613

100 block of North Washington Avenue, central city, looking north,
c. 1906. Courtesy of Norma Reese via Susan Pieroth.

CHAPTER I

Betting on Scranton

NEITHER OF JANE'S PARENTS had close family ties or any other connection to Scranton before they moved to what was, at the turn of the last century, one of Pennsylvania's most booming and bustling cities. Jane respected her father's judgment enormously, but she was confounded by his conclusion in 1906 that Scranton would continue to thrive. She contemplated and talked about her parents' carefully considered decision as she was writing *The Death and Life of Great American Cities* in the late 1950s and again in conceiving *The Economy of Cities*. In retrospect, the Butzners' choice to settle in Scranton seemed so inexplicable to their descendants and extended family—who knew firsthand or had heard of Scranton's long decline and leaching of population during the latter half of the twentieth century—that some told a story of the couple's putting the names of two cities in a hat and randomly extracting the one where they would live. This seemed as plausible an explanation as any for choosing Scranton.[1]

Had they known the anthracite capital when Jane's father, Dr. John Decker Butzner, first arrived there in 1906, they might have thought differently. Nestled in the Lackawanna River valley of northeastern Pennsylvania, Scranton supplied much of the nation's anthracite coal, turned out prodigious amounts of silk textiles, and had a spectrum of smaller industries and businesses found in large cities, including several ironworks. Making his permanent home in a good-size city was a novel experience for the young doctor. He had grown up in the South in a freethinking family that opposed slavery, secession from the Union, and the Civil War. Born on September 22, 1878, "Decker"—as his parents, William and Lucy, using Lucy's maiden name, called their oldest son—grew up on his parents' farm in rural Virginia, outside Fredericksburg. His family raised pigs and a variety of Scottish cattle called black Galloways, and they cultivated fruits and vegetables to feed themselves and the livestock. With about two hundred acres, they could earn a living from dairy farming and selling pork but could not afford to hire help. They did the work themselves. "Father often told us what a hard life farming was," Jane recalled. "The farm he grew up on in Virginia was the kind of farm that is much romanticized today. . . . He didn't romanticize it at all, and we knew very graphically how difficult it was."[2]

When they weren't helping on the farm, Decker and his brothers—along with a dozen or more of their cousins—were taught by a succession of young women relatives in a one-room schoolhouse. As each teacher married, another unmarried female took over. A rich uncle on Decker's mother's side recognized Decker's and his youngest brother's scholarly proclivities and saw to it that they went on to receive a top-notch college education. With an insatiable curiosity and a thirst for knowledge, Decker chose to study medicine at the University of Virginia in Charlottesville. In 1904, he graduated as a doctor, having received his B.A., M.A., and M.D. degrees from the university. In December 1905, he passed a comprehensive exam by Virginia's Medical Examining Board and earned his license to practice medicine. The three days of tests covered proficiency in obstetrics, gynecology, and surgery; histology, pathology, bacteriology, chemistry, and physiology; and anatomy, hygiene, therapeutics, materia medica, and medical jurisprudence—exams that were comparable to the general medical boards of today. In 1910, almost 90 percent of the students taking the exams passed the Virginia medical boards and could thus practice, but Dr. Butzner thirsted for greater knowledge and experience, traits his daughter Jane would acquire.[3]

Dr. Butzner received his training and license before the American Medical Association regulated the education of doctors. Although the AMA had begun its effort to improve medical education in 1904, educator Abraham Flexner did not publish his assessment of all 155 medical schools in the United States and Canada until 1910. The University of Virginia was one of the few schools that escaped Flexner's excoriation for failing to meet his stringent standards in the categories of entrance requirements, teaching staff, funding, laboratory facilities, and clinical facilities at a hospital. Prior to the exacting Flexner report's recommendations, it is quite likely that Decker knew of the AMA's Council on Medical Education and that the national organization questioned the quality of medical schools. On his own, the enthusiastic and diligent young physician decided to further his medical education by pursuing the present-day equivalent of a residency when it was not yet obligatory for practicing general medicine. Despite having graduated from one of the continent's top medical schools, Dr. Butzner chose to go above and beyond the requirements.[4]

As a licensed practitioner, Dr. Butzner set out for Philadelphia, the third-largest city in America, to gain proficiency at one of its preeminent hospitals. He was the oldest and only one of his parents' three children to venture beyond Virginia. William, his youngest brother by four years, studied law. He became a much-admired lawyer and well-known character in Fredericksburg. The middle brother, (James) Calvin, followed in his father's footsteps and remained a farmer in his native state. But the inquisitive, ambitious young doctor continued his training at what his daughter Jane would later refer to as "an important hospital in Philadelphia." In its "Medical News," the national *Journal of the American Medical Association* made note of his hospital appointment: Dr. John D. Butzner was one of five "elected resident physicians to the Polyclinic Hospital." Founded in 1882, the Philadelphia Polyclinic and College for Graduates in Medicine offered not only experience as a resident physician but also advanced instruction in medicine and surgery to graduates of established medical schools through six- and twelve-week courses "adapted to the needs of practitioners." In addition, the hospital ran an excellent training program for nurses.[5]

In the close quarters of the hospital, Dr. Butzner was particularly taken with one of these nurses. Elizabeth Mary Robison, called "Bessie" or "Bess," had received her nursing diploma from the Polyclinic Hospital School for Nurses in 1904 and stayed on to work as the night supervising nurse. She had come to Philadelphia from the village of Espy, Pennsylvania—about sixty miles southwest of Scranton—next to the town of Bloomsburg, where she was born on June 21, 1879. From a prominent family with considerable roots in this part of Pennsylvania, Bess grew up with eight siblings in a stately brick house along the old canal that paralleled the Susquehanna River. "Bess used to keep her favorite books in the cupola on top [of the house], and read there," Jane reminisced. "It was her hideaway." Bess's father was a highly respected lawyer, and her mother was a teacher, as was her older sister, Martha, and her aunt Hannah Breece. In 1897, like her aunt and sister before her, Bess graduated

Robison family home in Espy, Pennsylvania, with Jane's daughter, Burgin, and Jane's husband, Bob, May 1989. Estate of Jane Jacobs.

from the Bloomsburg State Normal School. By age twenty, she was teaching elementary school in and around Bloomsburg.[6]

Bess Robison was a member of the First Presbyterian Church of Bloomsburg, a brownstone edifice with stained-glass windows in the town's center, down the hill from the cemetery where earlier generations of her family were buried. Bess, who had grown up in a solid middle-class family but not in the lap of luxury, liked to joke to her granddaughter Jane Butzner Henderson that she considered herself "as always on the periphery of great wealth." This was because Bess's aunt Emily Robison had married George Markle, an anthracite-coal baron with extensive mines in Luzerne County, Pennsylvania. He was not beloved by the miners he employed and "barely escaped injury at the hands of the redoubtable Molly Maguires [a secret society of Irish immigrant miners who resorted to violence in disputes with coal operators], who had driven him into ambush." Their son John Markle, Bess's first cousin, followed in his father's footsteps and made millions by taking over the Jeddo-Highland Coal Company, where

Dr. John Decker Butzner, 1913.
Estate of Jane Jacobs.

Bess Robison (later Butzner),
c. 1904–1908. Estate of Jane Jacobs.

he "combatted strikes and arbitration with bitter pertinacity" and asserted that he "would rather fight than eat."[7]

While still in her twenties and already an experienced teacher, Bess Robison was drawn to nursing and to the metropolis of Philadelphia. For years, she told stories of assisting Dr. Decker at the Polyclinic when he performed appendectomies. Like all nurses at the time, one of her duties was to mend the doctors' uniforms. According to family lore, Decker liked her sewing and counted this among the qualities that attracted him to her. Jane Jacobs recalled her mother as a "very compassionate person" who, as a nurse, had worked with less fortunate people. "Most of the child patients that she had [at the Polyclinic Hospital] were from very poor areas of Philadelphia, and she would tell me how limited their lives were in many ways. She felt sorry about that." Since neither Bess nor Decker was listed in the Philadelphia city directories, they probably both lived in accommodations provided at the hospital, a common arrangement for doctors and nurses in that era. Consequently, they spent much time together and grew enamored of each other. No letters or stories tell us at what point they decided to marry.[8]

We do know that Decker had no intention of returning to rural Virginia or becoming a country doctor. In pondering the best city in which to set up a viable medical practice, he and Bess—both voracious readers—surely perused the plentiful newspaper and magazine accounts of various cities as well as the history books describing the development of particular American cities. In 1889, Joseph Curtis Platt, an original founder of Scranton, published his reminiscences of his city's early history. Two years later, a team of local historians, led by the Reverend David Craft, combined an account of Scranton's origins, its dramatic growth, institutions, and societies "down to the present time" with detailed documentation of current financial establishments and manufacturing enterprises. While we can't be sure the young couple was familiar with these books, we do know that in his library Dr. Butzner kept a copy of, at the time, the most complete chronicle of Scranton's development, *History of the Lackawanna Valley*, by fellow physician Dr. Horace Hollister. This thick volume covered the re-

gion's earliest Native American history through its first European settlers and Scranton's remarkably rapid growth period. Hollister's fifth
edition of the book, published in 1885, remains in the family today.[9]

Born on a farm in Wayne County, Pennsylvania, in 1822, Horace
Hollister lived in Scranton from the age of twenty-four until his
death, in 1893. Here he practiced medicine and gained more than a
local reputation as an author. Having graduated from the University
of the City of New York, he had spent time in the large and diverse
metropolis of New York City. In the appendix of Dr. Butzner's edition
of *History of the Lackawanna Valley,* Hollister contemplated Scranton's prospects: "With its two mammoth and best-managed Bessemer
steel-works in America, its busy silk-works, its street railway; with
its nineteen newspapers, its $400,000 in bank [*sic*] subject to check, its
scale, terra-cotta, and fire-brick for stoves; its electric lights, its internal revenue receipts of over $133,000, its factories, foundries, and
furnaces; its iron-, brass-, and glass-works, its button factory, its mills,
and its countless industries that enliven capital and labor, it is bound
to become one of the first cities of the Union." He noted that in the
previous year alone, fourteen hundred new buildings were erected
in Scranton—among them the new county jail, the Moses Taylor
Hospital, and the YMCA.[10]

Hollister's book may well have informed and influenced the young
couple's choice. Where Decker and Bess would settle was above all,
Jane conveyed to her son, "an economic decision." They tried to
discern what city held the greatest promise for continuing growth
and prosperity. After much deliberation about the economies of many
cities, they narrowed the contenders to Detroit and Scranton, the
two cities in the imaginary-hat story. Decker's interest in working
with victims of trauma tipped the scales slightly in favor of Scranton. With its coal-mining industry, Scranton was all too likely to
provide this opportunity. And for Bess, it would be a short trip by
train from this northeastern Pennsylvania city to see her relatives in
Bloomsburg. Decker and Bess placed their bets on Scranton.[11]

By the fall of 1906, Dr. J. D. Butzner had left Philadelphia and
arrived in Scranton to set up shop. The Scranton that greeted him

had almost 130,000 residents, nurturing vitality, density, diversity of people, and commercial activity—urban qualities that Jane would extol in *Death and Life.* Fine department stores and flourishing small businesses lined the main downtown streets. The coal, railroad, and silk industries employed the largest portion of the population. The wide assortment of smaller factories turned out everything from building materials to soap. Recent immigrants from Italy and Eastern Europe—often by way of New York—disembarked in Scranton, joining the earlier influx from Wales, Ireland, and Germany. When Dr. Butzner came to town, roughly a quarter of all Scrantonians were foreign-born. A small number of African Americans had settled in the city, too, and a few had established themselves as successful businessmen. Charles "Susky" Battle had made his way up from Maryland in 1886 and later opened the downtown Newport Hotel, in the alley between Lackawanna Avenue and Spruce Street, generously accommodating his "racial brethren" who looked to Scranton for an asylum and a livelihood. A few months after Dr. Butzner's arrival, the magnificent Beaux Arts–style Delaware, Lackawanna & Western (DL&W) train station opened, from which five major railroads linked the city to New York, Philadelphia, and the rest of the country. People from near and far flocked to Scranton to conduct business or partake of the city's cultural institutions, theaters, and shops. Choosing this city certainly made sense to the young doctor.[12]

Yet sixty-six years before Dr. Butzner landed in Scranton, there were no signs of a real settlement, much less a city or town, on the terrain from which Scranton would begin its meteoric rise. The narrow valley between West Mountain and the Moosic Ridge was only sparsely populated, with occasional farms and gristmills scattered about. The 1840 census takers found fewer than twelve hundred inhabitants on a tract of land some six miles square, the southeast quadrant of which included the area where Roaring Brook emptied into the lazy Lackawanna River. Back in 1800, the Slocum brothers had dammed the brook just above this juncture and built an iron forge upstream, but by 1822 they had ceased producing iron. Up until 1840, Slocum Hollow, as the future site of the city of Scranton

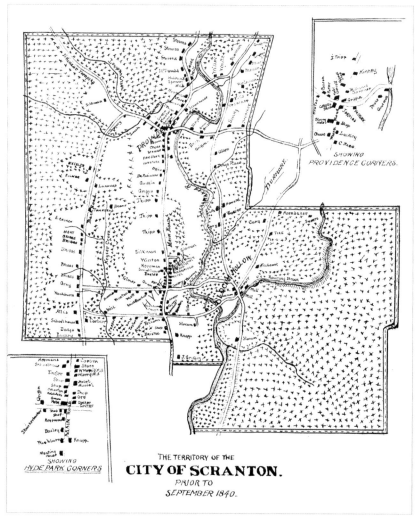

Edward Merrifield's 1895 map of the area 55 years earlier.
Scan obtained from Scranton Public Library.

was known, consisted of merely five houses, a school, a cooper shop, a sawmill, and a gristmill. The only clusters of buildings shown on Edward Merrifield's 1895 map of the "The Territory of the City of Scranton Prior to September 1840" indicate small settlements at the crossroads labeled Hyde Park and Providence, but none in Slocum Hollow.[13]

Contrary to accepted assumptions about how cities develop, Jane argued in her *Cities and the Wealth of Nations* that cities developed first and agriculture followed. The early history of Scranton supports her hypothesis. Newcomers and new ideas brought change to the area. Hoping to manufacture pig iron and nails using local iron, limestone, and coal, William Henry arrived in 1838 to purchase land on which to construct a forge in Slocum Hollow. Henry was a trained mineralogist and had operated the Oxford Furnace, an iron foundry in Belvidere, in northwestern New Jersey. Also an innovative engineer, he was the first American to make iron using the more efficient hot-blast method, which heats air before pumping it through the molten iron, thus requiring less fuel. He had learned of the hard coal that poked through the valley's surface, hinting at the world's largest deposits of anthracite buried below. Henry intended to build iron furnaces and fuel them with this local resource, a daring undertaking at a time when anthracite was not a common source of heat.[14]

But William Henry encountered financial setbacks and sent to New Jersey for his son-in-law, Selden T. Scranton, and Selden's brother George W. Scranton for help. In September 1840, the date in the title of Edward Merrifield's map, the Scranton brothers—originally from Madison, Connecticut—appeared on the scene, and the territory began its dramatic transformation. Presbyterians and teetotalers, Selden and George Scranton had successfully managed and prospered from the Oxford Furnace. They brought with them Sanford Grant, one of Belvidere's wealthiest citizens, as an investor. With the help of Grant's capital, the brothers purchased the land in Slocum Hollow to begin the manufacture of pig iron from what they thought were large quantities of iron ore in the mountains, using the abundant anthracite coal for the hot-blast method. Full of enthusiasm, great plans, and expectations, they formed Scrantons, Grant, and Company, and, as zealous Whigs—the party of moral reformers—they named the settlement Harrison, after the newly elected president. The locals, however, persisted in calling it "Scranton's Furnace." This first manufacturing took place on the site of what would one day be Lackawanna Avenue and the city's central business district.[15]

"September 11, 1840, is to this city what the Fourth of July is to our country," historian Frederick L. Hitchcock wrote in his 1914 *History of Scranton and Its People.* "It is the birthday of Scranton." On that date, Simon Ward, an artisan whom the Scranton brothers had summoned from New Jersey, sank the legendary first pick into the ground for the furnace's foundation. "This industrial beginning was the genesis of our municipal existence," Hitchcock declared. The enormous furnace, eight feet in diameter by thirty-five feet high, seemed to spring up almost overnight. But as it turned out, the amount of iron ore in the region was small and of poor quality, and limestone, necessary to remove the ore's impurities, could not be found nearby. These materials had to be hauled by wagon from fifty miles away. Nevertheless, by 1842 the entrepreneurs had succeeded in producing 374 tons of pig iron, in crude iron blocks to be recast into products. Two years later, the company tried turning out nails to be sold locally, but their inferior quality garnered little profit. The iron-manufacturing enterprise created more demand for coal from the surrounding valley's roughly one hundred small surface mines, leading to the excavation of the first mine shaft in the region in 1843.

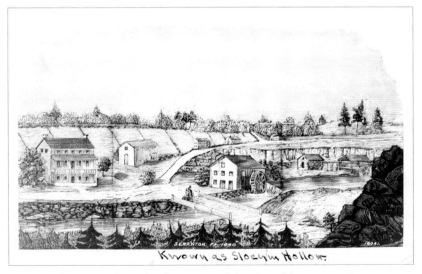

Slocum Hollow, the future site of the city of Scranton, 1840.
Author's collection.

Like the iron products, this coal had to be consumed in the area because there was no practical way to transport it to other markets.[16]

After what Hitchcock called "seven years of blood sweating," Scrantons, Grant, and Company's fortune changed. In 1847, joining his cousins Selden and George, successful businessman Joseph H. Scranton of Augusta, Georgia, moved to northeastern Pennsylvania. He injected additional money to help finance and run the company. That year, the New York & Erie Railroad desperately needed a huge order of T-shaped iron railroad tracks—known as "T rails"—to build a line connecting Port Jervis and Binghamton, New York. If the NY&E Railroad could get this job done, it could save itself from ruin. New York State had loaned the railroad three million dollars, on the condition that if the new track were finished before the end of 1848, they would forgive the loan. Britain dominated the market for manufacturing these rails, but the shipping costs and time involved spurred the NY&E to find a manufacturer closer to home. They approached the Scrantons, whose foundry lay only sixty miles from either end of the line. Although neither they nor any other American manufacturer had ever mass-produced this amount of track, George W. Scranton signed a million-dollar deal with the NY&E to fabricate twelve thousand tons of T rails. The company—now called Scrantons & Platt with the addition of Joseph Curtis Platt from Connecticut— employed eight hundred workers, including many Welsh, Irish, and German immigrants. In order to fulfill the order, it built two more blast furnaces and a rolling mill, used to shape the hot iron into tracks. "It was a contract that called for bravery and daring," *The Scranton Republican* crowed decades later, "but it was carried out [with just four days to spare], and it gave the mills the start that made them the biggest in the country for years."[17]

With plenty of iron products to export, the company required better transportation. In the 1850s, George W. Scranton invested in railroads and helped to establish the Delaware, Lackawanna & Western Railroad Company. Realizing that they could also make money selling the anthracite coal they used as fuel for the iron furnaces, the Scrantons added the mining and transporting of this local resource.

The railroad allowed for transporting greater quantities of coal to New Jersey and New York. In 1853, Scrantons & Platt reorganized and became the Lackawanna Iron and Coal Company. By 1857, they had built a total of five colossal blast furnaces, fueled by anthracite for the smelting of iron ore, and installed Bessemer converters, which enabled the production of steel. "These great furnaces, belching forth their lurid volcano-like fires," as Hitchcock described them, "lighted up the country for miles around." In 1865, the ironworks produced sixty thousand tons of rails annually, thus becoming the second-largest manufacturer of rails in the United States.[18]

As the Scrantons' iron, coal, and railroad ventures expanded, other individuals and companies opened similar and supporting businesses and rapidly recruited workers, many from afar. By 1870, over 45 percent of Scranton's growing population was foreign-born, with huge numbers from Wales and Ireland. Many immigrants found employment in the flourishing coal industry as laborers doing perilous work. Welsh immigrants who had worked in the anthracite mines of South Wales could sometimes obtain supervisory positions. The Welsh, unlike the Irish Catholics, could also use their Protestant ties to link hands with the coal operators and more easily become mine managers. But other Welshmen maintained their allegiance to the miners and became leaders in the coal unions, such as John Mitchell and John L. Lewis. Railroad companies used their profits to acquire coal mines and invest in coal-laden land. The DL&W controlled a network of anthracite mines that by 1868 had excavated and shipped two million tons of coal. In the early days of anthracite mining in northeastern Pennsylvania, this industry sometimes provided opportunities to work one's way to the top of the ladder. Canadian-born but of Scots-Irish descent, William Connell started as a boy mine-mule driver in the valley. In 1856, at age twenty-nine, having studied at night and risen through the ranks, he came to Scranton to manage the two mines belonging to the Susquehanna and Wyoming Valley Railroad. Connell purchased these mines fourteen years later, making him one of the largest shippers of coal from the valley and a multimillionaire.[19]

Alongside Scranton's foremost anthracite-mining industry rose the silk factories, where women toiled to supplement the wages of husbands and fathers employed in the mines. "The textile plants," Jane Jacobs noted in *Economy of Cities*, "for the most part, were transplanted industries located in Scranton because the wives and daughters of the coal miners provided a pool of very cheap labor." Scranton's silk industry began in the early 1870s with the Scranton Silk Manufacturing Company, which employed fewer than two hundred workers. "Then the business was but a struggling experiment, now it is an assured success," *The Scranton Republican* proclaimed on December 8, 1891. "In the beginning there were no skilled operatives in the city, now there are upwards of 2,000 on the South Side alone. . . . The plant [now taken over by] the Sauquoit Silk Mill employs 1,300 people in the three silk factories situated inside of the city limits. When the machinery in the new additions to the Sauquoit Silk Mill is put in motion . . . Scranton will contain the largest silk factory in the country, owned by the third largest silk manufacturing corporation in the United States. . . ." To make the "the finest grade silk dress goods in the markets," the Sauquoit Company imported raw silk from China, Italy, and Japan. They exported the finished fabrics to New York, Philadelphia, Boston, and Chicago. Scranton was engaged in both national and international trade.[20]

The city's steel industry developed at about the same time, and Scranton soon became, wrote Hitchcock, "one of the chief producers of this commodity in this country." In 1875, the Lackawanna Iron and Coal Company turned from manufacturing iron rails to steel rails, using the Bessemer method. Because they were stronger and lasted longer, steel rails became their main product within a couple of years. In 1883, Joseph H. Scranton's son William Walker Scranton quit the Lackawanna Iron and Coal Company to form the Scranton Steel Company with his brother Walter, erecting a steel mill not far away on the south side of Roaring Brook. The Scranton Steel Company became a major competitor, but the two companies resolved this by consolidating in 1891 as the Lackawanna Iron and Steel Company.[21]

During the three decades from 1860 to 1890, the city of Scranton grew by leaps and bounds. Industries and businesses multiplied, and, according to the U.S. Census, the population soared from 9,223 in 1860 (before the annexation of Providence and Hyde Park) to 75,215 in 1890. Hearing of the city's phenomenal growth and the opportunities that abounded, entrepreneurs came in droves from New England, New York, New Jersey, and small towns in northeastern Pennsylvania to seek their fortunes. They started additional foundries, steel mills, silk mills, stove works, carriage works, glass and lumber companies, an asphalt paving company, breweries, a jar and stopper company, a piano factory, and an underwear mill, to name but a few. Some of the new industries supported the existing industries—such as stove works or silk textiles for the railroads and the Dickson Company's machines for the mining industry. Other of these manufacturers replaced previously imported products. Investors arrived from the surrounding regional capitals to establish banks, building and loan associations, and insurance companies. By the turn of the nineteenth century, the city's population swelled to 102,026 people. Jane could have been talking about Scranton when she wrote, "Economic life develops by grace of innovating; it expands by grace of import-replacing."[22]

As Scranton's industry and businesses developed, so did its built environment. In 1841, the Scrantons had enlisted a surveyor to lay out a village grid near the blast furnaces, and they allowed workers to put up shanties there, creating the densest settlement around. Beginning in 1850, Scrantons & Platt hired Joel Amsden—an architect and engineer as well as a surveyor who had migrated westward from New Hampshire by way of New York State—to devise a plan for the central city with a grid of uniformly sized and spaced residential streets. To fit into the natural landscape between the rivers and the mountains, he tilted the grid's northern axis toward the northeast. Amsden, in consultation with the men who commissioned him, named the avenues running more or less north and south after notable Pennsylvanians and U.S. presidents, and the east-west streets after trees. Between all the downtown north-south avenues, and a few blocks between the east-west Lackawanna Avenue and Spruce Street, he inserted narrow unnamed alleys, which could be used for rear-door access, deliveries, and outbuildings. The alleys further divided the grid and added flexibility to access and uses in the downtown plan. In order to have wide thoroughfares to accommodate commercial activity, Amsden plotted Lackawanna Avenue and the north-south Wyoming Avenue and gave them the names of the area's two valleys (whose names had originally derived from local Native American words). The T-junction of these two main streets constituted the town's focal point and epicenter of activity. In 1851, locals finally settled on the official name of Scranton for the newly planned settlement.[23]

The industrial founders clearly had high hopes for Scranton. With the construction of the DL&W, Scrantons & Platt decided that the town needed a fine hotel that would be suitable for an important city. At Scranton's main intersection, they engaged Joel Amsden as the architect of the luxurious three-story brick Wyoming House, which he modeled after New York's renowned Astor House, designed by the nationally successful architect Isaiah Rogers. In 1852, Wyoming House opened to receive its first visitors. In 1855, the first president of the DL&W, John Jay Phelps, felt that the magnificent spectacle

Wyoming House, hotel designed by Joel Amsden, 1852,
corner of Lackawanna and Wyoming Avenues.
Courtesy of Lackawanna Historical Society.

of the railroad billowing steam as it left Scranton's first roundhouse and the nascent city behind should be commemorated by an artist. He commissioned prominent landscape painter George Inness to depict the bucolic scene with the city and its industry at the center of a large tableau titled *The Lackawanna Valley.*[24]

In 1856, Scranton incorporated as a borough, thus achieving official town status. Amsden himself drew a new street map, published a year later, ringed with detailed illustrations of stately homes, impressive churches, and substantial commercial blocks that were already filling in the grid. Amsden had designed at least five of these buildings, including the First Presbyterian Church, the Methodist Episcopal Church, George W. Scranton's house, and Public School #1. Two years hence, Scranton had eighty brick buildings. On April 23, 1866, merging with the neighboring boroughs of Hyde Park and Providence, Scranton incorporated as a city, with a footprint of almost twenty square miles and an estimated thirty thousand residents. Famous for its coal, iron, and railroad industries, the city of Scranton now had a popularly elected city government with the ability to tax its citizens to pay for policing and other services. It was on a steady course toward becoming the regional capital.[25]

The newly chartered city of Scranton was situated in the northern section of Luzerne County, of which Wilkes-Barre—incorporated as a borough in 1806 and for many decades the larger of the two cities—served as the county seat. Scranton's lawyers and other citizens, who now outnumbered those of the neighboring city down the valley, resented having to travel twenty miles to record deeds, attend lawsuits, and transact other county business. Residents of Wilkes-Barre resolutely resisted attempts by the northern county residents to secede, which would have meant taking with them the valuable coal deposits in and around Scranton. After almost forty years of contention, in 1878, a majority of the people in the proposed new county were finally able to vote to break away and form Lackawanna County. The first election of Lackawanna County officials took place the following year, and a decision was made to build a county courthouse befitting a first-class city.[26]

To provide a site for the new county's most important edifice, the Lackawanna Iron and Coal Company, along with the Susquehanna and Wyoming Valley Railroad and Coal Company, generously contributed a substantial tract of land along the edge of Scranton's original grid. The county determined it would erect a magnificent eclectic Victorian courthouse—complete with bartizans and Flemish gables—built of stone from the city's West Mountain and trimmed with Onondaga limestone from New York State. Construction on the extra-large, square block of donated land, however, posed some problems. "On April 14, 1881, ground for the court house was broken," *The Scranton Republican* reported. "The land had been the heart of a swamp, on which lads skated in the winter and in which frogs sang in the summer. But it was drained off and deep foundations laid for the heavy stone court house."[27]

With the foundation complete, in May 1882, Dr. Horace Hollister and more than one hundred other prominent men of the Lackawanna Valley took part in what Hitchcock later dubbed "the grand jollification banquet" at the Wyoming House following the cornerstone-laying ceremony for the courthouse. In high spirits, these leaders celebrated the separation of Lackawanna County from Luzerne, reveled in the significance of the splendid edifice-to-be, and contemplated the city's future. Dr. Hollister transcribed a number of speeches for the next edition of his history book. Responding to Edward Merrifield's opening toast, Judge Stanley Woodward waxed eloquent on what the ambitious project symbolized: "Perhaps a court-house, more than any other structure, does represent the civilization and morals of a community. It speaks for law, and order, and justice, and is a fair expression and exponent of the culture and thrift of the people who build it."[28]

Two years later, the monumental building opened to the public. Designed by Isaac G. Perry, the state architect of New York, the new courthouse was reminiscent of his completion of the New York State Capitol in Albany, with its Romanesque arches and steep roofs. The Lackawanna County Courthouse's surrounding grounds were adorned with monuments, and paths "lined both sides with settees for the accommodation of the public." While sitting or strolling in

Courthouse Square, citizens could marvel at the stunning symbolic centerpiece of the thriving city.[29]

Hollister believed that the city's growth and surge of building—including its many architectural gems—would naturally continue. ". . . Scranton, by the momentum of her population, by the inevitable operations of natural causes, is pushing up and down the valley with its building operations, and will, in the course of the next half-century, cover all the unoccupied territory." Did Bess and Decker concur with Hollister's assumption that one could examine a city's rise and, based on its previous rate of development, expect the momentum to continue?[30]

Besides recording the festive atmosphere of the cornerstone-laying celebration, Hollister captured the words of one individual who felt compelled to offer a cautionary toast regarding Scranton's future economy. William Walker Scranton, scion of Scranton's founding family, observed: "It seems to me that this community is based

Lackawanna County Courthouse, built 1884, postcard c. 1905.
Courtesy of Norma Reese via Susan Pieroth.

principally upon the mining of coal—half of it depends upon it. Now these mines are being worked out more and more, and, in my mind, it is not going to be forever. It will not be one hundred years before these are all worked out. To me it seems that a great many of us here are going to live to see the time when the growth of this town, so far as it depends upon mining, is not going to increase. When that time comes, we have got to fall back upon something else. It seems to me that we ought to provide, as far as possible, for our manufacturing interests. . . . " Jane would have endorsed this admonition.[31]

When W. W. Scranton spoke these words, he may already have been planning to launch the Scranton Steel Company the following year. Although this company went on to merge with the Lackawanna Iron and Coal Company in 1891, the resulting Lackawanna Iron and Steel Company—the second-largest steel-manufacturing facility in America—did not stay long in Scranton. The difficulty and expense of having to import iron ore, the major component of both iron and steel, had plagued Scranton's iron industry from its very beginning. After more than half a century in iron and steel manufacturing, the proprietors of the latest iteration of the business turned their sights elsewhere. In 1899, the Lackawanna Iron and Steel Company amassed land in Buffalo, New York, a first step in their dismantling and departure. A little more than two years later, on February 27, 1902, with the doors of the steel manufacturer's North Works already barred, a *Scranton Republican* headline tolled the death knell: "South Steel Mill Closed Suddenly." After years as the industrial core of the city, the Lackawanna Iron and Steel Company "rolled its last rail . . . and the big works from which over a thousand men have earned their livelihood for such a long period closed once [and] for all." Adding insult to injury, this occurred just as the steel industry was soaring nationwide.[32]

Just a few years before Dr. J. D. Butzner and Bess Robison carefully studied cities to choose the best one in which to live and work, Scranton's economy suffered this unforeseen and devastating blow. Scranton's prime industry, to which it owed its very existence, had abandoned the city. It was lured away to Buffalo, whose shipping port on Lake Erie was easily accessible via the Great Lakes to Minnesota's plentiful Mesabi iron-ore range and the burgeoning steel markets in the Midwest. The highly lucrative company, with two of the finest steel mills in the world, passed into oblivion, leaving the five huge blast furnaces behind as historic relics. A dozen years later, F. L. Hitchcock still mourned the city's loss: "This plant had built and occupied most of the south side of our city. It employed upwards of 5,000 men. It was the climax of sixty years' growth." When betting on Scranton, did Bess and Decker consider this recent event? Did they view the move optimistically, as *The Scranton Tribune* did, as a "blessing in disguise," making the ninety-seven acres once owned by the steel company available for a depot, freight yard, and power station for the railroads?[33]

With the mainstay of its existence abruptly wrenched from it, Scranton's economy relied more heavily than ever on its coal industry,

The Lackawanna Valley, George Inness, oil on canvas, c. 1856, in the National Gallery of Art, Washington, D.C.

the economic situation that William Walker Scranton had warned against. This younger Scranton family member understood the inherent problem of a "company town," of having an economy based on one product without creating other economic reasons for a town's existence. He also recognized the danger of fueling a city's economy by consuming its capital—that is to say, by depleting its finite natural resource of anthracite coal, which would one day be mined out. Jane Jacobs would have agreed with W. W. Scranton's observations and dismissed Hollister's notion that the rapid development of a city is an indication of its future success. The physician-historian had based his rosy prediction of Scranton's future on the spectacular growth he had witnessed in Scranton for four decades. But Hollister ignored what appeared obvious to W. W. Scranton.

Jane's parents' decision to move to Scranton, rather than Detroit or another city, was a continuing source of fascination and puzzlement for their younger daughter. Choosing a city, as Bess and Decker had, intrigued Jane Jacobs from an early age onward, and it contributed to her pondering what makes cities work. As a child growing up in Scranton, before she went on to examine other cities, Jane systematically observed the city around her and studied her Scranton history. She undoubtedly read her father's copy of Hollister's history in the family library and more than likely pored over Hitchcock's two-volume *History of Scranton and Its People*, the only comprehensive book about Scranton's development to follow Hollister's.

Jane's knowledge of Scranton's origins and history surfaces throughout her writings and interviews. She often turned to Scranton for source material for ideas and for concrete examples. In *The Economy of Cities*, Jane opened her chapter on "How Cities Start Growing" by reconstructing the tale of her parents' runner-up city of Detroit. Detroit, which would become the auto-manufacturing capital of America, she explained, had begun by exporting flour. The business of making and repairing gristmill machines sprang up, to which was added the building of steamships for the export of flour, and so on. In this "reciprocating system," "Detroit contained industries producing exports, and industries supplying the exporters."[34]

Jane followed with her grasp of her "own city's" history to illustrate "little cities that grow only briefly": "In Scranton, Pennsylvania, for example, which stagnated when it became a successful coal-mining city, the first export of the settlement was not coal, but iron and iron forgings. Among the local suppliers to producers of forgings were miners of anthracite coal, which forges used for fuel. The mining companies, having started as local suppliers began exporting the coal that was soon to become the city's chief export." Thus Jane used Scranton to characterize what would lead a city—which she defined as "a settlement that consistently generates its economic growth from its own local economy"—to change into a stagnant city, one that "formerly grew as a city, but stopped doing so." But Jane had the advantage of quite a few more decades of hindsight than her parents had to mull over the question of whether settling in Scranton in the nineteen-aughts was indeed a good bet.[35]

The grand Delaware, Lackawanna & Western train station,
built 1907, opened in 1908, photo 2008. Author's photo.

• • •

CHAPTER 2

Many Small Decisions

IN AUTUMN 1906, while Bess Robison remained in Philadelphia, employed as a high-ranking nurse at the Polyclinic Hospital, Dr. Butzner went ahead to Scranton to test the waters for launching a medical practice. He set up a small office and his residence, in an area where other physicians clustered, a few blocks north of the city's epicenter and just a ten-minute walk from the city's eagerly anticipated DL&W railroad station. The rooms he rented—from Dr. Frank Birchard, who also had his home and medical office in the building—were a stone's throw from the Scranton Private Hospital. Dr. Birchard had bought the two-and-a-half-story semidetached house on a block where a number of doctors resided, not surprisingly, since both the State and Moses Taylor hospitals were also within easy walking distance. Dr. Butzner's block resembled others nearby with their rows of brick town houses, "newly constructed and . . . deemed quite desirable," ready to accommodate the many entrepreneurs, including physicians, riding the wave of the city's prosperity and anticipating opportunities. At least one other physician in this emerging medical district, Dr. Thomas Wiles Kay, had moved into the YMCA's luxurious seven-story building, one block east, which had opened only a few years earlier on the original site of the Hahnemann Hospital. The magnificent new YMCA edifice reaped national praise. Dr. Kay rented a "large outside room with private bath" and could enjoy lectures and performances in the 720-person-capacity auditorium, or languish in the public reading room, parlors, gymnasium, or Turkish baths, as described in a full-page ad, hoping to attract New Yorkers, placed in the *New-York Daily Tribune*.[1]

Dr. T. W. Kay was a colorful character and would become an influential figure in Dr. Butzner's and, eventually, his daughter Jane's life. In fact, Dr. Kay probably played a role in Dr. J. D. Butzner's decision to move to Scranton. Kay himself had chosen this city seventeen years earlier. Decker's copy of Hollister's *History of the Lackawanna Valley* bears Dr. T. W. Kay's stamp with his first Scranton address, to which he moved at age thirty-one, in 1889. Since Dr. Kay lost no time in joining the Lackawanna County Medical Society, he would have become acquainted with and read the works of Dr. Horace Hollister, an active member of the society from its founding in 1878. Dr. Kay must have been intrigued by Hollister's *History*, whose "publication," the author hoped, "might possibly awaken an interest . . . [in] a region where nothing yet had been done in the way of gathering its local history." When, in the mid-nineteen-aughts, Dr. T. W. Kay was looking for a young doctor to join his practice, he put word out through friends and colleagues in Philadelphia. Hearing that Decker was considering Scranton as a place to practice medicine, he likely sent Hollister's engaging book about the city to spark his interest.[2]

Once Dr. Butzner relocated to Scranton, he effortlessly became part of the community and quickly caught the attention of the city's newspapers, which kept close tabs on news of all Scranton's citizens in those days. The young doctor must have been contemplating teaming up with Dr. Kay. As he became better acquainted with Dr. Kay, who was twenty years his senior, he discovered how much they had in common. Dr. Kay had also grown up in the Virginia countryside on a family farm. His father, Joseph Wiles Kay, and mother had raised their son, Thomas, and daughter, Georgia, on this farm, in Port Royal, Virginia, only twenty miles southeast of the Butzners'. Although Thomas Kay departed to pursue a medical career, he preserved his ties to his family and to southern culture. The Scranton

Y. M. C. A. Building,
Scranton, Pa.

YMCA, built 1903, corner of Washington Avenue and Mulberry Street,
where Dr. Thomas W. Kay resided, postcard c. 1905.
Courtesy of Norma Reese via Susan Pieroth.

newspapers frequently noted Dr. Kay's trips back home to "vacation in Virginia"—once for a six-week duck hunt—as well as his participation in Scranton's Southern Society, a social organization for "men of Dixie." Proud of their southern heritage, Drs. Kay and Butzner shared an amiability and easy manner. Dr. Kay's knowledge and intelligence, wide-ranging interests, and tales of traveling the world delighted his younger colleague.[3]

Dr. Kay became an unusually accomplished and internationally known physician. After completing his medical education in 1879 at the College of Physicians and Surgeons in Baltimore, Maryland, he spent a year heading the Baltimore Women's Hospital before building up "a lucrative practice" in Columbia, Pennsylvania, along the eastern Maryland border. Lured by the chance to see the world and study medical science in foreign countries, he accepted a chair in medicine at the Syrian Protestant College in Beirut. After five years, "because of his father's death," his colleagues wrote in his obituary, "he was forced to resign . . . and return to America taking the opportunity on his return journey of studying in a number of the large hospitals of Europe and particularly under Professor Pozzi at Paris." Dr. Kay's friend and mentor, the brilliant and flamboyant Samuel-Jean Pozzi, was not only a pioneer surgeon and president of the French Society of Anthropology but also a muse to composer Wagner and a paramour of actress Sarah Bernhardt. The esteemed John Singer Sargent painted his illustrious friend's full-length portrait in a scarlet dressing gown and titled it *Dr. Pozzi at Home*.[4]

Back in the States in 1889, Dr. T. W. Kay devoted a month to "look over his native land for a more auspicious location" in which to practice and, like Decker and Bess, "finally decided upon Scranton as the place for his best efforts." Within four years of landing in Scranton, Dr. Kay married Edna Fuller—the twenty-three-year-old daughter of the popular Methodist Episcopal minister Moses D. Fuller—who lived down the street from him on North Main Avenue, on the city's West Side. With his bride and in-laws, Dr. Kay became fully ensconced in his new city. The erudite physician's selection of Scranton as the best place for his medical practice may have helped sway Dr. Butzner in his choice of the city, and Dr. Kay's potential offer of a place in his practice probably sealed the deal.[5]

From the time he arrived in Scranton, the gregarious and adventurous Dr. Butzner plunged himself into the city's social life. With his southern drawl and manners, he made friends easily. In February 1907, a local newspaper reporter spotted Dr. Butzner along with his colleague Dr. Kay at the third annual gathering of the Southern Society, attended by what the *Republican* jokingly referred to as "fifty rebels." The article describes the convivial sense of southern pride yet an allegiance to the whole country. "While their numbers are small, yet there is no annual dinner of any society in the city which is as unique as the annual dinner of southern men. Speakers are heard from down south, where they make them. A Yankee is introduced to show the contrast in style. Then the southerner talks about chivalry and the northerner talks about enterprise . . . and every one explains that we are all part of one anyway and they sing 'America.'"[6]

Within a year and assumedly with the endorsement of his physician friend, Dr. Butzner joined the staff of the acclaimed Scranton Private Hospital—the first private hospital in the entire region—where Dr. Kay, a distinguished physician, also practiced. Founded in 1895, "the hospital specializes in many departments and cares for patients suffering from almost any of the accidents or ailments that flesh is heir to," wrote historian F. L. Hitchcock. "It is pleasing to note that the institution is a financial as well as professional success. It has maintained a good school for nurses for many years. . . . " From the start, Dr. Butzner's fellow physicians recognized his "skill both in diagnosis and in treatment." By the spring of 1908, *The Scranton Republican* mentioned that the new doctor was part of a "preeminent medical team" at the hospital. In addition to joining the local Lackawanna County Medical Society and the national American Medical Society, Dr. Butzner, like Dr. Kay, maintained his membership in the Southern Medical Society and his connection with his native state. The *Scranton Truth*'s "Evening Social Chat" column reported, "Dr. J. D. Butzner returned yesterday from a three weeks' professional trip to Virginia." Within two years of settling in Scranton, the young Dr. Butzner—one of almost two hundred physicians listed in the 1909 city directory—was a known personage to other medical professionals, as well as to the city's newspaper reporters.[7]

In less than a year, the afternoon paper took notice of another trip by the young physician. He was to join Bess Robison in Bloomsburg, Pennsylvania, but she set out before their arranged meeting. Bess's family had summoned her home because her father, James Boyd Robison, was seriously ill. The Civil War veteran, outstanding lawyer, and well-respected citizen died on March 2, 1909, at the age of seventy-one. The Columbia County Bar Association paid tribute to him in the local paper: "His high sense of honor and his fidelity to clients caused him to be held in high esteem by fellow members of the Bar, while his active interest in all matters pertaining to public affairs made him a man of force and influence in the community." But Bess's visit to her hometown served a happier purpose, too. As the *Scranton Truth* announced on March 24, 1909, "Dr. J. D. Butzner, of this city, went to Espy, Pa., yesterday, where he was married to Miss Elizabeth Robinson [*sic*] of that place, today. The couple will spend a few weeks at the doctor's former home in Fredericksburg, Va., then they will take up their residence on Taylor avenue in this city."[8]

For himself and his wife, Decker had rented one side of a two-family dwelling on a residential street of mainly single-family houses, a little more than a mile west of central city. Back from their southern honeymoon, they unwrapped wedding presents and discovered a large and tastefully framed etching labeled *Silver Sea and Silver Birches.* In delicate black lines on white paper, the print replicated a chromatic oil on canvas by the celebrated Scottish romantic landscape painter John MacWhirter. Bess's cousin, the coal baron John Markle, and his wife, Mary Robinson Markle, had sent the newlyweds the treasured gift, which is still displayed by the family.[9]

No longer living in the center of the city, Dr. Butzner felt he should acquire a motorcar, the latest equipment for general practitioners. Automobiles enabled physicians to make house calls and visit patients farther away. Aware of these potential buyers, car manufacturers targeted doctors directly through advertisements in medical journals. In 1910, at the dawn of the automobile age, car sales were rare and noteworthy enough to be featured in a city newspaper. The *Scranton Truth* ran a weekly column called "Automobile News and Gossip," presenting anything having to do with cars—clubs, long-distance races, fun facts about autos, new arrivals for sale in town, and even the names of people who purchased automobiles. On March 15, 1910, the column reported recent sales by the local Ford agent, G. S. Wrightnour, in his downtown office. Eight of twelve buyers were doctors, one of whom was Dr. Butzner. He had bought a roofless little red Ford, equipped with acetylene gas lamps for night driving. To make the purchase, Decker had withdrawn Bess's savings from the bank without informing her, which many years hence Jane Jacobs related

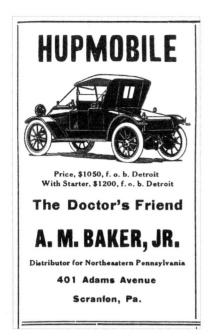

Automobile advertisements from *The Medical Society Reporter*, June 1914.
Courtesy of Geisinger Commonwealth Medical School Library
and Lackawanna County Medical Society.

to her niece. Bess had saved the money from working as a teacher and nurse. In those days when a woman married, her money automatically belonged to her husband, too. Bess was upset, not because her husband had spent roughly nine hundred dollars on a car that he needed for his practice, but because he had never consulted with her. She told her daughter-in-law Kay Schoen Butzner that the marriage was "never the same" after this incident. But the marriage had also taken an irreversible turn a few weeks prior for a joyous reason.[10]

On February 7, 1910, less than a year after Decker and Bess Butzner tied the knot, a child was born to the thirty-year-old mother and thirty-one-year-old father, relatively old first-time parents back then. They named the little girl Elizabeth Robison Butzner, after her mother and her great-grandmother, but family and, later, friends usually called her "Betty." With Betty as a member of the household, the apartment felt as if it were bursting at the seams. The new parents' thoughts naturally turned to finding more spacious quarters and, at the same time, a more permanent home of their own for a growing family. They undertook another decision as to where this would be.

In this era, Scranton's population, too, continued to grow by leaps and bounds. The 1910 census takers counted 129,867 people—27,841 more than in 1900. Much of this increase in population was due to the large influx of foreign-born immigrants to the city, especially in the latter part of the nineteen-aughts. Between 1906 and 1910, 6,600 foreign-born residents had arrived in town. In 1910, 35,122 people in Scranton—27 percent of the city's population—had been born outside the United States, with almost a quarter of them born in Russia (which still included Poland). Many other of the foreign-born were from Ireland, Germany, Wales, and Italy. Scranton's smaller-circulation and weekly newspapers reflected the makeup of the city's main immigrant groups—with two German-language papers, one Polish-language weekly (proudly advertising itself as the largest in Pennsylvania), *The Druid*, in English, for the Welsh population, and *The Catholic Light*, in English, for the Irish and other Roman Catholics. The recent foreign-born settlers joined the already considerable number of earlier immigrants who had come seeking work in the city's mines and factories or opportunities in business. Scranton's economy was strong and booming, and the word was out.

Of fascination to Jane Jacobs, these years "from about 1905 to 1920" she viewed as the period of Scranton's most "explosive growth." Every city, Jane concluded when writing *The Economy of Cities*, had one such period. Scranton's was "due to a combination of two causes. Its exports were growing . . . [e]specially coal, textiles, and a correspondence school. . . . It was also producing locally many humdrum former imports: beer (legally until Prohibition, illegally afterwards), stationery, tombstones, stock brokerage services, mattresses, potato chips . . . and so on. But other goods and services, apart from locally produced former imports, were rapidly added into Scranton's economy at that time too. Among them, I am glad to say—because they meant much to me as a child—were a zoo, a museum of natural history and a central public reference library. Several hospitals were added, several stuffy but imposing clubs, several department stores, such city departments as fire-fighting and public health services, and a trolley-car system." Jane drew upon her thorough knowledge and understanding of her hometown's history, buttressed by her own observations even as a child, to formulate her urban and economic theories.[11]

In this thriving economy, around 1910, Scrantonians, newly arrived or—like the Butzners—with growing families, looked for new places to live within the city. South Scranton, with its flat lowlands subject to flooding, was adjacent to and south of central city and Roaring Brook. With its older working-class dwellings close together on small lots—many home to people of German and Eastern European descent—the South Side absorbed additional immigrants. There were outbuildings, such as chicken houses or bakehouses, on the properties and small industry interspersed. Hyde Park and Prov-

Bill Steinke's illustration of Scranton's diverse industries, in *Steinke's Story of Scranton with Who's Who and Why in Cartoons,* 1914. Scan obtained from Scranton Public Library.

idence—the West Side, west of central city and the Lackawanna River, where a Welsh-language church persisted into the 1930s—accommodated many relatively recent arrivals, including a large number of Italians, some of whom had saved enough money to buy small houses. Not jurisdictionally part of Scranton, the independent and largely working-class borough of Dunmore lay to the east, with its own bite-size town center but plenty of undeveloped land covered with underbrush along its boundaries. Homes petered out in both municipalities as Scranton neared Dunmore. The section of Scranton known as Green Ridge—without delineation of borders or boundaries—lay beyond the city's industrial fringe along its northern edge as you followed the downtown avenues, such as Penn, Wyoming, and Washington, northward. This section within the city limits, once the property of coal companies and early big-time land speculators, had an abundance of plotted but empty lots for middle-class homes. Ten years into the new century, it was ripe for residential development and new buyers. The Butzners were among those whom it attracted.

Less than a half century earlier, the outer-city neighborhood of Green Ridge did not exist. "In 1868, Green Ridge had no name or being," Hollister mused in 1885. "Upon the ancient lands of John Dings, Joshua Griffin, Henry Whaling, and Michael Lutz, embracing a green slope on the east side of the Lackawanna, opposite the Indian meadow of Capoose [*sic*], a mile from the court-house, this village or appendage of Scranton has emerged within the last two decades. Hon. George Sanderson, the founder of it . . . [purchased] a portion of these acres several years ago, and encourage[d] a village, which tidy and hospitable . . . depends upon Scranton for its subsistence, trade, and mail."[12]

In the early nineteenth century, George Sanderson was one of many ambitious young middle- and upper-middle-class men from the Northeast who gradually migrated west in search of small growing cities with industry, banks, or commercial undertakings that promised rewarding business opportunities. Born in 1810 of Puritan stock and a graduate of the distinguished Boston Latin School, Sanderson was the key player in Green Ridge's development. As was customary in such a family, his oldest brother took over his father's business, in the remunerative West Indies trade, leaving the younger ones to find new ventures. George Sanderson felt "the new life of the West attract[ing] him," his *Scranton Republican* obituary claimed, luring him away from his ancestral home of Boston. "He traveled in New York State as a Universalist minister, editing a religious paper," before heading for northeastern Pennsylvania and settling in Towanda, Bradford County, sixty miles northwest of Scranton. Here he met and married Marion Kingsbury, the daughter of a large real estate owner. In the early 1850s, he represented this district in the state senate—thus earning the title "Honorable"—and met fellow state senator George W. Scranton, a founding father of the city that bore his name. Sanderson helped Scranton secure "passage of bills which placed the mining and manufacturing industries of Scranton . . . upon a firm and stable basis." Enticed by George Scranton's glowing reports of Scranton's economy, in 1855, at age forty-five, Sanderson pulled up stakes and moved to what his colleague had extolled as a boomtown. Wasting no time and clearly supplied with considerable funds, Sanderson founded the second bank in the city of Scranton, practiced law, and, like his father-in-law, became a successful real estate developer.[13]

In 1854, as his initial land venture in his new town—before committing to Scranton and moving his family—Sanderson acquired the Elisha Hitchcock farm, adjacent to the eastern edge of Scranton's commercial center, with its 220 acres of land extending from Roaring Brook into the surrounding hills. He paid the seller the hefty sum of $65,000. A few weeks later, he sold half the unplotted property to buyers from Philadelphia for the same amount he had paid. Sanderson had the rest of the tract surveyed and divided into sizable residential lots, which he sold individually to upper-middle-class families. Not only did Sanderson profit heartily but his decision to create substantial and thus costly lots determined the new neighborhood's affluent character for years to come. Successful entrepreneurs built impressive Victorian homes here, not far from downtown, in what was called "Sanderson's Hill" and, eventually, simply the "Hill Section." In 1856, Sanderson expanded the northern reach of the central

George Sanderson's first Scranton home, built 1856,
later owned by J. I. Blair, on future site of YMCA. Courtesy of
Norma Reese, from H. J. Sutherland's *The City of Scranton,
Pennsylvania, and Vicinity and Their Resources*, illustrated, 1894.

city by widening and extending Washington Avenue. He cut through
the pinewoods to the north, laid a log road across the swamp, and
built amid the stumps a handsome residence for himself, his wife,
and his children. Sanderson thus installed himself in the city and
literally blazed a trail at the same time.[14]

By now the town's major banker, Sanderson focused his sights
on the territory beyond Vine Street, which was parallel to and four
blocks north of Lackawanna Avenue, Scranton's main east-west commercial street. Past Vine Street, groups of buildings essentially ceased.
This sparsely settled area within the city limits was primarily wilderness, with occasional farms dotting the terrain. The land, with its coal
underneath, beckoned new industry. On the flatlands in the western
portion of this area along the Lackawanna River, the Delaware &
Hudson Railroad Company constructed the Von Storch coal breaker

in 1859 and, soon, the Manville and Dickson breakers nearby. Enticed by this area's potential, in 1865 Sanderson purchased the old Whaling Farm, an extensive tract of land, and erected a "palatial mansion" for himself and his wife on Seventh Street (later renamed Sanderson Avenue), between Marion Street and Green Ridge Avenue, about a dozen long blocks north of Vine.[15]

The Sanderson family became pioneer settlers in this budding suburb. Replete with the mixed-use elements of residences, factories, and stores—a natural stew that Jane Jacobs would extol—it was called "Green Ridge" after the oblong forty-foot-high by two-block-long verdant knoll, running north-south between Sanderson's mansion and the city. Since Sanderson built his home within a few blocks of the three existing breakers with their mammoth piles of refuse, Green Ridge's developer clearly had no objection to living near large industry, a visual reminder of the city's lifeblood. Within Sanderson's innately mixed-use neighborhood, Green Ridge's first commercial center—where Green Ridge Avenue crossed Sixth Street (later Dickson Avenue)—also took shape. Besides industry and commerce, Sanderson recognized another crucial ingredient for the development of Green Ridge: the need for transportation between Green Ridge and downtown. In 1866, he was one of nine men who obtained a charter to form the Scranton & Providence Passenger Railway Company. This horse-drawn railway ran from the DL&W depot on Lackawanna Avenue to the intersection of Sanderson Avenue and East Market Street in Green Ridge, once called Griffin's Corners for the site's original farm but now renamed Green Ridge Corners.[16]

Sanderson set about subdividing his vast land acquisition and extending and grading the avenues—converting the remaining wilderness into a suburb with eighty-foot-wide streets and single-family house lots. In April 1868, the *Morning Republican* ran a notice offering 250 lots for sale in Green Ridge from the banking house of George Sanderson: "These lots are on the main traveled road, and only good one, up the valley. They are larger than any lots offered for sale in the city . . . and . . . at less price than the small lots are now sold for. But little money is required to secure a desirable homestead; and in some cases none is required down. Four to six years are given to pay the purchase money. Street cars pass hourly. Trains for New York, Philadelphia, Wilkesbarre [*sic*] and Carbondale, arrive and depart from Green Ridge several times daily." Besides offering reasonable terms for his properties, affordable for a range of people, Sanderson, as his obituary noted, "adopted a liberal and public spirited policy towards settlers upon his lots, donated ground for school and church purposes, and served the young borough twice as burgess." He also gave land for the city's first public library, the Green Ridge Library, built in 1881. These donations may have stimulated lot sales, but they simultaneously contributed to community life.[17]

Another of the many New Englanders who came to take advantage of Scranton's booming economy and, in the process, helped build the city was Edward Baker Sturges. Born in Connecticut in 1845 and educated in New York City, he relocated to the newly incorporated city in the late 1860s. He practiced law and became a coal operator. In 1873, he, advantageously, married George Sanderson's daughter Marion and began speculating in Green Ridge's real estate. In about 1880, Sanderson, now Sturges's father-in-law, planned and oversaw the removal of the high knoll that separated the two flat tracts of land he had invested in, and filled the area's lowest terrain, toward the river, with soil from the knoll. The leveled landscape, over which the city's grid easily extended, was better suited for development. In the mid 1880s, Green Ridge's southern and central areas steadily gained residents, but its northern end was still sparsely populated. Sturges took as his real estate partner Robert E. Hurley, a successful civil engineer from thirty miles to the north. Hurley was well known for inventing the Hurley track-laying machine. With the capital these men accumulated from the city's railroad and coal industries, they were able to buy up dozens of undeveloped lots in northern Green Ridge.[18]

Large-upscale land developers—who were ultimately community builders—such as Sanderson, Sturges, and Hurley influenced the kind of neighborhood they created not only through the size of the subdivided lots they decided on but also through restrictions they placed

E. B. Sturges's home, built 1875, Edwin L. Walter, architect
(also of Scranton City Hall in 1888), photo 1880s. Courtesy of
Robert J. Walker, who bought and rehabbed it in 2008–2009.

in the deeds for lots sold. One such deed carried with it stipulations placed by the subdividers: "First. No intoxicating liquors shall be sold upon said lots." Any building had to be set back thirty feet from the front line of the lot, and "no barn or shed or other outbuilding" could be within fifty feet of this line. Furthermore, to ensure a respectable residential neighborhood, the developers required that the "lot only be used for dwelling purposes and not more than one single or double tenement to cost when built not less than two thousand dollars." The developers intended these lots in Green Ridge to be home to what they considered decent and upstanding citizens. They wanted to keep out such things as saloons, horses, other animals and smelly activities, and the people of the most meager means. By excluding elements they saw as undesirable, they would make their land more valuable. In short, they hoped to create a solid middle- and upper-middle-class neighborhood.[19]

The entrepreneurial Sturges saw the need for even faster, larger-capacity, and cleaner transit in and around Scranton, and he understood that an improvement over the horse-drawn variety would increase his profits from his land dealings. In 1885, when he learned that Belgian immigrant and inventor Charles Van Depoele had patented an electric railway, he commissioned him to design an electric streetcar for the new Scranton Suburban Street Railway Company, which Sturges helped organize and presided over. A year later, the first economically successful exclusively electric streetcar system in the United States made its maiden voyage between central city and the outlying neighborhood of Green Ridge. Not only was the trolley powered completely by electricity but it also had electric lights inside the car and ran on a regular schedule, thus upstaging attempts to establish electric streetcars in Richmond, Virginia; Montgomery, Alabama; and South Bend, Indiana. Green Ridge was now poised to become the finest "streetcar suburb" in the city.[20]

Along with electric streetcars, Scranton was quick to adopt electric lights, and the little metropolis's early technological prowess would inspire its long-standing nickname. Shortly after Edison's perfecting

Scranton's first electric streetcar, c. 1890.
Courtesy of Lackawanna Historical Society.

of the lightbulb and before he electrified and lit up an entire New York City block, Scranton had electric illumination at its Dickson Locomotive Works in 1880, its steel mills in 1881, and increasingly thereafter in its streets. In the mid- to late1880s, the Reverend David Spencer of the Penn Avenue Baptist Church first dubbed Scranton "the Electric City." The moniker quickly caught on. By 1889, *The Scranton Republican* laid claim to this technological achievement and its resulting appellation and lorded it over its neighbor city: "Scranton is known widely as the Electric city, and it is not surprising that all electrical improvements in this region are credited to that place. . . . The streets of this city were lighted by electricity some months before those of our neighboring city [of Carbondale], and incandescent lamps were in general use here first."[21]

New technology begot more residents. What growth the horse-drawn railway had started in Green Ridge, the electric streetcar accelerated, and with growth came new institutions bespeaking the diversity of the population. Episcopal, Presbyterian, Methodist, Baptist, and Catholic churches—handsome stone and brick edifices, all within a block of Green Ridge Avenue and few blocks from one another in central Green Ridge—were established by the new residents during the last three decades of the nineteenth century. Neighborhood children could attend the two-story public school, originally called the Green Ridge School, erected in 1870 at the corner of Dickson Avenue and Breaker Street, or St. Paul's Catholic School a half dozen blocks away. In 1902, the name "Electric Street" was also applied to Breaker Street, its continuation westward to the river. Replacing "Breaker" with "Electric" carried the concept of the Electric City and its association with modern technology from one end of Green Ridge to the other. By the turn of the twentieth century, passengers could ride electric streetcars from the heart of Scranton's downtown into neighborhoods throughout the city and transfer from one line to another. Beyond Green Ridge's center, the streetcar continued more than a mile farther north, past recently subdivided but largely empty lots.

After George Sanderson's death, in 1886, his second son, Col. George Sanderson, took over the Sanderson estate. The Pennsylvania Coal Company, which owned enormous tracts of land in the northeastern section of Green Ridge, offered a great number of lots for sale. At the northernmost end of the acreage they had plotted, they set aside a median strip of parkland opposite moderate-size lots on a street alluringly named Woodlawn Park and advertised them as "A New Departure for Attractive Homes." They configured smaller lots on nearby streets or at the end of blocks approaching thoroughfares where businesses sprang up. The land-planning decisions of the Pennsylvania Coal Company, the Sandersons, and other large developers, in fact, determined the general nature of the neighborhoods to come. After they laid out plots and streets, these major speculators—as exemplified by the 1898 *Atlas of Surveys of the City of Scranton & Borough of Dunmore*—sold lots to many individuals planning to construct a home for themselves and sometimes an additional one next door to help finance their own. But the recurring names of the owner of each land parcel in the vicinity also reveal that many smaller investors scooped up multiple lots, confident they could resell at a profit over time.[22]

Green Ridge, like other Scranton neighborhoods, came to be through a myriad of small decisions by many individuals looking to benefit from Scranton's boom economy. No overarching plans or the concept of zoning restricted them. This process of incremental development and growth made for a population with a diversity of incomes, a built environment of mixed residential and commercial uses, and housing of varied types and styles all in the same neighborhood. By 1898, Sturges and Hurley had bought up numerous lots north and east of Green Ridge Corners, including seventeen of the thirty-six lots on the unusually long block of the north side of Electric Street. It was here that the Butzners would move in 1910. The easy access via trolley made this undeveloped section of gently undulating land even more appealing to the Butzners and other middle-class families seeking new homes. Just before the turn of the century, however, only five of these thirty-six lots had houses on them.

People of relatively modest means could purchase lots in Green Ridge from well-heeled men like Sturges and Hurley. Some of the less recent immigrants had saved enough to buy property—a reliable investment for their hard-earned money. A sixteen-year-old Polish immigrant named Joseph S. Judicki arrived in America in 1888, married Polish-born Sibnea six years later, and became an American citizen in 1897. He worked as a salesman before becoming a butcher in his own right. By 1904, the local paper referred to him as "the well-known meat merchant of North Main avenue," with three assistants and a delivery wagon. Although his store was in Scranton's West Side neighborhood, he rented a humble dwelling on the east side of the Lackawanna River, in the rear of 702 Electric Street, for his family of six. In September 1906, he and his wife had saved enough money to buy a single moderate-size parcel of land down the block, at 815 Electric Street, between Boulevard and Capouse Avenues. A little more than a mile and a half north of City Hall, the parcel was one of scores of recently subdivided lots of assorted dimensions and shapes in Scranton's Green Ridge section, just a few blocks from the city line with Dunmore. The 50-by-135-foot lot had once been part, according to the deed, of a much larger "plot of lots . . . situated partly in the City of Scranton and partly in the Borough of Dunmore" and belonging to Edward B. Sturges and Robert E. Hurley, the real estate duo who had invested in numerous parcels they had bought from the Pennsylvania Coal Company.[23]

Judicki—"a quiet and industrious citizen," according to *The Scranton Republican*—had invested well. Land in Green Ridge continued to increase in value and created a chain of opportunities for modest investors. Three years later, in 1909, having withstood malicious charges that he was an "Italian anarchist"—on both counts a patently false accusation, meant as a slur, from his business partner, with whom he was parting ways—Joseph Judicki sold the unbuilt lot for twelve hundred dollars to Francis J. and Katherine H. Olver. Since 1894, the Olvers had lived in a small house at 723 Electric Street, the third building from the corner of Boulevard Avenue, on the same block. Mr. Olver was a former teamster who had become a mason and a carpenter. With

Jane's birthplace, 815 Electric Street, in Scranton's Green Ridge
neighborhood, 2014. Author's photo.

his construction skills, he himself most likely built, as a business venture, the practical two-story wooden single dwelling on the property.
Olver followed the plan of other houses nearby, making it simple and
serviceable, two rooms wide by two rooms deep on an ashlar masonry
foundation, with windows in the cellar. Except for a leaded-glass window at the foot of the hall stairs, the single-family residence lacked
ornamentation. Within a year, Olver had completed the building and
found a buyer. On October 21, 1910, Dr. J. D. Butzner signed the
purchase agreement for six thousand dollars—with no mention of a
mortgage—on his first home for Bess, eight-month-old Betty, and
himself. They moved in shortly after signing the deed.[24]

By late fall of 1910, when Decker, Bess, and Betty moved in, all
but two of the lots on either side of their block had been built upon.
Each house had a shallow front yard and at least enough land between
it and the neighbor's house for a driveway, although most households
did not yet have an automobile. The gently rolling terrain added
charm to the street and the neighborhood. In predominantly gridded
Green Ridge, Electric Street was something of an anomaly because

it conformed to the curves of the two and a half hilly, oval-shaped blocks across the street from the section in which the Butzners lived. In this splash of picturesque landscape set aside for grander houses, the north-south streets dead-ended into the south side of the oval blocks, prevented from cutting through to Electric Street and beyond. Thus, the Butzners' new home, on the north side of Electric Street, was situated on the area's longest block, spanning the equivalent of five short city blocks or roughly four-tenths of a mile.

As the Butzners headed out their front door and walked west down this extraordinarily long block, the terrain sloped gently downhill toward the Lackawanna River, and the homes turned humbler. With their eclectic roof styles, window arrangements, porch designs, and interior configurations, no two houses were exactly alike. Yet the houses lining this block of Electric Street formed a pleasing and cohesive streetscape full of individual variations. The houses'

Streetscape downhill from 815 Electric Street, with slate sidewalk, looking toward Green Ridge Corners, 2014. Author's photo.

occupants, too, were of assorted backgrounds and occupations but collectively formed a little community. On the Butzners' side of the street, Mr. D. E. Baldwin, a plaster contractor, lived next door to the west, then Mrs. Isabella Okell, an elderly widow, and Herbert Axford, an inspector for the DL&W Railroad. After passing these homes similar in size to theirs, the Butzners walked by a half dozen smaller, older dwellings—including that of Francis Olver, his wife, and two daughters—before reaching the thoroughfare of Boulevard Avenue, along which the streetcar ran. At the end of the block, Green Ridge Corners greeted them across the street. Although in 1898 only a few commercial enterprises existed at "the Corners," with the addition and extension of streetcar lines, a new array of businesses at Sanderson Avenue and East Market Street had grown up—among them the Green Ridge Bank, the diminutive Green Ridge Department Store, a grocer's, a butcher's, a shoemaker's, and two drugstores. Between the commercial blocks and the river, apartments above the stores and boardinghouses provided affordable living quarters for low-wage immigrants and native-born workers.

Nestled into the neighborhood but taking up considerable space, big industry was clearly visible within the adjacent blocks west of Green Ridge Corners—including the Nicholson Lumber Company and the Paragon Plaster & Supply Company. Dominating the industrial aspect of the landscape, massive angular coal breakers loomed beyond this section of Green Ridge. In 1912, the Scranton Board of Trade tallied twenty-seven working coal breakers (or collieries) in the city of Scranton itself. Three of them—already established when George Sanderson arrived—churned out the region's main export in the streetcar suburb's western section. The breakers continued operations until the 1950s, processing anthracite for almost a century.[25]

When Bess and Betty headed out of their house in the other direction, homes became finer the farther east they walked. They first encountered the home of their easterly next-door neighbor, Mr. Philo W. Butler, who, with other family members, managed a company providing coal breakers with pipes for steam, water, and gas.

Up the hill, they might cross paths with the family of Edson Blandin, manager of the Hitchner Biscuit Company, or with Seth Shoemaker, a textbook editor at the International Correspondence Schools, the large and successful institution Jane Jacobs credited as helping to fuel the city's "explosive growth" during this time. At the end of the extra-long block, they reached North Washington Avenue, the first in the series of avenues named for American presidents. Some of the city's wealthiest citizens, many with their live-in servants, resided on this stretch of North Washington, an extension of central city's spine and the last street before crossing into Dunmore. Most people on the hilly, picturesque south side of Electric also occupied fancier homes. People of diverse incomes and professions dwelled contentedly within a few blocks of one another. Apparently, none of these residents minded living in close proximity to commercial and industrial ventures.

A few years after the Butzners and many of their neighbors moved into Green Ridge, F. L. Hitchcock proclaimed this outer-city neighborhood "the finest suburb of Scranton." Although he worked as a lawyer in central city, Hitchcock himself had chosen to live in Green Ridge beginning in the late 1870s, only a decade after settlers started trickling in. From its earliest days, Green Ridge naturally contained

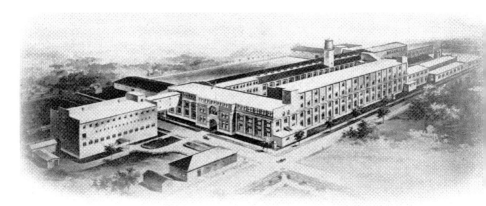

Scranton Lace Curtain Company, built 1891, on the western edge of Green Ridge, photo 1914. Courtesy of Margo Azzarelli.

the mixed uses and diversity whose value Jane Jacobs would argue for in *The Death and Life of Great American Cities.* Just a few blocks from George Sanderson's house, two other major industries flourished. The Scranton Glass Company occupied ten lots and had an eighty-five-man force to produce a prodigious number of bottles and glassware, as well as fill an ongoing order from Chicago for all the inkwells they could make. Thirty employees at the Green Ridge Iron Works manufactured about four thousand tons of wrought iron a year and reworked scrap iron. The sprawling Scranton Lace Company employed a considerable workforce. Managers and laborers alike could walk to their jobs at these plants, and they lived not far from one another. Unlike desirable suburbs today—which Jane Jacobs disdained because they lacked "the room for great differences among neighbors"—Scranton's finest suburb in the initial years of the twentieth century encompassed a population with a range of incomes and backgrounds, living adjacent to commercial and industrial activities all within a quick ride or moderate walk to downtown.[26]

Scranton's finest suburb had come about as a result of a multitude of decisions by diverse individuals, rich or of modest means, physicians or laborers, native- or foreign-born. They often lived cheek by jowl and were all reported on by the city's newspapers. The wealthy businessman and the industrious immigrant could acquire property and a home. It was George Sanderson, tapped by one of the city's founding fathers, who could be credited with first seeing the possibilities of Green Ridge's development as an expansion of the city. Having amassed wealth from his early real estate dealings, he felt a sense of civic duty and took it upon himself to contribute parcels of land for the common good, such as a libraries, schools, and churches. His opportunistic son-in-law continued to build the neighborhood that he had started. Scranton's outer city developed without large-scale plans or zoning restrictions. Like all the city's neighborhoods, Green Ridge grew organically over time. Even the earliest developers of Green Ridge, as they laid the groundwork for the kind of neighborhood they envisioned, varied the size of the lots they plotted and the restrictions they placed in the deeds. In an unplanned process, the many other individuals seeking opportunity in Scranton—like the Olvers and the Judickis—who bought the lots and put up houses, spontaneously fabricated a neighborhood by enlarging the city's grid with adaptive anomalies as they saw fit to encompass a lively mix of land uses, buildings, and people. Catholic churches and schools were mixed in among Protestant institutions. Mine whistles sounded not far from mansions. The incorporated city of Scranton was barely a half century old, full of promise and pride, and largely accommodating to all. Green Ridge was the community that the very young Jane would first experience and observe. It would leave a lasting imprint.

Green Ridge Presbyterian Church, corner of Green Ridge Street and Wyoming Avenue, 2011. Author's photo.

CHAPTER 3

Ties That Bind in the Great Mosaic

WHILE DR. BUTZNER'S PROFESSIONAL ties to the city strengthened, family and neighborhood life increasingly anchored Bess Robison Butzner in the community. Sinking roots ever more deeply into Scranton, Bess Butzner, in the early spring of 1912, officially joined the Green Ridge Presbyterian Church, a ten-minute walk from the Butzners' new home and across from the Green Ridge Public Library. Bess may have attended this church from the time she moved to Scranton, but formally giving up membership in her hometown church, to which she had belonged all her life—even during her years in Philadelphia—indicated she had made a serious commitment to her adopted city. To join, one had to apply to the new church and get a "letter of dismission" from the old. The Green Ridge church found the papers of "Miss Bessie May Robinson [*sic*] from the First Presbyterian Church of Bloomsburg" in order and received her into their membership.[1]

Decker Butzner also cemented his ties to the Electric City and to his friend and colleague Dr. Kay. On May Day of 1912, Drs. Butzner and Kay established their offices together in a suite on the top floor of the imposing Dime Bank Building, in the heart of downtown, fronting on both Spruce Street and Wyoming Avenue. The Richardsonian Romanesque-style red sandstone building had an exquisite bank lobby on the ground floor and a turret running up the full five stories at the corner. The two men shared office space, allowing Dr. Butzner to cover Dr. Kay's patients when he traveled, which he did quite frequently, to such places as Paris for a three-month course in medicine, or to circle the globe in 1916, returning via ocean liner from Yokohama to San Francisco. The doctors placed an ad that ran for two weeks in the daily paper so that no one could miss the announcement of the opening of their practice. The newspapers not only reflected and permanently recorded the city's intricate web of social ties but also served as the primary method of mass communication.[2]

Whether Dr. Kay's frequent and prolonged trips contributed to or were made possible by his estrangement from his wife, we can only speculate. Lackawanna County court records show Dr. T. W. Kay's divorce from his wife, Edna Fuller Kay, was finalized on June 1, 1912, and a public notice appeared in the *Republican* shortly afterward. Divorce was not unheard of in those days but was still unusual, with less than 10 percent of marriages ending in divorce. But to all eyes, Dr. Kay led an unconventional life—part of his aura that Jane found intriguing—and those close to him knew that by 1910 he had found quarters at a central-city boardinghouse where nine other men of varying professions—including a lawyer and a candy maker— resided, while Edna had gone to live with her parents in New York State. Other signs of the couple's whereabouts suggest they had separated several years before this. In October 1912, the *Scranton Truth* shared the divorcée's cheerful social news: "Mrs. Edna Kay, daughter of Rev. M. D. Fuller, formerly of this city, now of Minneapolis, has sent cards to her many friends, announcing [she had wed] George Hudson Strickland of International Falls, Minn."[3]

As active and recognized members of the Lackawanna County Medical Society, both Dr. Butzner and Dr. Kay presented papers to the membership on their research and helped organize its social events, all of which the newspapers followed. Dr. Butzner usually attended meetings and annual dinners, as did Dr. Kay when he was in town. But Dr. Kay was one of a small number of his colleagues who would pick up and go to Harrisburg for the State Medical Association convention, and he spoke more often than his office partner at professional gatherings. The elder doctor had published numerous scholarly articles on a vast array of medical topics in professional journals nationwide since at least 1888. The city agencies of Scranton, at times, looked to the county medical society for help with public-health matters, and the public-spirited and independent-minded Dr. Butzner could be counted on to answer the call.[4]

On March 13, 1912, in response to a request from Scranton's school board, physicians in the Lackawanna County Medical Society discussed at their monthly meeting whether to and how they would carry out the medical "inspection" of vision and hearing, and tuberculosis testing of 23,000 schoolchildren. They argued about how much each doctor should be paid for this service and what the school board could afford, comparing what the board paid their teachers and the school janitor to the small amount they would receive. Many physicians were in favor of fixing payment for an inspection at one dollar per pupil, the standard price of a visit to a doctor's office. Dr. Butzner, however, cut through the bickering and suggested that three doctors could do the job and devote their entire time to it. "If this course were pursued the danger of exploiting the public, the danger of a motive of graft would be removed. The rest of the men, sixteen or seventeen of us, would get nothing, but we would get a more efficient system." A vote by members of the society defeated the move for a dollar-per-pupil fixed payment, and the medical community came together as before.[5]

During this impassioned meeting of the medical society, one doctor admitted that "most of us make more than $3000 a year and the majority $4000 a year." At least some doctors felt they earned enough—or were generous regardless—to contribute to charitable causes and make investments in local companies. The local papers recorded numerous gifts by its physicians as well as the rest of the population. At whatever level they could afford, citizens supported others in need, and the papers acknowledged their good deeds. Dr. T. W. Kay donated to the city's playground fund, although he had no children, and to Scranton's semicentennial festivities and, as a member of Scranton's Board of Trade (the predecessor to the Chamber of Commerce), gave to the Belgian Relief Fund, providing food for German-occupied Belgium. Both he and Dr. Butzner gave to such things as the Board of Associated Charities' big benefit at the grand Poli Theatre.[6]

With a growing family, Dr. Butzner had reason to invest for the future. After his customary serious consideration, he put money into the Anthracite Trust Company, a local bank whose way of conducting business he approved of. Beginning in May 1915, he attended their annual banquet and birthday observance held for the officers, directors, and stockholders at the Hotel Casey. Banks with $250,000 capital typically had a hundred stockholders, but the Anthracite Trust Company had closer to four hundred stockholders, "each one of whom has always been made to feel that he is intimately connected with the welfare of the company," the *United States Investor* commented. "The result has been that stockholders have shown far more than ordinary interest in the affairs of the bank and have brought in a great many accounts. . . . The maintenance of this spirit of close co-operation seems destined to carry the Anthracite Trust Company to even greater prosperity." Dr. Butzner was drawn to this company that valued the participation of its many small investors. His daughter Jane would later applaud these kinds of relationships in business and community.[7]

On January 15, 1913, when Betty Butzner was almost three, her first sibling was born—a little boy named William Boyd Butzner. With a predilection for family history and recurring family names, Decker and Bess had an easy time choosing this baby's first name because of the many Williams on both sides of the genealogical tree. Decker's father and brother were named William, and there had been three Williams on Bess's side: her paternal grandfather, her great-great-grandfather, and her brother. Boyd was Bess's father's middle name and a family surname from erstwhile generations. Bess was the keeper of her family's genealogical records and kept track of her relations.[8]

One of Bess's relatives—a distant cousin who had grown up near her in Columbia County and now lived in Scranton—Dr. Edith Barton, likely came to visit the new baby. After graduating in 1902 from the Woman's Medical College of Pennsylvania—established in 1850, the world's second medical school to train women and grant them an M.D. degree—Dr. Barton had moved to Scranton in 1904, at age forty-two, to practice medicine and surgery. Her office and home were side by side in central city, close to Decker's and other doctors' offices. *The Scranton Republican* called her one of Scranton's "most prominent women physicians," revealing that she was not alone in her gender among doctors in the city. She was duly recognized nevertheless.[9]

The Barton branch of Bess's family, stemming from her paternal grandmother, Betsy Barton Robison, was descended from Thomas Barton, the original emigrant in 1760 from England, who came via Virginia to Pennsylvania. Edith's father, Henry Clay Barton, was proud to be related to Clara Barton, the Civil War nurse and founder of the American Red Cross. Bess spoke of Clara Barton as her relative and kept in touch with her cousin Edith, another remarkable woman among the unusually large number of professional females in Bess's extended family. Jane was aware of this legacy and admired these women. Like Bess and other of her female relatives, Edith Barton had graduated from the State Normal School at Bloomsburg and begun by teaching in the public schools. In 1913, a day shy of her fifty-first birthday, Dr. Barton died suddenly of endocarditis. Dr. J. D. Butzner was one of six pallbearers, all of whom were physicians, at her funeral. Members of societies to which she belonged—including the Foreign Missionary Society of the Elm Park (Methodist) Church, the Florence Crittenton Organization (for moral reform), and the Daughters of the American Revolution—formed part of the "large attendance," headlined by the *Republican*, at the service. Edith Barton shared the family penchant for helping the less fortunate through her church and social welfare societies, and a pride in her relation to her nation's early history.[10]

Although their cultural background differed vastly from the Robisons', Decker's parents, William and Lucy Isabel Butzner, and Bess had fond feelings for one another. Unlike Bess's parents, who were proper and "very Victorian in character," her grandson said, Decker's parents could embarrass both Bess and her husband with their country ways and expressions—such as casually describing the Virginia weather as "hot as six bitches in the summer." In July and August of 1913, Bess was happy to spend the summer months in Virginia at her in-laws' farm with her three-year-old daughter and infant son while Decker traveled in Europe for eight weeks as part of the Physician's Travel Study tour—"the Scranton physicians with the party being Dr. T. W. Kay and Dr. John D. Butzner," *The Scranton Republican* noted.[11]

While Dr. Butzner felt conflicted about leaving his family to go abroad for the summer, the worldwide adventurer Dr. Kay was footloose and fancy-free. Dr. Kay convinced his partner to explore European capitals he had never seen before and to meet his "professional brethren of Europe." The bon vivant Dr. Kay certainly made

Dr. Butzner (far left) and Dr. Kay (far right) on board ship for the Physician's Travel Study tour, 1913. Estate of Jane Jacobs.

an enjoyable traveling companion. Sailing from New York, the two Scranton doctors took part in clinics in Italy, Germany, England, and France, and attended the International Congress of Medicine in London. Before the congress convened in early August, committees of local doctors in Paris, Berlin, Vienna, Munich, Brussels, Frankfurt, Cologne, and Wiesbaden feted the visiting doctors and held lavish banquets in their honor. Dr. Kay had also invited along his Scranton friends Charles Seamans, a successful businessman and fellow Board of Trade member, his wife, Emma, and their niece, Blanche Gardner of Wilkes-Barre, who, though not in the medical profession, "were invited to all of the functions tendered the physicians." On August 15, Drs. Butzner and Kay and his friends boarded the *President Lincoln* in Southampton, England, for their eleven-day voyage back to New York before traveling by train to Scranton. This was the first and, apparently, only trip Decker ever made overseas. Bess began their family photo album with pages and pages of images of people Decker had traveled with—including a group portrait of sixty well-dressed passengers on a ship's deck—and places he had seen. When the county medical society convened in the fall, Decker regaled his colleagues with tales of the study tour and presented the paper he had given at the International Medical Congress.[12]

When parental or sibling emergencies arose, Decker made the three-hundred-mile trek to his family's farm in Virginia. In March 1915, he left for Fredericksburg to tend to his critically ill sixty-three-year-old father. He had been summoned previously to help with his family's medical crises and had once performed surgery on his brother. After a couple weeks' ministering to his father in Virginia, Decker returned to his wife and children. Within a fortnight, they received the news that Decker's father, William Joseph Butzner, had passed away.[13]

Only a few months later, when Decker's son, little William, was two and a half, he contracted a childhood illness—probably scarlet fever, because, despite Dr. Butzner's and his colleague Dr. E. L. Kiesel's efforts, William developed acute nephritis. Terrified of losing him and protective of Betty's health, his parents sent Betty to stay with her grandmother in Bloomsburg. Sadly, William died on August 5, 1915. He was buried in the family plot at the Creveling Cemetery, in the tiny village of Almedia, down the river road from the old Robison home in Espy. "He was a bright and interesting child," a short obituary read, and "was beloved by all who knew him." Betty was shocked and distraught when she learned of her brother's death. As children do, she blamed herself. Not long afterward, when Betty was in Sunday school, the teacher attempted to stimulate discussion in the class. "Do you know anything about God?" she inquired of her young students. Betty was quick to respond and did so earnestly: "I know that if your brother is sick and you go away, God takes your brother." For Betty, William's death was a deep loss and profoundly affected her for the rest of her life, her daughter observed. "She was always very protective of her other siblings and wanted to make sure

Mary Jane "Jennie" Breece Robison, Jane's grandmother, outside her home in Bloomsburg, 1920s. Estate of Jane Jacobs.

that nothing happened to them. As an adult, Betty talked about what the loss meant to her and often used to say, 'Life is temporary.'"[14]

In 1916, the Great War was raging in Europe, women in America still struggled for the right to vote, and Scranton celebrated a half century of cityhood. On a warm, showery May 4, Jane Isabel Butzner was born. Less than a year after the trauma of little William's death, the new baby was especially welcomed by Decker and Bess, now age thirty-seven and thirty-six, respectively. Betty, age six, was delighted to have another sibling—and a little sister, no less. Dr. Butzner signed his daughter Jane's birth certificate as the attending physician in his own home. As they had with their older children, Bess and Decker chose two recurring family names for the little girl—Jane after Bess's mother, Mary Jane Breece Robison, who went by "Jennie" (then a common nickname for Jane), and Bess's sister and aunt, both named

Betty, Jane, and Bess Butzner alongside garage in backyard of 815 Electric Street, 1917–1918. Estate of Jane Jacobs.

Jane. They selected Isabel because of Decker's mother's middle name, which derived from her grandmother, Isabel Richardson Walker.[15]

Jane's first city, the Scranton into which she was born, was itself still young for a municipality, but it was in its prime. Incorporated in 1866 with an estimated 30,000 people, fifty years later Scranton's population was estimated by the morning paper to have quintupled to 150,000. "It has five steam railroads and two electric railroads entering the city and a trolley service that covers the valley," *The Scranton Republican's* commemorative semicentennial insert took pride in enumerating. The city's economy thrived as exports increased and tonnage of coal mined neared its all-time peak in 1917.[16]

Despite the health of Scranton's economy, with their newborn Jane and a heightened awareness of the threat of childhood diseases, Decker and Bess kept careful track of newspaper reports of cases of infantile paralysis—as polio was known then—in both Pennsylvania and the rest of the country. When Jane was just two months old, they saw on *The Scranton Republican's* front page that this dreaded illness lurked too close for comfort. "One Death an Hour, Toll of N.Y. Plague: Infantile Paralysis Works Continued Terror—Thousands Leave the City," it virtually shouted. The article warned of "thousands of families who usually leave town for the summer" hastening their departure to escape the scourge. Scrantonians feared the New York refugees would come to their city and bring infantile paralysis with them. The disease had been around for decades, but this was its worst epidemic in America to date. Dr. Butzner, civic-minded and active in the community, was again ready to step up to the plate.[17]

Six days later, on July 12, Scranton's Director of Public Safety, Fred K. Derby, put out a boxed, front-page call in the morning *Republican* "request[ing] all physicians in the city to confer with the department of safety" on the best way of preventing an epidemic like New York's "in their own city." Sixty of the 213 physicians listed in the city directory answered Derby's summons by showing up in the City Hall council chambers that evening. "Addresses made by many of the physicians present [at the meeting] sought to have a more rigorous inspection of the children brought into this city from New York. . . ." Besides advocating sanitary living conditions and cleaning up the city, the doctors expressed their concerns about flies and open garbage cans in some sections of town. One of them singled out open manure piles near barns around the collieries, "where most of the flies [believed to be the source of disease at the time] in the city are bred." Dr. Butzner was not among the physicians who cast aspersions on the working class and the places where they worked and lived. He was cited, however, as a physician "prominent in the session" who had spoken at the meeting.[18]

The *Republican* reported that Scranton's first victim of infantile paralysis died the night that the doctors met with city officials. Eighteen-month-old, Harry Naso, a child of Italian immigrants, lived in a wooden tenement block on the West Side. Called the Carlucci building, it was home to fifteen families and seventy-five children, and bordered the railroad tracks along the river. Accompanying the news story, a photo spanned more than half the page directly below the paper's masthead, displaying the extensive back facade of the tenement strung with rows of porches. An *X* marked the apartment that the Naso family occupied. Despite calling attention to the crowded conditions of housing where poor immigrants lived, the caption praised the porches for affording "ample opportunity of enjoying fresh air" and pointed out that this healthful amenity—common to Scranton's multifamily housing—was not usually found in New York City's or other large cities' tenements.[19]

By the end of July, Dr. Butzner was attending to another case of infantile paralysis—this time that of a two-and-a-half-year-old named Gertrude Philbin in Dunmore, closer to his own residence. Cautiously and responsibly, he called in the state health department to confirm his diagnosis. They corroborated it and "ordered a general clean-up in the vicinity." On August 10, Dr. Butzner reported to the state Scranton's third case of infantile paralysis since the New York outbreak. He examined and treated four-month-old Harry Kalinosky of South Scranton. The infant's home was "placed under strict quarantine" and "a nurse was placed in charge of the house." Scranton City Hall now required that parents who wanted to travel with their children out of state obtain a certificate of good health from their family physician.[20]

Despite precautions—including strict quarantine orders—to prevent the spread of the disease, by August 25, twenty-three cases of infantile paralysis had been identified in the county: ten in Scranton, six in Dunmore, and the rest scattered in other boroughs. This time the state health board conferred with twenty-seven physicians on whether to close the schools and for how long. Some supported school closures, while others opposed the idea. Of course, Dr. Butzner took part and, with his sympathy toward people of all circumstances and his natural ability to take charge, raised an additional issue for consideration. As the *Republican*'s correspondent noted, "Dr. J. D. Butzner, also declared himself in favor of closing the schools for at least a month, but believed that the teachers should be paid for this time lost, not through a fault of their own, but by conditions. Dr. Butzner's plea that the teachers should be paid seemed to be the sentiment of the meeting." After the conference, the board decided to close all schools until September 18. Dr. G. J. Van Vechten, the board's superintendent, also ordered Sunday schools and local movie theaters closed to boys and girls under the age of sixteen.[21]

A decade after setting up practice in the Electric City, Dr. Butzner had become a leading physician in the Scranton area and an integral member of the medical community. Regular squibs in the newspaper showed that other well-respected doctors frequently called him in to consult on important cases. Medical professionals and citizens alike recognized his extraordinary diagnostic abilities. In an interview in 2002, his daughter Jane recalled, "[My father] was intellectually very curious, bright and independent. In some ways he was like a detective. He was locally very famous as a diagnostician, and a good diagnostician is a sort of detective. I loved to hear his stories about how he found out this and that." No doubt Jane heard his stories of the polio epidemic. Her father was civically engaged and a born leader, never hesitant to go against the grain. And Scranton was a manageable and medium-size city, where officials could sound an alarm and citizens could easily mobilize for the commonweal. The newspapers expressed the city's pride that some of its qualities were superior to those of a "great" city, such as New York or Philadelphia, where they saw overcrowding and disease as rampant.[22]

While Dr. Butzner participated fully in the civic and professional life of the city, Bess Butzner was pulled into the close-knit social fabric of neighborhood life in Green Ridge, a departure from her premarriage life as a professional teacher and nurse. Now she devoted a great deal of her energy to her children, but she also set aside time to help others. By the time Betty was two years old, "Evening Chat" in the *Scranton Truth* had noted Betty's presence, accompanied by her mother, at Amelia Kiesel's bon voyage party. Amelia was the daughter of Dr. Ernest L. Kiesel, another of Dr. Butzner's close physician friends. Her grandparents hosted the fancy party, handing out miniature traveling bags and steamer trunks as party favors. The next year, the newspaper spotted Betty at a more typical birthday party of neighbor Irvine Downing, along with other Electric Street children. Bess herself also took part in social occasions and belonged to organizations, both exclusively for women. Neighbor women invited Bess and other adult females to afternoon tea parties, often with musical programs and bridge games. Women tended to gather for their own functions, usually after lunch, when children were at school and husbands were at work, and they banded together to form their own charitable clubs. Bess, as a member of the Scranton branch of the Needlework Guild, assisted in a citywide project to raise funds to buy food for ten thousand starving children in Central Europe.[23]

As Decker and Bess ensconced themselves in the community, Betty expanded her world and ties to the neighborhood when she started at the local public grammar school around the time her little sister was born. Without crossing any streets, she could walk to the Robert Morris School #27, situated just minutes away on the same block where the Butzners lived. Because this part of town had no back alleys, Betty could cut through the ample backyards of her Electric

Street neighbors and those back-to-back on Columbia Street. Since 1895, the newer, larger three-story brick and stone Robert Morris School had stood at Boulevard Avenue and Columbia Street, the northwest corner of the emerging neighborhood, anticipating more students. It had replaced the old Green Ridge School when the school board acquired a new site through a land swap with the owners of the mine near the school's previous Dickson Avenue location. Behind the Butzners' house, Columbia Street still had uninhabited two-family houses on its south-side lots, once owned by the Pennsylvania Coal Company, as well as a couple of empty lots on its north side.[24]

Although Europe's Great War had broken out in July 1914, the United States did not join the triple entente of Britain, France, and Russia until almost three years later. On April 6, 1917, the U.S. Congress voted to declare war on Germany. Deeming this "a war to end all wars" and one that would "make the world safe for democracy," President Woodrow Wilson abandoned his stated position of neutrality and attached his signature to the war resolution. Jane's father heartily endorsed the president's action, even though he had not voted for him. Six months prior, Decker had joined fifty thousand college alumni in the Hughes National College League, which was "rapidly organizing branches in hundreds of cities" throughout the country. "College Men Work to Elect Hughes," declared the headline in *The Scranton Republican*. They were campaigning for Republican presidential candidate Charles Evans Hughes, a former governor of New York with a progressive record, backed by former President Theodore Roosevelt, a staunch proponent of entering the conflict against the Germans. Hughes challenged Wilson, the incumbent and a Democrat, but was unable to stop him from winning a second term. Nonetheless, events finally convinced Wilson to come around to Hughes's position on the war.[25]

The *Republican* approved of President Wilson's declaration of war and lauded the throngs of Scrantonians eager to join the cause. On June 9, 1917, the paper announced: "Sixty-five physicians, members of the Lackawanna County Medical Society, the majority of them

Contingent of Members Leaving C. R. R. of N. J. Station. Scranton. Pa., 1917. World War I
Left to Right—Dr. John B. Corser, Dr. Van Decker, Dr. F. Whitney Davies,
Dr. J. N. Douglas (deceased), Dr. John D. Butzner (deceased), Dr. D. J. Jenkins

Lackawanna County Medical Society members as army
volunteers, 1917; in *The Medical Society Reporter,* Oct. 1943.
Courtesy of Geisinger Commonwealth Medical School
Library and Lackawanna County Medical Society.

residents of Scranton, have volunteered for service in the American
field armies and have passed their examinations." There followed a
list with each physician's name and city of residence. Dr. Butzner, but
not the fifty-nine-year-old Dr. Kay, had volunteered. A contingent
of six county medical society members posed for a photographer
in front of the Central Railroad of New Jersey Station before they
boarded the train heading to their assignments. The mustachioed
Dr. John D. Butzner towered above his five colleagues, all dressed
in army uniforms with caps and knee-high leather boots and staring
earnestly into the camera.[26]

The train carried commissioned lieutenant Butzner to Fort Ogle-
thorpe, Georgia, for military training. He was then assigned to Camp

Gordon, outside Atlanta, "where he made a splendid record. Soon after taking up his work at Camp Gordon, Dr. Butzner was promoted to the rank of captain and placed in charge of the infirmary. Within a short time, his ability was recognized and he was appointed chief of the examining board of the large camp." For more than a year and a half, Dr. John Decker Butzner served his country as an army camp physician. While he was away from his family, he missed certain momentous occasions at home, and his family felt the absence of his large and cheerful presence. On October 2, 1917, four months after Dr. Butzner left for military service, John Decker Butzner, Jr., was born. Seven-and-a-half-year-old Betty could be of some help to her mother with the new baby and her little sister, Jane, who was only seventeen months old and toddling around. Bess named the new baby boy for his father, who was named after his great-grandfather, Johann Batzler or Butzler, born in Hennenberg, Bavaria, in 1790. Somehow, the last name of Johann's son George (Dr. Butzner's grandfather) had evolved—either through error or intention—into Butzner when he emigrated from Europe to America in the second quarter of the nineteenth century.[27]

Expecting to be shipped overseas soon and wishing to see his family and new baby son, Dr. Butzner went home on leave for a few days in early August 1918. By September, however, the army's plans for him had changed. With the advent of the flu, Dr. Butzner's overwhelming task was tending to soldiers afflicted with the deadly Spanish influenza. Military personnel spread the virus as they traveled from camp to camp, and the crowded conditions of the camps further exacerbated the outbreak. Influenza and pneumonia sickened between 20 and 40 percent of people in the army and navy and, in the end, claimed more American lives—both those of civilians and military personnel—than would all the twentieth-century wars. In late September, *Scranton Times* reporters discovered that an unusually high number of influenza and pneumonia cases in the Electric City had gone unreported to public officials. On October 1, Pennsylvania, one of the states hit hardest by the influenza outbreak, first ordered theaters and saloons to close and then all public and parochial schools. Compared to Philadelphia and Pittsburgh, Scranton did not have a huge number of cases, but the Green Ridge Presbyterian Church, where Bess and the children attended, decided as a precaution to close its doors for more than a month, from October 4 through November 7, when hospital beds were full and additional sufferers were treated at the Watres Armory. Although Scranton had managed to prevent a more catastrophic epidemic in the city, 913 Scrantonians died by the end of 1918. Fortunately, the Butzner family escaped the scourge.[28]

Bess's concern for Americans engaged in the war extended to her youngest and—as she told her children—favorite brother, Irvin A. Robison, who had taught her how to fish. Irvin served as an ambulance driver in France. Women back home, and young girls, too, looked for ways to contribute to the war effort. Through the following winter months, Betty took part in a children's club in Green Ridge with a project to aid the war effort. Their contribution made it into the newspaper: "The E.S.K. club of Green Ridge, composed of children ranging in age from 7 to [roughly 13] years, have completed a beautiful knitted afghan, which they have sent to Dr. Butzner for use in the hospital in Atlanta, Ga., where he is serving in the medical corps U.S.A." Since all five girls and two boys "contribut[ing] strips" to the afghan lived within a half block of the Butzners, Bess—with her needlework aptitude—seems to have been the organizer of a group of Betty's neighborhood friends for a fun yet beneficial purpose.[29]

Eight months later, the armistice with Germany was signed, and the Great War ended on November 11, 1918. In Scranton, ten thousand local officials, business owners, and other citizens turned out in the evening for a hastily organized but nevertheless highly spirited Victory Day Parade. While Bess looked forward to Decker's return, a week later she made a celebratory trip with Betty, Jane, and John to visit her mother in Bloomsburg, where her brother Irvin may already have landed. John junior was thirteen months old and had barely seen his father.[30]

On January 21, 1919, the *Republican* broadcast the joyous news that "Captain J. D. Butzner, who for the past year and a half, has been serving in the medical department of the army, has been [honorably] discharged from the service and returned home to resume his practice" in the office he shared with Dr. Kay in the Dime Bank Building. Wasting no time, the next evening, in his magnanimous way, "Dr. Thomas W. Kay, charter member of the Lackawanna County Medical Society, expert medical man, lecturer, worldwide traveler, author, humorist and one of the most interesting characters in the city, was the host . . . to eighty of his friends at a most delightful banquet," the morning paper reported. "Nine Scranton doctors, all wearing their army uniforms were guests of honor." Dr. Butzner was seated at the speakers' table with Dr. Kay. "The affair proved one to be long remembered. . . . Dr. Kay acted as toastmaster and he filled the role admirably. His brief introduction of the various speakers and his witty remarks was a pleasing feature of the evening." As it turned out, "the function also served as a fitting farewell party for Dr. Kay, as he plans to sail . . . to visit France, England, Italy, Belgium, and other war-devastated countries of Europe in an inspection tour of all the famous battlefields and to closely study reconstruction work." His friend and next-door neighbor attorney Cornelius Comegys gave the main address, expressing his appreciation for those who had served and sacrificed and for Dr. Kay, who was too old "to take up arms," yet he contributed money, bought Liberty Bonds and Victory Bonds, and generally lent moral support. The guests rose to toast the doctor in unison and wish him a well-earned vacation.[31]

After his journeys, Dr. Thomas Kay would return to share his travel experiences through tales, photographs, and exotic souvenirs that he brought back. "His experiences proved of great worth to his friends for whom he kept a record of his travels and at great trouble and expense he sought to illustrate them as views could be gotten to make his vivid descriptions seem more real," his friends wrote of him. The Butzner family looked forward to an evening with "old Dr. Kay," as they affectionately called him, learning about far-off lands and hearing his wonderful stories. The larger-than-life Dr. Kay became a character of lasting importance for Jane. Dr. Kay entertained

Lackawanna Avenue, looking east, Scranton's semicentennial celebration, 1916. Courtesy of Lackawanna Historical Society.

his colleagues as well, occasionally using the monthly meeting of the Lackawanna County Medical Society to this end. Fresh from the Middle East, he presented "an illustrated lecture on Palestine" as the "intended business of the regular meeting," much to the physicians' delight.[32]

The Great War left an indelible mark on its veterans, who sought ways to recognize and honor the war's heroes. As early as summer 1919, a group of physicians met in the Hotel Jermyn to form a local post of the American Legion. Dr. Butzner served on the executive committee that organized the Scranton branch. They decided to name the post after Dr. Reese Davis, a not quite twenty-four-year-old member of Scranton's State Hospital staff of physicians, who had been mortally wounded in France. Davis "enlisted early in the war, and lost his life on the first day of his service with the British medical corps—the only physician from Northeastern Pennsylvania to make the supreme sacrifice. Rudyard Kipling, in his story on 'The Irish Guards,' paid tribute to the Forest City doctor." Dr. Butzner would remain keenly involved with the post for the rest of his life. From time to time, members of the Lieutenant Reese Davis Post of the American Legion held a dinner in honor of the ladies, and Mrs. J. D. Butzner accompanied her husband. Even though Dr. Butzner—unlike his wife and children—never officially joined the Green Ridge Presbyterian Church, the governing elders paid tribute to him in their session record and entered his name among eighty "on their Roll of Honor of the Church of those who did service in the late war."[33]

Scranton's anthracite coal production had peaked during the war primarily because the U.S. Navy purchased huge quantities to power their submarines. The advantage of anthracite was that it burned hot and smokeless, so the smoke from submarines was not visible to enemy ships. After the war, Scranton's economy in general continued to grow rapidly, while the coal industry remained the region's economic base. With great public spirit to foster this momentum, a community fund had raised a million dollars to help industries in the city expand. Scranton-born editor John Oliver La Gorce wrote breathlessly in May 1919, "One factory turns out three million buttons a day. One-third of the nation's raw silk is carded and spooled in its metropolitan district. More than half a million people live within twenty miles of its court-house. Bees in a hive were never busier than the hustling, bustling go-ahead folk of the Electric city."[34]

In the postwar boom, smaller businesses sprouted throughout the city. By 1920, in the Butzners' Green Ridge neighborhood, the commercial center at Green Ridge Corners had blossomed with diverse offerings and attracted more people than ever, making it a community center, where people ran errands, crossed paths, and stopped to chat. Thanks to the rising popularity and availability of longer motion pictures and to a small entrepreneur named Michael Webber, the Corners now had Webber's Theater. This movie theater snaked all the way through the main commercial block from Sanderson to

Boulevard Avenues and could seat over three hundred people. To convey the respectability of his theater to upright citizens, Webber advertised: "No better pictures shown anywhere. A first-class theater in every respect." It was flanked at its rear, on Boulevard Avenue, by a paint store and vulcanizing shop. The theater's entrance faced Sanderson Avenue, with Thompson's drugstore and the Globe Grocery on either side. Across the street, behind two dwellings with commercial fronts, the Brown-Wright Dairy Company had moved in with its creamery and bottling plant. The triangular Corners had become—in Jane Jacobs's words—"a hearth," where locals on foot naturally encountered one another.[35]

Soon after New Year's Day, 1920, a census taker knocked at the door of 815 Electric Street and entered the data for John D. and Bess R. Butzner, ages forty-one and forty, respectively, and their three children, Betty, Jane, and John Jr., ages nine years, three years and eight months, and two years and three months, respectively. He also recorded Lucy Isabel Decker Butzner, Decker's mother, as a member of the household. The widowed Lucy had joined the family sometime after Jane was born. With her self-reliance and work ethic, Lucy Butzner must have been a great asset to Bess, taking care of the children and helping to run the house, especially if she was there while Decker served in the army. The children surely enjoyed having their grandmother living with them and the experience of being a three-generation family. At some point after the 1920 census, Lucy returned to Fredericksburg. She died there at the end of 1927, at age eighty-two.

We do not know whether Lucy stayed on to help when she learned that Bess was expecting another baby later that year, or if she stayed longer because she enjoyed living with the lively, growing family. But records attest that on November 10, 1920, James Irvin Butzner was born. He was the youngest and last child in Decker and Bess Butzner's family. His parents acknowledged several ancestors in choosing his first name: James Calvin Butzner (Decker's brother), James Boyd Robison (Bess's father), and James Boyd Robison, Jr. (Bess's older brother). They chose Irvin for Bess's brother (Irvin Robison) and her uncle (her mother's brother, Irvin Breece). The Butzner family affectionately called the baby "Jimmy." When Jimmy was fifteen, his cousin Irvin Andrew Robison, who was two years older than he, visited the Butzners. Jimmy and Irvin commiserated with each other over their shared name. "Perhaps you know that about twenty years ago I legally dropped my first name," (Irvin) Andrew Robison wrote to Jane Jacobs in 2003. "There was a book review in *Time* magazine of a book about names and their consequences, both objectively and subjectively. The last line in the book review was 'worst of all is Irvin.' I recall telling Jimmy upon learning that his middle name is Irvin . . . 'Shake hands, I thought I was the only one stuck with that handle.' I heard your Dad telling your Mother about that incident and enjoying it."[36]

Young Jane and her mother and brothers sometimes accompanied Betty as she walked to school. Like most children, Jane naturally observed everything around her. She looked with her own eyes and, most important, trusted what she saw. "In many cases, people don't see what is in front of their eyes because they've been told what they should be seeing," she explained to Canadian journalist Eleanor Wachtel in 2002 in response to a question about her "special qualities" of being inquisitive and seeing for herself. Jane attributed this lifelong practice of observation to her parents' fostering this habit and taking her seriously from the time she was a very young child. "Children do report what they see and are interested in, if they're not pooh-poohed and are listened to respectfully and [if] it seems that what the grown-ups usually hear is interesting. That's a way of encouraging people to look with their own eyes."[37]

Jane appreciated her parents' receptiveness to and their respect for what she had to say, and she, in turn, took them seriously, sometimes literally. "I remember once when I was very small," she wrote to her brother Jim in 1984, "hearing how March 21 would be the first day of spring, and how I leapt out of bed that morning expecting with full confidence to see flowers blooming and leaves on the trees. Mother had a lot of explaining to do."[38]

Jane, her brother John, and Aunt Emily Robison (?) in front of Electric Street house with velocipede and horse with wheels, 1919–1920. Estate of Jane Jacobs.

From her youngest years, Jane observed and experienced the components that made up the world outside her front door: the sidewalks, the houses up and down the street, the long and short blocks, and the rolling landscape and curving streets. An early impression of sidewalks was etched permanently in her mind and would become a theme in her adult writing. "My earliest memories, of course, are before [I was five] years old [in our house on Electric Street]," she divulged in Wachtel's interview. "It's the sidewalk in front of my house, and in our household we had four children. One of them, at that time, was in a baby carriage, but there were three who were older. We had two vehicles that my mother called velocipedes. They were really tricycles. And we had a little stuffed bear that stood about a foot and a half high. If you pulled a wire in the center, it squealed. I got very irritated at this bear. It had four wheels, and they were very tiny. Every time you hit a joint in the slate sidewalk, you had to pick it up and move it to the next slate. I would get exasperated at that. It was better than nothing on the sidewalk riding up and down, but I learned to get out in sufficient time to stake my claim on one of the velocipedes." Some people recalling such a childhood incident might have focused on the sibling competition for the tricycles. For Jane, this story was about sidewalks. In her adult life, observing city sidewalks would lead to Jane's coining one of her best-known and most frequently quoted concepts, "the sidewalk ballet," describing the ever-changing cast of characters and activities that appear throughout the day along an urban street.[39]

Scranton's sidewalks emblazoned themselves on the memory of another little girl, Mary Catharine "Kay" Schoen, born in 1920 and destined years later to join Jane's family as her sister-in-law, Kay Schoen Butzner. Kay vividly recalled the sidewalks of the city's West Side neighborhood where she grew up as an only child with her chemist father of German background and her mother—a teacher before her marriage—of Welsh descent from rural Bradford County, sixty miles northwest. "The sidewalks were often paved with flat square pieces of gray slate, quarried nearby. They were set closely together and formed a smooth surface for roller-skating," Kay remembered. A single unbroken square comprised the entire width of the path, but inevitably some cracks would widen enough to trip your skates if you weren't careful. With her eyes peeled on the ground, she "found occasional pieces of stone that had fossils of plant fronds or small insects embedded in them." Layers of slate often capped the coal beds, formed by compressing swampy forests over millions of years. Coal mines and the adjacent slate consequently contained a relatively large number of fossils. Throughout her life, Kay displayed on a shelf a fossil of a beautiful and intact fern she had found during childhood explorations with her father of a nearby mine closed on Sundays.[40]

Kay could easily skate or bike around her block and others in her neighborhood, but Jane spent her first few years on one of the city's longest, uninterrupted blocks. Finally, in 1920, the year Jane turned four, Green Ridge's Capouse Avenue was extended through parcels of land previously owned by Sturges and Hurley, thus crossing Electric Street and connecting with its continuation on the other side of the block. The superlong block was now divided into two shorter ones, around which people could walk more easily, providing people with more routes to access neighbors to the north, especially once backyard fences began to create barriers to free-form roaming. New houses squeezed into the cut-through block of Capouse. Jane may have watched the construction of the Capouse connector block. She certainly appreciated it, however, once she could circle the block on her early-model tricycle. Sidewalks and short versus long blocks, observed and experienced at an early age, would figure prominently in her seminal book.[41]

Dr. Butzner walked around the neighborhood, too, but because of his work, he had to travel throughout the city and the surrounding valley in his automobile. Besides performing surgery at the hospital and seeing patients during office hours, he spent long hours making house calls, frequently treating miners with traumatic injuries or black lung disease.[42]

Jane became acquainted with the city beyond her block and the Green Ridge section thanks to her father's work and to the observations about people and places that he shared with his family. "Another [early memory] is: my father was a doctor," Jane recalled for Wachtel. "He had one of the earliest automobiles in the neighborhood. Automobiles have never seemed glamorous to me because, after all, they were just a workaday thing. He needed it to make his calls, but sometimes he would take my mother and my brother and me with him while he was making his calls. I saw quite a bit of Scranton that way. . . . He had all kinds of patients, of course, and he would tell us about them, so my two brothers and my sister and I got quite a picture of Scranton as a great mosaic." Jane preferred to think of diverse groups of people coming together to form a mosaic, with discrete pieces composing a larger picture, rather than a pureed "melting pot," where everyone blends and forfeits their individual characteristics.[43]

"One thing I saw was what we called the "built-down" houses," Jane continued. "Scranton was a coal-mining city, and although there were laws about leaving coal in columns in [the mines] to support the ground up above, it would sometimes get too tempting to the mining companies, which were robber baron sort of companies, to do what was called 'robbing the pillars.' They would take out these supports, and then the ground would cave in up above them. If there were houses [above], the houses caved . . . into a hole. We called those the 'built-down' houses. So I learned about them quite early and what the cause of them was."[44]

Along with their fellow Scrantonians, Decker and Bess understood the danger posed by a city built atop underground mines. Many home buyers examining the deed to their property encountered long passages clearly specifying that a particular coal company retained the rights to any minerals buried below the ground as well as the rights to access and extract them. The deed of sale from Francis J. Olver et ux. to J. D. Butzner described the lot as "extending from the line of lands of the Pennsylvania Coal Company in the rear of said lot" . . . "[e]xcepting and reserving" ownership of "all coal and minerals beneath the surface of said lot with the sole right to mine and remove the same by any subterranean process without liability" . . . "under any circumstances whatever for any damage thereby done to the surface of said lot, or any buildings or improvements that may now or hereafter be placed thereon." Thus, the coal company absolved itself of any responsibility for damage to people or property caused by the cave-ins, or "subsidence," as it was politely euphemized. Since the Pennsylvania Coal Company owned land adjacent to the Butzners' house, mines may have underlaid the house, or new mines could be excavated.[45]

In the days before long-distance motorcar trips were commonplace and roads were still perilous, Dr. Butzner was accustomed to traveling in his little roadster, sometimes taking it, rather than the train, to Virginia to visit relatives or for vacations. Even so, this experienced driver suffered a terrible accident. On a foggy Saturday night in January 1921, as he was driving back from seeing patients in the outlying mining townships—perhaps in Dickson City or Olyphant— Dr. Butzner "miraculously escaped death when his automobile went over an eighty-foot embankment" along the Lackawanna River "on Boulevard avenue [at the corner of Raines Avenue] in the Green Ridge section of the city," *The Scranton Republican* reported. "Prompt action [of two police officers] probably saved [his] life. Pinned under his car, Dr. Butzner was just able to keep his head above the water. . . ." Although he "suffered considerable shock," he recovered remarkably quickly and was released from the State Hospital in barely a week's time. The accident was so terrifying and Dr. Butzner so beloved that the newspaper once again recounted his "narrow escape" three years later, when a similar mishap occurred at the same spot. Perhaps Jane's spirits lifted a little and she felt proud when, in reprising the terrifying incident, the reporter casually and assuredly identified her father as "one of the best known physicians of the county."[46]

As an early and voracious reader in a family that perused several papers a day, four-and-a-half-year-old Jane most likely read the newspaper story about her father's accident herself. She had learned to read at almost the same time as she learned to talk. Unlike most children, who begin to speak sometime around their first birthday and do not recall this experience, Jane remembered precisely when she uttered her first words. A little past her third birthday, when her relatives were worried because she had not said a word up to that point, she was standing on the porch of her grandmother's house in Bloomsburg, waiting for her mother to return. Jane remembered clearly articulating, "Look! There's mother coming," and witnessing her grandmother almost falling over backward. "It was as if a switched had been turned on," Jane recounted to her son. "My grandmother kept talking to me, and I could say anything. So I talked on and on until my mother got there. The rest is history." Shortly thereafter,

Bess, who had trained as a schoolteacher and for years taught young children, started in on instructing Jane to read.[47]

Jane delighted in reading and loved books, but she averred no interest in cars or learning to drive. In 2002—and consistently throughout her life—Jane dismissed cars as a functional contraption, lacking glamour. Her mother and siblings all learned to drive, and later her husband drove a car. Jane never obtained a driver's license or attempted to learn to operate an automobile. She stated in no uncertain terms that urban planners accommodated cars rather than people, which was to her an altogether misguided priority. One wonders, however, if her father's nearly fatal auto accident played a role in her negative association with cars, which early on disposed her unfavorably toward a machine that would dictate so much of the built environment for decades to come, one that she would attack vociferously over and over.

As the Butzner family expanded and deepened their ties to Scranton during their almost ten years in Electric Street's miniature mosaic of ethnic backgrounds, occupations, and income levels, neighbors had come and gone. More than half of those on the Butzners' side of Electric Street who had lived there when Decker, Bess, and Betty had arrived—especially those who rented properties down the hill, close to Green Ridge Corners—had moved elsewhere. At least five of the original neighboring families, however, had stayed on. Now in his early sixties, Francis Olver, the builder from whom the Butzners had bought their property, remained, while his daughters married and moved out to set up their own homes. Seth Shoemaker was promoted to director of the School of Agriculture at the International Correspondence Schools and later presided over Scranton's school board. Although the Baldwin, Axford, Blandin, and Shoemaker families—like the Butzners—had more children during the decade, they continued, whether because they had enough space or could not afford to buy a larger house, to live in their homes on Electric Street. The Butzners now had four children, and Decker's mother may still have lived with them. Less than a month after Dr. Butzner recovered from his accident, Bess and Decker, in February 1921, arranged to sell their first home and purchase a more spacious and handsome house on solid ground.

Jane and her family prepared to cross the city line into Dunmore, less than three-quarters of a mile to the east. Even in her earliest formative years in her close-knit community on Electric Street, Jane soaked up everything around her, albeit silently for her first three years. She meticulously observed and mentally recorded her surroundings—from the sidewalks on which she rode her velocipede to the stores the family frequented. The seeds of some of her ideas about cities had begun to germinate in the complex mosaic of Scranton.

View from Clay Avenue, Dunmore, toward Green
Ridge Breaker, with culm pile and Scranton beyond, c. 1910.
Courtesy of Lackawanna Historical Society.

• • •

CHAPTER 4

Crossing the Line into Dunmore and at School

THERE IS NOTHING THAT indicates when you have crossed the city line between Scranton and Dunmore. No body of water separates the city from the borough, no signs announce the change of jurisdiction, no city grid is interrupted, no street pavement or sidewalk abruptly morphs. "The near future will see the two municipalities united, as they already are territorially," Hitchcock, the seventy-seven-year-old who had lived in Scranton for six decades, predicted in his 1914 history of his city. Over a century later, Scranton and Dunmore remain distinct jurisdictions. In essence, during Jane's childhood, Dunmore was a smaller community within the encompassing Scranton, and the Butzners' new neighborhood would be a bite-size unit within the borough of Dunmore.[1]

In late February 1921, when Jane was a couple months shy of her fifth birthday, the Butzners bought a house at 1728 Monroe Avenue in Dunmore. Neither Jane nor the rest of her family felt that crossing the line into Dunmore and then walking four more short blocks to their new home meant they would be living in another city. In her conversations, writings, and interviews, Jane always identified her hometown as Scranton. When her parents looked for a place to settle and for Dr. Butzner to practice, Decker and Bess had deliberately chosen "the city of Scranton." They first purchased a house on the outskirts of the city, and when they outgrew it and could afford more room, they cast their sights on the nearby neighborhood with its somewhat larger lots and homes, and sidled over to Dunmore. Dr. Butzner kept his office in Scranton proper. From their Dunmore house, the Butzners continued to walk to the Green Ridge Library and attend the Green Ridge Presbyterian Church. Scranton city directories of that period included addresses for all of Dunmore, unobtrusively followed by the letter *D* to denote the borough. In its weekly "Suburban Church Directory," *The Scranton Republican* did not list Dunmore separately, suggesting the paper did not consider it a suburb or outside Scranton. The Community Chest conducted its annual charitable campaign in Scranton and Dunmore, unified as one area. The Girl Scouts grouped the two municipalities together seamlessly and did not classify Dunmore as an "outlying town." To many in the 1920s and 1930s, especially in the Dunmore neighborhood contiguous to Scranton, Dunmore felt like an extension of Scranton, not a separate or suburban town.[2]

By the turn of the twentieth century, development of suburban-style upper-middle-class homes, similar to those in the vicinity of North Washington Street at Scranton's eastern border, had begun to spill over into westernmost Dunmore, and individual builders constructed mostly capacious single-family dwellings. By 1898, all the lots had been plotted in the twelve-square-block Dunmore neighborhood, with two long blocks between east-west Electric and Green Ridge Streets and the six short blocks between north-south Adams and Webster Avenues. Only a quarter of the lots had houses. New development in this section proceeded gradually during the next two decades. By the 1920s, most lots had been built upon. The new homes were so close in character to those in Scranton's Green Ridge neighborhood that people referred to these blocks in Dunmore as part of Green Ridge. Because of its larger and fancier homes, Scrantonians, Dunmoreans, and real estate advertisers from the mid-1920s on would dub this the "Hollywood section," appending either "of Dunmore" or "of Green Ridge" interchangeably. This neighborhood, like some others, defied legal boundaries. One old-timer pointed out that "the name 'Green Ridge' had more cache"—because the rest of

Dunmore, with a high percentage of immigrants, retained its historic, predominantly working-class, and heavily Catholic makeup.[3]

Once covered with forests and underbrush, Dunmore owed its initial existence to a crossroads and Allsworth's late eighteenth-century inn at what was known as "The Corners." In 1849, when the Pennsylvania Coal Company was established—with the three thousand acres of land it acquired—the sleepy village of Dunmore embarked on a growth spurt. Under the leadership of John B. Smith, Pennsylvania Coal opened a gravity railroad in 1850, facilitating the shipping of its product. Thus the industry was poised to take off. Joining the early English, German, and Scots-Irish settlers, workers poured in mainly from Ireland, seeking employment in the mines. Supporting businesses and institutions, such as a blacksmith's, a general store, a hardware store, schools, and a post office, sprouted, as well. Dunmore grew rapidly and continuously, with coal mining as the chief occupation of its residents. If Scranton was too much of a company town, which would fail to diversify economically, Dunmore was even more so. Writing in 1868, historian Hollister observed that the Pennsylvania Coal Company "turned the sterile pasture-fields around it into a town liberal in the extent of its territory and diversified by every variety of life. . . . Dunmore can congratulate itself not so much upon the internal wealth of its hills, as upon the vigor of the men who furrowed them out, and thus encouraged a town at this time deriving its daily inspirations wholly from this source."[4]

In 1862, six years after Scranton incorporated as a borough, Dunmore followed suit. By 1875, enough children lived in the borough that five public grammar schools had opened, and by 1915, there were twelve, most of which were of decent size, with between eight and twelve rooms. Beginning in 1868, the "Old Brick" two-year high school provided further education. Middle-class and workers' houses proliferated from the center of town, widening the circle of development over the years. Facing each other at the intersection of Blakely and Drinker Streets, the Fidelity Deposit and Discount Bank and the First National Bank were founded in the nineteen-aughts.

The Butzners' house, 1728 (later renumbered as 1712) Monroe Avenue, stood out among the neighboring houses, photo 2008. Author's photo.

The banks formed the cornerstones of Dunmore's business district at Dunmore Corners, as it was known when the Butzners moved to Dunmore. Down the block from the banks were the Clarke Brothers department store, the Globe and A&P grocery stores, the Model Lunch restaurant, the Paragon Pharmacy, a butcher shop, a cigar store, and quite a few other small shops.[5]

The Butzners purchased the dozen-year-old house at 1728 Monroe Avenue from George and Margaret Jiencke. It was a special house, built, under the supervision of Mr. Jiencke himself, with care and fine materials. Perched at the highest point on the block, it stood out from other houses around not only because it was an imposing and decorous structure but also because it was the only brick house in sight. Three levels of white wooden balustraded porches and a balcony cascaded down the symmetrical front of the house, with the two lower porches stretching across the full width. Punctuating the span of the broad hipped roof, a Palladian window looked out from under the peaked roof of the centered third-floor dormer. Below, in the front yard, a deep lawn sloped up toward the entrance. The Dunmore lot, substantially larger than the Butzners' Electric Street property, allowed for a good-size backyard for the children, a garden, and a two-car garage.[6]

George Jiencke was no ordinary builder. He co-owned F. E. Sykes and Company, one of Scranton's largest and most successful general contracting firms, responsible for erecting schools, stores, banks, and hospitals as well as a large number of residences. His partner, Frederick E. Sykes, belonged to a respected family of builders specializing in cut stone, brick, and flagging. With the Sykeses' skills, Jiencke could erect an impressive brick house with stone steps and a retaining wall. Brick pillars along the sidewalk marked the corners of the property and framed the driveway and front steps.[7]

Jiencke—an enterprising, skilled worker with a southern German name—had emigrated from his native Germany to the United States when he was twenty-five years old, sailing from Bremen to New York in 1882. After working as a machinist in Philadelphia, he went to Scranton in 1888 with a business venture in mind, for he immediately set up a paint-manufacturing company. With Alexander McKee and Herman Roeper, Jiencke launched the Lackawanna Paint & Color Works. The following year, he married McKee's sister Margaret, whose parents had been born in Ireland, and in 1893, their only child, Hilda, was born. Business must have been good, because Jiencke soon bought properties to rent out, plus two unbuilt lots on Monroe Avenue in Dunmore. By 1900, he had acquired ten properties and was able to hire a Welsh immigrant girl as a servant in the household. In 1906, now sole proprietor of the paint company, Jiencke teamed up with Sykes and capitalized on the family's imprimatur.[8]

By 1909, this prospering German immigrant with two thriving companies had built and was living in the fine house at 1728 Monroe Avenue, on the lot he had bought in 1897 from the estate of coal baron Thomas Dickson. Jiencke used his contracting company and connections in the building industry to embellish his new home. He installed glorious stained-glass windows in the dining room and in the wall beneath the stairs to the second floor. A sizable mahogany mantel topped the central fireplace opposite the entrance, ball-and-dowel gingerbread hung from the ceiling, demarcating living rooms, and second-floor front bedrooms with double-hung windows opened onto an unroofed porch. "It was the kind of house that wrapped its arms around you," mused Barbara Gelder Kelley, who grew up there with her sister Margaret after her parents, Franklin and Juanita Gelder, bought the house from Bess Butzner in 1946. Down the block, Jiencke also owned a lot with a two-story frame dwelling at 1710 Monroe, which he or his nephew Carl, a dental student from Berlin, resided in for several years. But after enjoying the grand domicile for more than a decade and now in his sixties, Jiencke—the "well-known contractor," as *The Scranton Republican* identified him—was ready to cash in his nest egg. The timing was right for Decker and Bess, and the Jiencke house satisfied the crucial condition: It appeared to be safe from cave-ins. The area's largest coal vein lay under the lowlands in the middle of the valley, and Dunmore's elevation increased as one headed north from central city toward Electric Street. The Butzners noted the house was high up the hill. Furthermore, they consulted geological maps for existing mines or potential excavation underneath the property. They wished to avoid any chance of subsidence, of ending up in a "built-down" house. Jane felt warmly toward the house long into her adult years. When returning to Scranton with relatives after a family funeral in Bloomsburg, she would take them to see the house where she was brought up. "My room," Jane said, pointing it out in a photograph to her Toronto friend Max Allen, "was on the right side of the second floor, over the corner of the porch."[9]

The physical and mental transition from Scranton to Dunmore may have felt seamless, but residing in the jurisdictionally discrete borough mandated that the children would go to Dunmore's, rather than Scranton's, public schools. In September of 1921, Betty and Jane enrolled in the George Washington School #3—at the corner of Green Ridge Street and Madison Avenue, about three blocks from their house—and within a few years, John and Jimmy would be of

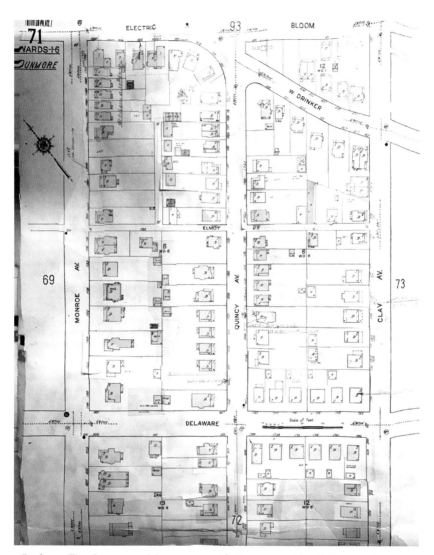

Sanborn Fire Insurance Map, 1919, with Butzners' side of Monroe Avenue, Dunmore (fifth house north of Delaware Street). Courtesy of Marywood University School of Architecture. Photo by Jarek Diehl.

age to attend also. Costing the borough the hefty sum of $100,000, the splendid redbrick and gray stone school had been erected between 1889 and 1898, awaiting the neighborhood's development. With its ornate bull's-eye dormers reminiscent of French châteaus and its other decorative elements, the building was architecturally captivating and may have helped lure prospective home buyers with school-age children. Because it was situated on the knoll of a hill, one could climb the two dozen stone steps—with two landings for relief—leading from Green Ridge Street to the main doors flanked by stone columns, or ascend the driveway on Madison Avenue to the rear entrance at ground level. The children and faculty more often than not used the rear doors. The school's last principal before the building was demolished in the mid-1970s, Al O'Donnell, called the Washington School "the most beautiful building in Dunmore, inside and out."[10]

Washington's floor plan was ingenious, and perfect for a grammar school. The building had a square footprint, with classrooms—one for each of its eight grades—at the corners of the two main floors. Grades one through four occupied the first-floor classrooms. The corner rooms, with their two perpendicular outside walls and tall windows, let the sunlight pour in from different directions. On all four sides of the school, between the classrooms were protruding central pavilions for stairwells and exterior double doors. The two side doors each opened on a straight flight of stairs directly to the second floor, while the main and rear doors gave access to the first floor, with interior back stairs, with a landing, alongside the rear door. During fire drills, all four doors served as exits. Above the classrooms' dark wainscoting, chalkboards stretched from end to end of the windowless interior cream-colored walls. Screwed into the hardwood floors, wooden desks—with cast-iron tracery sides, an inkwell, and a flip-up seat for the pupil in front—formed neat rows for up to sixty children per room. Each classroom had a cloakroom next to it, which students could enter from the hall and pass through into the classroom. Multigrade activities took place in the "big empty" space, the size of at least two classrooms, in the middle of the building, outside the classrooms on both floors. There was "an outpouching over the main entrance facing Green Ridge Street on the second floor for the principal's office," Al O'Donnell explained, "and we used the big space next to this like an auditorium for school assemblies." We stored furniture, such as extra or damaged desks, in the third-floor attic." He remi-

George Washington School #3, Dunmore, photo 1931,
demolished in the mid-1970s. Courtesy of MaryAnn Ferrario.

nisced about the golden days, when, as a principal, "you could just concentrate on education. You know why? There were no unions, no bus, and no cafeteria."[11]

Since the Washington School had no kindergarten and Jane, at age five, was an early reader and eager learner, she started first grade as eleven-year-old Betty began sixth. Jane met Marie Van Bergen in her first-grade class. Bound by a love of reading, they quickly became good friends. Both were tall and blue-eyed, Jane with straw-colored hair, and Marie's a more golden blond. Through grade school, Jane kept her hair cropped short—as did Betty—a version of the flapper style, called the "boyish bob," more commonly sported by modern young women. For the Butzner girls, both keen on swimming, short hair was a practical matter for quick drying and easy care. "Jane was not the frilly type. She leaned toward boyish things," Marie, who liked curls and pretty clothes, commented. Marie, like most of the children in the class, was almost a year older than Jane. She lived a block south of Green Ridge Street, and about a block east of the city line, at 1306 Marion Street, on the southern edge of the Hollywood section, just north of a working-class neighborhood called "the Patch." Marie's family owned a two-family house—"a duplex," as Marie called it, because the apartments were stacked rather than side by side. She and her parents and, ultimately, four younger sisters lived in the upstairs apartment. Her Van Bergen grandparents lived on the first floor. She loved this arrangement because she "adored her grandparents." Her father, Henry L. "Harry" Van Bergen was something of a rebel. His parents sent him to boarding school in New Jersey to get him away from "his gang at Scranton's Tech High, who were not interested in studying." Upon graduating, Harry went to work as a clerk in his father's store and sometimes drove the delivery truck.[12]

Jane and Marie shared a passion for local history. Marie's grandfather, Henry C. Van Bergen, descended from the mid-seventeenth-century Hudson River valley Dutch. From Cortland, in upstate New York, he had worked in his early twenties as a broker buying and selling goods along the DL&W Railroad line. In the mid-1870s, when one of his clients, the Lackawanna Iron and Coal Company store, offered him a job as their manager, he jumped at the opportunity to settle in the booming city of Scranton. A decade later, he married Emma Ward, head of the company's millinery department. Emma was the granddaughter of the legendary Simon Ward, who had come from northwestern New Jersey with George W. Scranton and Sanford Grant to build Scranton's first iron furnace. Ward went on to become a contractor responsible for, Marie said proudly, "building a lot of houses" around central city.[13]

In 1906, Marie's grandfather had gained experience and saved enough to establish a "fancy grocery store," named simply H. C. Van Bergen, at 1403 North Washington Street, close to some of the most extravagant properties in Green Ridge and across the side street from the Lackawanna County Prison, a location of no concern to him or his neighbors. The grocery store was located next to a butcher shop on the corner, and both stores were on the ground floor of the home

Central-city store where H. C. Van Bergen (third from left) got his start, late 19th century. Courtesy of Christopher Mansuy.

of Henry Kehrli, a German butcher. H. C. Van Bergen advertised widely in the papers "Staple and Fancy Groceries, Fruits and Vegetables, Butter and Eggs a Specialty." "My grandfather was a gentleman merchant who never lifted a carton," Marie recalled. "H. C. Van Bergen's customers could phone in their orders to be delivered by truck, which meant the grocer didn't have to keep everything in stock." He did, however, go to the "wholesale block," the 100 block of Lackawanna Avenue, to get fresh produce from local farms. His customers lived mainly in the Green Ridge or Hill sections of town. H. C. Van Bergen had a warm relationship with them and was a charitable man. When nuns came around with a horse-drawn cart, asking for contributions, he would pile it with groceries. "I would say, 'Grandpa, why are you giving them so much? You're not even Catholic.' And he replied, 'Maybe someday I'll need their help.'" From the Van Bergen house, it was a two-block walk west for Marie and her sisters to their grandfather's store or barely three blocks in the opposite direction to the George Washington School.[14]

Dunmore's Washington School—like all Scranton and Dunmore schools—was truly a neighborhood school. When the school board hired teachers, they usually assigned them to the school nearest where they lived. Almost all grammar school–age students within a fifteen- to twenty-minute walk attended the Washington School, except for the few children who went to Catholic or private schools. "The real rich kids went to the Country Day School," Marie observed. "William Warren Scranton, the governor of Pennsylvania, went there," as well as "other elites—children of doctors, lawyers, and the man who owned the gas company." But everyone else walked to the George Washington School—students, teachers, and the principal, Miss Nora O'Hara—because they all lived close to the school. One of the teachers, Miss May Mongan, literally lived next door, in a "gracious house," on the corner of Green Ridge and Monroe. Children and adult educators sometimes ran into one another along the way and walked together. Furthermore, everyone walked to the school twice a day, because they all went home for lunch. Jane and Betty Butzner walked down the hill along the slate sidewalks to and from school and, like the other kids, learned to time their walk perfectly to avoid waiting outside the building for the bell that signaled the start of the school morning or afternoon. Always commencing with the Pledge of Allegiance and a patriotic song, the school day ran from 9:00 A.M. to 4:00 P.M., with an hour and a half for lunch, beginning at noon. Each class also took a break for recess, but at staggered times because the playground was small. A tall cliff behind the school hemmed in the play area, and the students were forbidden to climb it. But the children were resourceful and made up games, played marbles or with balls, and jumped rope.[15]

Jane announced to Marie that "the two smartest teachers" she ever had were her first- and second-grade teachers, Miss Rose Hoffman and Miss Anna Taylor, respectively. In her late thirties, Miss

Hoffman was an experienced and devoted teacher who had taught at George Washington for twenty years before Jane and Marie started attending the school. From humble circumstances, she was the daughter of an Irish-born mother and German-born father. In 1920, she lived toward Dunmore Corners with her widowed mother and three younger siblings. Miss Hoffman was particularly active in Parent Teacher Association meetings and events, and she furthered her studies with summer classes at Penn State. She remained at the school long after all the Butzner children had finished there, and earned warm feelings not only from her students but also from their parents. Parents and teachers met monthly at the home of the elected head of the P.T.A., often hosting a scholarly speaker or a benefit for the school following "regular business." In 1936, Dunmore honored Miss Hoffman by hanging a banner in her classroom for having the "largest attendance of the children's parents at a P.T.A. meeting." Margaret Gelder (later Reese), who was in her first-grade class seven years after the banner was hung, recalled her as a "kindly and good teacher—with perfect handwriting and long, pointed shoes."[16]

Like Miss Hoffman, Miss Taylor had been at the school for quite a few years by the time Jane was in her class. Miss Taylor, like the majority of teachers, came from a modest background. She resided in Dunmore with her family near The Corners, and other relatives lived next door. Her father, Michael A. Taylor, whose parents were Irish immigrants, had worked as a machinist for a local railroad company, her younger brother was a surveyor in the coal mines, and her uncle, who lived with them, was a coal miner. Apparently, Miss Hoffman and Miss Taylor distinguished themselves so favorably from Jane's other elementary-school teachers that the discerning student spoke of them to her family—and even her children—for many decades to come.[17]

In Scranton (and in much of the country) in the 1920s and the 1930s, virtually all grade-school teachers were unmarried women. Those who married gave up their jobs—not necessarily because of a legal requirement, but more often because they were expected to focus undivided attention on their families, which included staying at home on school days when their children returned for lunch. Jane's future sister-in-law's mother was but one of many who followed this rule, whether written or not. Kay Schoen's mother, Norma Davis—in her mid twenties, with a teaching degree from Mansfield State Normal School—had come to Scranton from rural Bradford County to look for a job. Her uncle John H. Williams ran a wholesale grocery business and was on Scranton's Board of School Directors in 1912 and 1913. He used his school board position to get Norma a teaching job at a school on Scranton's West Side—an all too common form of nepotism in those days. When Norma married Carl Schoen circa 1917, she "automatically stopped teaching," she told her daughter Kay. Kay understood that in Scranton at that time, "you *had* to give up teaching if you got married." She remembered only one teacher who married in the middle of the year and stayed on to finish the school year.[18]

Barbara Gelder (later Kelley) spent her first twelve years on Quincy Avenue—with her younger sister Margaret—before moving to the next block over, the 1700 block of Monroe Avenue. She, Marie Van Bergen, and other Washington alums all agreed that students at the George Washington School could get a "very good education," thanks largely to the teachers. Many young women of Irish background in Dunmore had been well educated in Catholic schools, where perfect handwriting was de rigueur, and some had gone up the hill to Marywood College, the state's first Catholic college for women, which opened in 1915. They became teachers, thus earning a better and easier living, and gaining more respectability than some of their immigrant parents and grandparents. Quite a number of these teachers—"Miss [Rose] Hoffman, Miss [Agnes] Murray, Miss [May] Mongan, Miss [Catherine] Corcoran, and Miss [Anna L.] McGuire"—recalled Barbara, reeling off their names, "spent their entire careers at George Washington." These same women had taught at the school in 1919, before Jane and Betty started there, and were still in their classrooms when the Gelder sisters attended in the 1940s.

First-grade classroom at George Washington #3, 1954,
just as it looked several decades earlier. Courtesy of Sue Cantarella.

Perhaps some women derived such satisfaction from the teaching profession that it superseded their interest in finding a husband and having a family.[19]

"There was a great deal of holdover from the traditional Catholic education at the Washington School," Barbara Gelder Kelley commented. From first grade on up, the teachers drilled the students daily on handwriting skills, teaching them how to make printed and cursive letters. Children had to sit properly, with their forearms forming an upside-down *V* on the desk, paper slanted, fingers rounded, and pen held loosely. Besides handwriting and grammar, teachers emphasized memorizing poetry, which likely fueled Jane's passion for composing her own. Each month, Miss Agnes Murray had all her students memorize the same poem and recite it in front of the class.

"I remember learning Edgar Allan Poe's 'The Raven,' John Greenleaf Whittier's 'Snowbound,' and Joaquin Miller's 'Columbus,'" Barbara continued. "Miss Murray, the seventh-grade teacher, was a stickler for these poems and for grammar. She loved Poe and diagramming sentences. She sometimes made diagrams that were four blackboards long, covering two walls."[20]

Jane certainly was familiar with Miss Irene O'Boyle, who was to become her sixth-grade teacher for the first half of the year. Only two doors down from the Butzners, the O'Boyles lived in a rather plain thirteen-room wooden house, which included a small apartment in back. From Dunmore Corners, the O'Boyles had moved in a few years before the Butzners came to Monroe Avenue and a short time after Irene O'Boyle's father, Patrick O'Boyle, an immigrant from Ireland, had died. His widow, Mary, filled the large, serviceable home with their six daughters and a niece, and their married son with his wife and two young children. Irene had graduated from Bucknell, the prestigious four-year liberal arts college in Lewisburg, Pennsylvania, with the ambition of becoming a principal. In 1919, at age twenty-two, she began teaching fifth grade at Dunmore's Longfellow School #12. Four years later, the school board transferred her to the Washington School and assigned her to teach sixth grade. Miss O'Boyle "had the most perfect handwriting," Barbara marveled, "and could have made the long friezes of the upper- and lowercase cursive alphabet" that hung above all classroom blackboards for students to emulate. Miss O'Boyle's niece and Jane's friend Mary Evelyn Barrett (later "Evie" Brower), who was born and raised in the big house, described her aunt Irene as "a brilliant woman." The school board must have recognized this, for in a mere seven years, in the fall of 1926, the young and kindly Miss Mildred Gallagher took over the sixth-grade classroom because the tall and straight Miss O'Boyle had succeeded Miss O'Hara and ascended to the position of the George Washington School's principal. Miss O'Boyle held the reins there for more than three and a half decades, when mandatory retirement forced her out in 1962, at age sixty-five. A further provision of the unspoken decree regarding educators allowed women—single, at least through the 1940s—to become principals of grammar schools, but not until the 1960s was a woman made principal of Dunmore High.[21]

Al O'Donnell, a subsequent principal of the Washington School, characterized Miss O'Boyle as "the perfect, structured disciplinarian." Evie Brower concurred: "Teachers came back to thank her for her good work. Everyone loved her because of her strictness. She was strict but very good. Of course, since I was her niece, I got hit twice if I did something wrong," she said, laughing. Grade-school principals dealt out corporal punishment for what today would appear as minor infractions, and students saw—and feared—it as customary practice. According to Marie, "The principal, Miss O'Boyle, was very strict. You didn't cozy up to her, and you didn't act up in class. I can still remember going to her office and getting hit on the hand with a ruler. I had said something when the teacher was out of the room, when

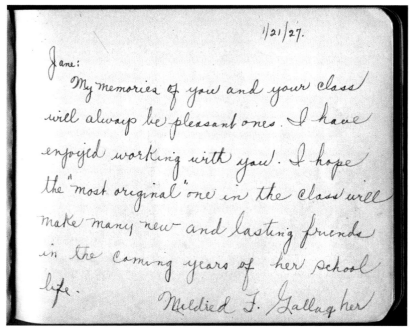

Jane's autograph book page with her sixth-grade
teacher's message, 1927. Estate of Jane Jacobs.

you were supposed to be quiet." "Sometimes you could hear cries coming from the principal's office," Barbara added.[22]

Miss Hoffman and Miss Taylor made the first two years of Jane's formal education the apex of her elementary-school experience, but it trended downhill from then on. After an auspicious beginning at George Washington, Jane, with her high standards, was impatient to learn and did not suffer fools. She marched to the beat of her own drum. When the teacher handed out the textbooks at the beginning of the year, Jane couldn't wait to read them, devouring the volumes from cover to cover in a couple of weeks. After she finished them, her mind would wander, and she grew bored. Jane "would doodle and was always drawing pictures in her notebook or on a tablet," her classmate Marie had noticed. "Jane seemed to assimilate things very quickly," but she was "an ordinary student," because she had no interest in receiving good grades. Miss Gallagher, however, recognized Jane as "the 'most original' one"—for better or worse. Marie, on the other hand, cared about being a good student and was, in her own words, "number one." "Jane didn't seem to pay much attention [at school]," Marie continued. "She was beyond them." Jane admitted as much, saying she "didn't listen much in class. I would try to, but I would get bored with it. . . . I just did enough to get by, really." Jane stared at the tin ceilings, out the tall windows on one side and the back of the class, or at Gilbert Stuart's iconic unfinished portrait of the man for whom the school was named, hanging at the front of the room, close to the American flag. Other students spent time gazing at this reproduction, too. "All the classes had a copy of the same famous painting of George Washington," Barbara commented. "I thought there were clouds at the bottom of the painting [the billowy-topped unpainted section of the canvas]."[23]

Both Marie and Jane were avid readers. "I read anything I could get my hands on," Marie declared. "When I heard the girls in the cloakroom talking about the Bobbsey Twins, I asked them [proudly] if they'd read *Huck Finn* yet." Apparently, no one in that group had. Jane, too, "read *anything* that came her way," her son Jim emphasized.

"There was nothing she would rather do," and she had wide-ranging tastes. She loved all of Mark Twain and *The Three Musketeers*, a book she felt was best read as a child, and Charles Dickens's *A Child's History of England*, a witty and cynical look at the royal family before Queen Victoria. The Butzners owned the prized 1911 edition of the thirty-two-book set of the *Encyclopaedia Britannica*. Propped in his lap, the huge volumes were her father's favorite bedtime reading and became a staple for young Jane, as well. She absorbed the learned essays on all sorts of historical, geographical, and scientific topics, which Dr. Butzner encouraged her to discuss with him. She read quickly and retained what she read. Always on the prowl for an interesting book, she made frequent trips to the Albright Library, the central public reference library, with a special section devoted to local history, or the smaller, neighborhood Green Ridge Library. She was well known to and befriended the librarians at both locations.[24]

The three oldest Butzner children walked to the George Washington School together from September 1923 to June 1924, when John was in first grade, Jane in third, and Betty in eighth. For Jane, third grade failed to live up to the first two years of her schooling, when she had actually, as she put it, "learned a great deal." Her teacher, Miss Catherine Corcoran, a likable and friendly young woman, had been teaching only a few years. Third grade was the year in which everyone abandoned printing and mastered the favored Palmer Method of penmanship for writing script. Using pens with metal nibs, which were dipped into the desks' built-in inkwells, and cheap paper, boys and girls made entire sheets, over and over, of push and pull strokes or ovals. Barbara was frustrated not only by the grueling repetition but also by the cheap paper, because the pens caught in the rough grain and messed up her practice sheets. And you never knew when Miss Corcoran would come around to tap your elbow or try to pull the pen from your hand to check your grip and position.[25]

Besides mulling over encyclopedia articles with his daughter, Dr. Butzner enjoyed discussing topics such as morals, a welcome antidote to practicing proper penmanship. The day after Jane had conversed with him about the importance of not making promises one could not keep, a guest speaker at assembly lectured the school's children on the proper care of their teeth. When the speaker asked everyone to raise their hands if they promised to brush their teeth morning and night every day for the rest of their lives, Jane considered her father's words and refused to make the unrealistic promise. Feeling convinced about this principle, she urged her schoolmates to join her in not making a promise they would surely break. Torn between obeying the speaker and accepting Jane's argument, the children raised and lowered their hands. Back in the classroom, the mortified and infuriated teacher felt Jane had crossed the line. Miss Corcoran could not tolerate such insubordination and promptly expelled her from the classroom. Reeling from this response to her speaking up sincerely, and hesitant to go home, seven-year-old Jane wandered down the hill to the Erie Railroad tracks, south of Marion Street, where the freight cars loaded with coal passed. On both sides of the tracks were high rock outcrops with loose rocks. It was extremely treacherous, and children were strictly forbidden to cross the tracks. In defiance, Jane scaled the rocks and survived to tell the tale. She returned home for lunch and received no admonitions from her family. "It gave me a feeling that I was independent," Jane recalled in a 1993 interview. From third grade on, Jane concluded that school was no longer a place of intellectual interest for her and mostly taught herself by reading books in her lap.[26]

Once Jane entered fourth grade, she was the older sister walking with one or both of her younger brothers. That year, Betty began her freshman year at Dunmore Senior High School, which accommodated about five hundred pupils. Recalling this school year, Marie perceived Jane as "nice, soft-spoken, never loud or belligerent," yet "opinionated in her own way and very self-assured." Their fourth-grade teacher, Miss Anna L. McGuire, had been teaching for at least sixteen years, and was known for her stern demeanor and authoritarian approach. She resided on the next block over, on Quincy Avenue, with her father—a clerk in a wholesale flour business—and five siblings, one of whom was married and had three young children. Both Gelder sisters referred to Miss McGuire as "a tyrant." The seasoned teacher managed to engage Jane's interest during a geography lesson when she offered what Jane recognized as "the standard line" that all cities developed around a waterfall. Already an observer and lover of cities, Jane could not resist taking issue, in her forthright rational manner, with what she considered a preposterous idea about why and how cities develop. "We were . . . taught it was always some natural feature like a waterfall that gave power," Jane said in 1997, recounting this clash. "I didn't believe that. . . . I was much more interested in how everybody was earning a living . . . and I could see there was a lot of interweaving of various kinds, and I thought that was more important. So I was really interested in this sort of thing from a very early age."[27]

The only waterfall in Scranton was in the city's largest recreational area, Nay Aug Park, where Roaring Brook plunged twenty feet amid a wooded area well upstream from the site of Scranton's genesis—its initial 1840s iron furnace. Marie remembered Jane's challenge and concurred that the falls had nothing to do with Scranton's economy. Everyone knew "that coal mines made the place," Marie said. The city ran on anthracite, and the ubiquitous presence of coal and the coal industry in the 1920s was hard to miss. Almost all the houses were heated with coal furnaces, and many families cooked with coal stoves. Coal breakers dotted the urban landscape, with more than a dozen mines and collieries within the Dunmore and Scranton city limits. Mountainous piles of waste coal, often conjoined with rock, known as "culm dumps," usually accompanied them. Even if you couldn't see the piles, you could smell the awful sulfur smell of the burning culm, often from spontaneous combustion. "Some of the culm dumps burned forever," Barbara complained.[28]

Jane took great interest in the city and region's history, and so did Marie. "I knew Scranton history well," Marie said, "because my family was part of it." History and geography were her favorite subjects, but local history was not part of the curriculum. Marie came from several generations of Scrantonians. She thought other students at the George Washington School "had a sense of the history," too. "Jane was always proud of the fact that she came from Scranton," Marie recalled. "And at that age, she was proud of her grandfather [Robison] fighting in the Civil War and being related to Clara Barton on her mother's side, and of her relatives from Virginia."[29]

Being in a classroom with the tyrannical Miss McGuire allowed Jane to hone her confidence, but, fortunately, Jane had to endure only a half year of fourth grade. At the time Jane and Marie entered school, everyone began a new grade in September. When they were in fourth grade, the school "gave [the Stanford Achievement Test] to all the students, and if you got a certain mark," Marie revealed, "you were put ahead a half a year." Thus both girls skipped a semester and entered the new fifth-grade "A" class in February. "We missed fractions because of this, so I was never any good at them." This test resulted in two graduating classes—one in June, the "B" class, and the other, the "A" class, in January. The January "A" class was the smaller of the two, with approximately twenty-five children per grade. Since there were only eight classrooms in the school, one for each grade, the two graduating classes met in the same room. There was one teacher for both the A and B groups in the class. She taught all the subjects and maintained perfect order, with students at each of the sixty desks. One group would study while the other received a lesson. Children could now start school either at the beginning of the school year or in the middle. Dunmore continued to have two graduating classes per year until the mid-1940s.[30]

When Marie and Jane and others who had scored well on the test joined the fifth grade at the beginning of February 1925, they encountered the component of students from the Dundell School. "It was a primitive little school in the middle of nowhere and had four rooms," recollected Florence Gillespie Brown, born in 1919 and a student there in the 1920s. "If you missed a spelling word, they hit you on the hands." With no separation of A and B classes, Dundell went only from the first through the fourth grade, so it funneled its graduates into Dunmore's Lincoln, Jefferson, and Washington schools. Located on Monroe Avenue, a few blocks downhill from Marion Street, the Dundell School served children in Dunmore's working-class Patch neighborhood. In and around Scranton, coal companies frequently built their own "patch" towns, with housing for their workers. Even after a patch had been filled in with noncompany houses, and laborers for other companies and industries moved in, an area where miners had once lived retained its character and was still known as a "patch." Originally called "Johnson's Patch," after the Johnson Breaker, for which the company housing was put up, in the 1920s Dunmore's Patch was home to people of Polish, Slovak, and Irish descent, with some Italians interspersed. As Dunmoreans such as Marie viewed it, "on the other side of the [Erie Railroad] tracks, in back [to the east]

Coal miners, with oil-wick lamps on their hats and lunch pails, outside a "patch" neighborhood, late 1910s to mid-1920s. Note outhouses in backyards, sewage and water run-off ditch, and poles for telegraph and telephone, not electricity. Scan obtained from Scranton Public Library.

Marie Van Bergen, age 7,
in her favorite outfit, 1922–1923.
Courtesy of Christopher Mansuy.

of the Erie Station on North Washington Street," lay the predominantly Catholic patch, with a high proportion of recent immigrants.
Children of laborers in the coal mines and other working-class kids
lived close to the breaker and culm pile—only half a mile from the
school—now owned by the Green Ridge Coal Company.[31]

From fifth grade on, some of these poorer children attended the
George Washington School. A number of neighbors on the Butzners' block in 1920 were also foreign-born, but they came from the
better-off Northern and Western European countries of Belgium,
Sweden, Austria, Ireland, Wales, Scotland, and England, and they had
emigrated longer ago. With the addition of the Dundell schoolchildren, the Washington school district—comprising the area between
Electric and Larch Streets, the northern and southern boundaries,

respectively, and Adams (the first avenue on the Dunmore side of the city line) and Webster to the east—had an ethnically and economically diverse population that ranged from children in a segment of the Hollywood section to fresh immigrants from Southern and Eastern Europe. In a similar way, many of Scranton's and Dunmore's public school districts funneled together students from small, adjacent, yet contrasting neighborhoods.

Jane accepted and enjoyed those schoolmates whose backgrounds were different from her own. She talked about them to her family and brought them home after school, but she was puzzled by some of her mother's comments about her friends and their families. Some people might have considered Jane's buddy Marie Van Bergen, who lived below the Hollywood section and was of "mixed parentage," of lower socioeconomic status. For their second-grade class photo, Marie had worn her favorite outfit—"a blue serge suit with a pleated skirt and Roman sash with red stripes" around the waist. Marie's mother, Josephine Lees Van Bergen, with her talent for sewing, had stitched the dress herself, copying an outfit another girl had bought in what Marie described as "a fancy store in New York City" where they could not have afforded to shop. Jane told Marie that her mother, Bess Butzner, thought "it was bad to copy the suit." [32]

Neither second grader knew quite what to make of this comment. Although Marie's father was an Episcopalian and of Dutch and English stock, he was easygoing and didn't mind flouting societal norms. He married Josephine Lees, of Irish Catholic descent. Thinking back to the 1920s, Kay Schoen Butzner remarked matter-of-factly, "Although families of different religions were good friends, parents didn't want their children to marry someone of another religion." Kay "really liked one of the McAndrew boys, who lived next door. Mother said to me, 'He has the map of Ireland on his face.' I understood what that meant. She was afraid I'd become attached to him and want to marry him." When I asked Kay how she reacted to this, she replied, "I didn't tell her about my friends after that." Harry and Josephine Van Bergen's five daughters were raised in the Catholic Church, with the younger ones attending parochial school. Jane and Marie wondered if Josephine's background had entered into Bess's opinion about the suit, an incident and question that perplexed Marie enough to remain with her ninety years later. As a child, Jane was aware that she herself "came from an old American family" and remembered sadly "how ashamed my classmates were that their parents were immigrants, and they tried to hide it. My parents were from America back before the Revolution." She added sympathetically, "So I didn't have this problem, but I could see that a lot of my classmates did." Clearly, prejudice existed, especially in Jane's and Kay's parents' generation, but in 1920s medium-size cities, such as Scranton, with their side-by-side exposure to others helped erase it among children growing up.[33]

In the 1920s, public schools in Dunmore and Scranton, and elsewhere around the country, concentrated not only on the three R's— reading, 'riting, and 'rithmetic—but also concerned themselves with instilling the virtues of thrift and savings, which would hold all students in good stead. In this culture of savings (rather than debt, which followed World War II), the schools set up what they called, simply, the "Christmas Club," where you "saved money at the school bank to buy Christmas presents," Marie recalled. Kids usually brought in a quarter, or occasionally two, each week, which the classroom teacher recorded and deposited. Before and after Christmas each year, the city's newspapers were filled with articles and advertisements about the adult versions of these popular savings clubs, encouraging new investors. In December 1921, *The Scranton Republican* announced, fifteen banks in Scranton and Dunmore held almost fifteen thousand Christmas Club accounts, and the banks were poised to "send out checks amounting to [a total of] $505,700." The ad for First National Bank of Dunmore (of which fifth-grade teacher Miss Mongan's father was president) conveyed to grown-ups what the schools aimed to impart to their pupils: "Christmas savings are simply a matter of putting as little or as much away each week as you can spare. Surprising how it adds up at the end of the year." Scranton's Peoples-Savings and Dime Bank and Trust Company incorporated the idea of the accounts

John Mitchell statue, erected 1924, in Courthouse
Square, photo 2012. Author's photo.

as models for children in their promotions: "Our Christmas Club
teaches the value of systematic savings. It is a splendid way to show
your children how small sums grow quickly in substantial amounts.
Money saved in the Christmas Club in most cases would otherwise
be spent." The schools created for children an easy way of saving for
a deferred goal, and they kept the money safe in a bona fide bank,
where, they demonstrated, it earned a modicum of interest. Even less
advantaged students managed to come up with a weekly contribution,
Marie confirmed.[34]

Besides Jane's mother's comments on the provenance of Marie's suit, Jane recalled her mother warning her that some of the children at the Washington School were "not nice." This time, Jane understood what she meant—she was referring to the Italian, Eastern European, and Irish kids, many of whom lived in the Patch. As early as third grade, Jane argued with her mother about issues of what she would later realize was bigotry. Through her observations and experience, Jane drew her own conclusions and set about educating her mother. She eventually brought her mother around to accepting people different from herself. Although these children might look different, Jane explained to Bess regarding some Chinese girls at her school, they were "just the same as you and me." In fact, Jane made friends among the heterogeneous group at school and in the neighborhood, brought them home, and was intrigued by what she learned from friends of another background. "The miners' children from a neighborhood near ours would, on a certain day in the year, be excused [from school] so they could march in the John Mitchell Day parade, a big event in Scranton," she recalled in 2002. "I once asked one of these classmates who John Mitchell was, and she said he was the greatest man in the world." As president of the United Mine Workers of America (UMWA) from 1898 to 1908—an unusually long run—Mitchell organized and led the anthracite coal workers and served on a commission with President Theodore Roosevelt during the strike of 1902, ultimately reaching an agreement that won the miners a shorter workday and increased wages and averted any major strikes for two decades.[35]

When asked as an adult if she had ever been bullied at school, Jane replied, "I went to a nice suburban public school and I had no such trouble. But I remember my brothers did." By the time Bess Butzner's youngest child, Jimmy, started at the Washington School, she had begun to revise her attitude toward the Patch. At a young age, Jimmy was afraid to walk through the Patch because kids there had thrown stones at him. As Kay Schoen Butzner remembered the story, Bess "purposely walked with him through the area so he would get used to it. She told him, 'You need to get to know these boys because someday you may be working with them.'" In what capacity Bess thought Jimmy might be working with them in the future, however, remains unclear.[36]

Conversely, Dr. Butzner treated patients from a wide range of backgrounds in and around Scranton. He took pleasure in getting to know people from all walks of life, from attorney R. A. Zimmerman, "prominent in civic and political life of the community," to miners and other laborers. Some of these patients saw him in his downtown office, and others he traveled to tend. He was the doctor to a group of Sicilians in the country town of Wyoming, north of Wilkes-Barre, allegedly a birthplace of the Mafia in America. He thoroughly enjoyed them. During hard times, they paid him in homemade red wine, which he had to hide from Bess, an ardent temperance supporter—largely on the grounds that male drinking harmed women's lives. There was a good chance that she would pour it down the sink if she discovered it. Bess was delighted when the Eighteenth Amendment passed, ushering in Prohibition in 1920.[37]

Some school activities at George Washington, such as assemblies and performances, brought most or all eight grades together. One of Marie's favorite aspects of school was its "wonderful dance program," where students learned traditional dances from nations around the world. Each grade worked on dances from a particular country and sewed the national folk costumes to add to the festivity. Marie remembered learning Dutch, Irish, and Scottish dances but could not recall incorporating traditional dances from the more recent Polish or Italian immigrants. Each year on May Day, at Memorial Park, near Dunmore's commercial center, all schools in Dunmore performed their numbers, mainly for their own enjoyment, although a few parents usually showed up.[38]

Occasionally, students invited a relative to come to their class and talk about something interesting they had done. Special visitors, often from out of town or of advanced age, shared memories of their experiences. Students were proud to bring their relatives. "My mother, Ruth McDonough, a schoolmate and an across-the-street neighbor of Jane," Barbara O'Malley said, "often told the story of bringing her grandfather John McDonough, a Civil War veteran, in his Union uniform to show-and-tell days at school. He would tell Civil War tales, particularly of his capture and escape. He showed a scar on his hand where a bullet passed through when he held his hands up to surrender, and he would sing war songs and dance. The way she described it he was quite a showman. His appearances were very well-received, which brought her great joy." One time when Jane was about eleven, her great-aunt Hannah Breece, who had taught school on Indian reservations and studied anthropology at the University of Chicago, spoke to the class about living among the native population of Alaska. She had gone there two decades earlier, "encumbered by long and voluminous skirts and petticoats," which women customarily wore. During her Alaskan adventure, she braved arctic cold and primitive comforts to teach Aleuts, Kenais, Athabaskans, Eskimos, and people of mixed native and European blood. At the Washington School, Hannah Breece either described totem poles so vividly or actually showed images to the students—Marie could not recall which— that Marie, at age ninety-six, could still picture them. Also leaving an enduring imprint on Marie was a presentation by a boy classmate's aunt from Louisiana, who explained how sugarcane grew and was made into sugar.[39]

Marie's mother not only came from a different ethnic group and religion than her father but, like the majority of Irish Catholics, also voted the Democratic ticket. Marie's Protestant father supported Republicans. These different views and backgrounds in her family fed her curiosity for history, geography, and politics. Both she and Jane— whose parents, Marie noticed, were both Republicans—belonged to a current events club at school. Club members had to pay to subscribe to an eight-page newspaper, received once a month, filled with national news, during the time of such momentous events as the Sacco and Vanzetti trial, the Scopes case, and Calvin Coolidge's landslide presidential victory. "After a while," Marie said, "the school decided it wasn't fair, since not everyone could afford the subscription, so they had the newspaper sent directly to our homes." The club convened at people's houses after school, with about eight girls participating. "The first meeting was at Jane's home," Marie recalled warmly. "Her mother served peanut butter and raisins on thick bread." Whenever the meetings were at Jane's house, the lunches were "much more elaborate." Their classmate Vita Barba, who lived two blocks from Marie on Marion Street, was a club member. She was Italian, and her father was a mailman. "Her mother made spaghetti, which I had thought only came in a can," Marie said, laughing. "Even after some kids had left George Washington, they still belonged to the current events club. We all wore different embroidered badges that some of the mothers had made."[40]

Activities outside school helped to sustain Jane when teachers stifled, rather than welcomed, her intellectual curiosity. Despite her restlessness and disappointment with school, Jane's fascination with cities and theories about them was taking hold, stoked by her insatiable reading, her father's intellectual stimulation, the city itself, and, occasionally, inadvertently by her teachers' inaccurate assertions. Perhaps because of Scranton's legendary meteoric rise and its continued importance as Pennsylvania's third-largest city, George Washington School #3's teachers worked topics about Scranton and cities in general into their lessons. A couple of years after Jane had finished at the school, her brother John, along with their neighbor Ruth McDonough and six other boys and girls, took part in Miss Gallagher's class debate on "Resolved, That Country Life Is More Beneficial Than City Life." The event was special enough and generated sufficient interest to make it into *The Scranton Republican*. Both Ruth and John were "negative defenders," proponents of urban life debating against the resolution.[41]

By the time Jane finished at the George Washington School, she had published her first poems. The world beyond school acknowledged her talent as a writer. A newspaper for children, offering yearly subscriptions, called *Picture World*—which Jane recalled as associated with the Presbyterian Church—printed "'A Mouse,' By Jane

I. Butzner, 10 years old." The refrain, "Dingsy, dangsy, dito," is interspersed between every line of the poem's three wry and bouncy couplets about a mouse's comeuppance after "gnawing a hole in the house" and wreaking havoc in the cupboard. The last couplet delivered the punch line: "The cat licked his chops when he finished his meal. / *Dingsy, dangsy, dito.* / If I ate a mouse, how sick I would feel! / *Dingsy, dangsy, dito.*" When Jane was eleven, Thomas Lomax Hunter invited readers of his weekly column, "The Waste Basket," in the Fredericksburg *Free Lance-Star* to "contribute pictures [i.e., verbal sketches] . . . of well-known people who will be recognized by everybody." T. L. Hunter, a Virginia lawyer and poet, practiced and wrote in the same town as Jane's colorful uncle William Butzner, a fellow attorney, who no doubt tipped Jane off about this opportunity to submit her verse. Two weeks later, Hunter placed Jane's "The Flapper" prominently in his Friday pastiche as a "picture for my Portrait Gallery," identifying the poetess, Jane Isabel Butzner, as a ten-year-old from Scranton. Jane portrayed the ostentatiously stylish "Flapper" in her fur, brocade, "Silk stockings rolled down, what a free show they made," and heavy makeup. Jane concluded the verse with a mocking twist: "And yet for all this a frown spread her face, / What's the matter? She lost her vanity case!" Below the poem, Hunter addressed words of praise to his readers and to the young writer: "I think [this poem] is astonishingly well done for ten years. Here is real power to see the details of a picture and skill in putting them together. You have a valuable talent, young lady. I hope you will cultivate it." In 1955, when Bess Butzner copyrighted at the Library of Congress a typed and hand-bound manuscript of twenty-eight of her daughter's childhood poems, she opened the collection with "A Mouse," presumably one of Jane's earliest verses, but she omitted "The Flapper." This would not have been a subject of which Bess approved.[42]

Although Jane at age ten or eleven was already reaching for the wider world, the microcosm of her Dunmore school provided invaluable experiences. Besides reinforcing a love of country, symbolized by the Pledge of Allegiance and Washington portraits, and instilling such values as thrift and respect, the grammar-school education engendered acceptance of others through association. Children of ethnically, socially, and economically diverse backgrounds intermingled at the neighborhood school, and, as Marie pointed out, "Everybody got along, and we learned from one another." The overwhelmingly Irish Catholic faculty and principals at the Washington School were well educated and devoted to teaching the fundamentals of learning through memorization and rote learning, and, at times, rough punishment. Whatever Jane's feelings about school, her teachers, and their method, and despite her crossing the line sporadically, she came away from grammar school with an early love of poetry, at least two published poems, and, of course, beautiful Palmeresque handwriting. Grammar school accomplished its eponymous goal: During Jane's lifelong and remarkable writing career, she would leave little work for any copy editor.[43]

Jane and her childhood home. "Photographed in May 1989,
but it looked the same," she wrote on reverse. Estate of Jane Jacobs.

• • •

CHAPTER 5

Eyes on Monroe Avenue

THE HOUSE TO WHICH Jane Jacobs dedicated two of her books remained not just a fond memory; it was a touchstone for the rest of her life. In her late eighties, Jane reflected on her Monroe Avenue home as "the house that [she] remember[ed] best" and had grown attached to in her most formative years. She cited it solely in the dedication of her first book, *Constitutional Chaff*, published when she was twenty-five, and foremost in *Systems of Survival*, a half century later. "A place where you live from the time you're four years old until you're eighteen years old is your childhood home, really," she reflected in 2002. "I loved the house."[1]

And with good reason, for the house was a place of gaiety, with both adult and child-age friends and relatives, neighbors, and out-of-towners coming and going. The first floor—with its living rooms, dining room, and kitchen flowing into one another—embraced family meals, gatherings, and grown-up guests. The children's friends became acquainted with the intimacy of the second floor, where the bedrooms clustered. From the front vestibule—with its exquisite patterns of small round, square, and triangular tiles—a quick jog to the right put them at the foot of the front stairs, with two steps up to a landing with a window, before turning left and proceeding along the side of the house to another landing, where the stairs snaked ninety degrees left again. Or from the kitchen in the rear of the house, they could climb the more utilitarian back stairs, designed by Jiencke for servants. As one of Jane's friends later observed, "We ten-year-olds always felt back stairs (and cupolas)" in addition to being a "sign of opulence in my eyes" . . . "had such a potential for play." Having front and back stairs between the two floors multiplied the possible escape routes during games such as hide-and-seek.[2]

At least for a while, Jane and Betty shared a bedroom, leaving one room for each brother and another for their parents. Three of the bedrooms, including Jane's at the house's southern corner, had windows looking down from high above—the crown of the hill plus the second floor's vantage point—affording a broad vista of Monroe Avenue. The fourth bedroom, an oversize bathroom the size of a bedroom, and a smaller room— used as a study or a bedroom but originally intended for a maid—looked out over the backyard garden and the rear of the homes on Quincy Avenue. Like the downstairs rooms, these upper chambers were spacious and comfortable. "The Butzner children all liked practical jokes, especially Jane and John, who were very close," Kay Schoen Butzner recalled. The house inspired their pranks. "One year, they tied a string to the Christmas tree and ran the other end up to a bedroom on the second floor above the entrance. You couldn't see the string. Someone would tug on it and shake the tree and spook the people below, which the children got a big kick out of."[3]

Although designed for utility, the basement with its cement floor also worked well for games. A large coal furnace commandeered the big open center of the basement, along with the hefty coal bin next to it. Through a cellar window on the driveway side of the house, a delivery truck poured anthracite down a chute to the bin. During heating season, ashes had to be removed and put in a dustbin every day. The Jienckes had partitioned two small spaces in the back of the cellar: One had a stone sink for laundry, and the other had a wooden sink with cupboards above and walls lined with shelves for storing home-canned vegetables, jams, and jellies. Another of the house's practical features was the miniature door in the rear first-floor wall,

Jane (far right) and neighborhood children, 1921. Estate of Jane Jacobs.

framed in the same manner as the windows, where the iceman, still with his horse and wagon, could place the delivery directly into the kitchen's icebox without going into the house.[4]

With a big oak tree and a profusion of lilacs, the Butzners' backyard was pleasant and shady—so shady that Bess could grow the forest-floor native jack-in-the-pulpits. The backyard accommodated any and all of the neighborhood kids who dropped by. "It was grassy and a little overgrown," Barbara Gelder Kelley recalled, but it was always inviting, since no fences separated neighbors on Monroe Avenue. This common, uninterrupted space ran through quite a few lots on both sides of the Butzners'. A low off-white picket fence symbolically bounded the back of the lot and supported the roses that crept over it. In the late 1930s, while working for the Dorothy Draper company as a textile and wallpaper designer in New York, Betty came up with a design based on the roses growing over the fence. Bess was delighted to convey the news to Marie that Draper had chosen Betty's design as their "pattern of the year."[5]

On Monroe Avenue, children of all ages and both genders played together after school. Evie Barrett, Principal O'Boyle's niece, who was even younger than Jimmy, came over from two houses down the block—where her aunt also lived—to "the Butzners' beautiful big home" for a game of tag or hopscotch with the younger brothers. "Mrs. Butzner was stocky and wore practical shoes. She was a lovely lady," she said, "and wonderful to the kids in the neighborhood. She would bake cookies and invite us kids over." When Jane's friend Marie—who was not only charming in manner but also tall and very attractive, even in her mid-nineties—visited, sometimes Jane's brother John and his friends were there, too. Afterward, Jane teased Marie by saying, "You know, John's friends thought you were pretty nice." Jane liked to go see the new babies at the Van Bergen house when another of Marie's four younger sisters was born. The Butzner siblings were also friends with the children of neighbors William McDonough, postmaster of Dunmore, and his wife, Agnes, whose parents were Irish immigrants. The McDonoughs with their children—Ruth McDonough, a Washington School classmate of John, and her older sister and brother—lived diagonally across Monroe Avenue from the Butzners. Sometime before Betty started high school, a large contingent of neighborhood children put on a play to raise money for "a good cause," Kay Schoen Butzner had heard from Jimmy. All four Butzner children participated in it, including Jimmy, the youngest, who could not have been more than three years old. The older Butzner siblings wrote and organized the play, and neighbors attended. From next door, merchant Michael Swift very likely came along with his wife, Etta, and their daughter, Laura, who was a schoolteacher. Since his young daughter, Eleanor, was Jane's good friend, Frank Stone, an engineer for the county, and his wife, Marion—next-door neighbors on the other side —had good reason to be there, too. "The play was something about a dog and was called 'Beauty Contest,'" Kay continued. "In the end, whichever dog earned the largest number of signatures won the contest." Such endeavors brought many people together in the little microcommunity of the 1700 block of Monroe Avenue to share the merriment.[6]

The Gelder sisters rhapsodized about growing up in this section of Dunmore, first on Quincy and then on Monroe Avenue. Being "neighborly," partaking in casual conversations, imparting news, and keeping an eye on the children were natural components of daily life. "We knew all the neighbors," Barbara attested, "everyone on the block, and still more in the vicinity. The kids knew all the adults, and the adults knew all the children. All the neighborhood children played till dark and would visit back and forth, although we didn't have dinner at each other's houses. Most mothers were home, and they knew where everyone was. My father [Franklin Gelder, an attorney for the Glen Alden Coal Company] walked around the block every evening, stopping to chat with people sitting on their porches. Everyone sat on the porches," Barbara remembered. "These are some of the things we've lost today, these connections," her sister Margaret added. "What we had in our neighborhood wasn't unusual. It was the same way in Green Ridge, West Scranton, South Scranton. . . ."[7]

Indeed, Kay Schoen Butzner portrayed her West Scranton community of Hyde Park as "a nice, close-knit residential area with a lot of people of Welsh background," as was her mother, née Norma Davis, but not her father, Carl Schoen, who was of German heritage. But like all Scranton neighborhoods, even those largely characterized by one national background, people who represented a variety of origins lived close together. In 1927, Kay's parents built a single-family home at 732 North Bromley Avenue, three blocks west of North Main Street. "They thought it would be a safe place to build a house because the neighbor on one side of the house, who was named Apgar, was a superintendent of the shops where they did mechanical work for the mines. Another neighbor, named Watkins, across the street was the superintendent of a mine, so we were probably safe from subsidence." There were also Italians, Irish, and Lithuanians nearby, some of whom were miners. After dinner, the children all roller-skated and rode their bikes together while the grown-ups sat on their porches and conversed with one another, sometimes talking across the street with other people on their porches taking the night air. Kay and her Lutheran father and Congregationalist mother formed a close relationship with their Irish Catholic neighbors next door, the McAndrews, who had four sons, and one daughter around Kay's age. Like most Catholics, the McAndrews were Democrats who read *The Scranton Times* and on Sunday got *The New York Times*. Kay's parents, like most Protestants, were Republicans—the nation's majority party from the Civil War until the late 1920s—and subscribed not only to *The Scranton Republican* but also to the Sunday *New York Herald Tribune*. The children exchanged parts of the newspapers; the McAndrew kids liked the *Herald Tribune*'s funnies, and the Schoens did the *Times* crossword puzzle.[8]

During the warmer seasons, neighborhood children all around Scranton and Dunmore rode bicycles. "Most kids," Marie stated, "if they could afford them, had bikes—first three-wheelers, then two. We usually rode in our own neighborhood, for fun, not transportation," because Scranton and its environs had so many hills. Like Kay and her friends on the West Side, Dunmore children roller-skated with the kind of skates that clamped onto your shoes. Marie sometimes roller-skated to Jane's house. In the winter, children sledded on the city streets near their homes, although parents warned them to stay away from busy streets and those that ran downhill into traffic. When enough snow fell for sledding, neighbors closed off Delaware Street between Monroe and Adams Avenues and put coal ashes, rather than salt or sand, on the road to slow the sleds before they reached the barricade at Adams. Neighborhood boys made their own toboggans from wood, "and if you were lucky, you got a ride," Kay joked. Boys and girls ice-skated in a swampy area off Electric Street that the borough flooded and let freeze for this purpose. Next to the improvised skating rink, people would build a fire so everyone could warm their hands. Margaret called this "neighborhood fun." Adults might drop off young children but did not usually join the skaters. "The big kids looked out for each other and watched over the little kids."[9]

People in the neighborhood noted that Jane could be quiet at times, lost in her book, reading in the warm weather on the front porch, while other children engaged in sports or games. The passion for reading ran in the family. Remembering her grandmother

Jane, Betty, Jimmy, and John Butzner (left to right) inside their front gate
on Monroe Avenue, c. winter 1925–1926. Estate of Jane Jacobs.

Mary Jane "Jennie" Breece Robison, whom she visited regularly in
the 1920s, in "the pretty and placid county seat" of Bloomsburg,
Jane wrote, "The two of us were typically engrossed in our books,
she in her rocking chair and I on the floor at her feet, a bowl of hard
candies on a table within reach of us both. Now and again we would
read good parts of our books to each other. . . . She spent most of her
time reading. She once told my older sister in my hearing that she
must read a great new writer named Ernest Hemingway, so I resolved
to read him too." In fact, all the Butzners read voraciously and had a
proclivity toward sharing the "good parts" of what they were reading, including passages from the newspapers. "In the morning," Jane
reminisced in her latter years, "[my father] would get his newspaper,
which was the *Public Ledger*, a Philadelphia paper, and put it up in
a wire contrivance that he had. But he didn't shut himself off with
this newspaper—he was always reading nuggets to us from it. He
had favorite columnists. I remember the name of one of them—Jay
House—and he would say, 'Let's see what Jay is saying today.' Then
he'd tell us if there was anything interesting." Bess, too, sometimes

read, to the exclusion of all else. At the Green Ridge Presbyterian Church, Marie once overheard a group of gossiping women who employed the same cleaning woman as Bess Butzner. When one of the church ladies asked the cleaning woman if Mrs. Butzner was a good housekeeper, she shrugged and replied, 'I don't know. All she does is read.'"[10]

Jane recalled her childhood home, beloved by her parents, too, as "a cheerful place" where "we did a lot of talking. My father worked long, long hours as a doctor, at first making [house] calls a great deal. Later on, with long office hours, including long ones in the evening, because that's when people often could come." In addition to ministering to patients, Dr. Butzner continued to spend time with the state and local medical societies, leading discussions after guest medical specialists lectured. Sometimes Jane's father went out of town for a period of study, such as in October 1922, when he took postgraduate courses at Indiana University. In 1925, he was especially busy as the elected vice-commander of the Reese Davis Post of the American Legion for the year and on occasion had to stand in for the commander, as well. Even so, he always made time to talk with his children. Some of these conversations became philosophical contemplations. "We were sitting on our front porch," Jane said, "when we got into [a] conversation and [my father] said, 'Look at that tree, that oak tree.' He pointed to the tree in our yard, and he said, 'What is its purpose? It's alive.' I made of the answer that the purpose of life is to live, and so I told him that's what I thought. He said, 'Yes, that tree has a great push to live—any healthy, living thing does.'"[11]

In his home, Dr. Butzner relished serious conversation with his medical colleagues as well as with his children. Some of these regular visitors figured prominently in the Butzner household, particularly the avuncular Dr. Thomas W. Kay. Jane had often gone to the office her father shared with him and sat in the waiting room, repulsed yet intrigued by the human skeletons and shelves of medical specimens floating in formaldehyde—including parts of people's anatomy from autopsies—preserved in glass jars with hand-inked labels. Belonging to Dr. Kay since his earliest years in practice, these specimens signified to his patients that his medical skills were well grounded in scientific knowledge, that he was no snake-oil salesman. The lurid array of samples did, however, kill any desire on Jane's part ever to eat organ meats.[12]

When Dr. Kay returned from his exotic travels and paid the Butzners a call, great excitement ensued. Not only did he have tales to tell but he also arrived bearing gifts for the family, with some selected specially for Jane. These objects of fascination tangibly illustrated his accounts of faraway countries and cultures, thus bringing them alive. Throughout her life, Jane treasured these objects and stored them safely behind glass-paned cabinet doors on the top shelves of her pine secretary. She called this collection her "museum." Eventually, Jane found or received more than 250 eclectic, captivating items that she deemed worthy of keeping in her museum. Some items were natural rarities, such as petrified wood. Others were ingeniously designed, represented world or family history, or held sentimental associations with the giver, owner, or maker. In Jane's museum—along with a chain carved from a single piece of wood by her grandfather James Boyd Robison in Libby Prison during the Civil War, moccasins brought from Alaska by Great Aunt Hannah, folk toys given by Uncle Calvin Butzner in Virginia, political campaign buttons, and

Objects in Jane's "museum" from Dr. Kay: Near Eastern water
bottle, Buddha incense burner, and olive-wood animals.
Photos by Caitlin Broms-Jacobs, 2006.

a family-heirloom jingle bell—were eighteen international objets d'art bestowed upon Jane by Dr. Kay. "It seems to me that if one has heirlooms," she wrote in adulthood to her mother, "the thing to do is keep them in top shape if possible, as a good museum would do."[13]

One can imagine the delight with which Jane first looked upon a tiny bronze Buddha with a disproportionately large bowl in his lap for burning incense. Not sure of its exact provenance, Jane distinctly recalled that it was the first Buddha she had ever seen. When Jane was "very little," old Dr. Kay brought wooden castanets from Spain, made in the early 1900s for tourists and resembling those used by Spanish dancers at the time. In the early 1920s, he gave Dr. Butzner a cleverly functional water bottle from the Near East with a woven reed cover, which, when soaked in water, kept the contents cool while traveling. He also presented the Butzners with such treasures as a woman's shoe from Brazil, a miniature llama made with llama wool from Bolivia, an opium pipe from Asia, a delicately painted porcelain cup from China, an African ornamental comb and a small clay figure of a woman with fabric for clothes and beaded jewelry, and a wooden figurine from Egypt. From the Holy Land came an inkwell carved from olive wood with a silver filigree pen, and a string of three toy-size olive-wood animals—a donkey with rider and two camels—linked with fine chain. Possibly following a cruise of the Mediterranean during the winter of 1923–1924, Dr. Kay returned to Scranton with his second wife, Olivette Luciani Kay, whose home had been in Marseille, France. Unfortunately, Mrs. Kay would return there sooner than she had anticipated.[14]

On October 3, 1924, Jane and the rest of her family were shocked and saddened when Dr. Kay died suddenly and unexpectedly of a heart attack at the age of sixty-six. "He and his wife had been at his office in the Dime Bank building at 10 o'clock and later Mrs. Kay went on a shopping tour," *The Scranton Republican* reported, chronicling the final day of "one of the city's best-known members of the medical profession." Dr. Kay did not feel well and went to his apartment at the Hotel Jermyn. Drs. J. D. Butzner and F. P. Hollister were called, but their efforts were futile. "[Dr. Kay] was a most pleasant, highly-esteemed gentleman with a wide circle of friends," a *Republican* columnist noted. Drs. Butzner, Hollister, and Kiesel paid tribute to their friend and colleague with an obituary in the *The Medical Society Reporter*, lauding "his delving nature" and "his life of unusual experience," not the least of which included serving—while residing in Syria —as one of Queen Victoria's three advisers on the affairs of Palestine. Although Jane was barely eight and a half years old when this gregarious, offbeat, and generous explorer of "practically every nation of importance" and "the wonders of every great city" died, he had made a deep and lasting impression on her and expanded her knowledge of the world. Dr. Kay left his substantial estate to his grandniece, other southern relatives, a trust to care for the cemetery in Virginia where his kin were buried, and—provided she did not remarry—his widow, Olivette. He bequeathed his surgical instruments and library to his office partner and close companion, Dr. John D. Butzner.[15]

Other visitors to 1728 Monroe Avenue arrived from points beyond Scranton. Many of them were relatives from Jane's extensive family, particularly from the prolific Robison side. Bess had six living siblings and dozens of aunts and uncles. From Berwick, in the Bloomsburg area, came Bess's older brother by three years, James Boyd Robison, Jr. (called "Boyd"), who worked first for a car company and later as a florist. He had six children, who were the cousins Jane and her siblings were closest to. The three youngest—David, Martha, and Irvin (who, in his sixties, legally changed his first name to his middle name, Andrew) Robison—dovetailed in age with Betty, Jane, John, and Jimmy. David Robison, two years younger than Betty, was a kind person, "somebody who very quietly help[ed] others," his daughter Mary Robison told Jane many years later. Boyd's daughter Martha was a couple of years older than Jane and had been intrigued by Jane's early fascination and facility with words. "You taught me," Martha recalled with amusement, 'You insignificant piece of inconvenience, how dare you insinuate that I should tolerate such a diabolical insult' and words such as antidisestablishmentarianism." In 1927, when these cousins got together, Jane penned one of her favorite quotations in Martha's autograph book: "Bite off more than you can chew—Then chew it—Plan more than you can do—Then do it. Tie your wagon to a star—Keep your seat and there you are." She signed it warmly, with humor, "Cousin Jane Butzy." In 1996, cousin Martha reflected that Jane herself had certainly lived by this advice. At age eighty-five, cousin Irvin/Andrew, two year's Jane's junior, looked back and effused about spending a few months with her family in Scranton when they were children. "Your father remarked that summer that 'he would like to adopt Irvin,'" he wrote. "It was an endearing thought that has been gold to me all these years."[16]

Traveling all the way from Virginia, Uncle William Butzner's middle child, Nancy, spent part of her summers in the Butzners' Monroe Avenue household. Betty declared Nancy her favorite cousin. Nancy's Fredericksburg schoolmates described her as "Tall. Well-proportioned, with beautiful hair" and "stunning." She had a "graciousness of manner" and "possesse[d] an endless supply of amiability which makes her universally popular." "Like Jane, she had an inquiring mind and a commanding presence," Nancy's daughter recalled. Nancy was "roughly Jane's age and so pretty and nice," Marie agreed. No wonder Marie, too, looked forward to Nancy's visits and having her join the community—as did cousin Irvin and other long-term guests—when school was out.[17]

In the interludes between their teaching and missionary work, Jane's great-aunt Hannah Breece and aunt Martha Robison stayed for extended periods with Jane's family. Tied to the demands of running a farm, the other Butzner cousins, the five children of Dr. Butzner's youngest brother, Calvin, were unlikely to make the trek. Jane and her family occasionally traveled to Virginia to see their relatives, but they—particularly the children—made more frequent trips to Bloomsburg, a place they grew to know well and appreciate. "That was a nice little town," Jane reminisced to her brother Jimmy. After her husband, James Boyd Robison, died, in 1909, their grandmother Jennie Robison moved from the fine house along the canal, in the neighboring village of Espy, into a humbler house in town, a few blocks from the

"Jennie" Breece Robison lived at West 3rd and Jefferson Streets, c. 1915–1930, photo 2014. Author's photo.

commercial center of Bloomsburg. In the 1920s, Grandmother Robison had a number of her children and grandchildren living with her. In the early part of the decade, sharing the three-story home, with its gingerbread porch wrapping the corner, were her oldest daughter, Martha Robison (born in 1874), who worked for the Presbyterian Church, and her youngest daughter, Emily Robison (born in 1886), a school librarian. Her youngest son, Irvin Robison (born in 1890)— back from France after the Great War and employed as an automobile salesman—had moved in, too, along with his wife, Elsie Hagenbuch Robison, the daughter of a Bloomsburg carpet-mill laborer. Much to everyone's dismay, Emily died of cancer in 1926, but Jane's cousin (as opposed to her aunt of the same name) Martha Robison moved in with their grandmother.[18]

The Bloomsburg house was filled with activity. Jane recalled Aunt Emily "grafting fruit trees or killing a chicken for dinner" in the backyard, while her grandmother "found time to make visiting grandchildren good things to eat"—especially fried tomatoes with gravy, Jane's favorite. Since Grandmother Robison had taught in a one-room school—from the age of sixteen, in 1864, until she married at twenty-six—and was a beloved teacher, she was "constantly visited by former students," Jane wrote. "[S]he proffered the candy and then talked politics with them—town, state and national politics," interests she helped instill in Jane, too. On summer evenings, members of the household and visitors would enjoy the air together on the porch, greeting any passersby. "You and I had a wonderful grandmother in Bloomsburg," Jane's cousin Irvin/Andrew wrote to her. "Grandma spoke lovingly of you on every visit. I remember seeing you at her funeral [in 1930]. We had wonderful aunts and uncles. . . . I loved Aunt Emily who took us on picnics." The Butzner children looked forward to attending the enormously popular annual Bloomsburg Fair in the early fall. It had begun in the mid-nineteenth century as an agricultural exhibition but, by the 1920s, had greatly expanded and diversified, even offering the novelty of airplane rides. Pooling all the money their parents had given them for the trip and well aware of Bess's disapproval of frivolous expenditures, Jane's brothers couldn't resist having their first airborne experience. After all, Charles Lindbergh had not long before, in 1927, made the first solo flight across the Atlantic. Dr. Butzner was undoubtedly proud of his sons' adventurous spirit.[19]

The Bloomsburg fairgrounds lay at one end of town, while the Bloomsburg State Normal School was at the other. In the center, the town hall, the Columbia County Courthouse, churches, banks, and stores radiated from the central crossroads, the intersection of Main and Market Streets. The town's largest mill—manufacturing carpets—stood opposite the railroad station along the Susquehanna River. Bloomsburg presented a marked contrast to Scranton and its outer borough of Dunmore in size and amenities. In 1920, Bloomsburg's population had reached 7,819, compared to 20,250 in Dunmore, Scranton's most populous and densest "suburb," or to 137,783 in Scranton itself.

Even though Dunmore had its central business district, all other sections of the independent borough were dotted with small stores. A profusion of mom-and-pop stores sprouted on the corners in the Hollywood section and other neighborhoods in Dunmore and Scranton. "Despite the Hollywood section's being [figuratively] ninety-nine percent residential, every couple of blocks, scattered here and there, was a little grocery or drugstore," recalled Bob Everly, the son of Spencer Everly, who bought H. C. Van Bergen's grocery and hired Marie's father to work there after her grandfather went out of business in 1928. "My grandfather was kindhearted and had so much out on credit," Marie explained, that he couldn't keep up. Bob Everly followed his father into the real estate business and was well acquainted with the area's nooks and crannies. "The South Side [inhabited primarily first by German, then by Polish and other immigrants] had bars or stores on almost every corner," he commented. By building a small addition with a large window on the front of their houses, people created storefronts as separate rooms in which to set up a business while they lived in the rear. Or sometimes they took part of their home and turned it into a commercial space, such as a small restaurant.[20]

Soon after the Butzners settled in Dunmore, Bess—who, like her mother, was an enthusiastic cook—enlisted her children to run errands to procure ingredients. From 1728 Monroe Avenue, abundant

Jane, Bess, Betty, and John Butzner (left to right) in their Monroe Avenue backyard, early 1920s. Estate of Jane Jacobs.

small stores selling groceries and fresh bread and milk plus a well-hidden food manufacturer of specialty products lay within a short walk. Similarly, from Marie's house, on Marion Street between Adams and Jefferson Avenues, it was an easy walk to several other grocery stores, a florist's, a barbershop, a drugstore, a butcher shop, and a plumbing shop. Not only networks of people but also businesses and small stores connected members of the community. "People walked to the grocery, walked to the florist and the drugstore," Margaret Gelder Reese emphasized. No hopping in the car for a quick sprint to the store or stocking up with a week's worth of food. They ran into neighbors along the way and chatted with others and the store clerk while making their purchases. The Hollywood section of Dunmore was glamorous enough, even with small commercial operations interspersed, to hold on to its nickname. In this largely residential neighborhood, businesses and light industry nestled among the homes, making it organically a "mixed-use" area, thus defying the segregation of uses often dictated by modern zoning.[21]

Jane loved to be sent to get a loaf of warm bread so she could sneak slices from the bottom of the loaf on the way home, hoping her mother might not notice them missing. Sometimes her mother asked her to go to the grocer's for dried chipped beef—a piece of thinly sliced salted beef that came in a jar. Bess prepared it by chopping and cooking it in a white sauce and serving it over biscuits. To the embarrassment of their mother, the children named it "piggy beef," because pork was preserved this way, too. For greater visibility to passersby, many entrepreneurs located their stores on the long and busier east-west streets. If Jane ventured up Monroe Avenue a half block north to Electric Street, she reached Sal Gallo's grocery store, Hoyt Jones's (by 1931, it became Jacob Scheibel's and, later, Kelly's) drugstore next to it as she turned right, and another grocery as she continued in the same direction, at the corner of Quincy and Electric. In the drugstore, she could mail letters or buy stamps at the U.S. Post Office substation. Three-quarters of a block west of Monroe, Henry Poinsard had a florist shop on the far side of Electric, near Madison. On Jefferson Avenue, the next block to the west, on both sides of Electric Street, Thomas B. McClintock had a prominent floral business with a sizable greenhouse for growing flowers and garden plants, and, in season, for selling decorative Christmas garlands and trees. McClintock's had opened at this location in 1888. He, and later his children, resided in the neighborhood when the Butzners lived there. Since the main entrance to Forest Hill Cemetery was just up the hill to the north, two adjacent florists did enough business to thrive. Next to McClintock's was a grocery store. William Rinaldi, a barber, rented space from the grocer and set up his shop there, too. Heading south and east from Monroe, on Delaware Street at the corner of Webster, Walter Crosa owned a medium-size grocery, which the Grand Union Tea Company took over in 1927 and the American Store Company bought in 1931. There was yet another grocery at Green Ridge Street and Clay Avenue.[22]

Because most of the grocery stores—so frequent and close together in one area—sold mainly nonperishable goods in jars and cans, they could coexist with one another while offering the neighborhood variety and convenience. Although almost all the stores were on through streets and at corners, a few were situated elsewhere. At the corner of an alley and Madison Avenue, the widow Adeline Beemer lived in a house and had turned the building in her backyard into a little grocery. Its entrance and display window faced the alley. As was customary with family-owned stores, the locals called it by the family's name, "Beemer's." Like the Butzners' house, Mrs. Beemer's property was in the middle of the long block between Delaware and Electric Streets, although one block over and on the opposite side of the street. Thanks to the subdividers of this part of town, Jane could take a shortcut through the block across the street to get there.[23]

When the subdividers of the Hollywood section of Dunmore planned the streets and lots, they imposed a grid over the hilly terrain. Long blocks on the north-south avenues and short ones on the east-west streets comprised the rigid plan. At the northernmost edge, Electric Street—a continuation of the same street on which the Butzners had lived previously in Scranton—bounded the neighborhood. This long east-west drag originated at the Lackawanna River and continued through Green Ridge Corners, ending on North Blakely Street, a block north of Dunmore Corners. It was an old thoroughfare with only sporadic cross streets as it skirted the Hollywood section. The electric-powered streetcar ran along here, before turning down Adams Avenue as it headed to central city. The driver picked up and discharged passengers at just about any corner. In this stretch, Electric Street had small lots on either side that made for modest homes squeezed together, side-by-side two-family dwellings, and, consequently, lower property values and rents. Because it was a relatively busy street with crosstown travelers, small businesses sprouted along it.[24]

A half block south and parallel to Electric, in the Butzners' section of the neighborhood, the subdividers had inserted a narrow alley that bisected several long blocks, including Monroe Avenue. It started halfway between Jefferson and Madison Avenues and stopped at Clay Avenue. Elmont Court—as it was elegantly named, although more often referred to as "the alley," to the disappointment of those whose homes abutted it—had dead-end extensions that headed north to Electric Street but did not cut all the way through. These cul-de-sacs allowed for outbuildings—such as sheds, stables, garages, and light industrial or commercial buildings—with off-street access. The lots and therefore the building types on the avenues between Electric Street and the alley resembled those on Electric. Single people, families with moderate incomes, and individuals not intending to stay for a long time lived here. Although these blocks were configured for generally less expensive housing as well as commercial and industrial uses, the alley and the resulting shorter blocks also created a choice of routes for pedestrians.[25]

Walking across the street, down the alley, and partway up the alley's northern cul-de-sac to Wickham Brothers' potato chip and peanut butter factory was one of Jane's fondest childhood memories. Here behind the McDonoughs' and other middle-class homes, in a diminutive brick building, located next to the Wickhams' three-story warehouse for "specialty groceries," the brothers produced these two foods on alternate days. The factory was so tucked away, "you would never know it was there," Marie marveled, but neighborhood residents, especially children, loved to go up to the little sales window on the front of the tiny factory. Jane had a "*huge* nostalgia for potato chips right out of the fryer," her son confirmed. "You brought your own bag to be filled, and it cost five cents to fill the bag, no matter what the size. They fried the chips in lard mixed with peanut oil, which had separated and was left over when they made peanut butter." Jane loved to watch the thick, nasty-looking peanut paste ooze from the blending machine's spout. The potato chips found their way into Jane's *Economy of Cities* as an example of a Scranton export "called Saratoga chips," she wrote, "because that was where they had first come from." Indeed, Wickham Brothers advertised them as "Saratoga Chips" and displayed them and all their "Scranton Made Pure Food Products" at the city's annual Industrial Exposition. No doubt, the ever curious Jane had inquired as to the meaning of the name. Marie's grandfather H. C. Van Bergen sold Wickham Brothers' specialties in his store, including a flavored mayonnaise they made with pickles, called "Tasty Naise." Alfred and Ezra Wickham and their

Wickham Brothers in alley bisecting 1700 blocks of Madison and Monroe Avenues, photo 2011, now demolished. Author's photo.

families lived in the neighborhood, and the Wickham kids attended the George Washington School #3.[26]

Hucksters, selling fruits, vegetables, and poultry from their gardens and farms, offered a way to buy superfresh food that the little groceries could not stock, and they stopped near the front of one's house. Although a handful of households grew tomatoes, not many people in Jane's or Marie's neighborhoods had vegetable gardens. People in the nearby Patch, however, all had vegetable gardens, and some even raised chickens. What they didn't eat, they turned into income. A few blocks from Marie's house, in Harmony Court, was a dense Italian settlement. "It had enclosed yards with vegetable gardens in the front of the houses," she noted. "Some residents were 'hucksters' with horse-drawn wagons—and, later, trucks—who went around selling produce." The Cascio family at the end of the court ran a grocery out of their house, which—like many owner-occupied stores—stayed open late, even on Sunday nights. "They were a big Italian family, all related, living in the same house," Marie added. "Some of them went on to become judges."[27]

Born in 1919, Leo Walczak, the son of two Polish immigrants who had become U.S. citizens a few years earlier, started working at age sixteen as a huckster of vegetables and poultry from his parents' farm. Having developed emphysema as a coal miner, his father, Jozef, in his mid-forties in 1929, sold their house in the borough of Dickson City and bought a farm in the nearby countryside in North Abington. Leo and his brother Vetz, who was three years older, had regular customers in Scranton, seven or eight miles away. They headed into the city with the farm's truck. "You just parked the truck on the street—you wouldn't blow a horn—and all the ladies would come to the truck," Leo regaled his nephew. "They would come from both sides of the street. On one street you'd make three stops. The prices would fluctuate from one week to the next. In the spring you'd have eggs, chickens, and ducks. When July would come, you'd have sweet corn, cabbage, carrots, and some early potatoes. In them days every farmer sold his own produce. They didn't have no fruit stand at the

Walczaks on Abington farm: (left to right) Joseph and Mary Walczak;
sons Juz and Vetz; grandchildren Suszanne and Lorraine, 1948.
Courtesy of Bill Walczak.

farm. You delivered into the city. The man who raised fruit, he delivered his apples, pears, and peaches. The vegetable farmer, he took his
vegetables down. But we were diversified. We had ducks, chickens,
and vegetables! That used to bring us about a hundred or two hundred
dollars a week. And that was a very good income [in those days]."[28]

Dairies, bakeries, and butcher shops also had workers meander-
ing through the neighborhood, purveying their wares by means of
horse-drawn wagons or trucks. The milkman made his way down
the street two or three times a week, and residents could arrange to
have certain dairy products delivered regularly. When the bakery
truck pulled up, buyers could walk inside to inspect the goods and
make choices. These hucksters had prescribed routes and schedules,
so people knew what days they would show up. The eyes on Monroe
Avenue would be looking for them. For fresh meats, they called the
butcher to place an order, which promptly appeared at their door.[29]

As hucksters—often immigrants or their children—rumbled
their way down the 1700 block of Monroe Avenue, neighbors poured

out to buy their products, bringing into contact small pieces of the great mosaic. In 1930, on this block alone, many residents were second-generation immigrants, while a number of the neighbors were foreign-born, having emigrated from England, Wales, Scotland, Ireland, Germany, Italy, Norway, Belgium, and Russia. Catholics, Protestants, and a few Jews lived side by side. Recently married by Scranton's chief rabbi, Henry Yitzak Guterman, Philip Swartz, whose Austrian-born parents resided in Scranton's well-to-do Hill Section, and his Russian-born Yiddish-speaking wife, Ethel "Ada" Alpert Swartz, bought a small single-family house, the third from the corner of Electric Street, on the same side as the Butzners'. Mr. Swartz was the manager and proprietor of the Universal Printing Company, which did both book and general printing. His wife had graduated from Central High School. *The Scranton Republican* noted, in their meticulous write-up of the wedding, that Ada was "popular among the younger set." Evie Barrett recalled Dr. Daniel E. Berney's wife as a memorable character on her block. Dr. Berney, a Great War veteran who served in France and was a respected physician in Scranton, had met and married Rose Marie Quittelier in Brussels, Belgium, in 1922. The couple's house, at 1702 Monroe, on the corner of Delaware Street, was "dark, Gothic, and spooky." Ruth McDonough thought the French-speaking lady was "mysterious" and remembered she had "definite ideas as to what were appropriate fashions for young women, such as when a veil on a hat or earrings were acceptable," her daughter Barbara O'Malley recounted.[30]

The places of worship radiating from Dunmore's center encapsulate the history of the borough's ethnic mosaic. Religious organizations distinguished themselves not only by religion and denomination but also by the nationality of the group that had founded them. The original English and Scottish settlers established the First Presbyterian Church of Dunmore, built in 1854, while the Germans erected their own German Presbyterian Church in 1858. The Irish, who had come to work in the mines, formed what became known as St. Mary of Mount Carmel Catholic Church in 1857, but, in 1891, Italians founded their own Catholic Church in Dunmore, St. Anthony's of Padua. Slovaks dedicated their All Saints Catholic Church in 1903. In 1911, the First Presbyterian Church sanctioned the use of their building by Italian immigrants to conduct services in their native tongue, giving rise to the Second Presbyterian Church of Dunmore for this purpose. That same year, early settlers from the Carpathian region of Czechoslovakia started St. Michael the Archangel Byzantine Church. Until they built Temple Israel, completed in 1925, for two decades Jews from Eastern Europe had been holding services in congregants' homes. Ninety-three Polish families founded St. Casimir's Church in 1929. In neighborhoods in and around Scranton, the churches and synagogues similarly reflected the ethnic diversity among religious groups as well as the arrival time of the region's immigrant groups.[31]

Although the Erie Railroad Company had, since 1893, employed hundreds of immigrant workers in their railcar "shops" along Mill Street in Dunmore, the largest portion of Dunmore's and Scranton's immigrants came to work in the mines. Once the earlier Irish, Welsh, and Germans climbed the ladder into management or out of the mines, in the late nineteenth century, coal companies recruited Sicilians who labored in the abominable conditions of the sulfur mines. By 1892, enough Italians from all regions had settled and thrived in Scranton and Dunmore to lobby and gain approval from the city for a monument dedicated to Christopher Columbus at Courthouse Square. Frank Carlucci, a successful stonemason and sculptor of the granite statue, conceived the project to commemorate the four hundredth anniversary of the Italian explorer's discovery of the New World. The statue simultaneously symbolized the ethnic pride of this recent immigrant group and its growing acceptance by the general community. In the early twentieth century, as Italians worked their way up to demanding increased wages and higher positions in the mines, the coal companies callously fired them so they could hire fresher immigrants and pay them less. Advertisements lured workers from Eastern Europe, where some were miners already, including

Poles, Slovaks, Hungarians, and Lithuanians. Thus, coal operators—as the miners generally and pejoratively referred to the bosses—pitted ethnic groups against one another as they vied for employment. Older immigrants resented the newcomers. United Mine Workers president John Mitchell, in helping to settle the anthracite strike of 1902, earned adoration from his union members by bridging language and cultural gaps and bringing the many immigrant groups together into the union to fight the operators.[32]

The meticulously collected statistics in the state of Pennsylvania's annual reports on the mining industry during the 1920s—with lists of coal companies and tons of coal mined, the number and nationality of persons employed, and occupations performed inside and outside—paint a vivid picture of the enormity of the presence of the coal industry in Scranton and the vicinity. With their figures on accidents, fatal and nonfatal, as well as widows and orphans bereft, they also reveal the constant dangers the industry posed to workers. Benedict "Benny" Holeva, the son of Polish immigrants, lived in Dickson City all his life and described his experience: "I started work with the Scranton Coal Company in 1923, when I was eighteen, and I worked there for thirty-four years. The shafts were a hundred feet deep. You'd go down in a carriage. When you were down there, you could stand up and walk around. . . . To get the coal, you'd dig a hole and dynamite. Where you worked was maybe a half a mile or a mile away from the shaft. You'd stay far away [from the explosion]. . . . The dust in the mines didn't help." He spoke of relatives working in the mines who developed terrible cataracts and others with asthma and black lung disease. The numerical data attest that work in the mine shafts and tunnels was treacherous in other ways, too, with falling coal, collapsing roofs, and explosions of gas or out-of-control blasting powder causing an alarming number of fatalities. Being caught in outside machinery or by hoisting carriages, or falling down shafts, accounted for many other deaths and injuries.[33]

Slightly down the hill southward from the Butzners', residents witnessed the risks to people living atop coal mines, where sections of the city and homes were literally undermined by the coal companies.

The wealthy George Brooks, who owned the brokerage firm J. H. Brooks and Company, and his family lived at the corner of Jefferson Avenue and Green Ridge Street. "They kept horses and cars in their carriage house," said Marie, shaking her head as she related the cautionary tale. "We called the place 'the Castle.' It subsided and had to be torn down, and became a lot where they sold Christmas trees. My father had delivered groceries to him. . . . My grandfather wouldn't buy property in Pennsylvania because he was afraid of subsidence." In addition to the "built-down houses," subterranean coal dust could catch fire, and in the winter, people could see the snow melting on the ground above. Carbon monoxide fumes from the underground mines seeped upward, an invisible and odorless threat.[34]

When examined sequentially, year by year, the state's statistical reports on mines in the 1920s divulge the creeping decline of the economic vitality of the hard-coal industry, even though most of the decade was a period of prosperity for much of the country—earning the era the moniker the Roaring Twenties. After anthracite's peak sales during the Great War, the economic base of the city started to erode. The New York City school system, a rapacious consumer of

Dunmore neighborhood children, 1920s. Estate of Jane Jacobs.

coal, and other institutional users scaled back their orders for anthracite as oil prices dropped. Homes and factories formerly dependent on anthracite—the most costly coal to mine and process—began to heat with cheaper fuels, such as coke, oil, gas, and bituminous coal. Simultaneously, the silk industry, the region's other large employer, shrank as people turned from natural fibers to synthetics. Even with the development of other businesses in Scranton, the area chiefly depended on the mining of anthracite. Scranton's economy began its slow descent, and the coal strikes—on hiatus for a decade—hastened the pace.[35]

Throughout the decade, the entire region felt the effects of the slackening demand and diminishing production of coal. Miners as well as consumers from all walks of life suffered from a series of strikes, compounding the economic downturn. In northeastern Pennsylvania, in 1922, the well-organized United Mine Workers, led by John L. Lewis, called a strike of the anthracite workers in April, and 550,000 miners in the region walked off the job. Because of the massive strike, anthracite production for the year was at its lowest since the strike of 1902. The negative financial impact to cities and communities extended far beyond the region, affecting not only coal-mining companies and their employees, and individual coal consumers, but also many industries, railroads, and business in general. President Warren G. Harding endorsed a compromise to end the strike and urged its acceptance "in the name of the public welfare." The miners and the small number of operators controlling the coalfields finally agreed to a settlement, opportunely, on Labor Day. A *Scranton Republican* editorial bemoaned that, because of the strike, "a considerable percentage of the anthracite market was surrendered to bituminous to meet the necessitous requirements of a fuel scarcity in the larger centers of demand," including many thousands of tons of coal imported from Britain. This was an early harbinger of anthracite's future. A year later, the United Mine Workers struck again, although they settled once more within a few months, in early December 1923, before the brunt of winter hit.[36]

Lasting for five months through a brutally cold winter, the anthracite strike, extending from September 1, 1925 to February 25, 1926, was the longest-lasting strike in the history of the industry thus far. Numerous big city newspapers followed the strike, and it remained indelible in the memories of all Scrantonians who lived through the ordeal. Jane wrote about it in her last book, *Dark Age Ahead*, equating its impact with that of the Depression. "In our little city, where the chief industry was mining expensive, high-grade anthracite coal, the Great Depression was intensified because, in effect, it had started four years early with a long and bitter strike and subsequent loss of markets." Soup kitchens sprang up in Scranton, Wilkes-Barre, Hazelton, and other anthracite cities. Coal prices skyrocketed, and thousands of residents—those who could afford to and had little loyalty to the miners—altered their heating apparatuses to run on other fuels for heat. The Butzners, the Van Bergens, the Schoens, and countless other Scranton families sympathized with the strikers and refused to switch fuels. Marie Van Bergen Mansuy exclaimed, "Everyone was freezing! You didn't know where you'd get coal to heat your house during the strike of 1925 to 1926. Sometimes you could get bootleg coal from out-of-work miners, but you didn't dare tell where you got it. I was told not to open my mouth." Mining families scavenged scrap wood and cast-off railroad ties or the best pickings from the culm piles. "We used to pick all our coal from the dump," Stephie Holeva, a Polish miner's wife who lost her brother in a mine explosion, recalled. "We'd sit in the cellar and cut the rock from the coal. We picked up the railroad ties and chopped 'em up. That's how we kept our house warm."[37]

Use of anthracite coal dwindled from this point on. The strike of 1925 to 1926 contributed to the downfall of the region by eliminating thousands of customers. Workers in the coal industry, out of work for six months, turned to other jobs. Almost fifty years later, Jane still thought about the strike. She wrote to her mother, "Do you remember how you scrunched and rolled up wet newspapers during a coal strike in Scranton? I can still see you in my mind's eye

View from Jane's bedroom window, looking west toward
Scranton and West Mountain; McDonough house is second
from right and next to alley, 2011. Author's photo.

dipping them into a bucket of water and drying them in the back
yard." The coal strikes and hard times united people from the block,
the immediate neighborhood, and the school district to the borough
and greater Scranton as a whole. Diverse neighbors—those who habitually looked out for one another, or periodically came together
for fun, or knew one another only casually or hardly at all—without
hesitation helped one another in large and small ways.[38]

Looking out from Monroe Avenue—observing people, activities,
and the built environment—as well as learning about the world from
books, from Dr. Kay, and from her extended family, Jane developed
a great interest in and an appreciation for variety of all kinds. She
enjoyed her neighbors of diverse national and religious backgrounds.
She was fascinated by "how everyone was earning their living." She
took notice of the spectrum of jobs comprising the city's economy
and of the people—including miners and hucksters—who worked
at them. She was intrigued by and began to understand the importance of manufacturing and selling a range of products. She liked the

array of small stores and light industry mixed in with residences. She valued diversity, all the way down to individual characteristics and minute components of community life, even kinds of families. "Who knows whether it isn't extremely important for some human beings to come from large families and some from small ones?" Jane responded to Leticia Kent in 1970 regarding the advocacy organization Zero Population Growth. "We ought to be wary of anything that tends to destroy human diversity. We surely need diversity in sizes and kinds of families just as much as we need diversity of talents, occupational preferences, and personalities. . . ."[39]

In her writing and interviews as an adult, Jane stressed the importance not only of all kinds of diversity but also of inclusive "networks of casual trust" in a community. These ideas grew from her early years in Dunmore and Scranton. In 1997, after describing her fourth-grade clash with Miss McGuire over why cities develop, Jane spoke about what helps form a community and, in turn, cities: "The most important thing is that there are networks of people who know each other and the more inclusive they are the better." She clarified that she was not speaking about "social relationships in the sense of who you invite to your home and who invites you. . . . [I]n order to have an efficient and inclusive network of people who know each other, the very basic thing about it is people knowing each other in a public and often in a very casual way. Like people who are walking along the street and stop and talk to somebody. Maybe they just say hello because they have seen each other four times. But eventually . . . they may come to feel these people . . . are part of their community." These communities can come together quickly if a threat arises. "I know that because I have lived in communities that suddenly had great threats to their existence, and suddenly these networks of casual trust become absolutely vital." Jane began formulating her ideas with her eyes on Monroe Avenue long before she peered from her window on Hudson Street in New York's Greenwich Village. She embraced the sense of community cohesion in Scranton during her childhood years as it had embraced her.[40]

Jane roasting a marshmallow at the Girls Scouts'
Camp Archbald, c. 1928. Estate of Jane Jacobs.

● ● ●

CHAPTER 6

The Liberating Ideology
of the Girl Scouts

LIKE SCHOOLS AND NEIGHBORHOODS in the first third of the twentieth century, Scranton's staggering number of clubs, societies, associations, and organizations fostered a sense of community and citizenship, and they, in many cases, expanded the universe of individuals in the city. For Jane, they also offered a welcome respite from the constraints of school and—especially Girl Scouts—helped develop her interests and instilled a means of investigating the world as well as a sense of a woman's boundless possibilities that she would carry with her throughout her life. Before the isolating factors of television and the dominance of the automobile—let alone the Internet—the dense organizational life in American cities comprised a highly influential component of a person's experience. Citizens, young and old, came together from beyond their immediate neighborhoods to form groups for a common purpose, a shared interest, or to reinforce similar beliefs. The clubs a person belonged to defined her or his life so well that obituaries routinely enumerated them.

Organizations existed for a wide variety of purposes, singular or combined— professional, social, educational, political, benevolent, or religious. They ranged from national secret societies with multiple branches, such as the Masons, to locally oriented benevolent societies, such as the Mothers Assistance Fund. Some of these organizations had further permutations corresponding to specific ethnic and religious groups. Adults often belonged to a multitude of clubs and organizations and spent several nights a week engaged in associational activity. The preponderance of these clubs was exclusively either for men or women, although the men's organizations frequently held special events to which they invited wives. The all-male Reese Davis Post of the American Legion and the virtually all-male Lackawanna County Medical Society—whose membership of more than two hundred male doctors had admitted two women physicians by 1926—occupied Dr. Butzner for many an evening and an occasional weekend afternoon. Weekend gatherings tended to be for such activities as an outing or golf match. Meanwhile, Bess Butzner organized and attended educational programs for the female-only members of the Anthracite chapter of the Delphian Society. She was especially active in the elite women's Century Club. Formed in 1911, when the prestigious men's Scranton Club refused to allow women members, the Century Club primarily focused on civic improvement, charitable activities, and lectures by prestigious guest speakers. Within the Century Club quarters, another exclusive organization, the Daughters of the American Revolution, met regularly. Bess belonged to the DAR and, with her literary predilection, helped judge its recurring essay contest.[1]

Bess, accompanied by her children, but rarely by her husband—whom Kay Schoen had always heard was "too busy with his work"—regularly participated in the life of the Green Ridge Presbyterian Church, one of the city's most prominent religious institutions, with its enfolded associations. Bess sent her children, from an early age, to its Sunday school. Young people generally took part in far fewer organizational activities —except at school and religious institutions—than their parents. But beginning early in the twentieth century, scouting emerged. The popularity of Boy Scouts and Girl Scouts in the United States far outstripped that of any other youth organization. When Jane joined the local Girl Scout troop in the fall of 1926, the number of American Girl Scouts had reached roughly 137,000. She became

Betty in uniform with Jane and cousins (?)
in Butzner backyard, c. 1921. Estate of Jane Jacobs.

part of a citywide, and ultimately national and international, organization, where she encountered girls from other Scranton schools and some from farther-flung parts of the state and, eventually, the country. In 1948, when interrogated for security clearance to work in the State Department, Jane cited Girl Scouts as one of two organizations to which she had previously belonged.[2]

Betty had preceded her sister, Jane, as an avid Girl Scout and member of Scranton's historic first troop. Jane watched with fascination as her big sister worked on scouting skills, badges, and projects. She listened intently as Betty recounted her adventures at Camp Archbald, the regional Girl Scouts camp. Jane was impressed that twelve-year-old Betty had arrived at camp for the first time, in 1922, "not knowing how to swim a stroke," *The Scranton Republican* reported, "and in less than two weeks she not only learned to swim sufficiently well to pass the Scout test of fifty yards, but also to pass the junior Red Cross life-saving test and to do the swan and corkscrew dives along with several other kinds." The prospect of learning subjects not taught in school and spending summers with swimming, campfires, and chores made fun, called "kamp kapers," captivated Jane.[3]

In September 1926, Jane and her friend Marie Van Bergen, both in the middle of sixth grade, had reached the minimum age of ten required to join the Girl Scouts. Together, they started going to Scout meetings each Friday after dinner at 7:30 p.m. at the Green Ridge Presbyterian Church. In the troop, they were with other girls their age who also attended the church: Gladys Baumann, and Jean Patterson, from the Robert Morris School, where Betty had gone when the Butzners lived on Electric Street. The Green Ridge church wholeheartedly supported the growing scouting movement. In 1916, the church officers had voted to host a Boy Scout troop, number 7, and the following year, they approved a petition for a Girl Scout troop, number 4, nicknamed—as was the custom then—"the Sunflower Troop."[4]

Betty had belonged to the Sunflower Troop for at least five years when Jane and Marie joined. Before either was old enough to join scouting, Betty and Jane had admired the older Girl Scouts in their khaki uniforms performing in church functions and, during Girl Scout Week, leading church services. Eager to get a taste of scouting, Jane had attended camp the summer before she joined the troop. In a heartfelt 1993 letter to her brother John after Betty died, Jane looked back on a cherished memory from that first year together with Betty at Camp Archbald: "I keep remembering Betty when she was sixteen years old, as Hiawatha in a pageant at camp. At the end of the pageant, just at sundown, she paddled a canoe out in the lake, right in the brilliant light-path of the setting sun, so fast and so far that she was finally a vigorous speck in the distance."[5]

More than a local or national organization, the Girl Scouts were part of a burgeoning international scouting movement. When Betty was a toddler, scouting for girls had first come to the United States from England, where in 1908 Sir Robert Baden-Powell launched the Boy Scout movement with his immensely popular book *Scouting for Boys: A Handbook for Instruction in Good Citizenship.* He had served as an officer in the British army in India and Africa for decades, specializing in reconnaissance, mapmaking, and knowledge of the woods and the great outdoors, known as "woodcraft." Having written a military-training manual, Baden-Powell decided to adapt it for teaching young boys to be outdoorsmen, explorers, and upstanding citizens. Appealingly written and illustrated, and interwoven with stories and games, the book for boys presented camping skills, from tracking to signaling; self-improvement techniques, from physical health to moral advice; and tips on how to help others, including lifesaving and patriotism. Complete with hints to instructors, Baden-Powell's book inspired boys to start their own troops. By the end of 1908, there were sixty thousand Boy Scouts in the United Kingdom. Troops began forming in British Empire countries, too, from Canada to Australia and India, and then in other nations around the globe. A testament to the endurance of the movement, *Scouting for Boys* would become the fourth-bestselling book of the twentieth century. Only the sales of the Bible, the Koran, and Mao's Little Red Book surpassed it.[6]

British girls exhibited such fervor for a female version of scouting that at first they organized their own informal troops. Then, in 1910, Sir Robert Baden-Powell's sister Agnes Baden-Powell founded the female, less militaristic counterpart of the Boy Scouts. She included domestic science and arts in the program, and aimed to create girls of character, brave yet womanly. Distinguishing them from Boy Scouts, she called them Girl Guides. Juliette Gordon Low—from a wealthy family in Savannah, Georgia, and freed from a catastrophic marriage by the death of her husband—made frequent trips to London, where she befriended Sir Robert Baden-Powell. She found herself collaborating with Agnes Baden-Powell on Girl Guiding. Two years after Boy Scouts of America began, the independent-minded, idealistic, and energetic Low brought the scouting-for-girls movement stateside and, in 1913, settled on the name Girl Scouts of the USA. The name she chose accentuated its association with Sir Robert's Scout movement. Beginning with the first troop, she included girls from various cultural, ethnic, and economic backgrounds as well as those with disabilities. Low formulated the core elements of the American organization. She designed the first uniforms for Girl Scouts and adapted Sir Robert's wording for the Girl Scout Promise—to serve God and country, help others, and uphold the Girl Scout Law. In 1916, Low authored her own edition of the Girl Scout handbook.[7]

Like girls who had formed troops in Stroudsburg, Jermyn, and other towns in northeastern Pennsylvania, a group of Scranton high school girls, who had read about Low and her Girl Scout organization, wrote, in 1916, to the first national headquarters, in Washington, D.C., for information. The girls then convinced Blanche Hull to be their leader. In her late thirties, single, and active in the city's Playground Association—an organization that believed in the moral and health benefits of fresh air and exercise for youth—Hull was granted permission by the Green Ridge Presbyterian Church to use its parlor for troop meetings. The newly formed Girl Scout Troop 4, with twenty-four members, became the first troop in the city of Scranton. Over the next decade, Girl Scout troops proliferated in the Electric City, including, in 1927, a second troop, number 5, at the Green Ridge Presbyterian Church.[8]

By May 1920, greater Scranton had a sufficient number of Girl Scout troops to organize representatives from each to create a council—one of an astounding almost one hundred in the United States formed in the eight years since the Girl Scouts' founding. The national headquarters in New York deemed the Scranton Girl Scouts Council important enough to warrant sending field director Miss Alice Conway for a several-day visit to the city. Miss Conway spoke to the council and representatives from other women's associations in Scranton. She delivered the encouraging news that thirty-six leading colleges—Smith, Wellesley, Bryn Mawr, and Barnard among them—now offered a Girl Scout training course. "Miss Conway explained the aims of scouting," *The Scranton Times* reported, "saying that it is a civic organization which is taking care of future members of grown up organizations. It is not an 'uplift' [moral reform] movement," evidenced by the fact that "the leaders play with the girls." Envisioning the desired Girl Scout, Miss Conway described strong and empowered girls: "Lydia Languish has died, and girls no longer faint and pose as sickly. . . . Scouting gives [the young girl] a splendid opportunity for working off [her] energy and helps her lose her self-consciousness. The laws and promises are the backbone of the organization, and they help a girl to play fair, keep her temper, and at the same time play to win."[9]

Although a few of Scranton's growing number of troops were based in community centers like the Weston Field House or workplaces like the Petersburg Silk Mill, churches and synagogues hosted the majority of Scout troops in Scranton and nationwide. Girls tended to join a Scout troop in their own family's house of worship. At the Green Ridge Presbyterian Church, Girl and Boy Scout leaders presented reports along with other committee heads at the session meetings of the church's ruling elders, of which Scranton historian F. L. Hitchcock was one. The church regarded the Scouts, organizationally, as a "department" or "society" of the church, and in 1934, it placed them under the church's Board of Christian Education. The Green Ridge Presbyterian Church congregation endorsed scouting and its values, and integrated the troops into the church and its programs. Blanche Hull's parents, Stephen P. and Mary Hull, had been members of the church since its inception in 1873, and Stephen had served as a longtime trustee. The Green Ridge Church Boy Scout committee invited "Men of the Congregation and parents of the boys [to] . . . meetings to see what the boys can do and are doing." Marie recalled the presence of adult female church congregants at Girl Scout meetings and activities, noting that although not affiliated with the Girl Scouts, "certain women in the church also helped our troop," but Bess Butzner was not among them.[10]

With a flourishing and well-heeled congregation, in 1893 the Green Ridge Presbyterian Church completed a magnificent new edifice. They had engaged Frederick Lord Brown to design it. One of Scranton's most prolific architects of homes, churches, schools, and other public buildings, he was born in Sag Harbor, Long Island, but

Green Ridge Presbyterian Church, home to several Scout troops, corner of Green Ridge Street and Wyoming Avenue, architect's sketch, 1892. Courtesy of Norma Reese.

began his practice in Scranton in 1885, three years after graduating from Cornell's highly reputable College of Architecture. As Brown was drawing up plans for the Green Ridge church, he was also developing Richmont Park, "a real residential Eden . . . in upper Green Ridge," two blocks north of the Butzner's first house, with his plans for "innumerable model, well appointed homes . . . for the best class of our citizens," the *Republican* effused in 1894.[11]

German-born Conrad Schroeder was the contractor, probably working with his frequent collaborator stonemason Frank Carlucci. As Scranton's foremost contractor, Schroeder had recently built the Coal Exchange Building, the Lackawanna County Jail, and City Hall. With an unusual mosaiclike facade of tightly fitting variegated flat stones with curvilinear outlines (most likely local stone from West Mountain), Romanesque arched windows and entrances, a conically capped bell tower (originally), and stunning stained-glass windows, the church was hailed by *The Scranton Republican* as "one of the most substantial and beautiful in the city." Fitted with the city's largest organ "of superior workmanship and power," the church drew its considerable, mainly upper-middle-class membership, or communicants, from the surrounding neighborhood in both Scranton and Dunmore.[12]

During the time Betty and Jane were ardent Girl Scouts, the Green Ridge Presbyterian Church thrived, and the number of communicants rose steadily from about a thousand in 1921 to a sizable thirteen hundred in 1934, allowing church members to maintain their efforts to carry out good works around the world. In these years, the church elders and the congregation were dedicated to supporting missionaries to foreign countries—mainly Korea, China, and India—as well as "home" missionaries to the indigenous peoples of Alaska and among the Jews in Brooklyn. They considered these groups in their own country outsiders in need of education, aid, and, potentially, conversion. Jane's great-aunt Hannah and aunt Martha were two such Presbyterian missionaries who devoted their lives to this work. The Green Ridge church also donated to Presbyterian churches serving recent immigrants, such as the "Dunmore Italian Church" and the West Side's "Magyar Church." Fervent advocates of temperance but following their church's protocol, church elders allowed the Anti-Saloon League to "present their cause" but not to collect money. The church raised money for disaster relief, such as for sufferers of the 1923 Japanese earthquake and the 1928 Puerto Rican hurricane, and for occasional "needy cases" of families or individuals. Not only because of shared values but also because Girl Scouts promoted interest in foreign countries and cultures (although without missionary motives), charitable works, and helping others, the Green Ridge church fully embraced them.[13]

Exceeding Sir Robert Baden-Powell's expectations but not his wildest dreams, the Girl Scout movement caught fire around the world. In his 1919 foreword to the Girl Scout handbook, following the armistice of the Great War, he expressed his vision of eradicating war through a borderless organization of women: "If the women of the different nations are to a large extent members of the same society and therefore in close touch and sympathy with each other, although belonging to different countries, they will make a real bond not merely between the governments, but between the Peoples themselves and they will see to it that it means Peace and that we have no more War." The First International Conference of Girl Guides and Girl Scouts took place in Oxford, England, in July 1920. At the Fifth International Conference in Hungary in 1928, delegates from twenty-six countries from four continents officially established the World Association of Girl Guides and Girl Scouts (WAGGGS), with a bureau in London.[14]

For Betty and Jane, joining Girl Scouts Troop 4 at the Green Ridge church constituted another activity in that familiar setting, but for her friend and classmate Marie, a Catholic, this church was terra incognita. Marie's neighbor Margaret Briggs, an active member of the church and Troop 4 captain since 1922, invited her to join the troop. A 1921 graduate of Columbia University's Teachers College, Margaret had studied during John Dewey's long tenure there and likely came into contact with his progressive educational philosophy and humanitarian ideals. She certainly incorporated these methods and principles in her work as a Scout captain.[15]

Margaret lived with her mother, Mary MacMillan Briggs, and lawyer father, Walter Briggs, in a commodious wood and stone house on Jefferson Avenue, around the corner from the Van Bergens' home. She had befriended Marie's family and taken Marie under her wing. "I became the only Catholic in the Girl Scout troop," Marie explained, "but Jane, and Lucille Parsons—who lived a block away in a two-family house like ours—and other friends from the Washington School belonged, so I was happy to be there. Catholics had their own troop in St. Peter's Cathedral downtown." Catholic classmate Vita Barba would soon join Troop 4, too. Like her troop mates, who adored their troop leader, Marie "thought the world of Margaret Briggs." She kept in touch with her long after Miss Briggs resigned as Scout captain in 1929. Dynamic and passionate, Margaret Briggs also taught domestic science and arts at North Scranton Junior High School and devoted her life to helping the community's less fortunate. Throughout her life, she worked for Lackawanna County's department of family services, the Red Cross, and a mental health clinic. Upon her death, at age ninety-five, in 1992, she endowed the Margaret Briggs Foundation to award college scholarships and assist Scranton area educational, human service, civic, and cultural organizations.[16]

For Jane and many other girls, Girl Scouts provided a welcome relief from the generally authoritarian nature of their formal education. Clearly articulated in the *Scouting for Girls* handbook, the Girl Scouts' hierarchical yet representative form of governance sought "plans and suggestions" from all the girls. Troops—preferably composed of about thirty-two Scouts, ages ten to sixteen—were divided into smaller units, called "patrols," of six to eight members. Each patrol congregated simultaneously in a particular corner of the meeting room, with a "patrol leader," elected by this small group, and a "second" to work closely with her. The patrol leader took counsel with her group, gathered ideas for activities, and proposed them at the Court of Honors. The Court of Honors was made up of the captain, later known as the "troop leader," who was at least twenty-one years old and approved by the national headquarters; the lieutenant or lieutenants assisting the captain, at least eighteen years old and also approved by the national headquarters; and the patrol leaders and, sometimes, their seconds. Convening at the close of each weekly troop meeting, the Court of Honors planned the patrol and troop activities, "carrie[d] on the business of the troop," and, in the process, allowed "the captain to learn the opinion of every member of the troop." What a breath of fresh air, Jane surely thought, to witness and be part of a democratic, participatory, and inclusive organizational system and have Miss Briggs as the captain.[17]

Grouped into patrols according to age and number of years as a Scout, Jane and her fellow Girl Scouts delved into intriguing subjects and acquired practical skills not touched upon in school. They learned such things as how to tie useful knots, send visual and audial signals from a distance, and practice the "habit of observation." Since Jane plowed through her school textbooks as soon as they were handed out, she undoubtedly had devoured Betty's copy of the Girl Scout hand-book at her first opportunity, before she attended Scout camp with her sister. Imagine her elation at discovering a chapter devoted to a com-monly undervalued activity she had enjoyed even before she learned to speak—called, simply, "Observation." "[The value of observation] cannot be over-estimated," the handbook plainly stated. "It makes the world more interesting, sharpens our wits and makes us more alive to all that goes on about us." Immediately following were several pages of Sir Robert Baden-Powell's instructions on stalking, tracking, and hiding one's self as a naturalist would when observing wildlife in the countryside. In minute detail, he described how to use one's eyes and other senses to notice small signs of activity and the surroundings, and how to analyze what one saw. The handbook also spelled out how in towns girls could hone their powers of observation just as well and practice remembering what they observed. Besides making mental note of different kinds of shops, the shop names, and contents of the display windows, "[t]he [Scouts] must also notice prominent buildings as landmarks," Sir Robert urged, "and the number of turnings of the street they are using." Such skills, Jane realized even then, could be applied to observing human activity and urban environments. In her later life, while writing *The Nature of Economies*, she would liken herself to a "city naturalist."[18]

Besides practicing the art of observation, new Girl Scouts mas-tered certain essential tasks, such as the proper hanging and care of the American flag. Even after the removal from the 1927 edition of *Scouting for Girls* of military and war references that had lingered after the Great War, the handbook continued to recount the history of the flag and outlined rules for respecting it. Well into the 1920s, *The Scranton Republican* still referred to the Girl Scouts as "a patriotic organization," because they had previously raised money for "the war effort" and Scouts in Scranton were now selling late-issue Liberty Bonds to support their country. Jane found knowledge of the flag practical and interesting. She could help her mother hang the family's early 1900s forty-eight-star flag from the front porch, in line with their neighbors' flags, for holidays like Independence Day or Armistice Day. Jane permanently retired the Butzners' flag, a valued family possession, to her "museum," along with treasures from Dr. Kay.[19]

As with troops across the country, each of Troop 4's patrols was assigned a part of the troop meeting room for its gatherings, dues collection (a modest twenty-five cents a year in the 1920s), attendance taking, lining up for inspection, and storage of books, pictures, tools, and records used in the work for rank tests and merit badges. Girl Scouts rose through a series of ranks, from Tenderfoot to Second Class to First Class, by completing requirements and earning badges. A girl herself chose to earn merit badges—no rules compelled her to—and she selected those that appealed to her. A sign of achievement, badges ran the gamut from an array of nature studies to aspects of nursing, domestic arts, and potential careers. Earning proficiency or merit badges required perseverance and occupied the greatest amount of the Scouts' time. *Scouting for Girls* emphasized "learning by doing"—also philosopher, social reformer, and educator John Dewey's mantra for the progressive education he advocated. This was a marked departure from the way things were taught in Scranton's and Dunmore's schools. Jane preferred the kind of education she experienced through scouting. It allowed girls to rise to leadership without being perceived as unruly or obstreperous.[20]

The national Girl Scout organization laid out the qualifications for receiving each badge, posed thought-provoking questions, and recommended a list of books for further reference. A number of girls within a patrol usually decided to work together on a merit or proficiency badge, making it a group experience and more fun. Classes held during troop time contributed information for specific badge work. During Jane's first year in Scouts, about a third of the troop decided to get their Citizen badge. "How can you help make your Government better?" the handbook posited. It suggested girls working on the badge read *The Subjection of Women*, by John Stuart Mill; *American Citizenship*, by Progressive reformers Charles and Mary Beard; and a dozen other relevant and weighty works. The Scouts also enlisted community members and institutions to lend their expertise to a badge's subject. Mrs. Polhamus, from the Octagon Soap Company, taught three lessons pertaining to the laundress badge. Mapping and nature classes frequently took place at Scranton's Everhart Museum in Nay Aug Park, with its extensive collection of taxidermied local wildlife.[21]

The active, cooperative, self-directed learning at Girl Scouts resonated with Jane, as did the self-motivation for earning badges and the method of ascertaining proficiency. "[Each badge] means, not that the wearer is an expert in the subject," the handbook explained, "but that she has taken enough intelligent interest in it to learn the main principles [of the badge's subject] and make practical use of them. . . . The real badge test is the use a Girl Scout makes of it when opportunity comes." Rather than written tests measuring rote knowledge, "[t]ests should, as far as possible, be oral and in the form of practical demonstration." We know that Jane thoroughly enjoyed Scout meetings, because at the end of her first year of scouting, she received a Silver Star award for attendance. The Silver Star signified that she had attended and been on time to 90 percent of the weekly Scout meetings—something, her family well knew, she would never have been eligible for if an equivalent award had existed at school. The extraordinarily high number of attendance awards earned by Troop 4—twelve Gold Stars, given for perfect punctuality and attendance of meetings, and sixteen Silver Stars, handed out at the annual Girl Scout rally in May 1927 at Scranton's Central High School—attested not only to the alluring projects the girls undertook but also to the admiration of the thirty-seven troop members for their leader, Margaret Briggs.[22]

The structure and governance of the Girl Scouts presented its members with "opportunities at leadership." During Jane's first year in Troop 4, Betty, who was seventeen, had been elected patrol leader and, simultaneously, troop scribe. A scribe was entrusted not only with delivering news of troop activities each week to the organization's Scranton headquarters but also with taking away a list of announcements to be read at the next troop meeting. Two years later, when Jane was twelve, her fellow troop members recognized her flair for writing and elected her to this position. Jane's troop news reports were never dry and straightforward—her enthusiasm for Scouts and high spirits shone through. The Scranton newspapers intermittently printed a sampling of Girl Scouts news penned by the scribes, and Jane's invariably stood out: "[Awarding badges] was followed by patrol corners, at which time the bull dog patrol appeared with celluloid bull dogs tied in their neckties," Jane chose to report. "Upon counting off we found that there were 31 girls present. It was with regret that we ended the meeting and sang taps." A month later, she let slip: "Another Friday night, and another Scout meeting! Hurrah! But though we felt happy we had to look solemn during lineup and inspection for it would never do to be seemingly laughing at an inspector. . . ."[23]

A less acclaimed but patently visible element of the Girl Scouts' mission in the 1920s and 1930s was its pervasive promotion of literacy and literature. *Scouting for Girls* concluded with an extensive list of "some of the best books in the world," grouped into eclectic categories, such as "History and Period Novels," "Nonsense," "Wonders of Science," and even "Government Bulletins and How to Get Them." At a time when Americans devoured periodicals in vast numbers— from H. L. Mencken's *American Mercury* to *The Saturday Evening Post* and *The Ladies' Home Journal*—the Girl Scouts launched its own. Beginning in 1920, the national organization put out a top-quality monthly specifically for girls. In an attractive layout bedecked with black-and-white photographs and illustrations, *The American Girl* packed its seventy pages with short stories (adventures, romance, mysteries, animal stories), serialized novels, poems, book reviews, craft instructions, and recipes, as well as features on Scout activities nationally and around the world. The magazine showcased the work of some of the leading writers of the day. A majority of the writing it printed was by women. The editor made sure to profile its highly regarded authors and artists, putting forward role models in the hope of stimulating interest in literary pursuits among its readership. Besides creating opportunities and inspiration for Jane to write, Girl Scouts helped feed her insatiable appetite for reading and motivated her to submit her own stories and poems for publication.[24]

Although its authors and illustrators were adults, *The American Girl* encouraged its audience to participate in the magazine. Referring to her readers as "assistant editors," editor Helen Ferris, herself a published author of books for young readers, ran an annual September "contest" she called "What I-Wish-in-My-Magazine," requesting that girls write to her about what they would like in the coming year's issues. She posted the results of the 1926 "ballots" in the December issue under the banner "These Stories and Features You Asked for Will Come in 1927." In addition, a sporadically appearing page called "The Beholder"—its title derived from the concept of "the eye of the beholder" —printed poetry, letters, and illustrations submitted by girls. Winners received books as prizes. The magazine also held occasional contests for Christmas cards, bookplates, photographs, essays, and poetry. Always the much-coveted prizes consisted of a book for the individual winner or, sometimes, for the girl's troop.[25]

Enacting literature formed an important part of the scouting program, too. In December 1926, the Girl Scouts in the Scranton Council held their annual winter citywide rally at the Central High School auditorium, where a group of girls performed a Christmas play in two acts called *A Pot of Red Geraniums*, written recently by Oleda Schrottky. Miss Schrottky, the Girl Scouts' national director of plays and pageants, who had visited the Scranton Council several times before, was in the audience and spoke at the performance. Betty was one of the actors in the play. Jane was there to see her sister and, at the same time, the dramatist. Miss Schrottky was well known not only as a playwright but also as an actor with the Provincetown Players and a speech instructor at Mount Holyoke College.[26]

Jane, whose "Mouse" poem was published around this time in the Presbyterian Church's children's newspaper, was on the lookout for places to publish her writing. In her short time as a Scout—at summer camp in 1926 and troop meetings the following fall—Jane's poetry had already caught the attention of Florence Yost, the Camp Archbald

Oleda Schrottky, playwright, actress, and Girl Scouts'
national director of plays, at Camp Archbald, 1921.
Courtesy of Mary Winslow, volunteer archivist with
Girl Scouts in the Heart of Pennsylvania.

director from 1922 to 1927 and the executive director of the Scranton
Council of Girl Scouts. During the camp reunion in the spring, Miss
Yost had someone read one of Jane's poems as part of the festivities.
By January 1927, Yost had written letters on Jane's behalf, first to
Miss Schrottky and then to Miss Ferris, with a few of Jane's poems
enclosed as submissions to *The American Girl*. "I read with a great deal
of interest the very nice poems which you wrote and which Miss Yost
sent me some little time ago," Oleda Schrottky replied to Jane on Jan-
uary 5. "I liked especially the ones about Halloween and the Harvest
Moon. I know Miss Ferris will be glad to read them too, although she
cannot publish everything which she likes." A couple of weeks later,
Jane opened a letter on national headquarters stationery from Miss
Ferris. "Miss Yost has just sent me some of the poetry which you have

written, and I want to tell you how much I like it," Jane read. "I only wish that I could use it all right away in The American Girl, but . . . it is not always possible for us to use all the splendid things that come to us, but you may be sure that I will use at least part of your poetry just as soon as we possibly can." Although no part of these poems ever appeared in the magazine, Jane had garnered an encouraging rejection letter from a highly respected editor. Beginning in 1929 and for the next three decades, Helen Ferris used her talent and high standards as the editor in chief of the Junior Literary Guild. She worked closely with Eleanor Roosevelt, a member of the Guild's editorial board, and with her coauthored *Partners: The United Nations and Youth.*[27]

Much as Jane relished Girl Scout meetings and gatherings throughout the school year, "the days [at Camp Archbald] seemed to pass on wings," Jane wrote in 1928. These idyllic days inspired Jane to compose poems about the camp's rituals, its natural beauty, and invented lore. In her poem "Around the Campfire," she described with skill beyond her years "all sounds heard" by "a band of Girls Scouts" sitting "In the dusky moonlight, / By the flickering fire, / Listening to the whispering leaves, / That never seem to tire. . . ." Another poem, titled "At Camp," bouncily chronicled a tent mate's cot collapsing during a rainstorm and the laughter and commotion that ensued, along with the forfeiture of swimming privileges the next day. The young poet, true to her nature, seemed to feel "the consequences we had to take," as she put it, were well worth the hilarity. Fairies and elves crept into Jane's nature poems "Indian Pipe" and "Our Secret Place," as she let her imagination run free. A half dozen of Jane's camp poems—along with "Halloween," which Helen Ferris complimented—live on at the Library of Congress in *Verses*, by Sabilla Bodine. To preserve her daughter's childhood writing, Bess Butzner copyrighted the collection under Jane's chosen pen name, borrowed from one of Bess's ancestors high up on the family's genealogical tree.[28]

Girl Scouts strove to offer young women a sense of adventure. In no setting was this more possible than at a summer camp, where they

Jane (right) in creek, with fellow Scouts at Camp
Archbald, c. 1927. Estate of Jane Jacobs.

lived together in the splendor of the great outdoors. While at camp,
they studied nature in what Sir Robert Baden-Powell called "the
proper way, because here you are face to face with nature at all hours
of the day and night." In 1920, the Scranton Council camp committee purchased land for a camp in the rolling countryside along Lake
Ely, near the tiny town of Brooklyn, thirty-five miles north of Scranton. They named the camp after the committee's chairperson, Mrs.
Thomas F. Archbald—wife of a Presbyterian, Yale-educated professor
of missions—and hosted the first campers the next year. Campers
could board the streetcar in the Electric City, which dropped them
a mile from camp. With bedrolls in hand, the girls either walked the
remaining distance or hopped into the camp truck for a bumpy ride.[29]
    When they arrived, the girls had the camp's 235 acres to explore
and to sharpen their observational skills on the natural world. Part of

observation, as the Girl Scout organization instructed, was keeping a record of what one saw. In the mid-1920s, they implemented a program of creating special "nature notebooks." In December 1927, Jane won the annual first prize from Scranton's Girl Scouts Council for her nature notebook and received an inscribed volume of National Geographics's *The Book of Wild Flowers*. The following April, Jane began the next year's nature notebook, meticulously describing in her crow-quill handwriting what she saw and on what dates. She observed nature in her backyard, her neighborhood, and up the hill on the grounds of the Home for the Friendless. Using colorful images from magazines and her own artwork, Jane illustrated her text. She infused her lists of flora and fauna with such notations as her portrayal of a "queer" bird, "almost a golden brown on top and . . . gray underneath . . . about as long as an English Sparrow, but much fatter, and . . . speckeled [*sic*] on his throat." Seeing two of these birds six days later, she added, "They seem to be ground birds because they hop around on the ground all the time, and we never see them on trees. . . . The squirrels never seem to fight the birds, but have a lot of fun hopping over them. One [squirrel] was especially funny and tried to turn somersaults in the air." Not only did backyard dramas emerge in her notebook but Jane, at times, burst into verse. Under a bird image cut from a magazine, she penned, "Cedar Waxwing has a little red crest/ with gaudy feathers, and lighter brest [*sic*]."[30]

Jane's first journalistic article appeared in a city newspaper soon thereafter, when she was but twelve years old. After her third summer at camp and at least two nature notebooks, Jane may well have been working on her Journalist Badge. She composed a substantial and striking piece that she submitted to the newspapers. Both city dailies and the Sunday paper habitually covered the goings-on at the Scout camps during July and August. *The Scranton Times* published Jane's account of her summer experience under the headline "Scout Writes Interestingly About Life at Camp Archbald." Conjuring up the site in prose, Jane waxed poetic: "Some of it is woodland; soft evergreen woods, fragrant with the smell of hemlock and yew, while

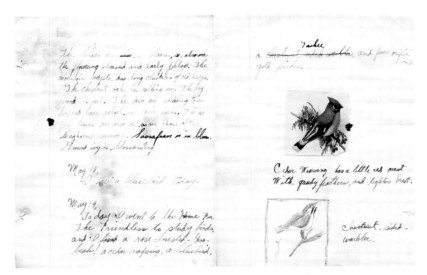

Front and back of page from Jane's nature notebook, 1928.
Estate of Jane Jacobs.

tiny streams sparkle and dance beneath the branches. The remainder consists of beautiful green fields dotted with yarrow, buttercups, daisies, and dozens of other flowers. In the tall grass are fascinating grasshoppers." Jane developed a passion for nature, just as she had for the city. She—and her sister, Betty, too—throughout their lives retained Girl Scouts guidebooks identifying plants and wildlife. Jane was fascinated by the interrelationship of the birds, insects, grass, sun, water, and other parts of the ecosystem coming together, as in her poem depicting "Our Secret Place . . . By the lake, at the mouth of a stream." In her adult writings, Jane employed what she had observed and learned from the natural world to understand and explain the city. After a "treasure hunt that began with the streets . . . I realized I was engaged in studying the ecology of cities," Jane wrote in her 1992 introduction to the Modern Library edition of *Death and Life*.[31]

In her article about camp life, Jane also "interestingly" described the discrete living units for different age groups of campers and each unit's connection with a literary classic the girls loved. The interweaving of themes from literature into the Camp Archbald experience captured the girls' imaginations and lent a sense of adventure to camp life. "The camp is divided into four encampments beginning with the Neverland and its jolly followers of Peter Pan," Jane wrote. "Then comes Hillcrest, a gypsy camp with the true scout spirit of the open. Up on the hill is Greenwood, where live the merry men of Robin Hood, while at some little distance from the main camp live the pioneers, the true disciples of the hemlock sprig, which is their emblem." During the day, there were "classes in nature lore, life-saving, mapping, judging, signaling, and woodcraft. . . . But our classes and kamp kapers took only a small part of the time, for there was swimming, rest hour, free time, hobbies and campfire . . . one of the nicest things we have at camp. . . . It was lovely to sit in the soft moonlight around a flickering campfire and look at the sky and lake so mysteriously alike and yet so unlike, and to hear taps floating skyward."[32]

In many respects, Camp Archbald focused on Lake Ely, which Jane characterized as "a delightful lake, big or small enough to suit anyone." On or within sight of the waterfront were the director's bungalow and "trading post," and buildings where all campers gathered—the dining hall and the stone and glass Schoonover Hall for performances, singing, games for all units, and rainy-day campfires in the huge fireplace. Swimming, canoeing, and lifesaving lessons were a popular part of camp. In 1925, the camp replaced the old dock and added a lifeguard tower and two diving boards. They hired Mary Louise Zimmerman, the champion high diver of the west coast of England, to take charge of aquatic events. Assured and fearless, Jane quickly became an astonishing diver and, even as an adult in Greenwich Village, would turn many a head in anticipation when she approached the end of the high diving board. Both Betty and Jane swam competitively at camp, in high school, and at citywide meets. Betty became a "swimming celebrity," as *The Scranton Republican* identified her, and won state and regional championships.[33]

Camp began on the last Monday in June and ran for eight weeks. Girls could sign up for a single week at the beginning or end of the summer term and for any or all of the three two-week sessions in

Republican Cameraman Visits Lake Ely

Photo by Prestwood

The Republican cameraman paid a visit Saturday to Lake Ely where Camp Archbald for Girl Scouts is located. The upper left shows a group of scouts at the diving board while at the upper right A. O. Tannebaum, Red Cross supervisor, is shown with a group that he is instructing in life saving. Seated left to right are: Marion Strunk, Jane Ferber, Janet Gleason, Sylvia Tannebaum, Peggy Oliver, Christine Purt; standing left to right, Janet Boyle, Betty Clark,

Cornelia Shafer, Helen Brundza, Mary Mackin, Camille Williams, swim master; Margaret Kerhli, swim staff; Mr. Tannenbaum; Martha Allen, swim staff; Priscilla Dean, swim staff; Betty Williams, Mary Oellgaard, Marion Brooks, Gertrude Mattes.

In the center left is shown a group of counsellors, left to right seated, Martha Allen, Lois Stetter, Josephine McClurg, Roberta Smith, Bonnie Christman, Winifred Kingsley, Margaret Christy, Kathryn Weist, second

row, Margaret Moffat, Margaret Atherton, Christine Cronwell, Katharine Mullen, Mrs. Esther Greener, Camille Williams, Rachel Jenkins, R. N., Sarah Engle; standing, Lettie M. Cole, Saralon Jordan, Margaret Kehril, Mary R. Mackin, P. Newcomb, dean; Mary Boland, Eleanor McCleary, Gladys Jackson, Grace Monie, Christine Purt; at the center right is shown one of a unit of four new buildings being erected and at the bottom are the campers all ready for their afternoon dip.

Camp Archbald and Lake Ely with swimmers, *Scranton Republican,*
July 27, 1931. Courtesy of Mary Winslow, volunteer archivist
with Girl Scouts in the Heart of Pennsylvania.

between. Archbald accommodated up to 160 campers and was often filled to capacity. Visitors were allowed only on Sundays from 3:00 to 5:00 P.M. Gates were closed at all other times. The new girls arrived on Mondays. Marie recalled that Jane was crazy about camp, and she marveled at the memory of "Jane going every year for the whole summer" without getting homesick. "It might have been because Betty was a counselor there, or maybe it was just Jane's personality," Marie mused. Marie suffered terribly from homesickness and, consequently, went home some weekends. Betty remained on the camp staff through 1932. Jane continued going to the camp well into high school, while Marie "dropped out" sooner.[34]

Remarkably tolerant in a time of anti-immigration sentiment and the rise of the Ku Klux Klan, Girl Scout "policy," as spelled out in the handbook, declared that "[the Girl Scout organization] is not only non-sectarian, but is open to all creeds" and should "[adjust] itself everywhere and always to local circumstances, and the habits and preferences of different groups." From its inception, Girl Scouts aimed to encompass girls from all walks of life. In 1912, Juliette Gordon Low began courting Catholic girls for her movement and strove to obtain approval of her organization from Baltimore's and New York's cardinals. In the early 1920s, Girl Scout troops began to form in Catholic churches, and churchwomen there signed up as leaders in the program. In 1917, the first troop for girls with disabilities began in New York City, and within a few years, troops of African American, Native American, and Mexican American girls were launched.[35]

Following its founder's tenets, the Scranton Girl Scout organization welcomed and sought diversity of religions, ethnic groups, and socioeconomic classes among its membership and within individual troops. Joining Jane and Marie in Troop 4 from the Washington School were Anne Safford and Thalia Barba, Vita's older sister by two years. These schoolmates, along with Jean Patterson and Gladys Baumann from Scranton's public Robert Morris School, got to know Gertrude Mattes, whose parents sent her to the private Country Day School. Longtime troop mates and all close in age, these Girl Scouts came from families of varying means and circumstances. Anne Safford's widowed mother worked to support her family; Jean Patterson's father sold insurance and provided the family with a modest home; Gertrude Mattes's father, a prominent lawyer, had bought a fine abode in a desirable section of Green Ridge. Mirroring the religious and ethnic clustering of local adult clubs, Scranton had a couple of Catholic troops, several Jewish troops, an African American troop, and a majority of troops in a variety of Protestant churches. Girl Scout rallies and events—such as holiday celebrations or Glee Club rehearsals—that took place at headquarters drew girls from all these troops, plus more from neighboring towns.[36]

In the 1920s and 1930s, Camp Archbald pulled Girl Scouts from the entire northeastern Pennsylvania region, mixing Scranton and its boroughs' troops with girls from Montrose, Honesdale, and other nearby small cities and towns. Occasionally, Scouts from afar spent some time at the camp, such as Jane's well-liked cousin Nancy Butzner, from Virginia, whose daughter reported she "absolutely loved the camp." Jane made a new friend in another girl from Virginia, who must have been a kindred spirit. "If there was ever a peach, a little devil, a good sport, a lovable kid, a great kid, or anything else imaginable, bound in one, Jane Butzner is it. Keep it up, kid," Charlotte Campbull [*sic*] from Clay Hill Stock Farm, Kernstown, wrote in Jane's autograph book. Archbald opened its gates to non-Scouts, too, although usually only a dozen or two attended each year. The region's Boy Scout Camp, Goose Pond, in Lake Ariel, Pennsylvania, where Jane's brothers spent their summers, must have attracted a significant number of religiously observant Jews, because it was known for having "one of only a handful of scout camp Kosher kitchens."[37]

The Scranton Girl Scouts Council's correspondence to national headquarters in the late 1920s and early 1930s expressed the local council's commitment to increasing the diversity of the city's troops. To plan a recruitment strategy, the council surveyed and tallied the city's ethnic and religious composition, summarizing that "[t]he community is largely composed of foreign-born men and women whose livelihood is dependent upon the coal mining industry." In 1918, a third of the city's population was of the Roman Catholic faith, the council noted, but by 1939—with additional immigrants from Italy, Poland, Lithuania, and Ireland—it had reached 70 percent. In 1932, the council's report to headquarters listed "religious affiliations of Girl Scouts" as 1,052 Protestants, 200 Catholics, and 125 Jews. A few years later, they identified the "predominating national and racial groups in the community: American-Scotch; Welsh; Polish; Italian; German-Irish; Lithuanian; Russian; Greek; Hebrew; Negro; Ukrainian," and the "distribution of Girl Scouts according to economic groups: high 10%; middle 75%; low 15%." Among its written "objectives," the council desired "new troops in all sections of the city, especially in the poorer sections." For years, the council desperately tried to attract more Catholics and "[felt the] need [on the council] of an active and representative Catholic member" to help accomplish this. But the Catholic Church, under the sway of the bishop, resisted and promoted the Junior Catholic Daughters of America rather than the Girl Scouts. The municipal school board, made up primarily of Catholics, was uncooperative and forbade using schools as Scout meeting places. In 1939, Bishop Hafey succeeded in organizing four Junior Catholic Daughters of America troops, "two Green [Irish] and two Polish," a division not condoned by the Girl Scouts. The Scranton Girl Scouts Council concluded their report to national headquarters optimistically: "But there are many Catholic children attending troops in Protestant churches." In 1927, the council didn't think twice about inviting Zenobia Dorsey, the leader of the Progressive Recreation Association's mainly African American troop, to the first training course given in Scranton to sixteen Girl Scout committee women.[38]

There were distinct limits, however, to Scrantonians' open-mindedness. Along with churches, schools, the YMCA, and the YMHA, the Girl Scouts regularly produced a form of entertainment people commonly called "minstrels." These ubiquitous and hugely popular vaudevillelike variety shows put on by numerous organizations attracted large crowds. They were also performed in movie theaters before the featured movies started. Inherently racist because of their origins and content, minstrel shows, by Jane's years in Scouts, had morphed into a series of skits, comedy, songs and other music, emceed by an "interlocutor." The minstrel shows used stock characters and a format that derived from the original minstrel shows of the early nineteenth century. When the Boy Scouts selected Jane's brother John for the coveted interlocutor role in their annual minstrel, an article about this coup appeared in newspaper, along with John's photograph. One of Jane's contemporaries recalled that "minstrels were a big thing in the 1920s and '30s. There were different acts. It didn't occur to me at the time that they were racist, just good entertainment. Blackface was just part of the routine, especially for the main performers, not necessarily for everybody." Perhaps having gained some understanding of racism since then, many people who remembered the shows today refrained from commenting on them. Records of the shows seemed to have been expunged from institutions that had held them.[39]

Camp Archbald maintained and increased its diverse group of campers by ensuring a variety of ways for girls to earn money toward camp tuition or to receive full scholarships. When Jane was a camper, camp cost seven dollars per week. The city's Community Chest provided most of the revenue for the Girl Scouts' operating expenses, but it did not include funds for the camp. Organized in 1921, when other Community Chests were forming around the country, the Community Chest of Scranton and Dunmore was a federation of thirty-four member organizations, whose welfare activities and social work the Community Welfare Association coordinated. The Girl Scouts organization was a member from the start—under the Chest's category of "character-building organizations." With the Chest's permission, the camp, too, solicited funds.[40]

The national staff of the Girl Scouts visited from New York and evaluated the camp yearly and, in 1931, specifically commended the Camp Archbald committee for the considerable financial aid and

Cover of *The American Girl* magazine, Nov. 1926.
Used with permission of the Girl Scouts
of the United States of America.

the number of scholarships they awarded. The Girl Scouts also allowed a girl to raise money to send herself to camp by selling *American Girl* magazine subscriptions, and many Scouts, past and present, endeavored to raise scholarship funds for others. Former members of Troop 4 of the Green Ridge Presbyterian Church gave a party to make money for camp scholarships. Current Scouts participated in baking and holding cookie sales for this purpose—before commercially baked Girl Scout cookies began selling nationally in 1937. In December 1933, Scranton's troops competed with one another to contribute the most financial aid for camp. "During the past week, Girl Scouts of the city sold doughnuts, the proceeds to go toward a fund to send girls to Camp Archbald next summer," *The Scranton Republican* reported. They expected to exceed their goal of selling one thousand groups of a dozen. Troop 10, at Temple Israel, led with 192 dozen. Troop scribes could win one-week scholarships to Camp Archbald for "their interesting, well-written and illustrated reports." In 1932, among the recipients were Duella Mitchell of Troop 34 at the African American community's Progressive Recreation Association, Marjorie Hetherson of Troop 41 at the Petersburg Silk Mill, and—for best patrol leader's notebook—Betty Tuck of Troop 10 at Temple Israel. Reflecting the success and popularity of Camp Archbald in these years, well over four hundred girls—and sometimes over five hundred—were able to attend the camp during the summer. "Scranton had a high percentage of Scouts in camp for one week or more," the council told headquarters in the early 1930s. "Girls have been coming back yearly for long periods."[41]

In return, Girl Scouts pitched in to raise money for Scranton's Community Chest. During the Chest's annual fund-raising campaigns, Girl Scouts threw themselves into distributing posters and leaflets, writing letters, speaking to contributors, and participating in special programs and activities on behalf of the Chest. A "number of scouts and leaders" ushered at the Community Chest fund-raising rally, which took place at the huge Masonic Temple. "Mrs. Greener, local director," the council proudly wrote, "indicates Girl Scouts have been asked to cooperate with thirty-two other organizations under the Scranton Community Chest in putting on a skit for Chest publicity this fall. . . ." In 1932, a group of Girl Scouts sold their own home-baked cookies at the Scranton Spring Brook Water Company and the Scranton Electric Company, garnering the hefty sum of $263 to donate to the Chest.[42]

Because the Community Chest was intricately connected to associations, businesses, and activities in the city, working for and with the Chest exposed Girl Scouts to many aspects of city life and plugged them into the community at large. In the process, girls assisted with everything from charitable organizations to volunteering to aid individuals. They saw firsthand how the city functioned, and the relationship of welfare agencies and organizational life. The city provided abundant opportunities for community service, which was part of the Girl Scout belief in helping others on a daily basis, and Girl Scouts responded. Notices in the *Republican* announced that "Girl Scouts wishing to do Community Service Work may report after school either to the Association of the Blind, to dictate lists, or to the Tuberculosis society in the Medical Arts Building and help with Christmas seals," or they could choose from "a list of shut-ins to whom scouts could read." Around the holidays, troops made and filled candy boxes for patients at the West Mountain sanitarium or "planned special entertainments"

Girl Scout award recipients at Nay Aug Park: Betty Butzner (third from left in top row); Jane Butzner (middle in first row), *Scranton Sun*, May 12, 1930. Courtesy of Mary Winslow, volunteer archivist with Girl Scouts in the Heart of Pennsylvania.

Counselors fetching water from the well at
Camp Archbald, late 1920s. Estate of Jane Jacobs.

at hospitals. Troops 5 and 45 from the Green Ridge Presbyterian
Church "ha[d] been sewing for the Visiting Nurse association."[43]

Deeply embedded in the Girl Scout movement, from its very beginning at the crescendo of the struggle for women's suffrage, lay the
core value of empowering girls through adventure, learning by doing,
and character building. *Scouting for Girls* made clear the movement's
aim to help girls and young women learn "in the happiest way how
to combine patriotism, outdoor activities, skill in every branch of domestic science, and high standards of community service." Holding up

exemplary women from American history, the handbook praised Sacajawea [*sic*], of Lewis and Clark expedition fame, Louisa May Alcott, and "[o]ur pioneer grandmothers . . . [who] knew an immense number of practical things. . . . And for pluck and resourcefulness in a tight place it is to be doubted that we could equal them."[44]

"The skills we learned at Girl Scouts made us feel more confident and instilled a sense of independence," Barbara Gelder Kelley, a devoted Girl Scout well into high school, recalled. "If things went wrong, we had survival skills and could take care of ourselves. In senior unit, we really learned to build a fire, since we cooked breakfast and supper out—but not the largest midday meal—every day." The girls gathered and split wood a day ahead in preparation. Since they slept in tents on platforms and cooked outdoors in a fireplace protected by an improvised canvas roof, "a cookhouse," they learned camp craft skills, such as lashing together saplings to make shelves and tables. "We had to use dangerous tools like an ax, hatchet, and knives. Now there are so many liability laws that prevent the teaching of such things." In Jane's and Betty's years, the campers had to haul water in pails from the pump, before an artesian well was dug in 1934. They had to send their laundry home via U.S. Mail in reusable cardboard boxes encased with canvas and girded with straps. Until 1941, ice harvested from the lake kept the camp's food from spoiling.[45]

Girl Scouts played an enormous role in Jane's own education and her engagement with the city. In scouting, Jane found the freedom to indulge her curiosity, imagination, and creativity, together with an opportunity to observe nature, people, and urban life. She made a point of crediting Scouts with playing a role in disseminating the "liberating ideology for women" in the 1920s. When asked in 2002 whether she thought it unusual in those days for a young woman to grow up with the idea that she could do anything, Jane replied emphatically, "No, it was not—it was quite common," but she added that this feeling of women's empowerment had ebbed and flowed from decade to decade. After the success of the women's suffrage movement, "we grew up in this kind of island of hope for women." Later, in the 1950s, "[t]here was a real going backwards; it was reflected in the Girl Scouts and in the magazines for girls, as well as in the atmosphere in general." In her day, "there was the idea that women were equal to men and they could do anything. In the Girl Scout troop that my sister and I belonged to, we had all sorts of merit badges, not just child care and hostess and all those things, but merit badges in astronomy and tree finding and making things of various kinds."[46]

As an adult who received worldwide renown for her books, Jane was offered a great many prestigious honors, but she never accepted any award solely for women. She insisted that her work be judged with that of men. She did not feel that being a woman distinguished her work in any way. It was her ideas that mattered.

George Washington School #1 (inside the School Administration
Building), built 1910, photo early 1950s. Author's collection.

CHAPTER 7

• • •

Eighth Grade at the
"Model School of the City"

AT THE BEGINNING OF February 1928, a few days after completing seventh grade at the George Washington School #3 in Dunmore, Jane Butzner took the streetcar into central city to start her final year of grammar school at Scranton's George Washington School #1. Located inside the School Administration Building, a fanciful crenellated Gothic Revival edifice, designed by local architect Lewis Hancock, Jr., the school went from kindergarten through eighth grade. This block was well-trodden territory for Jane—just south of the Girl Scouts' headquarters and across the avenue from one of her favorite destinations, the central Albright Library. Jane's eighth-grade year would further open her eyes to Scranton's immigrant life and the way schools helped assimilate children of varied socioeconomic backgrounds—some of whom lived in poverty or alongside vice—into the community and, eventually, the nation.

Students soon to enter eighth grade at Dunmore's Washington School and at other schools in Scranton's nearby boroughs and townships planned ahead for high school. Those who intended to matriculate at the rigorous and acclaimed Central High School in Scranton could do so by switching to one of two schools at this juncture. Some students went to North Scranton Junior High—with room for up to nineteen hundred students in grades seven through nine—newly opened with much fanfare in 1924. From North Scranton Junior

High, they could enter Central as sophomores. Others eager to begin Central High School as soon as possible were assigned to Washington #1 for eighth grade. Upon completing the grade and graduating from the grammar school in Scranton proper, they could enroll in Central as freshmen. Scranton's Central High was tuition-free only for Scranton residents, but in the opinion of Florence Gillespie Brown, who grew up in Dunmore's Patch with a father who worked for the Railway Mail Service, "It wasn't *that* expensive." For a variety of reasons, not the least of which was the free tuition, the majority of Jane's Dunmore schoolmates chose Dunmore High, like Marie Van Bergen, and Vita and Thalia Barba. Jane's sister, Betty, had gone there, too.[1]

Upon finishing Washington #3, Betty Butzner had headed off to Dunmore's only high school and would soon graduate. The "Central School," as it was also known, occupied a modest two-story stone edifice, rather plain except for its peaked central pavilion. By the time Marie attended, overcrowding had forced two pupils to squeeze into each flip-up seat, and lack of heat in the cold months required students to keep their coats on all day. Most disturbing to Dr. and Mrs. Butzner was their feeling that Betty, although a bright student who, among other achievements, gave a presentation at her school assembly on "Marshall and the Constitution" and was a "local aquatic star" athlete, had received a subpar education there. With only about fifty-five students in Betty's graduating class in June 1928, a smaller faculty, and lack of resources, Dunmore High could not come close to the extraordinarily rigorous academic standards and extracurricular opportunities of Scranton's Central High School.[2]

Despite praising the "marvelous teachers" at Dunmore High, Marie complained about the "split shifts, necessitated by too little room for the growing number of students." Florence Gillespie Brown, also at Dunmore High in the early 1930s, spoke of being assigned to the morning shift, from 8:00 A.M. until noon. "We had five classes, no gym or any extras," she said, sighing. The school was so cold in winter that "you took your exams with your gloves on." Some classes were held in the annex, in "the runway off the auditorium," and in the auditorium itself or on the balcony. "You didn't really know half the class because you never saw them." Florence had one friend "whose great-est claim to fame was that she'd never used the high school bathroom" because it was "so terrible." The teachers, she agreed, were excellent, and students managed to go on to "good colleges." But Florence also spoke of an anomaly she recalled: "It was unusual at Dunmore High to have Protestants. For class-president elections, a Protestant student and Catholic student often ran against each other." This reflected the general makeup of the Republican and Democratic parties, respec-tively. Of Scottish and German descent, Florence belonged to Pres-byterian churches throughout her life but delighted in having grown up with many Catholic friends in a heavily Catholic neighborhood. She appreciated Scranton's multicultural character.[3]

Because Dunmore had rejected annexation with Scranton in 1866 and had chosen to remain an independent borough—largely due to the influence of the dominant Pennsylvania Coal Company— Dunmore had to pay for its own schools and services, with no help from more prosperous Scranton. Soon after his election in 1922, Scranton's mayor, John F. Durkan, presented the City Council with a plan to add Dunmore to the city. Durkan was the only Democrat

Dunmore High School in the 1920s, built in 1908,
destroyed by fire in 2013. Courtesy of Dunmore Historical Society.

to have been elected mayor since Francis Allen Beamish in 1884. For the first time since 1866, Durkan proposed expanding the city's boundaries by annexing the borough, which happened to have a Democratic majority, due to its largely Catholic and working-class population. The Scranton city councilors heatedly and at length debated issues of Dunmore's "floating debt" and its need to improve its schools and to hard-top sixty-seven unpaved roads. Many citizens from both municipalities expressed strong views on the issue. "Nearly 250 men and women were present in the council chambers at city hall for the meeting," *The Scranton Republican* reported. Although Durkan gained the support of prominent organizations and individuals, such as the Chamber of Commerce, the Century Club (to which Bess Butzner belonged), City Solicitor P.V. Mattes (the father of Jane's Girl Scout friend Gertrude), and the auditor of the Dunmore school district, the all-Republican Scranton City Council unanimously voted down his idea. They felt annexation would be too costly to Scranton. Giving Dunmore "the same municipal and school service" as Scranton "would necessitate a tax boost," but no one mentioned the elephant in the room—the large number of Democratic voters that adding Dunmore would bring. Surprisingly, petitions signed for and against the proposal showed that the majority of Dunmoreans were not in favor of annexation. As Dunmore native Florence Gillespie Brown summed it up with local pride, "Scranton tried to adopt Dunmore, but Dunmore resisted." Following Mayor Durkan's thwarted effort, Dunmore's schools struggled with financial hardship. When the Depression hit, "[it] was bad, so bad that Dunmore High School teachers didn't get paid in cash, but received IOUs," Kay Schoen Butzner recalled. "My uncle William Davis was happy to teach at Scranton Central High, where this didn't happen."[4]

Jane's eighth-grade, 8A, class at Scranton's Washington School was comprised of a robust mixture of children from the neighborhood surrounding the school, plus a smaller component of "tuition students"—as June Carter (later Davies), one herself, called them—from the city's neighboring communities. Of the twenty-five students in the class, only Jane and one other girl, Carol MacAskie, from Elmhurst, a rural township east of South Scranton, were newcomers preparing to go on to Central High. "That year, Algebra and Latin had been added to the eighth grade curriculum," wrote June, who was in the preceding and overlapping 8B class that graduated in June 1928. "We were supposed to have a year of both these subjects before we entered a city high school." Carol's father had studied medicine at the University of Pennsylvania and was employed at the International Correspondence Schools, where he climbed his way up from department head to assistant director. To attend eighth grade, Carol commuted alongside her father, who went to work in central city via the DL&W train, which took passengers into Scranton once each weekday morning and back again by 6:00 P.M.[5]

But most of the Washington #1 8A class walked no more than ten minutes to get to their neighborhood school. The school stood on a block bounded on its northern edge by Vine Street, a long east-west through street, south of which lay the city's densest commercial district, where few families lived. The children of those who did dwell there also attended the Washington School, such as Miriam Parker, who was a year and a half behind Jane. Miriam's family owned Parker's Deli, the only Jewish Deli in Scranton at the time, and she, her parents, and her two older brothers lived above the family business and across the alley from Feigenbaum's poultry store. All Jane's and Carol's classmates resided with their families in the area from Vine Street north, in comparatively inexpensive housing close to or mixed in with industry. Some of these families moved to the alleys—which Amsden had placed in his original 1850 Scranton city plan to accommodate services and deliveries, not living quarters. Relabeled in the city directories, beginning in 1894, as "courts" with proper names, they sprouted rudimentary housing for immigrants pouring into the city. Now the alleys were closely infilled with domiciles between outbuildings and homespun commercial ventures. Other families rented flats or tiny to modest single- and multifamily dwellings on the streets. For the most part, these eighth graders in the same class as Jane—students who had been advanced by a semester or started school in the middle of the year—had grown up in humble circumstances, with hardworking parents in blue-collar jobs. Many of these students had foreign-born parents or were immigrants themselves, with English as their second language, such as Werner Rosteck.[6]

Werner Rosteck graduated at the end of the school year, in January 1929, as not only secretary but also valedictorian of the 8A class. He had left the old commercial and industrial city of Bremen, in northern Germany, in April 1925, a few days before his twelfth birthday. With his parents and two younger sisters, he landed in the port of New York en route to Scranton, where his great-uncle lived. Within two years, his father, Wilhelm, identified as a "workman" on the ship's passenger list, had Anglicized his name to William and obtained a job as a "creamery man," making butter at the Brown-Wright Dairy Company near Green Ridge Corners. As was customary with immigrant children who did not speak English, the school system placed Werner in a lower grade than he would have been in back in Germany so that he could learn the language. Starting eighth grade at age eleven, Jane was the youngest in the class, while Werner, at fourteen, was the oldest. From his family's rented flat five blocks from the Washington School, he could not only hear but also see the Erie Railroad freight cars crossing Myrtle Street a few doors down from the 900 block of North Washington Avenue. Werner's flat was back-to-back with the side-by-side two-family home of his German-speaking classmate, Carl Ellerman. Carl's parents and two older sisters had come from Germany in 1912, two years before he was born. In 1928, his recently widowed mother supported the household as a cleaner at the Scranton Life Building. Another classmate, Louis Louwerse, and his three brothers and widowed mother occupied the other half of the two-family dwelling. Louis's parents had both emigrated from Belgium but were of Dutch origin and spoke Dutch.[7]

Besides Werner, the other foreign-born student in the 8A class was Sam Zlatin, who had emigrated from Russia with his parents in 1918, when he was about four years old. After the birth of his two younger siblings, the family moved into close quarters at 613 Kressler Court, the alley between Adams and Jefferson Avenues, where the census taker noted their—and several of their neighbors'—"mother tongue" as "Jewish." By the time Sam was in eighth grade, his father, Joe Zlatin, drove a truck for a living and, a couple of years later, had his own scrap-metal business, while his wife, Ida, was employed as an "operator." For extra income, the Zlatins took in three boarders, all recent Russian Jewish immigrants.

A number of African American families had also settled on this block. Jane's classmate Cidonia Mitchell, an African American, with her Pennsylvania-born father—who was employed as a waiter at a hotel—and her New York–born mother inhabited a comparable building, at 624 Lee Court, in a parallel alley on the next block east. The Mitchells lived in snug quarters in a two-and-a-half-story double flat, many of which were crammed in a row. Outside of school, Cidonia played piano, performing at recitals at the Scranton Conservatory of Music, and acted in plays at the Bethel AME Church, the YWCA, and the Progressive Recreation Association. She and her younger sister, Duella, attended the Girl Scouts' Camp Archbald. Their next-door neighbors were from Poland and spoke "Hebrew."[8]

Eleven members of the 8A class residing in the Washington School #1 neighborhood (almost half of the twenty-five) were native-born children of two immigrant parents. The majority (seven) of these students had parents who had come recently, as adults, from Eastern Europe—Austria-Hungary, Poland, Lithuania, and Russia—and were of Jewish background. Saul Davis—despite his Welsh-sounding surname, probably changed at Ellis Island—was the son of David Davis, born in Poland, and Minnie, from Austria. The family rented an apartment, at 425 Adams Avenue, in a continuous line of two-family houses jammed shoulder-to-shoulder, a block east of school. Saul was active in the YMHA's Pals Club. Marion Cohen's parents, Sam and Breta, or Bertha, arrived in the United States as a married couple from Russia in 1904, the same year as Saul's, while Isadore Levinson's father and mother emigrated separately from Russia, landing in 1911 and 1913, respectively. All three classmates' fathers worked as tailors, a common occupation for men of their background. David Davis had succeeded in establishing his own tailor shop, while Sam Cohen worked as a tailor for the Crane Marks Company, which sold fine men's and women's clothing downtown on Lackawanna Avenue. Esther Schoenberg and Marie Weiss's Eastern European–born Jewish fathers made their livings as hucksters, and Frank Schwartz's father was a self-employed window cleaner. In all, one-third of the class was of Jewish background, and only one of these students had an American-born parent. Dark-haired and dark-eyed Murrel Levy was an active member of the YMHA and of Boy Scout Troop 65 at Temple Israel. His Russian-born father, Sam Levy, and Pennsylvania-born mother, Fannie, owned their house at 521 Pine Street. They also owned and ran the White Lily Lunch, a restaurant two blocks south of their house, serving downtown employees on Adams Avenue, near the Albright Library. Murrel would go on to work in the aircraft and aerospace industry and change his name to Mike Loring.[9]

Even before Scranton incorporated as a borough, its first wave of Jewish immigrants had arrived—as they did throughout the nation—from Germany to set up businesses. Kramer Brothers opened the initial incarnation of their long-lived store in 1849, and Lauer & Marks began their clothing shop two years later. Hollister noted in his 1885 history of the city that physician Isaac Cohen, a "Jewish Rabbi," had lived and practiced in Scranton for a year in 1857. Max and Simon Rice ran a "prosperous grocery store" beginning in the 1860s. Isaac E. "Ike" Oppenheim bought Jonas Long's department store and opened the Scranton Dry Goods Company in 1912, a department store second in size only to its competitor, the Gentile-owned Globe store. Born in the States in 1882 of German Jewish immigrant stock, he eventually settled in the city's fancy Hill Section and was known for his charitable deeds, kindness to employees, and efforts to find jobs for those in need.[10]

Jews who arrived from the 1880s through the 1920s, during the city's second Jewish influx, were more often from Eastern Europe and fleeing persecution and poverty. They took up residence in the crowded quarters—the small streets and alleys north of the Washington School—in central city, while some of the earlier, better-off German Jews had acquired properties not far away in the affluent Hill Section. Yet all Jews faced discrimination. In the 1920s, Scranton-raised Arnine Cumsky Weiss's grandfather bought a home on Jefferson Avenue, among mansions on the Hill. "One of the neighbors was so upset at living next to Jews that he offered [him] $5,000 over the purchase price if he would move elsewhere," Weiss wrote. "My grandfather was a businessman, so he took the offer and bought a bigger house." Through at least the 1930s, the International Correspondence Schools, banks, coal companies, and exclusive clubs refused to admit Jews.[11]

By 1930, Scranton experienced a downturn in the number of new immigrants. The census showed that a little less than one-fifth of the city's residents were "foreign-born." Many more residents had at least one parent born in another country. Florence Osterland, an 8A student from central city, who had only one American-born parent, was elected an officer of the downtown Elm Park Methodist Episcopal Church Sunday school. With her Swedish-born father, Edwin Osterland, a baker, and her mother, Augusta, of Swedish background, she lived in a three-family flat on Olive Street, with its long side facing Dix Court. Florence graduated as the class salutatorian and vice president.[12]

At the same time, less than two-fifths of Scrantonians came from families where both parents were born in the United States, and an even smaller proportion of Jane's classmates fell into this category. Only four children in the 8A class who resided in the Washington School #1 district had two native-born parents. But being of native-born stock did not necessarily coincide with economic prosperity. Classmate Harry Caryl, with two native-born parents, lived around the corner from school on Vine Street. His father worked as a "garage man," and the family took in four boarders to help make ends meet. The daughter of native Pennsylvanians, Kathryn Coyne was Harry's neighbor across the street. Her father, Thomas L. Coyne, of Irish parentage, was employed as a "bartender in a saloon," as recorded in the census just weeks before Prohibition took effect. Coyne became the proprietor of the Hotel Vine, on the corner of Wyoming Avenue, where Kathryn's mother also worked and where the whole family lived. Built in 1875 as the "large and commodious"

Home to one of Jane's classmates, Hotel Vine (formerly
Hotel Terrace) was a target of crackdowns during Prohibition.
Scan obtained from Scranton Public Library.

Hotel Terrace, one of the city's "leading hostelries," the Hotel Vine
was repeatedly raided during Prohibition and its doors padlocked
by federal agents. The feds saw it as a "drinking emporium," which,
they claimed, had become home to women from "disorderly houses"
and others connected with gambling operations. Although students
knew of these reports in the newspapers, the 8A class elected Kathryn
treasurer.[13]

Some of Jane's classmates endured especially difficult emotional
and economic situations. Anarita McNamara, another of Jane's 8A
classmates, was also of Irish descent but had native-born parents. Her
father had died when she was young, although her great-uncle, a lawyer, lived with the family in the 500 block of Adams and presumably
helped support his niece and two grandnieces. Like Harry, Kathryn,
and Anarita, Alice McGuire was the daughter of two native-born parents, but along with three other classmates, whose parents were not
both American-born, she resided at the far western edge of the school

district. This heavily industrial, hardscrabble section of the city was bounded by the Lackawanna River on one side and the Pinebrook Coal Breaker on the other. Between two sets of railroad tracks that served the adjacent industries, tiny workers' houses were wedged together on short streets running off Olive Street and had names such as Mineral, Mica, and Silex. Alice's father made a living dangerously as a molder in an iron foundry. The fathers of her classmates Peter Hawter and Anna Miller toiled nearby in the coal mines, while John Mychayliw's father, an Austrian-born immigrant who spoke Ukrainian, was a laborer for a railroad. Peter's father had arrived from Austria (a considerably larger territory at the time) and was of Polish background, and Anna's parents were Lithuanian by birth or parentage.

The only student in the 8A class residing in central city whose father worked a bona fide white-collar job was George T. Munchak. In the mid 1890s, young George's father, George Munchak, Sr., of Slovak extraction, had emigrated by himself as a penniless teenager from Nagy-Berezna in Austria-Hungary. By 1910, the enterprising George senior had married Tillie P. Kiever, born in Pennsylvania of Polish Slovak-speaking parents, and owned and ran a hotel in South Scranton. By 1920, he was vice president of the highly successful Bosak State Bank, founded by fellow Slovak Michael Bosak. Four years later, young George's parents engaged architect Theodore Preitz to build a three-story brick building on a vacant lot contiguous to an existing commercial building on the corner. One block south of the Erie Freight Depot, the new structure had two stores on the first floor and apartments above. Mr. and Mrs. Munchak took up residence there with their eight children. In addition to his prominence at the bank and as an insurance and real estate broker, the seemingly indefatigable George senior ran a hotel and opened a market in his new building. His son George and George's 8A classmate Murrel Levy took on the role of student speakers for the Community Chest campaign. Perceiving that young George's competence and leadership were similar to his father's, his class voted him class president in 1928. George also followed in his father's footsteps as an active participant in St. John's Greek Catholic Church.[14]

At the helm of the 8A class and the entire Washington School #1 in 1928 was the kind-faced, solidly built, forty-four-year-old Miss Stella Kinback. Standing as tall as the male teachers she oversaw, she not only had served as principal of the school for eight years already but also—along with the young Misses Mary Barrett and Dorothy Coyne—chose to instruct the motley eighth graders, an uncommon practice for a grammar-school principal. Miss Kinback's family on both sides came from German stock. Her paternal side was composed of skilled artisans of Protestant background, who were politically active but not particularly active in any church. Stella's father, Henry W. Kinback, born in 1850, had arrived in the United States at roughly age five, accompanied by his parents and baby brother from Darmstadt—a hotbed of revolutionary activity in 1848—in the central German principality of Hesse. In America, the Kinbacks joined their relative Julius F. Kinback, a refugee from nearby Suizheim, known for its liberalism and culture. In 1848, Julius had emigrated directly from there to flourishing Carbondale—fifteen miles up the valley from the fledgling Scranton—where he and Henry continued the family's trade as expert cabinetmakers.

The Kinbacks were likely among the "Forty-Eighters," those disillusioned or wanted citizens who joined the exodus following the failed revolutions throughout Europe that sought democratic governments and human-rights reforms. In Carbondale, Julius became a "foremost resident" and was elected alderman, serving in that position for twenty years. He died in 1891. By the late 1870s, Scranton had overtaken Carbondale in size and prosperity and had lured Henry W. Kinback, with some savings from cabinetmaking, and his recent-immigrant cousin George Kinback—who was exactly his age and had arrived in 1866—to try their hands in the hotel and restaurant business. Henry, known now as Harry, teamed up with J. J. Flanaghan as proprietors of the Globe Hotel on Wyoming Avenue, in central city, before he alone acquired the St. Cloud Hotel on the same block—an establishment with the "Finest Liquors, Ales and Cigars." George worked his way up at the venerable Wyoming House hotel and restaurant and sometimes roped his cousin into keeping the bar. In 1882, George held the position of county treasurer. The local Democratic district committee often met at what the newspapers dubbed "George Kinback's hotel." Joining other leading downtown businessmen, Harry became an avid Free and Accepted Mason in Union Lodge 291. All members of his lodge and its sister lodges were encouraged to attend Henry's untimely funeral in 1901 at his "late residence," when Stella was seventeen years old and had not yet finished Central High School.[15]

Upon the death of her father, Stella, an only child, and her mother, née Sadie Kann, a longtime Scrantonian of German immigrant parents, found themselves in serious financial straits. Sadie Kinback took on dressmaking work in her home, while Stella prepared for a career in teaching. After graduating from Central High in 1902, Stella, a "successful pupil," continued on to the city's Teachers' Training School for its three-year course of study. Meanwhile, appointed by the school board as part of a citywide program, she helped support her mother and herself by teaching foreign-born adults at night school, helping them learn English and "Americanizing" them "by grounding [them] in the fundamentals of good citizenship." The idealistic and empathetic daughter of first- and second-generation immigrants with liberal leanings, Stella threw herself into this work. Even as a working student, in 1905, she was "one of twenty-five young ladies to graduate" from the Training School. A year later, the school board assigned Stella Kinback a teaching position at the James Madison School #33, on Madison Avenue at the corner of Pine, coincidentally her grammar-school alma mater in 1898.[16]

In September 1911, when the new School Administration Building opened, *The Scranton Republican* declared it "a beautiful well appointed home [for the school district] for all time to come." In an effort to relieve "congestion in three wards of the school district," the school board made rooms in the building available for a central-city grammar school, which had yet to find a name. Stella Kinback was among the teachers—as was her cousin on her mother's side, Sadie Falkowsky— who were transferred or appointed to this new educational facility.

Furthermore, the board named Joseph Rafter principal of the school-children in the Administration Building and the twenty-seven-year-old Kinback assistant principal. In 1915, the school board organized Parents Day in the public schools so that adults could view schools and student work displays all over the city. The *Republican* remarked, using the school's gradually adopted name, "George Washington school, in the School Administration building, called the model school of the city, had over 1,000 visitors in the course of the day. Principal Robert Bruce Albert received parents and referred them to teachers, who escorted them about the building where the [fine and extensive] work of pupils was shown. . . . [The work] showed that teacher and pupils were on more than common grounds of understanding."[17]

The pupils at Scranton's "model school" couldn't help but be aware of the special aesthetics of the building that contributed to the harmonious feelings and important business that occurred inside. Teachers and students, along with school district officials and immigrants attending evening school, kept the building in use from early morning on into the night. The style of the smooth gray stone structure—with its Gothic arched windows and doorways, pinnacles at the corners, and an asymmetrical central pavilion with turret—recalled the architecture of Oxford University and the more recently constructed University of Chicago. The comparatively narrow facade belied the depth and capacity of the building. Inside, the inviting mosaic-tiled entranceway led to a wide winding staircase for children and an elevator for adults to access forty-four rooms, including an assembly room, a library, classrooms, offices, meeting rooms, and rooms for a "medical inspection" department and dental clinic for maintaining student health, something that schools saw as part of their responsibilities. The schoolchildren—with the exception of the kindergarteners in the basement—spent most of their time in the classrooms on the first two floors, sandwiched between the flurry of civic activity above and below. The third floor was reserved for the offices of the city's superintendent of public schools and all other school district officers, as well as Scranton's Teachers' Mutual Benefit Association, the school board assembly room, three committee rooms, and an office for the truant officers. The office of the super-intendent of repairs and the supply department were maintained in the basement.[18]

Stella Kinback worked diligently in the Administration Build-ing both day and night. When the school board expanded its adult-education night classes for immigrants to grammar-school sites, they chose the new building and again appointed Kinback as one of the teachers. Her 1922 class was composed of twenty students—mostly Eastern European Jewish immigrants and only one of them female—from the school's densely populated surrounding area. Passionate about her pupils, she attended what the *Republican* called the "very inspiring" citywide graduations, at Central High's auditorium, of students from the Americanization classes. In 1931, she lectured at the Scranton section of the National Council of Jewish Women at the YMHA on "What the Evening Schools Do for the Foreign Born Women." Some of Kinback's Americanization students had arrived in the States before the attitudes and laws regarding immigrants changed in the early 1920s. These immigrants had disembarked at Ellis Island in New York's harbor, where they were inspected for disease, interviewed about their intentions, and, after 1917, had to prove literacy in any language. The majority of those allowed into the country eagerly sought American citizenship in the place they chose to settle.[19]

Scranton held naturalization courts sporadically during the year but always in the weeks leading up to Election Day. In the 1890s and 1900s, newspaper accounts painted a vivid picture of Demo-cratic and Republican committee chairmen at the court welcoming hundreds of recent arrivals, vying for new members of their respec-tive parties, and then shepherding them through the naturalization process as the foreign-born renounced their previous national alle-giance and manifested their knowledge of the U.S. Constitution. The committee chairmen viewed the foreign newcomers—in 1891, largely Irish, many Poles, "a number of Hungarians, and some former subjects of the Czar"—as prospective voters for their respective par-ties, "and they wished to secure for them the rights of citizenship."

For the most part, Democrats courted and won over Catholics, while Republicans appealed more to Protestants, and to Italians—Catholics who, by and large, stood in opposition to their perceived competitors, the Irish. In 1921, in the aftermath of the Great War, when Germans had been designated "enemy aliens" and worry about Communists after the Russian Revolution combined with increased unemployment, Congress passed the Quota Act, limiting numbers of immigrants by country. Three years later, the Johnson-Reed Act further restricted the number of foreign-born immigrants. With fewer able to emigrate, those who desired relocation to the United States. had to go to the American embassies in their native countries, where they applied for immigration visas and went through the process previously carried out at Ellis Island.[20]

In the Americanization program, Stella Kinback met William Rogers, another idealistic public-school teacher in the Administration Building committed to teaching evening school. Rogers, the son of Welsh immigrants, whose coal miner father had died young, had worked as a carpenter before becoming a manual-training specialist in the city's Continuation School, a school set up to accommodate working children. He also taught woodworking at Scranton Technical High School. On October 28, 1950, Kinback's front-page obituary in *The Scranton Times* divulged what many people already knew, that since 1920, she had "kept company" with William Rogers. Perhaps because as a woman she could not marry and retain a job as a public-school teacher and principal, the calling to which she had devoted her life, the couple had put off marrying until she retired. Rogers and the sixty-six-year-old Kinback had procured a marriage license four days prior to her tragic death, but they had set no date for the wedding. According to a city detective, "[s]he 'fell or jumped' more than 80 feet down a stairwell from the sixth floor at the Florence Apartments . . . where she resided" on the second floor. Taking the elevator to the top floor twice that morning and leaving her coat on the upstairs banister hinted at suicide. Had the school system's tacit rules for women educators played a part in Kinback's death?

The *Times* obituary lauded Stella Kinback as "one of the best-known educators in the [Scranton] elementary schools" and noted that she had been in the "teaching force for 43 years" and, by the end of her life, had "served as principal at three institutions."[21]

During her long career as an educator, Miss Kinback had served as an ardent member of the Parent Teacher Association and the Teachers' Mutual Benefit Association. She proved her leadership in both organizations by writing letters to the newspapers on behalf of the P.T.A and helping to orchestrate a grand reception at the Hotel Jermyn for two hundred in the teachers' association. Recognizing her talent for teaching her favorite subject, the school board selected Kinback to be on a citywide committee charged with evaluating the "elementary course of study" in English. The energetic and well-respected Miss Kinback, in her mid-thirties, became the first woman to ascend to the position of principal at the George Washington School #1, taking the reins of a special institution. During the 1920s and early 1930s, with more than forty public schools in Scranton and Dunmore, the newspapers were disinclined to write up each and every elementary-school commencement, but the city's morning paper, the *Republican*, frequently covered the Washington School's midyear graduation of the 8A class. The newspaper and the people in the city recognized the excellence of the school and its students, and especially the A classes. The 8A class had many accomplished students, a higher percentage having been selected to advance by a semester, plus the tuition students like Jane, poised for Central High.[22]

Like other principals and teachers in and around the city, Stella Kinback resided just a few minutes' walk from her work. After her mother died in 1923, Stella, who had lived with her mother since her father died, rented a flat in the elegant limestone and brick Florence Apartments. Like the Administration Building, it was part of the building boom on the edge of central city shortly before the Great War. Advertised as "high-class" accommodations "at low-priced rentals," with an elevator and housekeeping services available to avoid the hassle of dealing with servants, the Colonial Revival Florence

North Scranton Junior High, built in 1924,
drew students citywide, photo 2011. Author's photo.

Apartments rose above the low-rise, mainly wooden domiciles near
the heart of the city, the area where her students also lived.[23]

As in Dunmore and all neighborhood schools, children and teachers walked home for lunch. North Scranton Junior High, drawing
students from the whole city and some from beyond, contained a
cafeteria, but the George Washington School #1, with mostly neighborhood pupils, did not. Jane Butzner and Carol MacAskie, as tuition
students, came from too far away to go home for a meal, so they
brought their lunches and used the hour-and-a-half break to explore
downtown—a welcome relief after being cooped up to focus on spelling, algebra, history and civics, Latin, and geography.[24]

During these lunchtime downtown exploratory jaunts, Jane took
on the role of ringleader. Carol and two of Carol's neighbors—Virginia "Vee" MacAskie, her cousin, and June Carter, both a semester
ahead of them—were the "half-witted audience" for the "clever, hilar-
iously funny and fearless" Jane. June was already well acquainted with
Jane, whom she recognized as "a free spirit." June's cousin Barbara

Lidstone had lived across the street from the Butzners since Jane's family first moved to Monroe Avenue. The children had all played together from a young age, so June felt she "knew [Jane] forever." Looking back, in 1995, at eighth grade with Jane, June exclaimed in her weekly local newspaper column, "Who can recall whether we learned Latin and algebra but we had an interesting time. . . . Jane saw to that!" These three friends of Jane had grown up in the tiny community of Elmhurst, upstream from Scranton along the Roaring Brook, whose power had given rise to a small chair factory, tannery, and lumber mill. In the early 1920s, city folks willing to commute to work began to move there with dreams of vegetable gardens, orchards, and raising chickens. With the railroad skirting the water's edge, the bucolic township attracted Scrantonians desiring a suburban life in an "outlying ward" with convenient train service to the city's business center. As their part of what June called the "Exploration Exchange," the three country-dwelling schoolmates occasionally were able to reciprocate by leading city visitors through the woods,

Looking south down North Washington Street toward Lackawanna Avenue, 1905–1920. Courtesy of Springfield College Archives and Special Collections, ark.digitalcommonwealth.org/ark:/50959/vm414fo5d.

crossing streams on slippery moss-covered rocks, and occasionally stranding them in a hayloft.[25]

Jane —and, apparently, her chums—had some uproarious times savoring the urban environment, with its mixture of opulence and grit. A far cry from Elmhurst and even Dunmore, at the doorstep of the Washington School lay a roughly twenty-four-square-block area, with six short blocks between the north-south Mifflin and Jefferson Avenues, and four long blocks between the east-west Lackawanna Avenue and Vine Street. This comprised the largest and most tightly packed commercial section of Scranton, which Scrantonians referred to as "central city," the locale of Amsden's original mid-nineteenth-century town plan. Its western edge still functioned as the wholesale district, while Washington and Wyoming Avenues, in the area's center, were home to the city's finest retail stores. The DL&W station at Jefferson and Lackawanna Avenues marked the central city's southeastern corner. Street addresses began with 100 at Lackawanna Avenue and proceeded both north and south—with the railroad tracks along Roaring Brook as the north-south dividing line—rolling over to the next hundred on each successive block. East-west address numbers began at 100 Mifflin Avenue, behind which lay more tracks and the river, and the numbers jumped to the next hundred with each westward block. By 1928, the bulk of the old wooden structures on the downtown section of these streets had been replaced by fireproof buildings constructed of brick and stone. In between the north-south avenues were back alleys filled with garages and other structures for storage and commercial purposes, some morally disreputable or even illegal, such as speakeasies.

Having finished their home-packed lunches at school, the four friends started down the school's front steps and assessed the progress of construction on the Masonic Temple directly across Washington Avenue. Excavation for the foundation—extending to a depth of almost forty feet below the first-floor level—of the massive project was almost finished, and the Grand Lodge officers of Pennsylvania were preparing for the cornerstone-laying ceremony in June, complete

Old Post Office, opposite Courthouse Square, early 1920s, demolished c. 1930. Scan obtained from Scranton Public Library.

with pageantry and full regalia. The girls headed south down North Washington Avenue to the first corner at Mulberry Street, alongside the glorious YMCA, where Dr. Kay had lived, and the men's tony Scranton Club and spired municipal building across the street. Having passed the new Thomas Building, containing both *The Scranton Republican* and the Powell School of Business, the girls reached the exuberant French Second Empire–style central post office, erected in the early 1890s, and gazed across the street at the nine-foot statue of George Washington, carved by Scranton's Carlucci stonemasons, gracing the northwest corner of Courthouse Square. Before Jane, June, Carol, and Vee passed the front facade of Scranton's pièce de résistance, the Lackawanna County Courthouse, they admired the eight-story Beaux Arts–style former Board of Trade Building—facing the northern edge of the square. Just two years earlier, the Scranton

Electric Company had purchased this steel-frame "first skyscraper" in the city and crowned it with the dazzlingly lighted ELECTRIC CITY sign.[26]

All during their walk, the four friends peered into ground-floor store windows—displaying everything from hardware and auto equipment to pianos and furs—with barbershops, beauty parlors, tailor shops, shoe-repair shops, cafeterias, and "lunchrooms" for downtown workers, and grocery stores, bakeries, and banks interspersed. Above the commercial medley of vitrines along the sidewalk were offices, warehouse space, and small apartments, often home to the proprietors of businesses below. The girls took in the rich texture of bays and bows, mansards, and surfaces of the second and third and, sometimes, fourth and fifth stories. Before crossing Spruce Street, they said hello to Columbus's stone likeness gesturing west. But what propelled Jane on this particular day was an idea she had involving the escalator in the Scranton Dry Goods store.

On the last block of North Washington Avenue, before turning right onto Lackawanna Avenue, the quartet of schoolgirls went by the extensive streetfront of the eight-story Connell Building, erected by the rags-to-riches coal baron William Connell. In 1894, Connell purchased a lot and razed its wooden house to put up a fireproof building. Within a short time, he bought two adjoining properties on its north side, hired architect Lansing Holden and contractor Conrad Schroeder, and put up another stone and brick building, before connecting and heightening the two. Thus, as the oldest structures in Amsden's grid became outmoded, they were individually and incrementally replaced with taller, more durable buildings, making for a mix of ages and a pleasing architectural variety of downtown buildings that Jane admired. Connelly & Wallace clothing and Joe Keller's cigar store now occupied the Connell Building's ground-level space, while many physicians—more than in any other building in the city—and dentists, lawyers, insurance companies, and other enterprises filled the floors above.[27]

Around the corner at the far end of the block, with an even larger footprint than the Connell Building, was Ike Oppenheim's Scranton

Dry Goods store, locally known as "the Dry." A few years after Oppenheim opened the department store and as recently as 1926, he had acquired lots on either side of its corner location at Lackawanna and Wyoming Avenues. With the new additions and renovations, his fashionable downtown anchor store had entrancing display windows—with men's and women's furnishings and household goods—on both streets, as well as a modernized and stylish interior. Often donning white gloves, women and girls dressed up to go shopping downtown. The Dry was the first store in Scranton to have a beauty salon, a cold-storage vault for furs, an air-conditioned tearoom, a restaurant for shoppers, a cafeteria for its employees, and, as June noted, "the only escalator in the city at that time." Jane envisioned a creative new use for the store's escalator. "Jane, to the half fright and half admiration of her followers, went up the down stairway of the escalator. No mean feat because the steps on that moving stairway were not too wide and . . . always crowded. . . . Her giggling friends gathered at the foot of the stairs were not conducive to the mercantile business! Consequently, the store floor walker, looking wrathful, was waiting for her at the top! Nothing drastic happened to her, as I recall. She wasn't even banned from the store!"[28]

Jane and her friends giggled all the way back to school, rounding the corner to the 100 block of Wyoming Avenue, home to elegant shoe and jewelry stores, and prominent banks. In the center of this block stood the Coal Exchange Building, the substantial centerpiece of one of central city's most prestigious blocks and one of the first ornate office buildings in the city. Financed by coal baron John Jermyn and designed by John A. Duckworth—an early Scranton architect of about six hundred commercial, residential, and church buildings in the area and a "large realty holder"—it was constructed by Schroeder in 1885. The Coal Exchange Building, as the girls well knew, was named for the city's raison d'être. At the far end of the block, at the corner of Spruce Street, the foursome likely stopped by Dr. Butzner's office in the Dime Bank Building to regale him with Jane's high jinks.[29]

Sometimes the girls' lunchtime adventures took them in the other direction, away from central city, past the Hotel Vine and up

Bill Steinke's caricature of International
Correspondence Schools founder, T. J. Foster,
1914. Scan obtained from Scranton Public Library.

to the 1000 block of Wyoming Avenue and the International Correspondence Schools (ICS), where Carol MacAskie's father worked.
Two edifices, spanning the length of a long block, faced each other
and housed the massive operations. The girls were enthralled by the
Tudor Revival building, reminiscent of King Henry VIII's Hampton Court, in buff-colored brick, which held the latest offshoot of
the ICS, called the Woman's Institute of Domestic Arts and Sci-
ences, offering on-site classes in such trades as dressmaking, cook-
ery, and millinery. Constructed in 1921, the new institute reflected
the success and startling growth of the company, which Thomas J.
Foster had begun as the School of Mines in 1891 in two rooms of
the Coal Exchange Building to help miners prepare for a new state-
required exam on mine safety. During the ensuing decades, the ICS

expanded its curriculum to include hundreds of courses for working men and women, geared to career advancement in a broad range of occupations.[30]

A subsidiary of the International Textbook Company—across the street in an 1898 building with state-of-the-art printing presses and a huge mailing department that backed onto the railroad tracks—the ICS relied on their textbooks as the vessels of each student's education. The books that they produced clearly elucidated a subject—even for the foreign-born—without extraneous information and were accompanied by "question papers." ICS's courses ranged from those on the engineering trades and commercial education to instruction in ornamental design. In 1930, the ICS had enrolled, cumulatively, four million students. If students encountered difficulties with a course, a special instructor contacted them directly. All this book-based education—a method Jane would later applaud—was made affordable to workers and made possible by an efficient postal service. By 1928, the company employed at least four or five thousand men and women, with deans and principals of each educational department. "Biggest employer of learned help in the state," Bill Steinke, a *Scranton Republican* cartoonist and reporter, branded them a decade and a half earlier, ". . . millions of people the world over are daily thanking [T. F. Foster] for giving them the lift." In her *Economy of Cities*, Jane would cite the "correspondence school that educated people by mail" as one of Scranton's largest exports during the city's boom period.[31]

Through her adult years, Jane continued to think highly of the practical, sensible, innovative education the ICS offered, exchanging news clippings about it with her brother Jim into the 1990s. Beginning in the 1920s, community colleges gradually supplanted the ICS by providing the same kind of technical and professional courses of study. Jim Butzner, who became a chemical engineer, was instrumental in founding Gloucester County Community College in New Jersey in 1971. "The Community College became my dad's consuming passion," Jane Butzner Henderson said regarding her father. "I can remember my dad meticulously researching job demand in the area

THE UNIVERSITY OF THE NIGHT

More than three thousand two hundred Industrial Companies and three hundred Railroads have entered into educational agreements with the International Correspondence Schools for the training of their employees in courses of instruction relative to their work. Six hundred schools and colleges are using I. C. S. Text in daily classroom work.

Write for catalog describing I. C. S. Business, Technical, Common and High School Courses

INTERNATIONAL
CORRESPONDENCE SCHOOLS
SCRANTON, PA.

Advertisement for ICS from Scranton City Directory, 1928.
Scan obtained from Scranton Public Library.

so that the course offerings would be relevant and students would be able to find employment, or go on to a four-year-degree program upon graduation."[32]

Enamored of downtown because of her school days spent in central city, Jane returned on weekends with her Dunmore friend Marie. "On Sunday afternoons we would go to the Erie Station, on the 700 block of North Washington, to watch the trains go in and out," Marie recounted, "or sometimes we went to the 'DL' [the nickname for the grand DL&W station] "to see who was coming and going. You *always* saw someone you knew. The station had a reputation for being beautiful, so beautiful that there were books [and articles] about the station." Circling the main waiting room was a frieze of thirty-six gorgeous Grueby Faience Company tile panels depicting, in Arts and Crafts style, scenes along the DL&W line. While Marie delighted in the train station's beauty, Jane was struck by "how things work." "It all came to me first hand," she recalled for Jim Kunstler. "I used to like

Interior waiting room of DL&W Railroad station with faience murals, restored, photo 2008. Author's photo.

to go to the railroad station in Scranton and watch the locomotives. I got a big bang out of seeing the locomotives and those pistons that moved the wheels. And that interested me in how they were moved by those things and then the connection of that with the steam inside and so on. In the meantime, along had come these locomotives that had skirts on them, and you couldn't see how the wheels moved and that disturbed me. And it was supposed to be for some aerodynamics reason, but that didn't make sense. And I began to notice how everything was being covered up and I thought that was kinda sick. . . . It was those skirts on the locomotives that I was thinking about [when I wrote parts of *The Death and Life of Great American Cities*] and how this had extended to 'we didn't care how our cities worked anymore.'"[33]

Even the city's streetcars lent themselves to adventure and a way to investigate the city. Kay Schoen Butzner, Jim Butzner's high school sweetheart, whom he later married, spoke wistfully about riding the electric streetcars on a Saturday afternoon. Her friend's father was the secretary to the president of the Scranton-Spring Brook Water Service, the municipal water company, which had an office downtown across from the DL. As a treat, he would give Kay and his daughter— both of whom lived on the West Side—tokens for the streetcar. "We would ride the streetcars for fun to places like Dunmore and then ride back again on the same token," she recalled, laughing.[34]

Besides learning the prescribed eighth-grade subjects, by the end of January 1929, George Washington School #1 8A students had spent a year studying the city, either through daily experiences, intentional observation, or everyday interactions with their classmates of diverse backgrounds. On Friday afternoon, February 1, "commencement and class day exercises were conducted in the assembly room in the School Administration building" with an audience of younger schoolmates, and family and friends of the twenty-five graduating pupils. The 8A graduates were in high spirits, having planned the celebration and selected a heterogeneous group of ten presenters, who had composed the traditional elements of the program. George Munchak, class president, welcomed the audience before Florence Osterland's salutatory address. Then the hilarity began. No doubt with characteristic wit and irreverence, Jane Butzner followed, lightening the occasion with the traditional "class alphabet," in which one inserted the name of each student—*A* is for Anna who . . . —along with a zinger or two in light verse. Anna Miller reflected upon the "class history" preceding the "class song," whose words she had also composed. Isadore Levinson displayed his fanciful cartoons of classmates; Harry Caryl delivered the "class prophesy," extrapolating on each classmate's likely fate; Kathryn Coyne read her "class poem," Anarita McNamara, in her "class will," bequeathed qualities, abilities, and objects to younger schoolmates. After Murrel Levy's "class presentations," Werner Rosteck concluded with the valedictory address. A mix of solemnity and levity from a motley group of talented students having come to an end, both the class and the audience were relieved when Miss Kinback "presented the certificates."[35]

School principal Stella Kinback (third from right) with first
group of schoolboy patrols, *Scranton Times*, Sept. 28, 1931.
Courtesy of (Scranton) *Times-Tribune* archives.

Almost half the class would go on to Central High, while no fewer
than five others continued their education at Tech. Of the eight pupils
not listed at either high school, some undoubtedly found full-time
employment and attended the Continuation School part-time. As of
1924 in Pennsylvania, state law mandated that children stay in school
until age sixteen, but if they had been in school for six years and
completed eighth grade, they could leave school and go to work, provided they attended Continuation School. In 1923, the newspaper had
taken special note that among the thirty-eight 8A students graduating
from the Washington School, "the outgoing students are registered
in equal numbers at both the Central and Technical High schools."
Partly because the Washington School #1 served as a springboard to
Central for tuition students, this central-city grammar school had a
consistently higher than average number of graduates on their way
to Central High.[36]

Students who matriculated at Central generally planned to go on
to college, while those attending Tech—with its choice of Commercial

or Manual Training programs—prepared for careers immediately after high school. The Central High–bound students as a group were somewhat, but not overwhelmingly, from more advantaged circumstances. Among the 8A graduates in January 1929, besides Jane Butzner and Carol MacAskie (the only "tuition students" and also the only classmates from Protestant professional families), those bound for Central were Kathryn Coyne, who lived at the often-raided Hotel Vine; Saul Davis, Isadore Levinson, Murrel Levy, and Frank Schwartz, children of Eastern European Jewish immigrants; Anarita McNamara, whose Irish lawyer uncle supported her widowed mother; George Munchak, with a successful entrepreneurial Slovakian father and seven upwardly mobile siblings; and Florence Osterland, of Swedish stock and a baker father employed by the A&P. Robert Lynott dropped out of Central after only one semester. Harry Caryl struggled academically at Central and stayed an extra year to graduate. Perhaps his father's death had something to do with this. The 8A classmates headed for the equally excellent but vocational education at Tech were of similarly varied ethnic backgrounds but were, without exception, from working-class families. African American Cidonia Mitchell and Jewish Sam Zlatin, who lived one block apart in the courts, attended Tech. Their other Washington School classmates at Tech were Carl Ellerman, Marion Cohen, and Peter Hawter—all second-generation immigrants, and Peter was a coal miner's son. Stellar student and recent immigrant Werner Rosteck moved out of state with his family by 1930, after the multicity Woodlawn Dairy bought his father's employer, the Brown-Wright Dairy Company. According to newspaper accounts, within a year, Dutch-speaking Louis Louwerse fell afoul of the law and, along with his older brother, was arrested and charged with theft and burglary.[37]

For the most part, however, these graduating central-city eighth-graders brimmed with ambition and headed for satisfying careers. Quality public schooling, passionate teachers, and having the central city as a living educational laboratory helped stoke their determination. Three female schoolmates would go on to journalistic careers.

Following high school, Jane Butzner effectively "interned" at *The Scranton Republican*; Florence Osterland became a local correspondent for several years at its successor, *The Scranton Tribune*; and June Carter, in 1960, bought, re-created, and edited a successful weekly newspaper in nearby Moscow, Pennsylvania, called *The Villager*. She wrote features and editorials, and appeared on a local radio talk show called *Two Editors Share a Microphone* until her death, at age ninety, in 2005, the year before Jane passed away.[38]

During Jane's formative years, education for all was of utmost importance to the entire community. City officials and ordinary citizens, parents and children alike, put a high value on education for a broad spectrum of the population, ranging from special schools for working children to grammar schools and college-prep and vocational high schools to adult education for immigrants eager to learn English and qualify for better jobs. In her last book, *Dark Age Ahead*, Jane underscored the importance of education to society with the caveat that "a degree and an education are not necessarily synonymous." She went on to say, "A vigorous culture capable of making corrective, stabilizing changes depends heavily on its educated people, and especially upon their critical capacities and depth of understanding." Remembering her own encounters at school, she cited the necessities of having "students who are passionate about learning" and "faculty members who love their subjects passionately and are eager to teach what they know and to plumb its depths further. . . ." Not only passionate teachers like Stella Kinback but also learning from and about a rich multiplicity of striving classmates, glimpses of the adult Americanization classes, lunchtime jaunts, and even the commute to and from school constituted the education of the pupils at Scranton's "model school."[39]

John T. and Florence Lilly's family plot near the Bell family's plot, Forest Hill Cemetery, 2016. Author's photo.

CHAPTER 8

• • •

The African American
Community in the
Heart of the City

AFTER SCHOOL OR ON WEEKENDS, Jane's explorations of the city
sometimes took her to Forest Hill Cemetery, up the hill to the north
on Jefferson Avenue, a stone's throw from her Monroe Avenue home.
The cemetery's curving lanes and undulating landscape afforded a
commanding view of the city and a quiet place to ponder the urban
scene below. Unbeknownst to Jane and many Scrantonians, here on
the hill lay African Americans and Caucasians, buried side by side,
since Forest Hill's founding in 1870, soon after Scranton was incorporated. George Sanderson had yet again proved himself "a man of
strong, good sense and great public spirit," as the historian and his
contemporary Dr. Horace Hollister described him. He, along with
his relatives and friends, conceived the cemetery for everybody, and
the tradition has continued uninterrupted to the present day. Blacks
and whites have laid their loved ones to rest in single graves or family plots without regard for the race of those interred next to them.
While this practice has occurred in particular eras in some parts of
the country, in Scranton the custom has never ceased. Norma Vail
Reese, the caretaker, manager, and ardent historian of Forest Hill
Cemetery, has lived in its entrance lodge since 1990. With roots in the
region since the early nineteenth century, when her English ancestors
migrated from New England in search of more farmland, Norma is

a keen observer of the area and a passionate archivist. She has researched the lives of a substantial number of the eighteen thousand
people interred at Forest Hill since its inception. "When someone
came for a single grave or a lot, they could choose their site. It's nice
to think people in Scranton did not have a strong feeling of prejudice," she commented. "Mayor [of Scranton 1875–1878] McKune's
grave is right near Helen Louise Mitchell Brown's [the city's first
African American schoolteacher in 1953]." The Caucasian Bell family chose their family plot just below African Americans John T. and
Florence Lilly's stately obelisk.[1]

The juxtaposition of blacks and whites at Forest Hill Cemetery
mirrors the interweaving of African Americans with other ethnic
groups throughout the city's history. In the first half of the twentieth
century, most blacks lived in and around central city, although others
could be found in nearly every part of town, recalled Dorothy "Dottie" Walker Smith, one of Scranton's public characters from the 1940s
on. Dottie was highly visible, knew everybody, and took an active role
in both the African American community and the city as a whole.
She remembered that blacks shared the same classrooms as whites,
belonged to Girl and Boy Scouts, shopped at the same downtown
stores, and read and appeared in the same daily newspapers. Jane's
brother Jim Butzner would later tell his daughter that when he was
growing up, blacks had not been the "lowest group in Scranton."
That distinction, he claimed wryly, was bestowed on immigrants from
certain Eastern European countries.[2]

Even prior to eighth grade, Jane Butzner, like her grammar-school
friend Marie Van Bergen, was well aware of the relatively small yet
perceptible and integral presence of African Americans in Scranton
in the heart of the city. At that time, the greatest concentration of
blacks lived on the blocks behind Central High School or in the
courts between the avenues on the periphery of central city, places
Jane and Marie would have regularly traversed on their way downtown, to swimming at Weston Field, or to special events at Girl Scout
headquarters. The girls took part in activities with African Americans

their own age in school and at Scouts. Scrantonians of all ages and backgrounds gathered in and enjoyed the large, public Nay Aug Park. Adult African Americans, who tended to work in service jobs rather than as laborers, were also present in the girls' daily lives. Marie spoke fondly of a man she knew as Tom Burke, even though his last name was Franklin. He worked as a chauffeur for the well-to-do Burke family in Dunmore and often drove the Burke children, along with their neighborhood friends. He was a familiar and admired presence in the young friends' lives.[3]

The arrival of Pennsylvania's first African Americans can be verified as far back as 1639. Brought by European settlers, they came to the Delaware River valley in the colony's southeastern corner as "indentured servants." Unlike their white counterparts, however, they were actually slaves, because they could not earn their way out of servitude. By 1700, roughly one thousand African American slaves resided in Pennsylvania, most of them transported from the West Indies by Philadelphia merchants. But the large Quaker population, some of whom had owned slaves, sympathized with the enslaved people, and in 1712, they helped pass legislation in the Colonial Assembly banning slavery, although England subsequently repealed the law. In 1780, Pennsylvania became the first state in the new nation to pass a law emancipating slaves, albeit gradually, and it overturned a prohibition of interracial marriage. The Pennsylvania Quakers' questioning of the morality of slavery played a crucial role in these decisions. By 1850, the census reported no slaves in the state.[4]

Pennsylvania's long history of tolerance and abolition made the state a destination for those fleeing slavery in southern states. Blacks first came to the vicinity of Scranton in about 1840, when the Electric City was but a twinkle in the eye of Slocum Hollow. They arrived in Waverly, Pennsylvania, mainly from Maryland and Virginia, via the Underground Railroad's eastern network. One route from Philadelphia and another from Harrisburg passed through Waverly—home to devout Baptists who were ardent abolitionists—situated in the rolling country about ten miles north of the future Scranton. By 1844, eight formerly enslaved people, free of the fear of pursuit, had stopped at the "station" of Waverly and decided to settle there. In 1854, they had formed a large-enough community there to build an African Methodist Episcopal church in the African American neighborhood. Before the Civil War began, Waverly had seventy-five African American settlers. From the start, these early black settlers did not seek jobs in the anthracite region's mines. Instead, they farmed, cared for racehorses, or sometimes—like Ed Keyes, the barber, or Tom Crummel, the cider mill proprietor—started their own small businesses. The townspeople who had helped guide the blacks to freedom made land available to them on "easy terms" to build modest houses and pursue their occupations.[5]

Although few African Americans relocated to Waverly after the Civil War, the number of descendants of the first settlers continued to swell. Thomas Burkett, who came in 1844, had twelve children, and his son Benjamin had at least as many. Negroes were first recorded as living in Scranton in 1870. Like white settlers from the eastern states and immigrants from Europe, many blacks from Waverly sought the economic opportunities of Scranton once it blossomed into a thriving city. Having worked "good jobs" in Waverly, all but a few African Americans avoided Scranton's mines and found safer, better-paying service jobs as coachmen, butlers, and chauffeurs. In 1874, a local newspaper reported that the Wyoming House "put in its dining room last week a full corps of first-class colored men waiters. This will be a decided improvement on [white] girl waiters, and will further advance the popularity" of the hotel. When the elegant Hotel Casey opened its doors in 1912, many African American men were hired to work as waiters and bellmen, and women to work as domestics. By 1920, only six Negroes remained in Waverly.[6]

In the last quarter of the nineteenth century, a small number of blacks migrated to Scranton from places other than Waverly. The most prominent among these was John Thurlow Lilly. Born before the Civil War, in 1849, in Chester, South Carolina, Lilly had represented his district in his state's legislature during the period of Reconstruction.

When the militant white supremacist and anti-Reconstruction Democrat Wade Hampton was elected governor of South Carolina in 1876, Lilly fled to Scranton with his wife and two young daughters. As the *Republican* described him, Lilly was "a born leader . . . well educated and . . . very successful in business." In 1886, he opened—and lived in—the American Hotel, just steps from the Central Railroad of New Jersey station on West Lackawanna Avenue. He had as many as twenty-seven boarders, some of whom were white men, and he employed whites as well as blacks. The city, however, denied his hotel a liquor license because of allegations of disorderly activities there, even though Lilly was acquitted of these charges, which the jury viewed as a "spite action." After his death, in 1893, his wife, Florence, and older daughter Lulu's husband, Charles C. Smith, carried on the hotel's flourishing business.[7]

In the first decades of the twentieth century, African Americans in search of better jobs flocked from the South to the larger U.S. towns and cities in the North. This first wave of the Great Migration brought an influx of blacks to various sections of Scranton, but the largest proportion settled in the courts on the edge of or near central city—mainly Kressler Court, Lee Court, and Dix Court, but others, too, such as Oakford and Dupont, scattered around town. "You can call them courts if you want," Dottie Smith commented, "but they were alleys. You could see the back end of houses and garages and small—though not that run-down—houses interspersed where African Americans lived." When Jane and Marie were growing up in the 1920s and 1930s, working-class whites—especially recent Italian, Russian Jewish, and Greek immigrants—also lived in the courts. The modest dwellings in the courts were plain wooden structures, usually two stories high, with their front facades crammed against the narrow alley's edge. In contrast, a small number of black families, like the G. W. Browns—who owned and ran a successful trucking company and for whom Dottie's husband, Granville Smith, came to work— bought larger houses that fronted on streets. The black community considered the street dwellers "the elite."[8]

Some newcomers from the Great Migration fondly remembered life in the courts. Ezekiel and Elizabeth Simms moved from rural North Carolina to Scranton in 1928, when their only child, Matilda, was eight years old. "When we moved [here]," Matilda recalled in her memoir, "there were very few Negro people," especially in comparison to the Carolinas, where both her parents' families came from. In Scranton, her father found employment with the railroad as a porter, considered a prestigious job in the black community. "He made pretty good money—[Mama and Daddy] gave me the best they could. . . . When I was a kid we played tag in front of [our] house on 525 New Street [at the corner of Lee Court]. I played with Jenny Marrow or Gertrude Hudson." Jenny was one of nine children of Italian immigrant parents. Gertrude had five siblings, who lived with their single mother of English origin. Matilda "grew up in the Pine Street Baptist [Church]" and taught Sunday school there for many years. Here she made friends with Evelyn Franklin, Tom Franklin's daughter. "I'd get with Evelyn Franklin, and we'd walk to Washington Avenue to the ice cream parlour and get sundaes." When Matilda was in high school, the Simmses moved to Forest Court, between Washington and Wyoming Avenues, into "a seven-room home," large enough to invite southern relatives and roomers to live with them.[9]

"Nobody was too rich, nobody was too poor" in the black community of Scranton, Nira Blue Madison reminisced. "Everybody was in the same category." Nira—named for FDR's National Industrial Recovery Act—grew up on Lee Court in the 1930s with her parents, Paul and Alice Blue, her two older siblings, and her maternal grandmother. They lived in a three-story house with a living room, dining room, pantry, three bedrooms, and two more rooms in the attic—one her brother used as his bedroom; the other was used for storage. The family rented the house from a white man who lived in the house that was back-to-back with theirs and faced Adams Avenue. Although some courts were more residential, in the middle of their block was a moving company, owned by white people who did not live in the court. Next door to the Blue family was a large garage containing big

Newport Hotel and Alamanza Porter's advertisements in *The Pennsylvania Negro Business Directory*, 1910. Courtesy of Dorothy Walker Smith.

trucks, and on the Blues' other side was a root beer–bottling company. A few blocks away, on the streets and avenues, were an A&P grocery store, a laundry, barbershops, tailor shops, and an ice-cream parlor, just about everything one needed day to day, she said. To buy clothing and larger items, Nira and her friends and family walked the five or six blocks to the fine downtown stores. "We were very fashionable in those days," she said, chuckling. "We wore hats and white gloves to go downtown shopping." Among the department stores, she especially liked the Globe and Samter's, but she tended to go to Lewis and Reilly's for practical shoes.[10]

Two decades before Nira was born and Matilda arrived in Scranton, the *Pennsylvania Negro Business Directory*, 1910, compiled by blacks, took stock of the achievements of contemporary African Americans and the elements that nurtured them. Touting the Keystone State as "the first northern State in point of Negro population" and for its exceptional opportunities for blacks, it also acknowledged the help of "friendly whites." It stated that "many corporations throughout the State give employment to Negro labor, skilled and common. It is evident that the labor market is an open field, where a man's color has but little if any effect against his chances as a bread winner." The business directory tallied Scranton's black population at four hundred (which included blacks elsewhere in Lackawanna County), praised its "mixed" schools and six public-service employees, and highlighted five Negro-owned businesses in the city: Charles Battle's Newport Hotel, Alamanza Porter's wholesale paper and rag trade—the largest in northeastern Pennsylvania—Edward Myers's barbershop, and two draying (hauling) businesses. Not long after coming to Scranton from Maryland in 1882, when he was almost thirty, George W. Brown, a drayman and rigger, had started one of these draying businesses, "the largest and most complete in eastern Pennsylvania," his company's advertisement claimed. By 1910, G. W. Brown had "every description of furniture vans and wagons for heavy and light hauling." He owned a four-story brick storage warehouse, eleven double teams of horses

G. W. Brown Storage and Draying Company, c. 1920. Photo by John Horgan, Jr. Courtesy of Dorothy Walker Smith.

and two singles, and employed twenty to thirty men. When he died, at age sixty-nine, in 1923, his forty-year-old second wife, Louise Tanner Brown, took over the business, which had acquired four motor trucks and was pulling in $35,000 each year. Although the *Pennsylvania Negro Business Directory* bore a date in its title, no prior or subsequent volumes were ever published. Its opening "Comment" exhorted Negroes of Pennsylvania to support one another and make further strides: ". . . by their thrift and energy, being about the poorest paid labor in the State, hav[ing] amassed the immense sum of $15,000,000, it is up to them to learn to combine their powers and so invest their money in the establishment of business and industrial enterprises that will give employment to the Negro people."[11]

From 1925 to 1930, with blacks moving to Scranton primarily from the South, the city's number of African Americans reached 544 in the 1930 census, and was only .04 percent of Scranton's total population, although another estimate put the figure at almost one thousand. The importance, strength, and cohesiveness of Scranton's African American community during Jane's and Marie's school days belied its small number of people and evidenced itself in its churches and numerous social and political organizations. Almost all the members of the community belonged to either the African Methodist Episcopal church or the Baptist church, and sometimes congregants went back and forth between the churches, depending on how they felt about the current pastor.[12]

The first black Baptist church in Scranton formed in the late nineteenth century. By 1916, its congregation was able to build a new church on Pine Street, at the corner of Kressler Court, and named it the Pine Street Baptist Church. The Bethel African Methodist Episcopal Church usually had the somewhat larger membership of the two churches. The Bethel AME Church was organized in 1870, when the first African Americans arrived from Waverly. Fifteen years later, Caucasian men from the First Presbyterian Church of Scranton helped raise money to buy land and construct a church on Howard Place. Thomas Burkett's son, Benjamin Burgett, helped found the church and signed the original deed. In January 1912, at a mass meeting at the venerable Elm Park Methodist Episcopal Church, black and white ministers solicited funds from a mixed, but largely white, audience to build a new "institutional church [with a component akin to a YMCA or YWCA] for colored people." This new church, the African American Reverend George T. Smith asserted, would afford young people of color arriving in the city a place to spend a social evening, a reading room, a gymnasium, and a place to sleep other than "Battle's [hotel] down in Center street . . . the only place they have to go." "It is no reflection on the place," Dr. Smith explained. "Any colored man takes his reputation in his hands when he turns off Wyoming avenue into Center street," with its often vile environment. "While the best hotels were open to [blacks], the middle grade hotels were not." The Presbyterian Reverend Griffin W. Bull, who was white, spoke to the crowd: "The white people of Scranton [have] a duty to perform in providing for the spiritual, intellectual and industrial manhood of the colored man." The white Scrantonians answered the call with generous contributions, along with pledges from their black fellow citizens. Within the year, the Bethel AME Church had opened its brick and limestone building, designed by the up-and-coming Scranton architect Edward Langley, two blocks north of Central High, closest to where the majority of blacks resided. Both the AME and Baptist churches spawned vital Sunday schools, choirs, and a variety of clubs.[13]

Even after the Bethel AME Church opened its doors, Battle's Newport Hotel, at 307 Center Street, not only provided accommodations for travelers and boarding for lodgers but also remained a gathering place for years to come. Despite its tenderloin location with ladies of the night and other illicit activities on the street, Charles "Susky" Battle's establishment was an important fixture in the African American community, with its cabaret showcasing "a colored jazz orchestra and entertainers." Moreover, its proprietor was hailed as "the benefactor of the colored people hereabouts. His hotel . . . was their headquarters, and his helping hand was always outstretched to members of his race who were less fortunate. His business was very successful and but for the workings of his big heart, he would have died wealthy." Susky Battle was buried in an unmarked grave at Forest Hill Cemetery, perhaps a decision by his estranged wife. After his death, others took over running the Newport Hotel until "Prohibition scored another victory" and closed its doors in 1924.[14]

Born in Knoxville, Maryland, in 1869, the illustrious Susky Battle died a mysterious and untimely death at age forty-two. He had arrived in Scranton in 1886, almost a decade after John Lilly, although Susky was twenty years his junior. Saving part of his wages as a waiter, Susky invested in a poolroom and, in 1906, had amassed enough to open the Newport Hotel. His biggest claim to fame was discovering the future world heavyweight boxing champion Jack Johnson, who was working in the livery stables of Scranton and Pittston and "scrapping now and then for a few dollars." Susky spotted Johnson's talent, became his manager, and gave him the money he needed to compete. Were it not for one of Susky's substantial gifts, Jack Johnson might never have had a chance at the world title. In December 1908, the Scranton hotel proprietor handed the "Galveston Giant" five hundred dollars to go to Australia, where he wrested the world heavyweight title from white boxer Tommy Burns in an unusual biracial match. In 1909 and again in 1910, the first black world heavyweight champ, Jack Johnson, roared into the Electric City "in his big touring car" and spent the night at the Newport Hotel, where fans had flocked to catch a glimpse of the man who had become, in Ken Burns's words, "the most famous and the most notorious African American on Earth."[15]

Many African American social organizations and clubs arose in Scranton in the 1920s. After the churches, the organization with the greatest impact within the African American community was the Progressive Recreation and Social Service Association. It "was the hub of Negro activity in its early years," Marcella Martin, a graduate of Central High in 1965, wrote the following year. The association continued for decades as one of the most important social and cultural—and since 1969, primarily social service—centers in the city.

It had started, in 1923, when members of the Bethel AME Church, wanted to form "a recreation and social club in the Negro community," Marcella explained. Aided by Scranton's Bureau of Recreation, the Progressive Recreation and Social Service Association began with playground equipment and several open spaces in the black community. The Bureau of Recreation's superintendent appointed thirty-seven-year-old Mrs. Elvira R. King, an active committee member of the AME Church, as the association's first playground teacher. She had moved into Oakford Court upon arriving in Scranton from Virginia and married John T. King, a trustee of the church and a self-employed bootblack twenty-five-years her senior. Despite her humble circumstances, Elvira must have proven her competency. The bureau soon hired her to be on its "summer instructional staff " of about sixty men and women from diverse backgrounds in one of Scranton's most highly regarded citywide youth programs at neighborhood playgrounds. John Lilly's granddaughter, Esther Myers, assisted Elvira King at the North Washington Street playground. The volunteer efforts of Elvira and many others in the community brought recognition to the new association. "At a recent meeting in the city hall, the activities of the Progressive Civic and Recreation association were endorsed by leading citizens," *The Scranton Republican* reported. "A resolution was adopted which embodied a proposal for a membership drive with the purpose of opening the association to all interested citizens and raising funds for a year around [*sic*] program." In fall 1926, the Community Chest announced prominently in the *Republican* that it was adding the Progressive Recreation and Social Service Association to the roster of worthy organizations under its auspices, thus joining the Bureau of Recreation in financially supporting the growing organization.[16]

By October 1928, the Progressive Center, as it would come to be called, was headquartered across from the Pine Street Baptist Church. It offered a full range of classes and activities to children of all ages and to adults. For children, there were music lessons, sewing classes, sports teams, and much more, while adults could learn skills such as nursing and first aid. The association had a board of directors, some elected, some appointed, and some recruited from out of town. Following a public performance of the chorus and dramatic class to "a very appreciative audience, " the *Republican* noted, Zenobia R. Jackson (later Dorsey), executive director, "made a very impressive talk about the work and the aim of the Progressive Recreation Association to build character through recreational phases [such] as music, dramatics, athletics, sewing, supervised games and scouting. The point was emphatically brought out that through this program, better citizens were developed among the colored population of Scranton."[17]

During the fall of 1929, when Jane Butzner was a second-semester freshman at Central, interest in the Progressive Center's activities, the *Scranton Republican* opined, was "on the rise." The center worked together with other city organizations for meetings and events, taking part in pageants at the YWCA, or holding their performances at the Y's Platt-Woolworth Auditorium for a larger public audience. In an unusual occurrence—the paper rarely printed bylines and even more rarely printed articles by high school students—the city's morning newspaper ran an article with the byline "Miss Dorothy Tucker, Central High Student." Dorothy was almost exactly the same age as Jane and surely crossed paths with her at Central or at Girl Scouts. She lived in Kressler Court with an adult couple—whose last name was different from hers—and three children with different last names listed as "roomers." The male head of household was employed as a laborer in a construction company, and his wife did not work. All evidence suggests a family of meager means but enormously kind hearts.[18]

Dorothy Tucker was an involved member of the Bethel AME Church, participated in such activities as Girl Scout Troop 34 at the Progressive Center, and was a leading athlete at Central High. Whether Dorothy submitted the piece or was asked to write it, we do not know, but it was headlined "Association Meeting Needs of Community." Miss Tucker generously acknowledged the uplifting effects of the Progressive Recreation Association on Scranton's African American community and, in turn, the community's allegiance to Scranton. "Scranton's colored population is not large," she wrote, "when compared to other cities of its size, but nowhere will you find a higher type of citizen. The colored citizens of Scranton and Dunmore are proud of their community and are striving to be worthy citizens of it. Through the Progressive Recreation and Social Service association . . . it has been possible for these citizens to make great strides forward in the last few years. . . . There are 250 members enrolled in the Progressive association, 150 of them being boys and girls. Activities are provided for all ages. Wholesome recreation, properly supervised, and instruction such as provided in the scout troops, handicraft, music and drama classes, will develop members who are a credit to themselves, the association and their city. . . . Direct results can already be traced to the helpful influence of the association and as time goes on, the development of better citizens will result."[19]

After graduating from high school, Dorothy Tucker moved to New York. In July 1936, Joe Polakoff, sports editor for *The Scranton Republican*, conveyed news of her athletic accomplishments and Scranton's impact on her: "Dot Tucker is entered in the Spanish Olympics as a 100-meter sprinter, broad jumper and eight-pound shot putter. . . . She is the only girl in a group of 10 American athletes touring Scotland, England, France and Spain. Her first taste of athletics was at the Progressive Center here and at the North Washington Avenue Playground." Elvira King had been Dot's instructor at both venues.[20]

Both the Progressive Center's boys and girls basketball teams made the news. Elvira King managed the girls team, the Progressive Swift Six, which earned fame enough as the 1930 Church League champions that Baltimore's *The Afro-American*—"The Nation's Biggest All-Negro Weekly"—recorded its success in its national roundup. *The Scranton Republican* frequently gave accounts of the "[b]asketball team playing as the Scranton Five . . . under the management of Mr.

Paul Blue, dressed for work at the Masonic
Temple, 1971. Courtesy of Nira Blue Madison.

Paul Blue and under the direction of the Progressive Recreation and
Social Service Association." Born in 1905 in nearby Pittston, Paul
Blue—Nira Blue's father—had been a four-star athlete at Scranton's
Central High. After commencement in the early 1920s, he played
semipro basketball. Nira remembered her father working for the city
of Scranton during the day as a horticulturalist in Nay Aug Park's
greenhouse and for special occasions at night as the Masonic Temple's
doorman, resplendent in a top hat and tails. Many evenings, as a labor
of love alongside dozens of other volunteers at the Progressive Center,
he taught basketball, tennis, and golf to girls and boys. Instrumental
at the center from its start, Elvira King also remained dedicated to the
organization until her death, in 1963, at age seventy-seven. Through
dint of hard work, she and her husband had become street dwellers in

a three-story house in Scranton's Lower Hill Section. After her husband died at age sixty-four, in 1926, she resided there for the rest of her life, renting to her friends the second- and third-floor apartments with back-porch views of Nay Aug Park. As the Progressive Center's executive director for many of those years, she became a prominent figure in the city. Paul Blue served as her assistant executive director in the 1940s.[21]

In May 1930, the Progressive Center invited the public to a three-day celebration of the unveiling of its permanent quarters in a two-story building at 414 Olive Street (which today remains part of the center's evolution). A "capacity crowd" showed up to view the former residence's twelve rooms, eight of which were "converted into recreational units and equipped for requirements of the association." Leona Bray, executive secretary, presided over a program of speeches and musical performances. The Progressive Center's board had persuaded Mrs. Bray, a graduate of Fisk University, to come from Youngstown, Ohio, where she had been a youth social worker, to lead the center.[22]

In May 1932, while Jane Butzner was a senior in high school, the civically dedicated and highly energetic Elisha R. Johnson was elected president of the Progressive Recreation and Social Service Association at their membership meeting, and was reelected two years later. Born in 1878 in Waverly, Pennsylvania, E. R. Johnson, as he called himself, had passed the civil service exam in Scranton in 1907. Five years later, he was secretary of the newly chartered Afro-American Realty Company of Scranton, with the Reverend George T. Smith as its president. Not surprisingly, given his close involvement with the Reverend Smith, when the AME church opened, E.R. was one of its first officers; he also worked as a chauffeur and served on the executive committee of the Lincoln Non-Partisan club, committed to "bringing out the Negro vote of the city in coming election." By 1920, E.R. and his wife, Julia, owned and ran a grocery store and lived at 1345 Adams Avenue, not in the courts.[23]

One of the numerous other black Scrantonians devoted to the Progressive Center, Margaret Lilly Myers was an independent businesswoman of means, prominence, and great style. Driving around town in her two-door Ford with a stick shift on the floor, she waved to everyone she knew. She joined the center's board of directors in 1932, four years after her husband died prematurely. She chaired their health and civics committees, organized the women sewing for the Red Cross, and served in the annual membership drive (which, in the mid-1930s, set an ambitious goal of achieving five hundred members). M. L. Myers, as she often gave her name, in the manner of professional males, was the younger daughter of wealthy entrepreneur John Thurlow Lilly, a man said in 1910 to have "the [second-] largest estate owned by any of Scranton's colored people." (The first had been Susky Battle.) Margaret Lilly must have recognized the

The prominent and stylish businesswoman
Margaret Lilly Myers, born 1874, photo 1940s.
Courtesy of Dorothy Walker Smith.

promise of the young Edward Scott Myers, a porter at her father's hotel, who had grown up in the courts, although he and his brothers and widowed mother had originally come from Baltimore. In June 1900, twenty-four-year-old Margaret married Myers. The *Republican* reported on the wedding as they would have any "pretty marriage" of whites. Held in a parlor "elaborately decorated with palms," the bride was "attired in white silk, trimmed with duchesse lace, with a diamond brooch at the throat. . . ." By 1907—about the time Dr. J. D. Butzner initially arrived in the city—Edward S. Myers established a highly successful barbershop in Scranton, probably with the help of Lilly family money. Margaret and Edward's only surviving child, Esther, born in 1909, would marry the Reverend Malcolm Gray Dade in 1929 and move to Boston and ultimately Detroit. The Reverend Dade would become a noted Detroit black clergyman and community leader, appointed by five of its mayors to many municipal advisory committees during the civil rights movement.[24]

Jane and Marie would have strolled by the black churches on their way to central city, and as avid newspaper readers from an early age, they would have come upon many articles about activities at the churches, the Progressive Center, and the web of other African American organizations. Among the earliest black social groups in the area was Scranton's Oriental Lodge No. 80 of the Free and Accepted Masons. In 1905, David T. Brown, son of and manager for successful businessman George W. Brown, formed this chapter of the Prince Hall Masons, for black men demonstrating leadership, with its mission to support the black churches, provide scholarships, and foster business and social connections in the community. Black Freemasonry dated back to the American Revolution, when Prince Hall and fourteen other free black men were initiated into the order in Boston.[25]

The Black Elks spun off from the Benevolent and Protective Order of the Elks of the World, adding "Improved" to the beginning of their name. Scranton's chapter of the Black Elks, or Improved Benevolent and Protective Order of the Elks of the World (IBPOEW), started the same year as the Prince Hall Mason's Oriental Lodge No.

80. Like other fraternal orders, they aimed to provide spiritual and emotional support for the all-male membership and to raise money for charitable contributions. Inspired by the first inclusive Order of Elks—founded in 1898 in Cincinnati, Ohio, by B. F. Howard and former slave Arthur J. Riggs, who had been denied membership in the all-white BPOE—black men in Scranton created this fraternal organization, the "Colored Elks, Anthracite Lodge 57," with its headquarters among the modest houses and businesses on Lee Court. Charles "Susky" Battle was elected a trustee soon after the chapter's inception. Both Prince Hall Masons and the IBPOEW had their corresponding women's auxiliary organizations.[26]

From its earliest days, Scranton's black community took part in national and local politics. "At a meeting of the colored citizens of Scranton, held at the residence of D. E. Thompson," a Scranton newspaper announced in 1876, "Edward Roderick was elected a delegate to the Equal Rights League convention to be held at Philadelphia, August 13th." African Americans formed their own political groups, which grew or fizzled and were replaced by new organizations. The Keystone Republican Club began in 1878 and quickly gained popularity, but by 1905 its membership had dwindled to three. "For some time past, there has been a tendency . . . to start a strong, active political organization among the colored people," a *Scranton Republican* reporter observed in 1905. "Inspired by a strong desire to meet the coming issues and assist the Republican organization in Lackawanna [County]," he continued, "the present movement [to reestablish a Colored Young Men's Republican Club] was decided upon." At its meeting held at the AME church, a speaker urged, "We had better stick to the Republican party . . . the party of Lincoln, McKinley, and Roosevelt." Two decades later, in 1926, twenty-two African Americans gathered once again to revive and establish a permanent Keystone Republican Club, with headquarters a block from the Baptist church. By June 1934, with the Depression and the election of President Franklin Roosevelt, a number of blacks bolted the GOP and organized the Lackawanna County Colored Democratic Club. Some African Americans, such as Sam J. Porter, whose family owned an antique shop on North Ninth Street, emerged as political leaders "among other Negroes who were active politically in the area," according to Marcella Martin. Although blacks threw their support behind candidates, none, however, ran for office.[27]

In contrast to organizations intended solely for the black community, some citywide associations strove to include all ethnic and racial groups. The YMCA, YWCA, and the Central Boys' Club, from its beginning in 1899, all embraced African American members. The nation's oldest civil rights organization, the NAACP, was launched in 1909 by both blacks and whites, appalled by the practice of lynching. Zenobia Jackson Dorsey founded Scranton's branch sometime in the 1920s. It remained active through the 1930s, with Mrs. Bessie Smith, of Kressler Court, serving as chapter president and presiding over its "monthly mass meeting" at the Progressive Center.[28]

During Jane's childhood in Scranton, the city's newspapers reflected the contradictory attitudes that white Americans held toward African Americans. As a matter of course, the morning and evening dailies routinely printed news of local black organizations and individuals of color among other news stories and short items. In contrast to this practice, sensational stories of lynchings in Mississippi, Texas, Indiana, and other states jumped out from the front page. The papers' editorials decried "this form of lawlessness." Jane and Marie would also have noticed page-one reports of crimes in Scranton committed by people of color, almost all of whom came from out of town. But more often than not, these stories initially identified the perpetrator as "the Negro" or, less frequently, "darky," not mentioning the person's actual name until far down in the column.[29]

In the same edition of the newspaper, however, Jane and Marie could find a long and touching profile of an African American woman, complete with photograph, such as "Ex-Slave at 93 Sews Quilts and Reads Her Bible: Aunt Fannie, Born on a Virginia Plantation, Speaks with Charm Typical of Southern Gentlefolk of Civil War Days; Recalls Girlhood." The two bright and curious girls no doubt glanced at the "Social" column of the paper, with its brief color-blind accounts of births, parties, who was in or out of town visiting, and weddings. The Progressive Center's director Zenobia R. Jackson's marriage to Charles A. Dorsey was one of many in the "Marriage Licenses" feature on the women's page, with no identification of race. Among the prominent citizens whose social activities the paper followed repeatedly were African Americans. "Mrs. George W. Brown, Prescott avenue, is entertaining as her house guest Mrs. D. Ivison Hoage, wife of the successful New York physician," *The Scranton Republican* reported. "Mr. and Mrs. James Taylor, Penn avenue, entertained last night in honor of Mrs. Hoage. Other guests include: Mr. and Mrs. H. Lee Dorsey . . . Mrs. Margaret L. Myers, Mrs. Walter Robinson, Mrs. Cassie Jenkins . . . Dr. and Mrs. J. L. Davis and E. R. Johnson." All the individuals named happened to be African Americans, but the writer made no distinction. "There was a subtle racism," Dottie Smith recollected, "but you never had to sit any place special, like in a theater, and you did what you wanted to do. People lived close together and went to the same schools, which helped, too."[30]

Black children, from their first arrival in the city, had been integrated into the Scranton public grammar and high schools at a time when other towns and cities in Pennsylvania, such as Philadelphia, still had segregated schools. "The quality of all the [local grammar] schools was excellent, and teachers took their work seriously," Marie contended, and others agreed, "so you could get a good education at whatever school you went to." Since students attended the grammar school closest to where they lived, the largest number of black children enrolled at the well-regarded George Washington School #1, in central city, where Jane Butzner attended eighth grade. Because the overall number of African Americans in Scranton was small, only a fraction of the students at the Washington School were of African American background, despite its being thought of as the "main black school." The next-largest number of black children lived nearer to the James Madison School #33, in the Lower Hill Section, and went there. A few attended the William Prescott School #38, in the Petersburg neighborhood to the east, and other schools here and there.

Despite the integration of black students, the Scranton and Dunmore public school boards did not hire any African American teachers until 1953, when they "welcome[d] the first colored teacher," Helen Louise Mitchell, a twenty-two-year-old graduate of the local Marywood College.[31]

Jane and Marie certainly came into contact with African American girls through Girl Scout activities and camp. By 1926, the year Jane Butzner joined the Scouts, the Progressive Recreation Association had Brownie, Girl, and Boy Scout troops up and running, with a large enrollment and some "outstanding scouts." "The Girl Scout troop [#34 at the Progressive Center] is developing very satisfactorily," a report to national headquarters stated. "Four patrols of girls have . . . pass[ed] their tenderfoot tests. . . . While this troop is the youngest in our city, Miss Ella Walker, bugler, is exceptionally good. Miss Dorothy Murphy is taking lessons in drumming. . . ." Troops from around the city gathered at the Girl Scouts' central-city headquarters or in Central High School's auditorium for the annual

Elvira King and children from the Progressive Center
at Weston Field auditorium, 1940s. Courtesy of Dorothy Walker Smith.

rally. In December 1931, Elvira King, who was also the Progressive Center's Girl Scout troop leader, proudly related the news: "The Girl Scouts are very active at the center. At Central High School a few nights ago there were three girls from this group who received five year service stripes." Like other Scouts in Scranton, African American Girl Scouts raised money to buy uniforms—for instance, by holding "a Dutch supper"—or to go to the Girl Scout's Camp Archbald for part of the summer. The national Girl Scouts organization encouraged regional offices not only to welcome but also to recruit African American Girl Scouts for camp. In response, Scranton's Girl Scout administrators stepped up efforts to enlist more girls through the Progressive Center, which it recognized as an association working for the benefit of girls, along with the YWCA and the YWHA.[32]

The few African Americans Jane and Marie got to know in their own Dunmore neighborhood worked nearby as liveried chauffeurs for wealthy families. The girls became well acquainted with Thomas J. Franklin, a church and political club leader in the black community, whom Dottie Smith described as "six feet two and lanky, with large hands, and looked like Abraham Lincoln." He chauffeured the Burke children, down Marion Street from Marie, with whom they played. Francis X. Burke, a contractor for coal mines, lived with his wife and three sons in a grand house, and had five or six cars, all property recently inherited from his well-known railroad-contractor father. Like a parent to all, Tom would have the neighborhood children pile into a car and drive them to a Dunmore drugstore with a soda fountain, where they could sit at the counter on swivel stools. "He'd buy us all ice-cream cones or soda," Marie recalled with a smile before her tone changed. "I really resented the soda clerk, who would only let Tom drink from a special glass he kept for him." She was angered by the clerk's prejudice against blacks and other remarks she had heard. People didn't want blacks living on their block, she said, but "this, fortunately, wasn't usually an issue because there were very few [in Dunmore]. *Everyone* accepted Tom Burke—that's what we called him." To Marie, calling him "Tom Burke" signified that she considered him a member of the family, but other people who called him that may have avoided recognizing who he really was. "Tom was a wonderful, special person. If he drove by while I was waiting at the bus stop, he would insist that he give me a ride. He would always stop to pick people up if he knew them. When other kids saw me riding in a chauffeured car, they would tease me," as if she were from a rich family. Marcella Martin shared Marie's impression of Tom Franklin. "Deacon Franklin," as she called him, because of his position at the Baptist church, "was very charismatic and had great class. Being a chauffeur in those days was an honor."[33]

At George Washington School #1 in central city, which a majority of the African American children attended, Cidonia Mitchell happened to be the only African American student in Jane's particular class, but other classes had more. The city's two high schools bookended the city's densest black neighborhood at its northern and southern limits, only three blocks apart. Both Central High School, the southern bookend, and Scranton Technical High School, its bookend to the north, drew students from all over the city. Most black students chose to go to Tech "usually because their friends were there," several people concurred, but "a handful"—between two and eight—selected Central each year. The majority of students attending Central, whether they were black or white, decided to go there because they were academically inclined and intended to go to college. Students at the vocationally geared Tech more likely considered the school as final training for jobs, such as stenographers or mechanics, although some did go on to college.[34]

Because of the relatively small proportion of blacks in the city, the high schools—like the public grammar schools in the 1920s and 1930s—were predominantly white, but no matter what their background, all students mingled in homerooms, classrooms, and extracurricular activities. "All students were treated the same at Central," Nira Blue Madison said of both her and her father's experiences there. "There was less prejudice [back then]. You didn't think black and white." Kay Schoen agreed. When pressed to recall black classmates at Central in the mid-1930s, she said she "didn't usually think that way," but upon reflection, she remembered two African Americans in her grade: Hilda, the daughter of a mailman, in her Latin class and another "nice girl in [her] English class." Kay and Jim's class photo shows there was also at least one black male among the 325 graduating students in June 1938. Two years younger than Kay, Evelyn Franklin—Tom and Minnie Franklin's only child, born in 1922—attended Central after graduating from Tech, in order to take extra science courses required for admission to nursing school. The Franklins lived on Lee Court, a few blocks from the high school. Evelyn's friend Matilda Simms overlapped with her at Central High. Matilda had been an honor-roll student at George Washington School #1, and her parents encouraged her to choose the college-preparatory school. Alice Elizabeth Porter's experience at Central may have motivated her to become a teacher. Born in 1915 to hotel porter William and his wife, Teresa Porter, who owned their house on Sanderson Avenue, Alice graduated from high school, having completed the Classical course in June 1933, the same year as Jane but as part of the B class.

Parran Foster III and his mother, Alice Porter Foster, longtime Scranton schoolteacher, 2011. Courtesy of Parran Foster III.

Four years later, Alice Porter (later Foster) earned a degree in education from the State Normal School at Cheyney, Pennsylvania's first institution of higher learning for African Americans. She taught in Maryland for two years before returning to Scranton to marry and raise seven children. In 1962, she became one of the city's three black teachers at the time. For twenty-three years, she taught fifth and sixth graders.[35]

Even though students felt they were treated as equals in high school, African Americans encountered racism in Scranton and elsewhere. Many persevered. When Evelyn Franklin applied to nursing school in Scranton, she was turned down with the stock phrase "We don't think you'd feel comfortable here." Undeterred, she gained admission to the Harlem Hospital School of Nursing, in New York City, and stayed to work as a nurse there for more than thirty years. Nira Blue, an excellent student who had followed the Scientific course at Central, attended college in preparation for a career as a medical technician. For many years, she was the first and only African American medical researcher in all of Scranton's hospitals.[36]

Perhaps it helped that these young black women had grown up in Scranton, where other African Americans had succeeded in the medical profession. Dr. James Edward Foster, Scranton's only black general practitioner when the Butzners lived there, was among the first generation of African Americans to enter the medical profession. Born about 1880, he relocated from the South and practiced as a licensed physician in Harrisburg, Pennsylvania, before settling in Scranton around 1912. Not only African American patients but also plenty of Caucasian ones went to see him, Dottie Smith recollected. Dr. Foster became a highly involved citizen in the black community and the city as a whole. In 1925, *The Scranton Republican* reported that at a meeting to discuss the city's housing problem, held at St. Luke's Episcopal Church, he introduced the representative from the health department. He assisted Thomas Franklin, president of the Lackawanna County Colored Republican Club, in presiding over the club meetings.[37]

In fact, black and white doctors set up their practices on the same block. During the 1920s and 1930s, Dr. J. E. Foster kept the public apprised through notices in the daily papers as to when his office was open and its location. In 1932, he posted an announcement that he had moved his office to 310 North Washington Avenue, which was across the street from the Medical Arts Building, where Dr. Butzner and other white doctors practiced. Like Dr. Butzner, he drove an automobile to make house calls to patients. Dr. Foster and his wife, Mabel M. Foster, resided at the same address as his office, and they attracted the attention of the *Republican's* women's page writer in September 1933: "Mrs. J. E. Foster recently entertained at a birthday party at her home on North Washington Avenue in honor of her husband, Dr. Foster. Present were . . ." A long list of guests' names followed, including those of African Americans and whites, one of whom was a relative of Jane's classmate of Italian background at Central. As in the paper's other social columns, the writer made no mention of anyone's race or the fact that Mrs. Foster was white. Jane Butzner, who was then the assistant to the women's page editor, may well have written this entry.[38]

Scranton's other black doctor at this time was Dr. James L. Davis, who was born about 1878 in Virginia. He owned a home at 409 Franklin Avenue and maintained a private practice there as a chiropodist. He and his wife, Mattie Davis, were active in the Progressive Center's member drives and, from time to time, appeared on the newspaper's society page. Despite their acceptance by Scranton's community as a whole, neither of these doctors appears to have been a member of the Lackawanna County Medical Society.[39]

For part of the 1930s, Scranton also had an African American dentist. Raised in Scranton from his birth, circa 1905, Birchard "Bert" Goodall spent his childhood in Kressler Court with his parents and two brothers. Edgar N. Goodall, his father, worked as a waiter at the Hotel Jermyn for fifty-three years. As a youth, Bert performed in piano and song recitals at the Scranton Conservatory of Music, where the majority of students were white. He received his dental degree from Howard University and came back to Scranton to set up an office in his parents' home on Olive Street, across from the Progressive Center. His niece, Angi Goodall Johnston, remembered that the family proudly referred to him as "Uncle Doc." After marrying Leona Warner, whose relatives lived in the New York metropolitan area, he moved to Paterson, New Jersey. He practiced dentistry in Paterson and Hackensack, New Jersey, for many years. Compared to Scranton, Philadelphia—the state's largest city—in 1910 had a huge African American population, close to 80,000, and was home to 131 African American medical doctors. Yet with the highest number of blacks in the state, Philadelphia did not have integrated public schools or black doctors ministering to whites.[40]

Black Scrantonians overcame major racial and gender hurdles to succeed in other occupations, too. In 1930, Ethel A. Miller, a Caucasian secretary at Scranton's YWCA, lauded one such person in her article entitled "A Successful Woman in a Man's Game" in the National Urban League's magazine *Opportunity: Journal of Negro Life*. In that year, Miller wrote that Mrs. G. W. Brown had successfully grown her deceased husband's company, which now owned fourteen trucks she called "speed wagons," conducted $72,000 worth of business annually, and employed twenty-two persons as drivers, helpers, and office workers. When some of her white truck driver employees—undoubtedly all men— "asserted they would not work for a colored woman," she persuaded them to drop their objections by signing a union agreement with them. From then on, she paid union-scale wages and hired equal numbers of blacks and whites. The nattily dressed and well-respected E. R. Johnson was her company's manager. The trucks, with "G. W. Brown, Drayman, Scranton" elegantly painted on the cab's red doors, could be spotted around the city, moving households or making deliveries to and from the department stores. It was quite a coup when G. W. Brown Trucking became the contract hauler for the A&P stores through the 1930s and 1940s, at a time when, with the advent of refrigeration, trucks could transport produce and dairy products to city markets from farther away. "This meant you couldn't

Born in Waverly, civically active E. R. Johnson
was the G. W. Brown Company's manager in
the 1930s. Courtesy of Dorothy Walker Smith.

work for anyone else [in trucking]," Dottie Smith explained, "and the A&P's northeast regional headquarters was in Scranton." A minister's daughter originally from Beaver, Pennsylvania, upriver from Pittsburgh, Louise Tanner Brown was generous with her time and money in helping her adopted hometown. Among many other pursuits, she taught Sunday school at the Bethel AME Church, served on the board of the Progressive Center, and was president of the YWCA's Fidelis Club for black women. An excellent public speaker, Louise Brown delighted crowds throughout the state with her readings of

Dorothy Winifred Walker, age 22, and Granville
Clark Smith, age 32, wedding photo, Dec. 4,
1945. Courtesy of Dorothy Walker Smith.

Negro poetry. In 1933, the National Association of Colored Women
in Washington, D.C., honored her as the "most outstanding business
woman in Pennsylvania."[41]

Not only did they persevere but Granville and Dottie Smith also
made a habit of ignoring racial roadblocks and charging ahead. From
a small town outside Pittsburgh and recently graduated from the all-
black Wilberforce College, Granville Clark Smith eagerly pursued
and landed the job as manager—following E. R. Johnson—of the G.
W. Brown company. His boss, Louise Tanner Brown, rented a room
in her house in the Petersburg neighborhood to her new employee. A

few years later, Granville was able to buy his own house in Scranton's prestigious Hill Section and brought his mother and handicapped sister to live with him. Soon his new bride moved in, too—née Dorothy Winifred Walker, from Wilkes-Barre, a smaller anthracite city roughly twenty miles down the valley or forty-five minutes via the interurban Laurel Line from Scranton. Dottie's father drove a truck and, thanks to the union, made a good living for his family. "We were never hungry, had shoes, didn't have to buy coal by the bushel, and had a furnace—not a coal stove. That's how you judged things in those days," Dottie recounted amusedly. She was "in line for a four-year scholarship" to Wilson College, a Presbyterian women's college in Chambersburg, Pennsylvania, but they denied her admission at the last minute when they met to interview her and realized she was African American. They claimed "it would be hard to find roommates for her." With her indomitable spirit and her mind set on a college education, she quickly rebounded and went to Bucknell University Junior College, "a ten-minute bicycle ride" from her home in Wilkes-Barre. She spent her last two years at Bennett College, a historically black women's college, in Greensboro, North Carolina, and majored in chemistry.[42]

Granville and Dottie Smith became "street dwellers" at 921 Pine Street, in a thirteen-room "mansion," said Dottie, in the Hill Section, once home to coal barons and other wealthy businessmen. Granville taught shorthand classes at the Progressive Center, joined the Jewish Community Center, became Scranton's first black Kiwanian, and was a force in the entire city, serving on numerous boards, including that of the Scranton Public Library. Dottie taught for fifteen years at the Department of Chemical Engineering at the International Correspondence Schools, where she was the ICS's first black instructor. "Why was I the first?" she demanded. "Because no African American before me had ever asked for work there!" She also served as a Girl Scout cookie chairman, a leader in the James Madison School PTA, and, with a nod from Mrs. Nathanial Cowdrey— Pennsylvania governor William Scranton's aunt—in the 1950s, became the first (and only) black member of the exclusive Century Club. Mrs. Cowdrey had called Dottie beforehand and said, "I hear your name is before the board. I'd appreciate your letting me know if you have any difficulty." Dottie and Granville sent their children to Sunday school at the Green Ridge Presbyterian Church—to which the Butzner family had belonged throughout their years in Scranton—and became the first blacks to join the congregation. They became close friends with Pastor Brewer Burnett, who had led the church in the 1940s, when Bess Butzner was still a member. "Scranton was kind of unique," Dottie reminisced. "It was a small city with [relatively] few blacks. People in Scranton were receptive to what you were trying to accomplish. We couldn't have made the friends we did if we hadn't been in Scranton."[43]

Two Scrantonians, John Strader and Gwendolyn Jones—like Dr. James E. Foster and his wife, Mabel, a generation earlier—challenged the most deeply entrenched racial prejudice. Born the same year as Jane Butzner, John E. Strader had spent his early years with his stepfather, Joseph Strader, a coal miner and trustee of the black Keystone Republican Club, and his mother in the 600 block of Dix Court. John's mother was Bertha Burgette, a descendant of the once-enslaved Burgettes who had found refuge in Waverly. After his stepfather died, John resided with his mother and brothers across from the county prison. Soon after leaving Tech High School, John—like his older and younger brothers—was hired as a doorman at the grand Hotel Casey. In 1940, he met nineteen-year-old Gwendolyn Jones, a waitress in one of the hotel's restaurants. Gwen had been born and raised in the anthracite-mining town of Blakely, eight miles northeast of Scranton, and sought work while her father, a mining engineer, was unemployed. Gwen's parents, Maud and Robert Jones, were both children of Welsh immigrants who had come to work in the mines. John Strader and Gwen Jones married in 1942, when thirty out of forty-eight states (but not Pennsylvania) still had laws forbidding interracial marriage. At first, Gwen's parents would have nothing to do with her, but eventually their relationship "did mend to a certain

John Strader, Jr. (wearing pointy hat in back row) at his birthday party, in front of Progressive Center, 1951. Courtesy of Dorothy Walker Smith.

degree," her daughter Cathy Ann Hardaway said. Because Gwen felt her five children would be perceived as black, she decided to raise them in the black community. Both John and Gwen joined the board of the Progressive Center. After John died, prematurely and suddenly, in 1968, Gwen stayed on in the community and eventually became, she told Dottie Smith with a chuckle, "the oldest living member of the Bethel AME Church." The African American community embraced Gwen, and many retained warm memories of her. "She liked to talk to everyone in the community," Marcella Martin reminisced, "and [as a young person] I *loved* to talk to her."[44]

Jane's awareness and knowledge of blacks and their culture and community clearly began during her childhood in Scranton. Although Scranton was a relatively tolerant city, Jane could not help but observe, in her daily life, the problems of prejudice that blacks encountered. In the 1920s and 1930s, African Americans in Scranton formed a tight-knit and supportive group, where virtually everyone attended one of two churches, and a great proportion came together at the Progressive Center. "There were so many wonderful people in

Scranton, it spoiled me," Marcella said. "I don't think I would have fared as well without the community. It wrapped its arms around us." Marcella Martin "went on to serve humanity" as a human services professional and minister "and empower thousands to walk out their purpose on this journey of life."[45]

With their long history in the city stemming from the Underground Railroad, many African Americans during Jane's time in Scranton held relatively good jobs. Dottie Smith defined a good job as "one where you could go to work dressed up." Those involved in these occupations ranged from professionals, businesspeople, and federal and city employees to hotel and restaurant workers. Black children went to school with whites and were treated "like everyone else," a number of black Scrantonians commented. Some went on to college and prestigious careers. Black families lived in decent houses, albeit largely in the alleys in an informally circumscribed area at the edge of central city, but in close proximity and often next door to whites. In Scranton's patchwork quilt of ethnic groups, Scranton's African Americans were an active and integral part of the fabric of everyday life. Non–African American citizens, churches, and other organizations lent a hand to the black community. The city government and Community Chest supported their community center. Prejudice existed, however, although it was "not blatant," as Nira Blue Madison put it. Perhaps the relatively small number of blacks made it easier for whites to get to know and appreciate them as individuals. The small proportion of blacks in the city made it simpler, natural, and logical to have integrated schools and a tradition, originating before the Civil War, for inclusion and acceptance of blacks.[46]

The Butzner family—from Dr. Butzner and Bess's earliest days in Scranton in the 1910s, throughout the 1920s, and into the 1930s—was surely familiar with the city's strong black community through the city newspapers, chance encounters, and at least casual contact. Having known and observed African Americans from a young age, Jane—along with her siblings—was conscious of the injustices and extra challenges they faced solely because of their skin color. She had seen the vibrancy of the kind of neighborhood that urban renewal aimed to eradicate. She had grown up with individuals who would be uprooted in the process of wholesale demolition. Besides making a case for the value of dense and diverse urban neighborhoods, in her first book about cities, Jane could not help but point out—even though it was not the book's subject—what she termed "our country's most serious social problem—segregation and discrimination." By 1969, in her next book, *The Economy of Cities*, she cranked up the volume against "[Blacks having] been kept in their economic subjugation by discrimination in cities." Scranton's black community must also have provided the seed—nurtured by trips to Butzner relatives in Virginia—for her brother John's illustrious career dedicated to advocating for the rights of African Americans. John Butzner would become a civil rights lawyer, appointed in 1962 by President John F. Kennedy as a federal district judge overseeing important civil rights decisions, and promoted by President Lyndon Johnson in 1967 to the Fourth Circuit Court of Appeals. As law professor and journalist Garrett Epps wrote, John D. Butzner, Jr., was one of the lawyers and judges whose opinions on school desegregation and employment discrimination "helped lift the curse of official apartheid from the South."[47]

Front facade of Scranton's Central High School,
with girls' entrance on left, 2008. Author's photo.

• • •

CHAPTER 9

The City's
"Best Investment"

THE JANUARY GRADUATES OF George Washington #1's 8A class of 1929 had no summer break in which to imagine what the teeming, citywide high school might hold in store for them. Less than a week after their commencement revelries, two-thirds of the fellow alums trundled off, dressed for snow—girls wearing black boots with buckles, leaving them undone, so they flapped noisily. On Wednesday morning, February 6, they were headed either to Central High School, the classical high school on Vine Street, around the corner from their alma mater, or to Technical High School, the vocational high school a scant three blocks farther up North Washington Avenue. Jane Butzner and eleven of her eighth-grade classmates were among the roughly 221 students who had registered to begin their freshman year at Central High that day. Most of these incoming freshmen were familiar with Central's monumental structure from the outside—the four-story Beaux-Arts building, topped with a steep black-tiled roof and spiky central spire. It took up most of the city block on the gently rising slope retreating from central city. The school's rear windows looked out over the homes of a goodly number of the city's African American community.[1]

Still three months shy of her thirteenth birthday, Jane felt a mixture of optimism and dread as she joined some two thousand students heading for Central High, freshman through seniors, in either the A (graduating in January) or B (graduating in June) classes. Although she was averse to the requirements, confinement, and memorization of public schools, she looked forward to encountering many more students than she had ever seen at once and to choosing among Central's extracurricular activities. Within the high school's walls, Jane would discover a small community of diverse, hardworking youth, as well as teachers of varying backgrounds who went way beyond the call of duty to aid immigrant and working-class students. Almost all Central's pupils engaged in a cornucopia of activities and experiences in and outside the classroom. The community at large—including municipal officials, the press, taxpayers, and the general population—supported the city's public high schools, and the students, in turn, found themselves increasingly involved in the city and civic endeavors. For many a pupil, the school provided an invaluable stepping-stone to advancement in life. Fifty years after graduating, alums displayed their school spirit at their respective reunions, which even iconoclastic Jane attended.[2]

On this first day of the new semester, teachers and administrators—as was their wont—entered through the school's commanding central portal, adorned with ironwork and granite steps leading to the first floor. The entryways for students were distinguished by two words—*Girls* and *Boys*—carved in formal Fraktur in stone above the doors. Coming by foot or streetcar from all points of the city and beyond, girls—who always wore skirts or dresses—poured into the arched entrance at the leftmost ground level of the facade, and boys—in their jackets and ties—found their way into the mirror-image counterpart on the right. Jane would soon hear older girls recommend approaching the school from Adams Avenue for a chance to walk by the boys' entrance on the way. Inside the doors on each side were mazelike rows of lockers, secured by losable keys until combination locks finally arrived. Girls or boys hung their coats and stashed their lunches, if they brought them, and some books. Jane caught glimpses of her new classmates stopping at their assigned lockers.[3]

The pupils proceeded from the locker room past the changing room for the adjacent gym and up the stairs to the first floor. Voices and footsteps reverberated in the wide corridors with their high ceilings, dark woodwork, gorgeous decorative tile floors, and light-colored walls adorned with plaster bas-reliefs of goddesses and Roman soldiers on horseback. Amid the hubbub, Jane found her gender-segregated homeroom, with Miss Henrietta Lettieri, a teacher of mathematics, in charge. The girls settled into their designated desks, in alphabetical order, while their teacher took attendance, made announcements, and recorded tardiness. In keeping with the homeroom system, the school's attendance records and course grades were also organized by gender and alphabetically, all in a beautiful cursive hand in leather-bound books. Although classes were coed, the school went to lengths to set boys and girls apart in assessing their achievement. Such things as the list of graduates and names of honor-roll students appeared in the local newspapers with separate groupings of boys and girls, the way school officials had conveyed the lists to reporters. The penchant for comparing girls and boys lent an air of competition between the sexes. Speaking of the 150 students who would graduate in the February 1931 class, Central's principal, Professor Albert T. Jones, disclosed, "Contrary to the usual list of honor students [with an average of 90 percent or higher], this semester's honor group includes 5 boys and 6 girls. In former years the girls have gained a higher representation on the honor roll in comparison to male students." Evidently, girls consistently outranked boys academically, and they exceeded boys in the number of pupils enrolled.[4]

Central High's curriculum required four years to complete in order for a student to graduate. Students could choose one of three courses of study at the school: Classical, Scientific, or General, but "you *did* get to know people who were following other courses," Kay Schoen, who began Central in September 1934, clarified. Students in each of these programs were mixed together in the homerooms and in certain classes, such as English. Kay was in the Classical program, the most popular, although looking back, she felt she should have pursued the Scientific course, as Jim Butzner, Jane's brother, did. Kay and Jim met in their freshman science class, and they both aspired to careers as chemical engineers. In the General course, students took academic classes but also learned "useful" skills. This program, according to Kay, was in least demand at Central High. The Scientific course was comprised almost exclusively of boys, while girls predominated in the other two. Just about every student in all three programs at this high school studied some Latin.[5]

Students, in consultation with their parents, decided on which of the city's two public high schools they would attend. After Betty Butzner's subpar experience at Dunmore's classical high school, Jane and her parents hoped that Central would hold Jane's interest and provide a more solid education. With its three years of Latin, three more of a modern language, and courses in English, science, and history, the Classical course prepared students for the standard four-year liberal arts college. The Scientific course trained students for engineering schools, while the General course was adapted to those planning to attend "normal" schools—named for establishing norms in teaching—two-year colleges that were later called "teachers'" colleges. In the General course, students who were going to be secretaries could learn typing, shorthand, and bookkeeping. Although Central turned out boys and girls ready for college, not all its graduates went on to higher education. The high school, nevertheless, prepared them well for the "active duties of life," professions, or business. "If you wanted to be a bookkeeper or an auto mechanic, you went to Tech," Kay explained. "Tech was more diverse, and far more girls than boys enrolled." The Technical High School offered two courses of study: Commercial and Manual Training/Industrial." Besides excellent academic classes—aimed at teaching maximum practice and minimum theory—for both programs, girls could learn such skills as garment making, plain and fancy cooking, laundry work, and art applied to functional and ornamental items for the home. Attracting even more pupils than Central, Tech was hardly a mediocre second high school. Its programs and training were every bit as rigorous as those at the renowned Central. Even though the school was geared to vocational education, it offered courses such as Latin, modern languages, and English, and its students produced the *Tech Quarterly*, which won first

Scranton's Technical High School, with William T. Smith Manual Training School on left, c. 1910. Courtesy of Norma Reese via Susan Pieroth.

place in the national school-publications competition's category for technical high schools.[6]

Entering Central a year before Jane, Carl Marzani had emigrated from Italy in 1924, at age twelve. In his four-volume 1990s memoir, *The Education of a Reluctant Radical*, he paid tribute to the reputation of Scranton's Central High as "one of the finest high schools in the country." Marzani was also struck by the high value the city placed on education and, consequently, on the architecture of its school buildings. He had come to Central from North Scranton Junior High—the largest single feeder school for Central—whose ninth-grade graduates represented a significant number of the students in Central High's sophomore classes. "North Scranton Junior High was a magnificent edifice with an imposing façade of sculpted portals and mullioned windows," he wrote. "The school . . . was set back on a slight hill and had impressive lawns in front and a big playground in the back—an amazingly prodigal use of urban land. In style and munificence our junior high was a precursor of schools in suburbia, only ours was in the middle of a working-class area—and a considerable investment, of which the city was justly proud." The city's investment in such glorious school buildings was a testament to the pervasive belief among the community's residents in the intrinsic worth of a good education.[7]

Three decades before the city had put up the dazzling junior high, the school board had engaged the highly regarded New York City architectural firm Little & O'Connor to design the new Scranton High School, as it was called then. Michael J. O'Connor, an 1884 graduate of Columbia University's School of Architecture, and his partner and fellow alum, Willard Parker Little, created the facade's variety of colors and textures with native stone from West Mountain. Sparing no expense, they planned the high school's ornament accen-

Albright Library, entrance, across Vine Street from Central High, built 1893, modeled after Hôtel de Cluny in Paris. Scan obtained from Scranton Public Library.

tuating the front entrances and focal windows to complement that of the Albright Library. The elaborate and eclectic new high school building opened in September 1896. The *Republican* pronounced the high school building "the best investment ever made by the city of Scranton." Hundreds of people gathered for the dedicatory exercises, where the principal proclaimed, "The dedication of a high school building of such proportions as this marks the dawn of a future, educationally speaking, that cannot be measured. . . . [It] means that we are passing through a commercial age and entering upon a reflective one, where culture and education are to take a deeper hold of our citizen-life and thus shall be evolved a generation of increased power and usefulness."[8]

The new high school replaced Scranton's first public high school, built in 1858, on the same site. Although the erstwhile school had "command[ed] a view of the whole city," it was in a "very ordinary school building" and only "a few of the more ambitious students . . . secure[d] the advantages of the two or three additional years of instruction offered by that institution," historian Hitchcock wrote. With a flood of matriculating students, in 1903 the new Scranton High School adopted a four-year curriculum for all pupils. After the school board decided to put the vocational programs in an autonomous location, they erected Technical High School in 1905 and renamed Scranton High School Central High School. In 1922, Edward Langley designed a substantial expansion of Central, increasing the number of rooms and adding the elegant and large-capacity auditorium, directly opposite the main entrance, easily accessed by public audiences attending plays, concerts, and Scout rallies held there.[9]

Throughout the newly and beautifully expanded edifice, bells resounded after the brief homeroom meeting, signaling first period. Typically serious and motivated, the students sprang from their seats and sorted themselves among the school's forty-six rooms on the three main floors, including rooms dedicated to particular subjects and purposes. Central's facilities far surpassed any they had seen in their grammar schools or junior highs. In addition to traditional classrooms, there were art studios, double-size music rehearsal rooms, secretarial classrooms outfitted with typewriters and business equipment, and science laboratories manned by lab assistants, sometimes recent Central female graduates, like Dorothy Burkhouse. Pupils could spend study periods in a small but well-stocked library above the main entrance on the second floor. For gym periods, boys and girls returned to their respective locker rooms on the ground floor to change into uniforms before showing up in the gymnasium, toward the back of the building. Girls had to take part in gymnastics on parallel bars and leather horses and had to climb thick, abrasive ropes hanging from the ceiling. When the school formed its first girls swim team, Jane tried out and easily qualified. Boys could join football, track, basketball, softball, and tennis teams. Jim Butzner would become a high school tennis champ. Football and tennis were the students' most preferred sports and lured crowds of spectators.[10]

Students in Central High School Library, boys in ties, girls in skirts, *Impressions* magazine, Mar. 1929. Courtesy of Donna Zaleski, Scranton High School Library.

At lunchtime, most students ate in the school cafeteria, even if they brought their own food. Although the school employed a cafeteria manager and supplied excellent lunches at low cost, most kids brought sandwiches from home. Students were assigned to a certain time for lunch, and the allotted slot was far too short. "By the time you got your lunch out of your locker and sat down or went up to the counter to get something to drink," Kay recalled, "there wasn't much time left." Barbara Gelder admitted that she sometimes was so rushed that she "ate on the fly" as she stood in front of her locker. Without enough time to explore the city during lunch break, Jane—true to form—turned her energy to amusing herself and her schoolmates. One day at the cafeteria, she blew up a paper bag and popped it loudly. Consequently, Jane was sent to the principal's office. The principal made a point of calling parents to enlist support and administer punishment to the child in question, so he called Dr. Butzner at his office and related the incident. Having listened politely, Dr. Butzner bluntly informed the principal, "I am a busy man taking care of my business. You take care of yours." The next time Jane got into trouble, she was told that her father "was a very busy man" and the school wouldn't bother calling him. Maybe the principal tolerated Jane's mischief because she was so talented and bright, Kay posited. The students got a kick out of Jane, and at least some of the school personnel must have, too.[11]

During their lunch period, students were permitted to leave the school. Some boys and a few girls made a brief foray to the drugstore for a soda or ice cream, and some "snuck a smoke" behind the Albright Library. "You weren't allowed to smoke at school. I don't think their parents knew, and I doubt they would have liked it," Kay stated. "Both these groups of kids must have had quite a bit of spending money." Although her parents gave her money to take the streetcar from their West Side home, Kay more often than not walked the half-hour to school. She and her friend Anna Manno, who came from an Italian family a few blocks "up the mountain" and with whom she often walked, would save up their carfare—and combine it with money from babysitting—to treat themselves to an occasional hot dog at the foot of the Linden Street Bridge across the Lackawanna River.[12]

For Anna and Kay, saving money led to adventures and a chance to glimpse the city's raunchier side, a source of great curiosity. On the way to school, at the top of the hill near the corner of North Main Avenue and Linden Street, there was a Greek Orthodox church. "You could cut behind the church and walk by the washhouse below, where miners getting off work from a mine nearby showered, changed their clothes, and emptied their lamps," Kay recounted. "The washhouse was made of cinder blocks, and the miners would knock their lamps on the side of the building to dump the ashes from them. Sometimes the lanterns had been burning all night. Parents told their children, 'Don't walk by the washhouse,' but you walked by it with all your friends. Continuing downhill on Linden toward the river, you passed the culm dumps on one side and a deserted brewery on the other.[13]

The culm dumps consisted of partially mined or burned coal. Some of the coal caught fire. Homeless people slept on top of culm piles to keep warm, although the burning culm gave off carbon monoxide." Kay paused and added, "Sometimes they wouldn't wake up." Across the street was the abandoned brewery where the "bottle gang" —the guys who hung out next to the brewery—congregated. They were harmless to passersby. "I never heard of anyone being attacked. . . . They were poor miners with miners' disease and would cough and spit up all kinds of things." From the bridge over the river, Anna and Kay could see the water, black from ashes. Kay remembered her father wisecracking that the ashes in the river kept the sewage from smelling so awful. Across the bridge, at the western edge of central city, Kay's route to school skirted the area where the "disorderly houses" clustered. "Everyone in town was aware of the red-light district," Kay volunteered. It was on Penn Avenue, and her grandmother Schoen's house on Capouse Avenue was parallel to it and one street over. Anna's father, a city detective, instructed the girls to "walk straight by the red-light district." He knew exactly where the houses were and warned the girls not to stray down those blocks.[14]

While some working- and middle-class girls attending Central High babysat to earn spending money, boys of this same status tended to have paper routes, rising early before school to deliver the morning newspaper. Some students from more strapped households held full-time jobs and managed to keep up their grades at Central, but others were forced to drop out. From the age of fourteen, Carl Marzani had worked summers for an Italian baker in the nearby borough of Jessup, and during high school, in addition to a full load of classes and extracurricular activities, he worked eight hours—from 4:00 P.M. to midnight—seven days a week at a gas station. He was paid a dollar a day at his after-school job, and his father contributed three dollars a week, rounding out the weekly sum to ten dollars for deposit in Carl's savings account, earmarked for college.[15]

From the day he arrived in America, Carl was industrious and ambitious. Fleeing Mussolini's fascism, Carl's socialist father, Gabriel Marzani, had left a "responsible post office position in Rome" for the village of Peckville—seven miles up the valley from Scranton. Ten months later, he sent for his wife and two children. Gabriel's uncle had sponsored the family's immigration, taught Gabriel the tailor trade, and given him work in his tailor shop. After five months of concerted effort and approaching his thirteenth birthday, Carl had learned enough English from Peckville's kindhearted postmistress, librarians at the hole-in-the-wall local library, Saturday-afternoon motion pictures, and comic strips to begin first grade at Peckville Elementary School in January 1925. Having mastered sufficient additional vocabulary, he was promoted to second grade a month later. He was proficient enough in English to begin fifth grade in September. Two weeks before the school year's end in 1926, after progressing from grade to grade, he had reached the first semester of eighth grade in Peckville, so he was able to start the second semester in September 1926 at North Scranton Junior High—in the West Side neighborhood where his parents had just moved. One year later, after only four years in the United States, Gabriel Marzani—through ingenuity and frugality—bought a small house and opened his own tailor shop next door, within two blocks of the junior high. No longer skipping grades now that he had caught up in age with his classmates, Carl began the school's ninth grade at age fifteen in the spring of 1927. He graduated with the second-highest grade-point average in his 9A class.[16]

When Carl Marzani entered Central High as a sophomore in February 1928, he was among other first-generation immigrants at the school, but Marzani thought of himself as "*the* immigrant," the freshest off the boat and with the thickest accent. Nevertheless, he quickly found a place in the heterogeneous student body reflecting Scranton's mosaic. Like Kay Schoen, Carl Marzani lived on the West Side, although in the North Scranton neighborhood, walked to Central, and also had the culm dumps etched in his memory: "mountains of black slag . . . [that] hemmed in the view," he wrote. Central's pupils came primarily from Scranton's neighborhoods, ranging in character from the heavily ethnic South Side to the central-city courts, where many African Americans and Jewish immigrants lived, to the northern edge of Green Ridge, home to students like Gertrude Mattes, who had gone to private school, like the scions of the founding-father Scranton family. For most of Central High's student body, their schooling came at no cost whatsoever. Pennsylvania's free textbook law, enacted in 1893, required the school district to furnish all books and school supplies without any expense to residents. A small contingent of parents of children from Scranton's adjacent boroughs or outlying towns was willing to pay the very reasonable annual tuition of roughly $75 for the high-caliber education at Central. Interestingly, Central had the reputation—which scanning lists of students' names would seem to support—of having a disproportionately higher percentage of Jews than in the city's general population, perhaps reflecting their culture's especially strong emphasis on academic achievement.[17]

This diverse array of students' socioeconomic backgrounds included a handful of rich kids, like the entitled daughter—in Carl's grade—of the lawyer who owned the gas station that employed Carl Marzani as well as kids such as Robert Lynott, Jane's eighth-grade classmate, whose family fell into terrible financial straits. Robert left

Central after his first semester, having completed only his gym, health education, and freshman general science classes, with barely passing grades. The majority of students, however, were somewhere on the economic spectrum between the two extremes. Carl was well aware of class differences among the student population, but he was struck by the equal treatment principals and teachers afforded to all. "In class and after-school activities, working-class children like myself," Carl wrote, "rubbed shoulders with the sons and daughters of investment bankers. The only favoritism shown by our middle-class teachers was toward those students who worked hard. Because the school system was so excellent, very few of the wealthy sent their children to private schools."[18]

Jane, Carl, and Barbara Gelder all fondly remembered Miss Louise Howitz, a teacher still in her twenties when Jane and Carl were at Central High. The daughter of Charles Howitz, a special tax agent for a coal company and treasurer of the Green Ridge Presbyterian Church, Miss Howitz, like others on the Central faculty, had been an honor-roll student at Central High. She graduated about 1920 and went on to Bryn Mawr College. She continued to live in Jane's Dunmore neighborhood and belong to the same church as the Butzners. Miss Howitz had begun her long career in education as a public-speaking teacher and drama coach (also called "oral expression"). Howitz was "an incredible teacher of English and social studies!" Barbara exclaimed. "She would give a topic each week about which to write a three- to five-page essay, with such imaginative topics as 'elbows' or 'teacups.' This all added up to a lot of practice in writing." In addition, Miss Howitz taught a class called Problems of Democracy, analyzing politics, propaganda, and communications. "Her exams encouraged students to think, with four or five ads to comment on, based on what they had studied. And," Barbara added, "before Christmas, she would read aloud a Christmas story that would absolutely enthrall you."[19]

Louise Howitz, whom Carl referred to as "our dramatic director" because she oversaw Central's Thespis Dramatic Club, went to great lengths to find roles for him in the sophisticated and well-attended high school theatrical productions presented each fall. Following his successful debut in the nonspeaking but histrionic role as a Chinese murder victim, she cast him as the eponymous debonair lead in Booth Tarkington's *Monsieur Beaucaire* largely because she decided his heavy accent would lend credibility to the French-speaking character. Concerned afterward that she had exploited Carl's foible instead of helping to remedy it, "Louise tutored [Carl] daily in a nook of the library," giving him lists of words they called "dems and doses" to practice enunciating. Carl likened himself to Eliza Doolittle in George Bernard Shaw's *Pygmalion* and expressed gratitude to Miss Howitz for improving his speech so that it was "as crisp as any WASP's."[20]

Of the sixty or so faculty members, one of the "two preeminent teachers" at Central in the late 1920s and early 1930s, Carl Marzani maintained, was Professor Michael H. Jordan, "nearing seventy and refus[ing] to retire . . . a formidable old man of huge proportions—hands like baseball mitts." Jordan had begun his career in 1889 in the local public grade schools, before teaching at Dunmore High and at St. Thomas College for a brief time. The school board appointed Jordan vice principal of Central in 1906, and two years later had considered him for superintendent of all public schools. His title of "Professor" indicated he had earned an advanced degree. Professor Jordan also headed Central's math department, with its dozen instructors, although he taught only advanced algebra. This seasoned veteran had been a teacher to all Scrantonians on the faculty when Carl and Jane were there, including the principal, Dr. John H. Dyer. With his office close to the main entrance, Jordan "kept an eye on everything and was held in awe." From Carl's first year at Central, Professor Jordan took a special interest in him. He pulled Carl aside to inform him that colleges frequently provided scholarships to students in need—a most welcome revelation to this foreigner unfamiliar with the American educational system—and recommended he concentrate on after-school activities during his last semester of senior year. Carl credited Professor Jordan with having "steered him to Williams College."[21]

Among the students, rumors abounded that Central's longtime vice principal—whose aunt was a nun—had never married, had trained to be a man of the cloth but flunked out, and carried a torch for a woman who had spurned him. Little did they know that Michael H. Jordan was born in August 1868 to Irish immigrants, the fourth of eight surviving children, and grew up in a patch community on Shanty Hill in Carbondale, where his father labored in the mines. At twenty-one, Michael Jordan had married Elizabeth, the daughter of two German immigrants, and they raised three children. The vice principal kept his origins and personal life to himself, which allowed the rumors to flourish. After years of renting in Scranton's working-class neighborhoods, he was able to buy a house in Dunmore's fine Hollywood section, where, after he was widowed in the 1930s, he lived with his married daughter Mercedes O'Brien and her husband and children. When the school year ended, Professor Jordan headed up Scranton's summer school program, open to students in all years at Tech and Central and to ninth graders at North Scranton Junior High who had failed their June exams. Held at Central five mornings a week for six weeks, the summer session allowed only so-called delinquents to attend, with a chance to take "the delinquent exams at the end of August" and thus proceed to the next grade or to graduate. When Professor Jordan finally retired in 1936, after forty-seven years, a *Scranton Republican* editorial proclaimed him "a man of striking appearance, fine address, courtesy and charm of manner" and "one of the widely known and most successful among local educators."[22]

Carl considered an English teacher named Miss Adelaide Hunt the other preeminent teacher at Central High School. Miss Hunt had graduated from Central in 1910 and had gone on to Wilson College in Chambersburg, Pennsylvania, the college that declined admission to the more than qualified Dottie Smith on racial grounds. In her late thirties, Adelaide Hunt resided in a large, comfortable house in the Green Ridge neighborhood with her mother and father, a vice president of a local bank, who had worked his way up from cashier. Carl remembered Miss Hunt as "a very attractive woman, just short of beautiful . . . and she was very fond of me. She had a car, a Pontiac coupe. . . . We would go for long rambling rides, always with a justification—to look at the fall colors, the fresh snow, the first crocuses of spring. . . ." She took pleasure in matching her favorite students with one another and succeeded in forging fast friendships. With this end in mind, Miss Hunt arranged for Eugene Morley, from the class of 1927—a brilliant former student of literature and editor of the school's *Impressions* magazine—to meet Carl, who was three years his junior. After high school, Eugene had moved to New York's Greenwich Village to become a painter—although Miss Hunt had counted on his becoming a writer—and live a bohemian life. Carl passed long hours in the salonlike atmosphere of Miss Hunt's living room, talking over tea with two of her other favorite students, Jack Duro, the son of a lace-factory worker, who became a pianist and composer, and Harriet Voris, an aspiring poet and painter, and daughter of a stockbroker.[23]

For some time, Miss Hunt and her colleague Miss Howitz had teamed up to dissuade Carl from pursuing what they felt would be a dull career in science and gently guided the young scholar toward becoming a writer, which they saw as a more fitting, creative, and rewarding profession for him. Although Carl had signed up for Central's Scientific course of study because he was good at math and science, he was well read and passionate about literature and drama. "They thought they had a budding Sinclair Lewis or Maxwell Anderson on their hands," Carl scoffed, adding that he had never really written much of anything. Despite the stock market crash on October 29, 1929, and the start of the Great Depression—and Scranton's hard times preceding this—these teachers held the work of writers and other artists in high regard and encouraged their students whose talents lay in this arena.[24]

In late December 1930, with Carl as the number-three student in the high school and his graduation only a month away, Professor Michael Jordan weighed in on the young man's future. Jordan acknowledged Carl's facility with math, but he was of the opinion that Carl "might make a good novelist or dramatist." With enough good scientists around, the country needed more good writers. Concluding that the most pressing task at the moment, however, was to find Carl a top-notch liberal arts college "to broaden his mind," Professor Jordan reached into his desk drawer and pulled out two college application forms. Both Hamilton and Williams College accepted Carl with unusual speed, likely due to Professor Jordan's relationships with them. Williams, which offered the more attractive scholarship, stipulated that Carl complete a third year of Latin before entering in the fall. Because the magnanimous Latin teacher met with him every day all day throughout June, Carl "nail[ed] down the scholarship with full tuition and dormitory room." The "boy from the slag heaps and dilapidated working-class houses of North Scranton," Carl recounted, was on his way to one of the best colleges and, ultimately, to becoming a writer.[25]

In his memoir, Carl wrote that he had read and admired Jane's books before he discovered that the author was his high school friend Jane Butzner, writing under her married name of Jane Jacobs. Although they were two years apart in school and four in age, Jane and Carl had been together in classes and were well acquainted through after-school activities. They both had strong opinions and no problem expressing unorthodox views. Like Jane, Carl was an astute observer of his physical environment and the people and culture around him. He was dismayed by the "violence [that] was endemic to America," which he experienced at the hands of young toughs acting as "self-appointed mentors of street mores," and the struggles between socioeconomic classes and coal bosses and miners. All those years later, Carl "remembered [Jane as being] on the tall side, a bit gawky and socially shy, but very assertive in class." They struck up a correspondence in their old age. Carl was thrilled when Jane wrote a letter to him complimenting his first volume of *The Education of a Reluctant Radical* quartet: "*Roman Holiday* is terrific. I look forward to the next volume in the series." Carl mused in the second book, *Growing Up American*, "Such praise [as Jane's] is balm to a writer's soul." The two Central schoolmates of vastly different backgrounds shared similar views, preferring the least amount of government and abhorring the brutality of the coal company police and state troopers protecting the nonunion "scabs" during coal strikes.[26]

Although Jane's grades would never land her at the top of her class or even on the honor roll, her Central classmate J. Milton Swartz and schoolmate Miriam Parker, a couple of years behind her, both remembered her as "really smart." Consistent with her attitudes in grammar school, Jane preferred reading and thinking on her own to studying for tests and trying to achieve good grades. If a particular subject and the way it was taught piqued her interest, she worked diligently on her assignments. Her highest marks were in English and history. Judging from the grades she received, junior year European history must have riveted her, but math courses, Latin, and French did not. Jane would later regale her children with the tale of "going to war with the French teacher," who demanded that students reel off the French word for the image on the cards she held up, or face the consequences. When Jane's turn came, the teacher showed a picture of a car. Jane thought quickly and replied brazenly, "Chevrolet coupé!" Apparently, Jane's cleverness and wit allowed her to get off on a technicality and spared her the teacher's wrath. Often in high school, Jane felt frustrated and impatient. One day, bored to tears, she told her niece Nancy McBride, she walked out of the school and sat on the hill by herself, looking out over downtown, with city neighborhoods beyond. She was observing and contemplating the subject that most intrigued her, and later would connect so many of her interests.[27]

Dr. Butzner recognized and fostered Jane's wide-ranging curiosity. At home, as a high school student, Jane would sit out of sight at the top of the stairs until the wee hours of the morning, listening to her father and his colleagues' discussions in the parlor below. One time, her father had a guest from the University of Virginia, someone he had gone to medical school with. The two doctors mulled over mental illness, the friend's specialty. At other times, four or five doctors convened. During these informal meetings, the doctors considered unusual and original medical ideas. They pondered such topics as whether cancer was one disease or many, and they rejected

Freud's fashionable theories that psychiatric disorders, like manic depression, were solely of experiential origins. They agreed that mental illness might have a chemical or organic basis. Dr. Butzner didn't mind letting Jane listen, since he was happy to talk about these ideas with her, but he felt his colleagues might have found it odd to have a young teenager witnessing their debates.[28]

In a remark that could have applied to Jane at any point in her life, Jason Epstein, her friend and lifelong editor, while trying to conjure up Jane, told a 2011 gathering, "Jane was very strong-minded. She knew exactly where she was going and how to get there. And she had a real gift for saying what she meant." Jane's father, along with the women in her family, the Girl Scouts, and the culture in high school and the city, reinforced her self-assuredness. "The years when I was growing up, in the 1920s, were not like the 1950s," Jane told journalist Mark Feeney. "I did grow up with the idea that women could do things, and in my own family I was treated much the same as my brothers. . . . The male-domination thing affected me externally, and I resented it. But I didn't resent it in this corrosive way because it wasn't affecting me internally."[29]

Enough of Jane's teachers and peers perceived her intelligence, powers of reasoning, and strength as a writer that she became a star student in her own way—rather than by being on the honor roll. She was sufficiently confident not to care about doing well in school but to pursue her interests, especially reading and writing. Jane's mother, however, expressed disappointment with Jane's academic achievement. "Jane would take her report card to her father first," Kay had heard. "If it wasn't very good, he was more likely to be sympathetic." The report for the school year 1929–1930 of days absent and days tardy conveys Jane's lack of enthusiasm for school. Compared to the future class valedictorian, Charles Moesel, who was never absent or tardy, Jane missed eight days of school and was late eleven times. By commencement, the school ranked Jane as ninety-eighth in the class, with a grade-point average of 80.73, which landed her right in the middle of the 198-person graduating class. In other words, Jane was a perfectly average student, quite a remarkable feat for someone who made limited scholastic effort. Furthermore, "[t]he Class of January, 1933, ha[d] maintained an unusually high grade of scholarship during their course in Central," the school magazine noted in December 1932. "Fourteen per cent of their number has been on the honor roll for four years." In 1933—the year of Jane's graduation from Central and the worst of the Depression—a friend asked Jane's mother what was the most difficult thing she had done that year. "Getting Jane to graduate," she replied.[30]

The school's extracurricular activities—an assortment of clubs, dramatic performances, musical groups, school publications, and athletic teams—did, however, appeal to Jane. Besides the daily roster of academic classes, these additional offerings provided an important aspect of a student's education. Some activities actually took place during the school day, while others occurred after classes ended at 3:30 P.M. Virtually all students participated in these voluntary pursuits. A student editorial in *Impressions* expressed an opinion held by many schoolmates: "Every student in the school who enjoys physical recreation in an organized way is almost sure to find some athletic niche into which he can fit. The various art organizations in the school, such as the Dramatic Club, the Writing Club, the Book Club, the Orchestra, all afford an ample field upon which the student may satisfy his ambitions. The student who neglects to take part in any of the scholastic activities misses some of the finest and best things in school life by so doing." These activities brought students from all years and graduating classes together and comprised a wealth of learning experiences. The brief profiles of graduating high school seniors proudly listed the student's club affiliations and whether s/he was one of the officers. Central High School did have some sororities and fraternities, but they attracted only a tiny portion of students and were viewed as exclusive. Kay decided to join one because she "was asked to" and went to their monthly meetings "but that was about it." Neither Jane nor her brothers belonged. Marie Van Bergen recalled rather disdainfully that Hugh Ellsworth Rodham—the future father of Hillary Rodham Clinton —who was a couple of years ahead of her, "was known as a frat boy."[31]

Within the microcosm of the school, clubs were added or discontinued according to demand. The Book Club started in fall 1930 with avid readers and budding reviewers, and a year later was given its own "Back Shelf" page, dedicated to the subject of books, in *Impressions.* Jane signed up for Book Club and, later, both her brothers were elected officers. A year later, the Chess Club began with tournaments scheduled and twenty eager members. "Under the guidance of Mr. Quevedo," head of the Spanish department, several students formed the Archery Club, of which John Butzner was elected secretary. Pupils excited by whichever language they were studying—French, Spanish, German, or Latin—might join the respective club. The French Club held annual Christmas meetings, and the Spanish Club presented a Spanish play in the auditorium. Washington #1 alumna Florence Osterland became a member and eventually vice president of the German Club. She and her classmate George Munchak took part in the school orchestra, while Kay and Anna Manno—each a musician's daughter—were in the band together. Kay's mother played piano, and Anna's mother was a cellist and singer well known in the city. Band practice took place after school and sometimes lasted so late that Kay's father, having finished work in his lab two blocks away, walked them home. Other of their musical friends sang in the school Glee Club and chorus.[32]

The "many successful amateur theatricals" staged by the Thespis Dramatic Club created quite a stir in the school, the city, and the press. Each year in late fall, thespians, under Miss Howitz's direction, put together a first-rate production of a notable play. In Jane's senior year, she and many other girls and boys from all years auditioned for roles in Shaw's *The Devil's Disciple*, an irreverent play that would "require special attention" in costuming, staging, scenery, and lighting. The shows were so highly anticipated that students and Reisman's bookstore sold tickets in advance. The city's newspapers apprised their readers of casting decisions and the progress of rehearsals, and ran photos and reviews of the performances. The much-admired Miss Howitz selected Jane Butzner (in the role of Mrs. Titus Dudgeon) as a member of the large cast, as well as her brother John, in his sophomore year, who also helped on the properties committee. Florence Osterland had a minor part and chaired the publicity committee. An appreciator of good theater, Jane acted in quite a few plays both at school and in Girl Scouts. She enjoyed bringing literature to life as well as the camaraderie of the process.[33]

In her junior year, in December 1931, the high school magazine listed Jane among the seven "especially active members" of the newly formed Writing Club. Two other club members were her eighth-grade lunchtime, city-exploring buddy June Carter and their new friend John F. Kane, both half a year ahead of Jane in school. The Kanes had emigrated in the 1860s from Ireland's County Mayo and settled in Minooka—a township adjacent to Scranton's South Side and the site of the Greenwood Colliery, employer to the predominantly Irish population that settled there. John's father had died before John turned five, so he lived on the South Side with his Irish-born grandmother, his mother, and an uncle, who supported the household as an agent for the DL&W Railroad. At Central, John shined as a writer, playwright, and actor. For May Day in 1932, Writing Club stalwarts John Kane, Jane Butzner, June Carter, and James McAndrew—one of the five sons of Kay Schoen's next-door neighbors—tackled a controversial topic for presentation in the auditorium before the entire student body. They must have had much fun coauthoring what even the conservative *Scranton Republican* applauded as "an entertaining program depicting May Day in old and contemporary New England and in modern Russia." Introducing the play's three scenes, another club member explained the origin of the Soviet Union's public holiday, begun in 1918, known as the Day of International Solidarity with Workers, an occasion that had sparked sympathetic celebrations worldwide. Generally, Writing Club members wrote and staged plays and provided the bulk of the material for *Impressions*, the school literary and news magazine, which had evolved from the school newspaper at least a decade earlier.[34]

The city took a keen interest in *Impressions*, the premier student publication of the superb classical high school. The roughly forty-page (half text, half advertisements providing revenue) glossy

Cover of *Impressions* magazine, Nov. 1932. Courtesy
of Donna Zaleski, Scranton High School Library.

bound magazine, with artful covers designed by students, appeared
six times a year. *The Scranton Republican* regularly disseminated news
and editorials about the contents, staffing changes, and production
of this publication. One of its editorials praised the November 1931
issue, "notable for its big [Christmas] advertising display and . . . a
very fine tribute to Dr. Albert H. Welles," Central's longtime principal, who had recently died. It also specified five contributors to
look for: Jane Butzner, June Carter, and James McAndrew among
them. A few months later, demonstrating it kept a close eye on the
magazine, the morning paper reported, "[*Impressions's*] contents show
a vast improvement due to . . . bimonthly meetings . . . by the staff
and several of the faculty to assist the students in the publication."
Available to all students and anyone willing to pay the seventy-five

cents for a year's subscription, the magazine presented poems, stories, book reviews, interviews, school and athletic news, class and alumni notes, and pensive editorials. Because the publication's circulation hovered at only five hundred, an editorial expressed hope that soon "every student [would] be an 'Impressions' supporter." Finally, in 1933, during Jane's graduation year, Central won second place in the Columbia Scholastic Press Association's national competition of student newspapers and magazines by classical high schools. With this honor and a charitable subsidy of forty cents per subscription, *Impressions's* number of subscribers soared to eighteen hundred.[35]

A dedicated and tireless group of students, working together with a common passion, made the magazine's success possible. Carl Marzani was one of these devotees voluntarily staying late at school to produce an issue. Miss Adelaide Hunt, Miss Jeannette Evans, and Mr. Robert Hughes, faculty advisers to *Impressions*, offered guidance and a sounding board. In December 1931, John Kane was elected assistant editor and then editor in chief the following spring. Other editorial positions covered alumni news, athletics, and class news, although no staff focused on poetry or humor. Despite the increased popularity and quality of *Impressions*, the editors and advisers of the "magazine of and for the student" had to exhort students for submissions.[36]

Like her fellow *Impressions* enthusiasts and poetesses Florence Osterland, June Carter, and Betty Toatley, Jane responded to this plea. Toward the end of Jane's junior year, her writing, in the form of a poem, first appeared in the school magazine. The sophisticated verse, titled "There Are So Many Things I Love," gathered images from nature to evoke her desire for experience beyond the path to or through school. She revealed: ". . . But always have I loved the water best. / Small puddles, token of a rainy day, / Have always lured me from my schoolward way." Fifteen-year-old Jane had also entered this poem in the Girl Scouts' *American Girl* poetry contest, open to any female reader (not necessarily a Girl Scout) of the magazine. Three winning entries would be printed in *American Girl's* November issue, and books were cited as prizes. The call for entries entreated girls to first carefully read their article "Why Poetry?"—which de-

scribed poems as "thoughts flowering into lovely and colorful words
. . . [that] should be set away to cool after they are written." Girls
should avoid "what someone has termed 'O Thou poems'—rhap-
sodic ravings without any spine." From a larger-than-expected pool
of "quality" poems, Jane's verse garnered third prize. The judges
were well-recognized poets: Joseph Auslander, who would become
the Library of Congress's first poetry consultant (a position that became the poet laureate); the National Girl Scouts' president at that
time, Mrs. Frederick Edey (Sarah Birdsall Otis), also a published
poet; and one other poet. Auslander noted that the second- and third-
place winners "press[ed] each other closely. . . . Miss Butzner's poem
is very good, indeed; but it suffers from an overcrowding of material
and an unnecessary, flat couplet." They awarded Jane a copy of Sara
Teasdale's *Stars Tonight*.[37]

The city's newspapers continually kept track of, recognized, and
commended its young people for their accomplishments. Three
months after *The American Girl* printed Jane's winning poem, *The
Scranton Republican* announced another honor for the young Central
student and for a recent Central graduate: "Miss Jane Butzner and
Miss Harriet Voris, two of the city's most promising poets, have one
and three poems respectively in an anthology of verse compiled by
Nellie B. Sergent, teacher in the department of English, Evander
Childs High School, New York." For her four-hundred-plus-page
book, *Younger Poets: An Anthology of American Secondary School Verse*,
Sergent selected student writers from "all the states, Alaska, and Ha-
waii, and twenty-two different nationalities," and printed the name of
each student's school and a short biography of the student, based on
Sergent's inquiries. Jane's verse "Fairy Tales" appeared in the section
of poems about "Childhood": "Fiery dragons, hoary, old, / Ancient
treasures, hidden gold. / Woven into mystic veil, / Named and called
a fairy tale." From whatever answers Jane had offered, Sergent noted
that Jane's ancestors were of English, Scottish, Dutch, and German
descent, most arriving in the late seventeenth century. Her paternal
and maternal grandfathers had fought on opposite sides in the Civil
War. "Her ambition is to be a writer. . . ."[38]

Like *Younger Poets*, the *American Girl* article "Why Poetry?" recommended that girls steep themselves in fine poetry. Above all, they should read the works of several poets, among them Rupert Brooke, a twenty-seven-year-old British Great War casualty and one of Jane's most beloved poets. Her poem "To Rupert Brooke" won Central's Book Week Contest and appeared in *Impressions* in December 1931. After articulating her frustration when writing verse, in this poem she declared, "—And then I read your poems; they give birth / To glorious exultation, boundless dreams; / I hope and strive again; you give me food. / For man, they say, has conquered air and earth, / But by a poet stars have been subdued."[39]

After Jane had submitted to and worked on *Impressions* for a year, the staff revised its organizational structure and established editorial positions for a poetry editor and a humor editor. They elected Jane the magazine's first poetry editor and initially credited her as such in the November 1932 issue, although she may have taken the lead in vetting poems before this. *Impressions* gave Jane her first experience as an editor. Relishing the role, she added an erudite and humorous subtitle to the poetry page, which sent many readers to the dictionary: "Expressions: A Poetaster's [an inferior poet with pretensions] Paradise." She not only chose the poems on the double-page spread but introduced the verses by addressing her readers and engaging them in her process: "It is common knowledge that the more difficult a thing is to compose, the more easily it seems to have been written. I hope that as you read this it conjures visions of long yellow pencils, easy chairs, and potted plants on window sills. As a matter of fact, my pencil is a stubby, chewed affair, and I am using a typewriter anyway. I am sitting on the floor, and the window sill is hardly wide enough to support the papers with which it is burdened. But I am surrounded by smiles of the Muse, and so am happy (and amused)."[40]

Enjoying the opportunity of her new appointment, the cleverly rebellious Jane placed her own poem "To a Teacher" in the December 1932 issue. Something of a rebuke, the final two lines of the short verse contained the zinger: "Without a light to help explore, / Some

And Still More Expressions

L'APRES MIDI d'UN FAUNE

With Apologies to Claude Debussy
Gershon Legman

Upon the rolling pleasant lawn
Of a decrepit manse in ruin,
There stood a bronze-cast deity,
Who sweetly piped his muted tune

A little child with joyous cries
And bubbling laughs a garland threw
Around the satyr's neck, and danced
About this monster thrice her size
And laughed with eyes of sky-like blue.

A dog that drank the bitter dregs
Of anger at a fine feast's theft,
Upon the figure vent its wrath;
Snapped at the faun's unfeeling legs,
And then with downcast mien it left.

A sad and sorrowing road back
From some loved grave I saw traced then.
The mourner sighs before the faun
And seemed to hear a dirge so black
From its reed pipes—'tis hard to pen.

Two lovers arm in arm went by,
Of love's sweet cup they took fond sips;
They saw the faun, together smiled.
(That love as Pan might never die!)
And sealed their love with press of lips.

The laughing, joyant, childhood path;
The puny hate of helpless wrath;
The mourner's soulful, doleful sigh;
Love's all enrapt ecstatic cry;
The homely sentiment and thought—
All these before the faun were brought.

On a flight with a coy sort of miss,
An airman attempted to kiss,
She faintly resisted,
But still he insisted.
¡¡¡¡siɥʇ ǝʞıl sɐʍ ǝlɐʇ ǝɥʇ ɟo puǝ ǝɥꞱ

TO-NIGHT

Betty Lou Toatley

Night!
How I wait for you to come,
So I can wander off,
Beneath the stars, my dull thoughts flee.
The friendly shadows of the trees,
Around me close their arms so tight
And yet so loose that I can flee.
I wonder at the darkness of the night,
The stars, the moon, the earth.
How beautiful is night.

DAWN

Betty Lou Toatley

I love to see you come,
Sweet Child of Dawn,
Soft in your gauzy gown
All scattered with diamonds.
I'm glad to see you go
When daylight comes,
I wait impatiently
To be alone again,
With shadows and the stars.

APRIL

Jane Butzner

I looked into a crystal pool
And searched the limits of the sky.
I saw a cloud all whitely cool
Throw kisses as the sun went by.

How could I help but fall in love
With anyone or anything?
With sky below and sky above,
And all the ecstasies of spring?

There was a man
With careless feet,
Who tried to cross
A busy street;
There was a man—

Page with poems by Gershon Legman, Betty Toatley,
and Jane Butzner, *Impressions* magazine, May 1932.
Courtesy of Donna Zaleski, Scranton High School Library.

things seem clearer than before." In the same issue, *Impressions* also printed several of Jane's short stories and an interview—in essay rather than conversational form—with Joseph Auslander, the poet and a judge for the *American Girl* poetry competition. Jane did not let the reader know the circumstances of her encounter with Auslander, but she made no attempt to damp down her delight: "To meet a man who can speak so beautifully and so truthfully is, in my eyes, like meeting Orpheus himself." Auslander told Jane, "It is the dreamers who have found the solutions before, and it is the dreamers who will find them again; our hope is in the poets. It is the poets who see the beauty in the machine age, and it is the poets who grant rescue from the machines. . . ." Offering advice that Jane could apply to disciplines other than poetry, Auslander stated, ". . . if [young poets] find a need for new forms, they should create them; but forms should never be made merely for the sake of modernity. . . ." Jane concluded the interview by asking "the question . . . nearest my heart, and by which I judge mankind," whether Auslander liked Rupert Brooke. "I adore him," he replied.[41]

The "smiles of the Muse" to which Jane referred in her poetry page's introduction were the verses she selected from fellow students. Because she repeatedly chose poems by Betty Lou Toatley and Gershon Legman, they must have been among her favorite Central High poets. Betty composed mellifluous poems based in nature and tending toward free verse, with titles such as "Dawn" and "Clouded Day." Gershon penned wry observations, as in "L'Après Midi d'Un Faune: With Apologies to Claude Debussy," and clever humor, in an untitled limerick. Gershon was a year behind Jane at Central, of Eastern European Jewish origin, and had been valedictorian of Scranton's William Prescott grammar-school class. His father, a clerk for the DL&W Railroad, had arrived from Austria-Hungary in 1907, as had his mother a year later. They hoped their son would be a rabbi. Swearing off college for autodidacticism, Gershon would bring origami to North America in the early 1950s and open "the field of erotic folklore to scholarly study." In adulthood, Jane followed this audacious renegade in the newspapers and kept in touch with him through letters.[42]

Betty Toatley—who was two years older than Jane, a semester behind her, and in the Classical course—had come to Scranton from South Carolina with her parents, two brothers, and uncles in the late nineteen teens. Like a good number of Scranton's African Americans, they had originally lived in the courts, but became "street dwellers" by the time Betty was in high school. Her father worked as a chauffeur and then a mechanic, while her uncles labored in a textile mill. Betty was particularly active in the Progressive Center (as was her father), the YWCA, the Girl Scouts, and the Bethel AME and Westminster Presbyterian churches. In January 1936, Betty Toatley and Jane's brother John—after each had graduated from Central— took part in a young people's panel discussion at the seventh annual Mid-Winter Institute at the Elm Park Methodist Episcopal Church on "What's Wrong and What's Right in Our City?" Representing "Gentiles and the Jews, the white and the colored races," *The Scranton Republican* reported, the panelists discussed the economic future of young people in the Scranton area. "John Butzner declared that the city provides little or no opportunity for the employment of youth in work which they could accept as a career. While admitting that this condition was general throughout the country, he was of the opinion that young people should not look so much to the established industries, such as coal and silk, but should direct their efforts into bringing new industrial plants to the city," the newspaper continued. "Betty Toatley gave an expression of the colored youth's problem. She said that colored boys and girls cannot find employment, no matter what their education, except in positions as servants. She said further that colored families are forced to live in the courts of the city." Betty's words and forthrightness no doubt moved John, who would devote his life's work to civil rights.[43]

Not only clubs and *Impressions* but also athletics assumed a major role in the lives of Central High School students. The school gym could not accommodate all sports classes, practices, and matches, but the city's Weston Field was only a mile away. "Weston Field [was] a large athletic park with two baseball diamonds, three tennis courts, a swimming pool, and a fine gym with a regulation-size basketball court," wrote Carl Marzani, who frequented the facilities. "In winter the tennis courts were flooded for ice skating and hockey. Weston Field was located on valuable land between North Scranton and the city center. It was named for the philanthropist whose money had built it, but its many acres had been donated by the municipality. . . . I think of its tennis courts, then rare in public parks, opening an upper-class sport to working-class kids like myself." Some tennis fans showed up to watch, but football, the passion of northeastern Pennsylvania—played at Memorial Stadium, on the way to Weston Field from Central—drew big crowds of students and parents. Kay's father, Carl Schoen, a Central alum, class of 1905, was a regular at the games. Jane often cheered in the stands at the school football games. "Being tennis players, neither John nor Jim played football," Kay reported, "but they attended. Everybody did."[44]

There was a spirited rivalry against Tech High School in football, and emotions ran particularly high when Central played Tech on Thanksgiving Day. The climactic game marked the end of the season. Kay played trumpet in the marching band, which performed at all the football games. It was so cold by the Central-Tech game that her lips would stick to the trumpet. "One time Jane was standing and cheering for the team and someone behind her yelled, 'Sit down in front.'" Kay laughed. "She was always quick with a retort, so Jane shot back, 'I'm not made that way.' In other words, she couldn't bend forward 'in front.'" Dr. and Mrs. Butzner showed up for some of the girls' swimming team's matches at Weston Field pool, where Jane often excelled. Perhaps they witnessed her victory at the end of her senior year, when she came in first in the hundred-yard breaststroke. Girls could also compete in intramural basketball, a volleyball tournament, an indoor track meet, an archery contest, and indoor baseball.[45]

Through athletics, extracurricular activities, and classes, Jane made new friends at Central, but she also mingled with old friends from Girl Scouts. Mary Oellgaard, a "tuition student" from the more affluent outlying town of Clarks Summit, whom Jane knew from Camp Archbald, was on the *Impressions* news staff and in Book Club with her. Jane teasingly dubbed Mary's father, a real estate manager

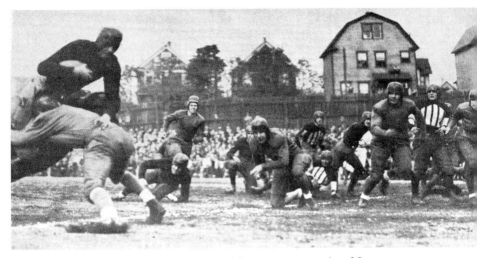

"Central . . . Defeating Dunmore, 12–6," *Impressions* magazine, Nov. 1931.
Courtesy of Donna Zaleski, Scranton High School Library.

born in Denmark whose first name was Axel, "Oily Axel Guard."
High school girls who continued scouting—and only a small but ardent group did—earned a new designation: "Senior Scouts." Scranton
had only "one older girls' troop," national headquarters reported,
Senior Troop 31, which met in central city at the Westminster Presbyterian Church, drawing girls in high school or older from all over
the city. Jane was one, along with her former Troop 4 friends—now
Central schoolmates—Anne Safford, Gertrude Mattes, Jean Patterson, Gladys Baumann, and Lucille Parsons. Troop 31's captain was
Mrs. Warren Edson, who lived in the Green Ridge neighborhood and
was married to a civil engineer. Her lieutenants, later called "assistant leaders," were Jane Butzner, Gertrude Mattes, and Lois Dakin,
a graduate of Wells College, near Ithaca, New York. Senior troop
members continued to work on merit badges. This group decided
on bird study, first aid, and minstrels as subjects to investigate. Introduced in 1929, the minstrel badge—despite the connotation of its
name—encouraged the study of traditional music and required learning words, melodies, and a musical instrument for playing English
and Appalachian mountain folk songs, cowboy songs, Indian songs,
and Negro spirituals.[46]

Not known for devoting her time to activities she did not enjoy, Jane, like her sister, Betty, was "very much interested in girl scout work," as she told Nellie Sergent when interviewed. Betty had been one of Scranton's first Senior Scouts. During Jane's freshman and sophomore years in high school, the Scranton Girl Scout Council hired Betty as one of two field captains, considered "important posts" as part of the executive staff, to work immediately under the local director. In September 1931, Betty went off to Philadelphia to attend the Pennsylvania Museum School of Industrial Art, but she maintained her ties with scouting by heading up a Brownie pack in that city. A month before Betty left to study interior design, Jane and Gertrude Mattes had the honor of spending two weeks at Camp Andrée Clark, the National Girl Scout camp in Briarcliff Manor, New York, where Betty had once been an instructor. Two campers from each of the forty-eight states were chosen to attend this "experimental and demonstration center" for girls fourteen years of age or older who were interested in becoming Girl Scout leaders. At Camp Andrée, Jane made a friend for life, a girl from Connecticut who shared similar interests, Miriam Camp, who, coincidentally, would later marry a man named Camps, as Jane wrote to her mother decades later. Miriam, like Jane, would go on to work for the State Department during World War II, and to write books in the 1960s on European unification.[47]

In April 1934, more than a year after her high school graduation and following in her sister's footsteps from seven years earlier, Jane joined the select few Senior Scouts who attained the Girl Scouts highest honor. In a formal ceremony complete with color guard at Girl Scout headquarters with the other Senior Girl Scouts in attendance, Jane received the Golden Eaglet emblem. Mrs. Reyburn Watres, then captain of the senior troop and a member of one of the city's wealthiest families, "presented Miss Butzner for the award, which was based on twenty-one proficiency badges in addition to those earned for the first-class Girl Scout badge, character and service to scouting and the community as a whole." The national headquarter's standards committee made the final decisions after reviewing nominations from the local councils. At their New York offices, the headquarters staff kept an index card of each and every Eaglet recipient. During the previous August at Camp Archbald, because they were about to leave for college, three of Jane's high school friends—Gladys Baumann, Lucille Parsons, and Gertrude Mattes—had also been awarded the Golden Eaglet.[48]

Before any equivalent for girls existed, the city of Scranton dedicated seven days each May to what was called "Boys' Week," part of a national movement begun in 1920, which spread to every state and major city. "This particular week is set aside . . . ," Scranton's mayor F. K. Derby proclaimed, "for developing in these boys the fundamentals of good character building for better citizenship . . . [and] advocating for every boy an equal chance and opportunity to weave his own destiny. . . ." Besides setting up the week's program for all boys, cities selected boys to serve in city government for a brief portion of a day. Based on merit, not status, Carl Marzani noted, "seniors

Carl Marzani (top row, second from left) with other
Boys' Week selectees, 1930. Author's collection.

took written tests on civic subjects, and the dozen or so top scorers served as municipal officials for one hour. I was one of them. As commissioner of public health, I sat in my office and signed various documents, then made a field inspection tour with my deputy—an adult." In 1933, during the city's fifth annual Boys' Week, "Central was again honored by having a large share of the boys' cabinet [and the office of mayor]," an *Impressions* editorial commented. "For all boys, the fellows who held no offices or positions of honor during the week, an extensive and well-mapped-out program was planned." On Monday, they could visit a local newspaper office; Tuesday, a silk mill; Wednesday, the telephone exchange; Thursday, an ice-cream factory and bakeries. The boy mayor and his cabinet were sworn in and got to ride in the police's "Black Maria," usually reserved for transporting people to jail. Friday was a "slack day," and Saturday was reserved for the Boys' Week parade, in which, in 1932, fifteen thousand boys marched. A sign of a dawning consciousness, the first annual Girls' Week was initiated in October 1933, after Jane graduated from high school.[49]

Central High students also became involved in citywide endeavors stretching well beyond the school community, especially the annual drive to collect for the Community Chest. For one week each November, Scrantonians—through churches, scouting, all levels and kinds of schools, and a vast array of organizations, as well as individuals going door-to-door—worked to fill the Community Chest with money and in-kind donations. Central students participated wholeheartedly—perhaps with extra intensity, given the pall of the Depression—and with good-natured competition between teachers and students and among homerooms, to see who could meet their quota and how quickly. *Impressions* reported on all this and noted those who went to extraordinary lengths: "The members of the Senior 'A' class showed their fine spirit when a special appeal was made to them on the Friday afternoon before the close of the drive. Each student in the graduating class willingly offered to try to sell ten tickets for the benefit of the Community Chest's Unemployment Fund. Central certainly did its best to make the Chest drive successful." Emphasizing the theme of inclusivity, a pamphlet produced by the Chest in 1922, its second year of existence—in a section called "The Greatest Week of the Year"—declared, "There is not a single individual in our midst today who does not come within the scope of the [Community Chest's] influence. Every one [in Scranton and Dunmore] either helps or is helped by it. . . . This is a work that knows neither race nor creed." The Chest's 1928 annual report expressed satisfaction in Scranton's "community cooperation" and "city pride" and having "brought together in an interdenominational corporation the Jewish, Catholic and Protestant citizens which made for broadmindedness and neighborly friendship" and "financial success of the Chest year after year." That same year, on behalf of women's

Cover of Community Chest campaign brochure,
early 1920s. Courtesy of United Way of
Lackawanna and Wayne Counties.

organizations and "girls work activities," the Chest advocated for the unprecedented hiring of a policewoman to be part of the City Bureau of Police. In 1929, I. E. Oppenheim, owner of the city's centerpiece Scranton Dry Goods department store and of Jewish background, became president of the Community Chest. Samuel Samter, C. S. Woolworth, and other of Scranton's prominent businessmen served as Chest officers or on its board of trustees.[50]

At the same time, the Community Chest provided practical educational experiences for Scranton's and Dunmore's students. A Chest committee selected forty-five students from Central, Tech, and Dunmore high schools and from Marywood and St. Thomas colleges (for women and men, respectively) to write promotional pieces for the 1931 fund-raising drive. Jane Butzner, June Carter, and Gertrude Mattes were among the nine pupils chosen from Central. At the Chamber of Commerce building, the student writers gathered for a group photograph and to hear the associate editor of *The Scranton Times*, Thomas Murphy, and member of the news staff of *The Scranton Republican* Reginald A. Williams give advice on preparing newspaper articles for Community Chest campaign publicity. Three reporters—one from each of the city's three local daily papers —would judge the articles, and "fountain pens [would] be awarded to the six students who [wrote] the best articles." This opportunity honored the young writers and served the community as well by encouraging citywide civic spirit.[51]

Like the George Washington School #1, Central High brimmed with activity well past school hours. Not only was the school auditorium used for presentations to the whole student body during the day—for example, an assembly where several Civil War veterans spoke and answered questions—but it also opened its doors to the city's population for occasions like musical performances at night. "Central's spring concert has been an annual event for a number of years," *The Scranton Republican* stated. "The school musicians [from the Glee Club and orchestra] are directed by Prof. W. W. Jones, music supervisor of the Scranton schools. The concert this year is open to all Central students, and their parents and friends. Musical organizations of the city and Parent-Teacher association have also been invited to attend." Jeanne Madden's photo adorned the article and helped draw a capacity audience. The daughter of Harry Madden, a successful singer who toured the country and owned and lived in the downtown Hotel Holland on Adams Avenue, Jeanne had earned the reputation as the "leading vocalist of the school." A classmate whom Jane considered a good friend, she sang regularly in the Glee Club, a popular extracurricular activity that included Jane's friend Gertrude Mattes and an African American schoolmate, Alice Porter. Within a few years of her graduating from Central, Scranton claimed her as the "City's Own Movie Star." On August 28, 1936, *Stage Struck*, her first film, had its world premiere in the Electric City, with Jeanne on stage at the Strand Theatre to "tell in her own words a few of her experiences in making the picture in which Joan Blondell, Dick Powell, Warren William and Frank McHugh also appear." Mayor Stanley Davis proclaimed the day as "Jeanne Madden Day" and acknowledged Scranton's "great pride in the achievement of this young star, who has brought national prominence to her home city. . . ."[52]

While Jane Butzner, Jeanne Madden, and their Central classmates progressed through high school, they could not miss observing, a half block away, the coming to fruition of the city's newest spectacular edifice, the Masonic Temple and Scottish Rite Cathedral. Jane had seen some of the city's gradual changes—individual teardowns and replacements, such as the old central post office's larger Art Deco successor—and she had read about others before her time. She knew from a bronze plaque in the Albright Library's entrance that the public-spirited industrialist John Joseph Albright had erected the central library in memory of his parents. He and his siblings— Jane Albright Bennell, Marie Albright Archbald, and Henry Clay Albright—had razed their own family homestead in 1890 and donated the site in order to create an important public institution. Along its south side remained two-story wooden shells of "old residences that had once graced North Washington Avenue." In the last several years, the Masons—a private organization of elite professionals and businessmen—had bought and demolished two of these former mansions on adjacent plots closest to the library to make way for another civic project. Although the Masons spearheaded this building project for their fraternal functions, they intended from the project's conception to make a substantial part of the more than 180,000 square feet of interior space available to the general public. High school students and all Scrantonians would have an auditorium more spacious than Central's in which to enjoy meticulously produced plays, the popular Community Concerts, and other crowd-drawing events.[53]

Because this building would be a public asset, the Masonic Temple Building Fund committee sought donations from all citizens, promoting the ideal of civic unity toward a shared goal, akin to the Community Chest drive. In an advertisement headlined "Will You Help?" the Masonic committee reasoned that "All Scranton [will] be proud of the new Masonic Temple . . . [and will] have use of the new Temple [and] its great, modern Auditorium, its banquet hall and ball room, and its splendid exhibition hall. . . ." The ad mentioned that "more than five hundred citizens [who were] not members of

Masonic Temple, by architect of New York's Radio City Music Hall, Raymond Hood, 1927–1930, rehabbed as Scranton Cultural Center, 1989. Courtesy of Lackawanna Historical Society.

the Masonic Fraternity" had already offered their financial support in the campaign. It presented quotes from editorials from each of the three city dailies—the *Republican*, the *Times*, and the *Sun*—endorsing this worthy construction project by a private but civically minded organization and urging the community's help in meeting the "Victory Quota." "No building enterprise in the history of Scranton," *The Scranton Sun* averred, "has ever held greater promise of contribution to the civic and cultural life of the city than this."[54]

In April 1927, almost three years after ground was broken, this magnificent building, with a mix of the contemporary Art Deco and the spiritually associated French Gothic Revival styles of architecture, welcomed the public into its lavish main theater. Below the bas-relief of dragons unfurling their wings, visitors passed through the sixty-five-foot-high arched entryway as they crossed the threshold of the ten-story building, four of whose floors were belowground. Inside, they admired the Roman travertine marble, Indiana limestone, ornamental plaster, chandeliers, paneling, and timbered ceilings with intricate designs. Floors were of stone, tile, and marble. Carved and stenciled Masonic iconography, such as stylized lions and eagles, bedecked walls and ceilings. Both the banquet hall and the eighteen-hundred-seat theater—two units cleverly separated by a sliding wall—were on the same floor. Combining the units made for seating for four thousand at gala events. Declaring it "a revelation in beauty and utility," the *Republican* had previewed the opening breathlessly: "At 3 o'clock Monday afternoon, the new Masonic Temple theater will open its doors to the public revealing one of the newest and most imposing theater structures in the entire United States; a theater that marks a great stride forward in the civic life of our city. Built at a cost approaching three million dollars, it stands as a monument to those whose vision, courage and civic-spirited enterprise made this magnificent edifice possible. With public service uppermost in mind, the men who planned, built and equipped the new Masonic Temple have made every provision for the comfort, safety and enjoyment of its patrons."[55]

The opulent Masonic Temple and the optimism that inspired it stood in stark contrast to the crushing times Scrantonians were experiencing. The city's economy had never fully recovered from the coal strike of 1925–1926, and the coal industry had continued to decline as demand for other fuels grew and mines closed. Men in the mines and in the coal companies' management and women in the companies' offices lost their jobs. When they could, the destitute moved in with relatives. After the stock market crash in late October 1929, during Jane's freshman year at Central and shortly before the completion of the Masonic Temple, the entire nation plunged into economic depression. Kay Schoen Butzner, who was still in grammar school on Scranton's West Side at the beginning of the Great Depression, remembered teachers calling children up to their desks and privately questioning them about what they had eaten for breakfast. Kay's father, who employed two young men at his Scranton Chemical Laboratory—which primarily analyzed the percentage of ash in coal for the industry and tested paint for lead—had to let one of them go when he lost the Glidden Paint contract. Kay had friends whose families were forced to ask the neighborhood grocer for credit in order to buy food. "I imagine grocers often absorbed these losses because their customers were never able to repay them. People couldn't pay their mortgages and lost their houses, but sometimes the bank let the family stay in the house and collected rent from them."[56]

Not only institutions and local businesspeople but also teachers and students throughout the city did what they could to help their community during the Depression. "Approximately ninety-three teachers at [Technical High] donated $3 apiece each year to aid worthy students whose parents are unable properly to care for them during their high school careers," the *Republican* reported. They succeeded in collecting more than one thousand dollars "since the plan was adopted." The fund was put toward lunches, graduation outfits, and clothes for cold weather. "Names of students receiving aid are never revealed outside of the teachers' committee," the article noted. Collecting for the Community Chest's Unemployment Fund enabled Central High School students to work to benefit the burgeoning

number of families in dire straits. The reverberations of a large segment of the population out of work touched everyone. Recalling
the Depression, Jane wrote in her last book, "For individuals, the
worst side effect of unemployment was repeated rejection, with its
burden of shame and failure. Many quietly despaired that the world
had a place for them. . . . Few of my father's patients were able to
pay him, as the effects of mass unemployment spread." In the November 1932 issue of *Impressions*, the editor, William Bayless—whom
the school had voted most outstanding pupil and whose father was
president of the Pennsylvania Appraisal Company—felt compelled
to confront the spreading and worsening of hard times: "Within the
past few years, our country, and every other country upon earth, has
been thrown into the midst of economic and social chaos, the like
of which has never been known before." In the upcoming national
and state elections, he advised, people should vote for the candidate
they believe in, not who they think can win. "The status of the world
today has brought into the political limelight many minor parties."
The editor urged students "that we closely follow the happenings of
the next few months upon the political front."[57]

On January 26, 1933, in an uncharacteristically somber commencement address, Scranton's school superintendent (and Central's
former principal), Dr. John H. Dyer, warned Central's graduating
seniors that they faced "exceptionally difficult economic problems."
Two evenings before, he had told Tech's graduates "the world's economic machinery is out of gear." Although Central's auditorium was
festooned with the customary blue and gold lights, of the 302 students who had entered Central in February 1929 alongside Jane or
joined the class from North Scranton Junior High a year later as
sophomores, approximately a third had dropped out or moved away,
and a few would graduate during the upcoming year. Only 105 boys
and 93 girls received their diplomas that night, and a mere half of
these students would go on to college.[58]

Jane Butzner and Jeanne Madden were among the dozen or so
students chosen to participate in the graduation program. Jane, although not an academic star, was a recognized literary talent and

Jane's high school friend Jeanne Madden, mid-1930s. Courtesy of Marnie Azzarelli.

Jane's high school graduation photo, January 1933. Estate of Jane Jacobs.

someone to whom students looked for leadership and ingenuity. She presented an imaginative and entertaining class prophecy, and Jeanne performed the class songs exquisitely. Charles Moesel delivered the valedictory address. From a working-class German family, son of a harness-shop manager, Charles was a well-rounded student in the Scientific course and achieved a 95.47 grade-point average, contributed humorous stories to *Impressions*, including one called "On Caring for a Furnace," and was a dedicated Boy Scout. He went off to Lehigh University, then earned a Ph.D. from MIT. He eventually moved to Washington, D.C., and worked as a project engineer for the Atomic Energy Commission. Salutatorian Leah Sahm, who followed the Classical course, was the daughter of a German-born father who worked as a salesman (first of shoes, then insurance) and a Russian-born mother. Leah would graduate from Cornell University, where she belonged to a Jewish sorority, before she moved to New York City and took a job as a secretary at a real estate office and married a dentist. Jeanne preceded Leah in going to New York, where she studied voice with the well-known soprano Queena Mario of the Metropolitan Opera. Despite her parents' preference that she continue her education, Jane, who was "thoroughly sick of attending school and eager to get a job, writing or reporting," decided not to go to college.[59]

Meanwhile, Marie Van Bergen, Jane's friend since grammar school, received her diploma from Dunmore Senior High School in January 1933 at commencement exercises held on a different day in the Central High auditorium because Dunmore High lacked a suitable space. That year, half the banks were failing, and there was a 30 percent unemployment rate nationwide. Almost eighty years later, Marie asked pointedly, "Can you imagine a worse time to graduate?" She paused before answering her own question with measured emotion. "It was during the height of the Depression. You were graduating into *nothing*. Only a few students from Dunmore High went to college." Marie "knew [she] wouldn't go to college." Some years earlier, Jane "had come to me to say she had found a college in Virginia that didn't cost too much, that [my family] could afford, and we talked about going there." Always at the top of her class, and despite her love of literature and history, Marie had tried to protect herself from unemployment by switching from the Classical to the Commercial course of study and gaining business skills in addition to studying academic subjects. She ended up finding a job right out of high school at "an upper-class shoe store called the Paramount on the 100 block of Wyoming Avenue." Marie worked in their credit office until she married. She went back to work there off and on after her son was born, around the same time as Jane's first child.[60]

During the Depression, some of Scranton's high school graduates, like Jane Butzner and even Carl Marzani, thanks to a college scholarship, could venture forth with skills, knowledge, self-confidence, and enough means to pursue their dreams. Others were not so lucky. Hard times would thwart their opportunities and, as few then realized, mark the end of Scranton's era of promise.

The Powell School of Business

This certifies that

Jane Butzner

Has honorably completed the Secretarial Course in this School and has attained satisfactory proficiency in the prescribed studies.

In Testimony Whereof This

DIPLOMA

is awarded her as an evidence of her scholarly attainments this 23ʳᵈ day of June A.D. 1933, at Scranton, Pennsylvania.

Principal

Jane's diploma from the Powell School of Business,
in the Thomas Building (pictured above), June 1933.
Jane Jacobs Papers, John J. Burns Library, Boston College.

· · ·

CHAPTER 10

"First to Be a Newspaper Reporter"

AT AGE FIFTEEN, Jane Butzner had already formulated a precise career plan. When she conveyed to poetry compiler Nellie B. Sergent
her intention of being a writer, she knew—as Jason Epstein characterized Jane's modus operandi—"exactly where she was going and how
to get there." She specified the steps to Sergent: She intended "first to
be a newspaper reporter, and later to do writing of other kinds."
Newspapers had always played an integral part in the Butzners' family
life. Decker and Bess and their children read interesting "nuggets"
from the paper to one another at breakfast, and Bess clipped articles
to send to relatives and friends or to save for the scrapbooks she
assembled. All together, the family scoured several papers a day for
world, national, and local news.[1]

For Jane, newspaper reporting would combine her penchant
for exploration and observation, her fascination with cities, and her
love of language and writing, and, in the long run, it would help
frame her thinking about "the kind of problem a city is." Working
at one of Scranton's daily papers would allow Jane exposure to the
scope of issues facing Scranton, total immersion in the complexity
of her city's components, and a chance to contemplate the way those
components interacted. She would learn not only about societal and
cultural events but also about Scranton's seamy side, the struggles

of its people, and the underworld. In effect, Jane's experience at the *Republican* would provide her with an intensive course in how a city functioned, and she could learn in the way she preferred, by observing, analyzing, and writing. At the same time, she would become well acquainted—and, in some cases, form lasting bonds—with people whose passion was uncovering and conveying news and information to the metropolitan community. In addition to hard news, the papers broadcast such occurrences as parties held, vacations taken, organizational activities engaged in, and scholastic prizes earned. From presenting international stories to following the local news to marking the comings and goings and achievements of vast numbers of Scrantonians from varied backgrounds and circumstances, the daily morning and afternoon papers—also known as the "evening papers" because of when people generally read them—were receptacles of a wealth of information and, collectively over the years, comprised a comprehensive and frozen-in-time historical record akin to no other. Newspapers were the eyes on the city and of the city. Working- and middle-class reporters from all over the region, the more affluent managers, and the editors in between joined forces to watch attentively and communicate accurately.[2]

Since Jane had turned down her parents' offer to put her through college, they strongly advised her to gain practical skills to fall back on so she could earn a living until she succeeded as a writer. Like many of Scranton's other high school graduates—including William Ratchford, from her Central class of January 1933, an honor student and humor editor of *Impressions* when Jane was poetry editor—Jane enrolled in the Powell School of Business in the spring of 1933. There she applied herself to perfecting her typing and learning stenography, also known as shorthand, for taking notes with special symbols as quickly as a person could speak.[3]

Some fifteen years earlier, when he was in his late fifties, Charles R. Powell had founded the Powell School of Business. Born in 1861 in South Wales, Powell at age two had come with his brother, mother, and coal miner father to what is now Coaldale, Pennsylvania, at the southern end of the anthracite valley. His father worked his way up to foreman in a coal mine. During school vacation months, nine-year-old Charles began as a breaker boy and quit school at age twelve to labor in the mines until he was twenty. Through his concerted efforts, he educated himself and gained entrance to the Bloomsburg State Normal School, where Jane's mother, aunts, and other Robison relatives had studied. Charles graduated in 1883 and worked in Johnstown, Pennsylvania, as a stenographer and teacher. Having survived Johnstown's catastrophic flood, in 1898 Charles Powell, along with his wife, Mary, and four children, moved to Scranton as a typewriter salesman. He soon found employment with the International Correspondence Schools and, a few years later, joined the faculty at Central High. When Technical High School opened in 1905, Powell became one of its original faculty members, "teaching stenography, commercial law, typewriting, bookkeeping and business details."[4]

As World War I ended, Powell opened his innovative business school in central city. In its first five years, the school met with enough enthusiastic response from Scranton's business community and a steady stream of enrollees to be able to take up quarters, in 1924, in the spanking new Thomas Building, the three-story edifice next to City Hall, a couple of blocks down North Washington Avenue from Central High. Powell served as principal of the school and, "assisted by his son, Elwood Powell, and an efficient faculty," the *Republican* commented, "has a large and successful school housed in roomy and attractive quarters. . . ." In both its day and night programs, the Powell School featured a system of instruction "which enables students to progress according to their ability. A student who is brighter than the average, who shows special aptitude for the work, will not be held back by others who cannot go along quite so rapidly but will be allowed to cover the work in as short time as is consistent with thoroughness." Students could choose from various programs of study: secretarial (a combination of several programs), typewriting, bookkeeping, accountancy, shorthand, and CPA training. Although the school advertised "training for high school and college graduates" and programs that began each year in early September, these policies were also flexible and thus much to Jane's liking. They allowed such bright and eager students as William Ratchford and her to start midyear, proceed at their own pace, and graduate with the rest of the class.[5]

On the evening of June 23, 1933, using Central's auditorium and rituals befitting a fine educational institution, Charles R. Powell addressed parents and handed out his school's diplomas to 112 students at the fifteenth annual commencement exercises. From the Green Ridge Presbyterian Church, where he had served on the board of elders for many years, Powell had invited the Reverend Charles T. Leber, "who was associated for a number of years with . . . Technical High School," as the keynote speaker. In the summer of 1933, to lure prospective students, the Powell School of Business placed multiple small ads masquerading as notices throughout *The Scranton Republican*, touting their graduates' success in finding employment. Some typical snippets read: "Seven Powell School graduates are now acting as secretaries to Superintendents and Principals of High Schools in this vicinity," or "Hollis Jackson, a June 1933, graduate of The Powell School, has secured a position in the office of an automobile company." With the Depression in full swing, some students matriculated from out of town, and the school aided them in finding room and board.[6]

While acquiring her secretarial skills and diploma at the Powell School of Business, Jane never ceased pursuing her passion for poetry. Just two weeks after commencement at Central, the Century Club hosted an unforgettable occasion. Bess Butzner had belonged to this women's club since the mid-1920s, and Betty Butzner, but not Jane, had joined its Junior Division when she was seventeen. Although Jane later referred to the club as one of "several stuffy but imposing clubs" arising during Scranton's explosive growth period, she could not resist a chance to see the poet Robert Frost, whom *The Scranton Republican* identified as "America's foremost poet." Since the previous August, Mrs. Jessie M. Wainwright, the head of the Century Club's Literature Department, had corresponded with Frost's wife, Elinor, to arrange the engagement. The poet requested a "quiet lunch . . . before going on the platform" because, as Elinor made clear, he "always enjoys seeing people *after* a reading—but not *before*.*"* A huge event in her life to date, on February 9, 1933, Jane was in the packed audience and thrilled to see Robert Frost, one of her best loved in her pantheon of poets. She hung on his every word as "he read from his own works, and interspersed his readings with comments on his own writing, frequently disagreeing with critics who have attributed to his works certain characteristics which Mr. Frost claims are not accurate," the *Republican* noted. "In all of his poems, Mr. Frost said, there is a person in the background, and his poems are not mere scenes or pictures. . . . He said that writing free verse is like playing hand ball with no wall, or like playing tennis without a net. Mr. Frost prefers experimenting with given forms and favors iambics. He is fond of

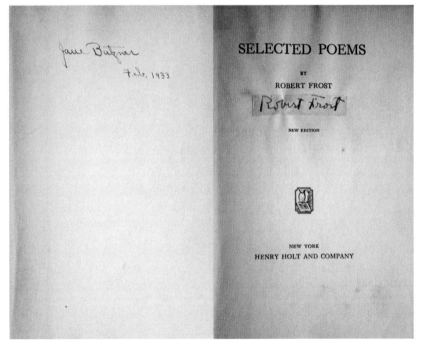

Pages from Jane's autographed copy of Robert Frost's *Selected Poems.*
Estate of Jane Jacobs.

blank verse, and said that poetry is an excess of feeling that must be written in an exclamatory style, yet it is excess in harness, being held in by forms as metaphor, which he likes best: rhyme and meter. Free verse, he characterized as being excess without a harness."[7]

Mesmerized by Frost's presentation, Jane realized at the tea afterward that she had forgotten to bring a book for the poet to autograph. Sympathetic and resourceful, Frost suggested he sign a piece of paper and wrote his name three times, one below another. Jane painstakingly cut the signatures apart and gave the other two to friends, one of whom was Jeanne Madden. At home, with her copy of Henry Holt's new edition of *Selected Poems*, on the first blank page, she inscribed her name and "Feb. 1933" with her prized fountain pen in her most careful script. On the title page, she pasted the neatly trimmed Robert Frost autograph below his printed name, and on the back inside cover, she glued a large photographic portrait of the dashing fifty-eight-year-old poet. Of the fifty-seven poems appearing in this volume from *A Boy's Will*, *North of Boston*, *Mountain Interval*, and *New Hampshire*—with the poet's illuminating comments fresh in her mind—Jane chose to unravel the intricate rhyme scheme of "The Runaway," annotating each line with a lowercase letter in the right margin to match rhyming lines.[8]

Perhaps Jane's encounter with Robert Frost further inspired her to submit her poetry to publications and competitions. Later that spring, she received notice that her poem "Of a Friend, Dead" had won honorable mention plus five dollars in the prestigious Witter Bynner National Poetry Contest, not an inconsiderable sum in those days. Her Central High friends and fellow *Impressions* staff members announced in the June 1933 issue of *Impressions* magazine: "Jane Butzner Wins Prize in Nation Wide Contest." They published the verse, underscoring, "This is an enviable honor as there were thousands of contestants from all over the country" who entered this competition, conducted by the Poetry Society of America.[9]

All through the spring of 1933, on her way up the stairs to the Powell School of Business on the top floor, Jane had walked by the offices of the Scranton Republican Publishing Company below. Catching glimpses of constant activity when the doors with frosted glass flashed open, she kept her first goal in sight and considered obtaining a writing position at her family's and one of the state's most-read morning newspapers. In April 1928, a fire had driven the newspaper out of the home it had occupied since at least 1915. Within a week, the *Republican* had bought the fireproof, well-lit and -ventilated Thomas Building down the block and across the street and began moving its operations there. The editors expressed their relief at being able to stay close to some of Scranton's most important institutions. Alongside City Hall and opposite the new Chamber of Commerce building that had opened in 1926, the newspaper offices and plant were at the center of a circle whose two-block radius encompassed the Courthouse, the central Post Office, the School Administration Building, the YMCA, the Scranton Club, the Elks and Engineers' clubs, the Masonic Temple, the Albright Library, Central High School, and the Christian Science church.[10]

In this formerly outlying section of central city, Jane observed the densification and filling in of empty spaces, processes Jane would one day describe as healthy for a growing city. A year after the *Republican* occupied its new quarters, another modern structure arose directly across the street: the Art Deco–inspired, ten-story Medical Arts Building, equipped with two high-speed elevators and a marble-floored lobby. A firm originating in Virginia erected medical buildings in Richmond, Baltimore, and Wilmington, and now Scranton. The architect, Marcellus E. Wright of Richmond, Virginia, allowed for four stores on the ground floor and filled the rest of the floors with suites and individual offices specifically designed for the needs of the medical profession. The *Republican* praised the new building, calling it "substantial, solid, and permanent," and "another architectural glory of Scranton . . . as tall as any building in the city." Discussing the ongoing incremental development of outer downtown, the article referred to the medical building's location as "the civic center" of the city "in line with the advance northward of trade" as business moved in that

Betty Butzner's watercolor of view from her father's office window,
looking west, 1932. Courtesy of Carol Manson Bier.

direction. When the Medical Arts Building opened in April 1929, it attracted scores of dentists and physicians, including the African American physician Dr. James E. Foster and Jane's father, Dr. John Decker Butzner. From his ninth-floor office overlooking the city, Dr. Butzner relished the glorious view almost as much as he enjoyed crossing paths, on the street below, with the reporters scurrying in and out of the *Republican*'s headquarters.[11]

An affable and loquacious man, Dr. Butzner struck up friendships among the newspapermen. "He became well known to the staff of [the morning newspaper] whose offices were directly across [from his on] Washington Avenue," Jim Butzner recalled in 1969. Among the reporters he befriended was the twenty-five-year-old go-getter Joseph Polakoff, who at age three in 1911 had emigrated from Russia with his parents and older brother. At seventeen, as a first-semester Central High School senior following the Commercial course, he started at the *Republican* as a messenger and office boy before taking "post-graduate" classes at Central. He then attended

St. Thomas College, where he gained experience as associate editor of the college magazine, and as a sportswriter and managing editor of the college newspaper. Before he had earned his A.B. degree, the *Republican* published his first bylined article, in 1927, a half-page appreciation and history of, as the headline crowed, the "Most Beautiful Building in City," with "200,000 Books in Circulation"—otherwise known as the Albright Library. The following year, the bespectacled Polakoff, with his big head of dark hair, became a *Republican* staff reporter. He went on to become its sports editor and to have his own column, beginning in 1934, which he named "Polley's Chatter," and ended up as city editor. Proud of his heritage, Polakoff noted that he was "the first Jew to hold those jobs" at the newspaper—although it routinely ran Happy [Jewish] New Year ads with greetings from the city's businesses and politicians.[12]

"Medicine was his work, sports his hobby," Polakoff wrote, describing his friend Dr. Butzner. An avid athletics fan and happy to offer his opinions on sundry sports, the doctor rubbed shoulders with newspapermen as they gathered to watch live reenactments of professional baseball games on the magnetic scoreboard on the facade of the Thomas Building, which the *Republican*—and later the *Tribune*—"operated for years prior to TV." Decades afterward, Jane reminisced about the "vertical playing field" in front of which she and her brothers would frequently join their father. "Daily during baseball months," Polakoff recalled, "Dr. Butzner crossed to [the newspaper's] scoreboard to watch the returns in the league games." In October 1933, during the World Series, a crowd of five thousand along North Washington Avenue perched on window ledges and roofs, and impeded traffic in the street to view a replicated game between the New York Giants and the Washington Senators. "With four amplifying horns [audible a block away] blaring the inning by inning accounts, spectacular plays and intimate touches from the Polo Grounds diamond," the *Republican*'s first-page story trumpeted, "the spectators were enabled to follow the action as rapidly as each batter faced the pitcher. The double announcing and diamond reproduction

300 block of North Washington Avenue with Thomas Building, home of *Scranton Republican*, next to City Hall, 2014. Author's photo.

with the roving ball left little to the imagination." Operators of the scoreboard cleverly assisted in realistic effects, "puff[ing] a gust of smoke through the first base loophole that looked for all the world like the whirlpool surrounding a sliding runner." The reporter also observed that passing "[m]otormen moved the trolleys at a snail's pace while craning their necks to steal a glance at the board." Fans whose view they blocked "roared their disapproval."[13]

Whether Jane's father's familiarity with the *Republican*'s staff had anything to do with her getting her first job or whether her articles in *Impressions* and her determination convinced the paper to take her on, we can't be sure. But we do know that in the summer of 1933, Scranton—and therefore all its interconnected businesses, including its newspapers—was feeling the viselike grip of the Depression, making it even more difficult for her than it had been for Joe Polakoff to land a position at the *Republican* just five years earlier. She never mentioned that being female might also have diminished her employment opportunities. Undoubtedly, Jane was creative in her strategy to convince the editors to give her a job. In her last book, when speaking of the Depression and the resourceful ways people lived through it, Jane told the story of the newspaper's hiring her: "I got a job without pay, for a year, on the Scranton, Pennsylvania, morning paper. The editor needed another reporter but lacked money to hire one. I earned his staff's generous tutoring by producing news items and articles the paper used. Although the paper was unionized . . . nobody objected to my Depression make-do barter agreement."[14]

In August 1933, Jane started her first job, doing what she had hoped to do. Although she joked that the paper asked her primarily to write "routine items about weddings, parties, and the meetings of the Women of the Moose and the Ladies' Nest of Owls No. 3," she gratefully recalled that she "was also given a free hand to find feature stories, write them, and they got printed." Jane's academic year of newspaper reporting lasted until May 1934. "[T]his was my apprenticeship, an equivalent to attending journalism school, part of my education," she explained. Jane worked as an assistant to Miss Wilhelmina Weichel, social editor of the paper, who oversaw the daily Women's, Society and Club News page, covering "social events" as well as "the activities of various women's organizations and clubs." Social editors, like Scranton's schoolteachers, were almost exclusively unmarried women and often quite young. Miss Weichel, a Central High alum, was the same age as Jane's sister, Betty, and had received a bachelor of science degree in journalism from Syracuse University in June 1930. Within weeks of finishing college, Miss Weichel obtained the position of social editor at the *Republican* after her predecessor, Miss Josephine Bull, resigned shortly after she married. The paper introduced Miss Weichel, the daughter of the assistant general manager of the Hudson Coal Company, as "a popular member of the younger social set of the city." An active participant of the Junior Century Club, organizing benefits and teas—along with Betty

Butzner and young poet Harriet Voris—Wilhelmina performed in local theater and had a serious interest in playwriting. She won the Century Club's prize for best playlet while also writing bylined reviews of plays and films for the *Republican*. She also produced fluffy pieces on such subjects as Christmas shopping and Valentine's Day. Judging from a jubilant *Republican* article on the eve of the legalization of beer in Pennsylvania in which Wilhelmina was the main source of information about beer parties being "all the rage tonight," Jane must have enjoyed certain aspects of her superior's personality.[15]

From the social editor's typewriter, set apart from the clusters of abutting desks, where men in shirtsleeves and ties sat in the second-floor city newsroom preparing local news for publication, Miss Weichel did, at first, assign Jane the task of writing up the myriad tidbits of social news that knit together the community—such items as Scrantonians going on trips and to soirees, or getting married. Jane became an ace wedding writer. In a scrapbook of her articles from that year, she saved a sample clipping of one of her typical accounts of a marriage, the union of Miss Jean Biesecker and Dr. Harry L. Houck at Elm Park church. Based on details obtained in advance, Jane painted in brilliant prose the bride "gowned in ivory satin with cowl neck and basque jacket" and the chapel "simply decorated in ferns and evergreens. Tall candelabra with lighted tapers will stand on either side of the altar." Jane also posted notices and composed brief paragraphs on the latest meetings of organizations—both unknown as well as those quite familiar to her—from the Slavonic Republican League to the Scranton Bird Club (for which her brother John led walks) and the Daughters of the American Revolution (for which Bess Robison, a regular attendee, judged annual essay contests). Before long, the young women's page apprentice was covering events at the Century Club and the Girl Scouts, whose large organization and numerous activities earned it a regular "Girls Scout News" feature on the women's page. With her flair for words and her ability to pour passion into the seemingly mundane, Jane pumped life into otherwise dry material. In reporting on the Girl Scouts (in which she remained an active member), she at times had the opportunity to highlight the accomplishments of those she admired, such as her friend and troop mate Gertrude Mattes's attaining the rank of Golden Eaglet and the revered Troop 4 captain Margaret Briggs's lecturing Girl Scouts on career possibilities for women.[16]

After Jane had been at the paper for two months, during the first week of October, at the Masonic Temple, the ninth annual Scranton Republican Cooking School took place. Announcing "new culinary ideas from the great De Both model kitchen in Chicago," the four-day affair attracted "over ten thousand housewives." Building on the enthusiasm for the cooking school, the editors launched a special weekly section ten days later called the "Homemakers Page," to appear each Friday. It was a logical offshoot of Louise Bennett Weaver's syndicated column "Helping the Homemaker," which had appeared on the women's page since 1928. Advertised as "helpful to every housewife in suggesting planning and table hints," the "Homemakers Page" expanded the concept of Weaver's column and filled an entire sheet or more with household tips, nutrition information, and menus and recipes that would help stretch a dollar and keep a family healthy during tough times. An Iowa native, Miss Weaver had begun her successful writing career by authoring a popular series of books that uniquely combined a novelistic approach and charming illustrations of family life with a multitude of recipes by one of her fictitious characters. The first in the series was called *A Thousand Ways to Please a Husband with Bettina's Best Recipes.* In 1922, at age thirty-four, Miss Weaver married fellow journalist Alexander George, who worked for the Associated Press (AP) news, and moved to Washington, D.C. Louise Weaver became the AP's home-section editor, and her popular column was syndicated in *The Scranton Republican* and many other papers in cities nationwide.[17]

For a recurring column on the new "Homemakers Page," in early November the *Republican* invited readers to submit for publication their "home-tested recipes which have proved satisfactory." Recognizing Jane's competence in writing all sorts of articles, Miss

Weichel asked Jane to come up with material for this page, too. Having noticed the shortage of recipe submissions, Jane made up her mind to put together one of her own. She concocted—using her imagination rather than actual ingredients—a dessert she fancifully thought of as Normandy Apple Cake. Jane's recipe was printed alongside several recipes carefully proven in a kitchen. When Jane's mother came upon the apple cake instructions and components (calling for five tablespoons of lard and disproportionate amounts of flour and milk), she pronounced the formula unworkable. She scolded Jane for causing people to waste ingredients, especially homemakers who could ill afford to do so. Thus ended Jane's foray into creative recipe writing, but with her collective articles, she had turned a number of male reporters' heads, including the head of the *Republican*'s local-news reporters, city-news editor Brychan B. Powell. Respected for his high standards, Powell had Jane apply her literary skills to a wide array of assignments.[18]

Looking back, Jane referred to B. B. Powell—as he was known—as her "boss" during her time at the newspaper. He would become the managing editor of the *Republican* for many years and "a legend among the journalists whose lives he had touched." During her internship at the paper, Jane clearly got along well and shared an outlook with him. "Powell was a teacher as much as an editor and he imparted his wisdom, provided direction and gave instruction in a quiet but forceful way," a veteran journalist wrote in his obituary in 1983. "He was literary and had . . . [a] love of music and poetry. He was witty. He knew and understood human nature. He prized ambition and industry, had little tolerance for laziness or indifference."[19]

B.B., like many of the *Republican*'s staff, had grown up on the city's West Side, in the northernmost section of North Scranton. Born in 1896, he was the youngest of ten surviving children, the oldest five of whom had been born in South Wales. Howell Powell, the children's father, worked as a carpenter, often at the coal breakers. Edwin G. Powell, Brychan's older brother by less than two years, dreamed of becoming a newspaperman, and as a young boy, he set up a printing press in their house. The two brothers produced their own homemade paper. At fifteen, Edwin pestered the *Republican* for a "real job," until they finally hired him as an office boy. Without attending college, he quickly worked his way up to reporter and then was hired by the *Philadelphia Press,* where he rose to assistant sports editor. In the meantime, Brychan worked as a copyboy, running errands and carrying copy from desk to desk at the *Scranton Truth,* an afternoon newspaper, before going off to Mansfield State Normal School, where he assumed the editorship of the college magazine. After graduating in 1917, he served in the Great War in the medical corps and remained in the States. Edwin was less fortunate. Deployed to France, he was killed in action at age twenty-three, just ten days before the armistice was signed. The community and his family deeply mourned the loss of the endearing and industrious young man, and they paid great tribute to him in the press and public ceremonies as a war hero.[20]

B.B. followed his brother's footsteps into the journalistic world, joining the *Republican* staff and rising quickly from reporter to correspondence editor—in charge of any correspondence to the newspaper, including letters to the editor—and then city editor in 1924. Wishing to be a reporter again, beginning in 1926 he took a job with *The Scranton Times* for two years—with city hall, the state legislature, and politics as his beat—before resuming his post as city editor at the *Republican.* Married to fellow Mansfield alum and art teacher Lillian Naumann and raising a family, B. B. Powell was appointed as interim school board director in May 1933. In the next primary election, in September, he ran as a Republican candidate for a six-year term on Scranton's school board.[21]

Both the city's largest-circulation dailies focused extensive coverage on this hotly contested local primary election. Working full-time at the city's—true to its name—Republican paper, Jane found herself following politics more closely than ever. Her parents, who tended to vote Republican, had always been passionate about local and national elections, and they subscribed to *The Scranton Republican.* The *Republican* boasted that it not only had "the distinction of being Scranton's oldest daily newspaper" but also was "the outstanding Republican journal in Northeastern Pennsylvania." Prior to election days, it promoted Republican candidates and printed the party ticket for Lackawanna County on its editorial page. From the paper's inception, the owners, editors, and managers saw supporting the Republican Party as an essential part of their mission. The editors of the evening paper, *The Scranton Times*, on the other hand, generally supported the Democratic Party. From the time the *American Newspaper Directory* first appeared in the late 1860s, it listed not only basic information, such as ownership, officers, size, frequency, and cost of the publication, but also its political and ethnic affiliations, which was expected of all newspapers. In Scranton, English and Welsh Protestants ran and tended to read the *Republican,* while Irish Catholic Democrats inclined toward the *Times.* There existed a friendly rivalry between the two main papers—as exemplified in the tradition of *Times* versus *Republican* baseball games—but also a spirit of cooperation and generosity. Even as the fire of April 1928 was destroying the *Republican*'s facility, the *Times* let the *Republican* set up temporary headquarters and use its presses to print the morning edition—and all other editions until it could move into its new space—so that *Republican* readers never missed an issue.[22]

In the fall of 1933, political observers waited to see how Republican candidates would fare after "the Roosevelt-Democratic attack of last year," the morning paper commented, referring to FDR's winning his first term as president in 1932. Under a recent law allowing mayors to succeed themselves, Republican mayor Fred K. Derby planned to seek reelection but first had to win his party's candidacy against fellow Republican Stanley J. Davis, his challenger on the City Council. Another new law permitted candidates to "cross-file," thus switching party registration, so in the primary, Davis ran on the Democratic ticket, as well. Davis lost to Derby as the Republican nominee but won the Democratic nomination. Therefore, two Republicans were pitted against each other in the November election. The mayoralty race turned into "one of the most bitter in the city's history," *The Scranton Republican* observed. On election eves, the newspaper would significantly increase its staff to "tabulat[e] figures as quickly as they are received" to bring the news to its readers with almost the same speed and excitement as their vertical playing field did with baseball. The morning paper blasted the upset victory: Davis defeated Derby, with final results showing a lead of a mere 650 votes. In years to come, both John and Jim Butzner—who also shared the extended family's (including their grandmother Robison's) keen interest in politics— temporarily "worked on special election night assignments on the paper and acquired their Social Security cards from this employment." Among the objects of intrigue that found their way into Jane's "museum" collection were an impressive number of political campaign buttons, including a 1928 campaign badge for Herbert Hoover ironically proclaiming, "Good for Four Years of Prosperity."[23]

By mid-October, Jane had yet to report on hard political news, when B. B. Powell charged her with the task of covering an event of much importance to the whole city and particularly for budding young women. From October 7 through 14, the city conducted its first Girls' Week—the equivalent of the established Boys' Week—to take place in the state of Pennsylvania. With great panache, Jane led off her account of the highlight of the week's activities: "Regulations were upset, routine was blown out of rhythm momentarily, and attaches of the Scranton municipal chambers enjoyed a brisk two-hour Roman holiday while this city's young womanhood yesterday grasped daintily onto the steering apparatus of the ship of state and directed the execution of the civic duties of the city." Jane described how the girls took over the municipal offices, including those of the mayor, public health director, public safety director, and City Council members, as well as the uproarious occurrences in the process. One girl "spent the rest of the afternoon riding in state upon a clanging fire engine, where she aroused the envy of hundreds of small boys." Sponsored by the Girls' Council of the Council of Social Agencies— comprised of "all the organizations in the city affiliated with girls work," including the Big Sister organization, Catholic Women's Club, Girl Scouts, Progressive Recreation and Social Service Association, YWCA, and YWHA—and with the cooperation of the city's schools,

Girls' Week demonstrated to one Central High senior that "[g]irls are just as important as boys, so shouldn't a week be devoted to them? . . . Is not the secretary of labor a woman?" Earlier that year, President Roosevelt had appointed Frances Perkins, the first woman to hold a U.S. cabinet position.[24]

The November 7 local election results proved to be momentous: B. B. Powell lost his bid for the school board to a Democrat, the *Republican* declared the "Democrats Winners in the County," Stanley J. Davis succeeded in his maneuvers to win the mayoralty, and Pennsylvania, along with Utah and Ohio, joined the "Wets"— bringing the total number of "wet" states to thirty-six—to nullify the Eighteenth Amendment and eviscerate Prohibition. And, from about this time forward, Jane, the young journalist apprentice, had proved her worth in covering news items. In addition, she was from then on entrusted with other assignments close to her literary and artistic heart: reviewing plays, books, concerts, and dance performances.[25]

Just before Election Day in November, Jane—as a young reporter—saw her first bylined article. The *Republican* rarely attached bylines to staff-written articles, reserving them instead for non–newspaper personnel, columnists, and pieces of special significance. Thus Jane must have been pleased to see her name in print on a review of a play presented by one of Scranton's dramatic groups. The article appeared in *The Scrantonian*, the city's only Sunday paper and under the same management as the *Republican*. Acknowledging the present economic circumstances in her critique of a local theatrical production, Jane began, "If the depression and its accompanying upsets have brought us anything, it is a number of excellent satires. This spirit of good humored, witty, and frequently sharp ridicule, managed deftly by [playwright] Fred Ballard, is responsible for one of the best plays Scranton theater goers have been privileged to see, 'Ladies of the Jury,' presented . . . by the Little Theater guild at the Y.M.H.A." After succinctly yet vividly conveying the plot and characters, the young reviewer homed in on a tantalizing detail: "One of the most delightfully comic scenes occurs . . . when each jury member reveals himself through the food he chooses and his manner of eating it." Jane's piece must have met with appreciation, for during the remainder of November, she turned out quite a few others, among them two more bylined theater reviews and an article on a talk by a Lafayette College professor advocating public colleges. At the Century Club, Jane heralded a lecture-recital by prominent music critic, composer, and magazine editor A. Walter Kramer, and at the same venue soon thereafter, she reviewed actress Dorothy Sands's presentation, to an audience of four hundred, on "Styles in Acting" from "the early eighteenth century up to the present Mae West era," Jane wrote. Weaving her passion for and knowledge of theater into her evocation of the evening, Jane continued, "Wearing the 'plumes of tragedy,' Miss Sands became 'Almahide,' in 'The Conquest of Granada,' by John Dryden; a tiny hat and a very large bustle transformed her into Nellie Hathaway in 'The Silver King,' by Henry Arthur Jones. As 'Anna Christie,' in Eugene O'Neill's play by the same name, Miss Sands showed the influence of the great war upon the theater, and its resultant effect on the present-day drama with its stark realism and truth." All were published within a few weeks of one another.[26]

Jane made sure to report on dramatic productions at her alma mater, too. Each year, *The Scranton Republican* closely covered and stirred up enthusiasm for the annual Central High School pre-Christmas play. Having been thoroughly immersed in this endeavor a year before, Jane experienced this year's production, A. A. Milne's *The Perfect Alibi*, as a member of the paper's news staff with a still-fresh connection to the Thespis club, some of its present members, and its leader, Miss Louise Howitz. Beginning on November 10, the *Republican* ran no fewer than nine articles on this play—stylistically similar and therefore likely authored by Jane Butzner, though only the last had a byline to substantiate this. Most of these pieces appeared on the women's page. The initial article noted that the student playing the female lead had previously chaired the "stage group" for last year's *Devil's Disciple* and acted in *The Rivals* two years ago. A separate profile highlighted Eugene McAndrew, a younger brother of Jane's classmate and Kay

Nay Aug Park in Spring, by Scranton artist Margaret L. Oettinger,
oil on canvas, c. 1949. Courtesy of the Everhart Museum
(depicted above), Scranton, Pennsylvania. Photo by Joshua Mann.

Schoen's next-door crush, who took on the role of the fetching male
lead. First performed in London under the title *The Fourth Wall* in
February 1928, the three-act detective comedy, the writer explained,
"is concerned with the murder of Arthur Ludgrove, an English gentleman, in his home at Sussex, England, by two clever criminals. Although the two murderers have established an apparently perfect alibi,
Susan, Mr. Ludgrove's ward, refuses to accept the verdict of suicide
which is substantiated by almost undeniable evidence." Then the reviewer sounds unmistakably like Jane: "Consequently, she follows her
intuition and detects the guilty ones by keen observations and logical
deductions." Going behind the scenes, Jane, in the final article about
the play, reveals the script's stage instructions "so obviously fathered
by the glorifier of Christopher Robin" that on the chair, desk, and
shelves are to be books by A. A. Milne.[27]

Of special appeal to Jane were chances to visit and report on one of her favorite destinations, the Everhart Museum in verdant Nay Aug Park, along Roaring Brook at the city's eastern edge. In 1908, Dr. Isaiah F. Everhart, a physician and expert taxidermist, had built and endowed this museum of natural history, one of the goods and services, Jane later specified, that were "added into Scranton's economy" during its heyday from 1905 to 1920. With its dioramas of local wildlife and extensive collection of stuffed birds "from everywhere," as Kay Schoen described them, the museum—and the pond and swans in front—drew throngs of citizens on Sunday afternoons. As a longtime reader of and now a regular writer for the *Republican* and its Sunday iteration, *The Scrantonian*, Jane followed the thoughtful and poetically scribed Monday column called "Museum Musings," by Everhart Museum director R. N. Davis, among syndicated features on the editorial page. In one entry titled "Fossil Words," Davis mused first on the plant fossils' helping us visualize the swamps that had formed the region's coal beds before he segued to the origins of three English words—lacquer, sincere, and Japan—related to products derived from fossilized materials. After devoting the museum solely to natural history for twenty years, Dr. Everhart realized his original vision for the museum and sought to expand the building to house science and art exhibitions, as well. On the top floor of the new three-story museum, he added "specially lighted" painting galleries—the first "real inlet" for Scranton's "public interest in art"—with significant wall space showcasing the work of Dunmore-native painter John Willard Raught. After Raught died in January 1931, in the house in which he was born, his friends and relatives established in these rooms "a most fitting memorial" to the internationally known artist.[28]

Born to "pioneer Dunmore settlers" in 1857, Raught left his job as a telegraph operator to study art in the 1880s at New York's National Academy of Design and overseas at the Académie Julian in Paris. As a painter working in the Impressionist style *en plein air*, he lived in New York around the turn of the nineteenth century and achieved modest success. But Scranton's pastoral surroundings as well

Brisbin Coal Breaker, by Scranton artist John Willard Raught,
oil on canvas, 1915. Courtesy of the Everhart Museum,
Scranton, Pennsylvania. Photo by Joshua Mann.

as its industrial environment lured him back to his roots. His greatest
supporters were also in Scranton, including his childhood friend and
publisher of *The Scranton Times,* E. J. Lynett, and coal operator John
M. Robertson. Besides producing commissioned portraits of prominent citizens, sometime in 1911 Raught took it upon himself to paint
in somber colors emotionally imbued portraits of isolated, ghostly,
yet monumental breakers. He created artworks of almost every large
breaker in the area. Reviewing his largest show to date—sixty-four
canvases at the Century Club in early October 1915—*The Scranton
Times* hailed the "breaker pictures" as "entirely new in art" and stated
that "Mr. Raught stands pre-eminent in the field." Working from his
studio on the same block as the *Scranton Republican* offices, Raught
also continued to portray the natural landscape. In the pamphlet for
his 1928 annual exhibition, he articulated what he aimed to convey
in his large canvas *The City of Scranton* and the beauty that inspired
him: "Mountains, steep hillsides, rocks, and the great sweep of the

valley, with the late afternoon sunlight throwing its golden glow over the central city and a portion of south Scranton."²⁹

From 1927 to 1930, Scranton's premier artist wrote eloquent articles, which appeared on the *Republican*'s editorial pages. In his piece "The Tragedy of Coal Mining," he bemoaned "the air of tragedy always hovering over the coal lands . . . the continual sacrifice of human life in the mines . . . and the heartrending catastrophes that have taken place . . . in the black underground depths." But harking back to the region's more prosperous times, he also expressed nostalgia for "the old black wooden structures with their lofty towers and many gables . . . more picturesque [than the new steel, glass, and concrete structures] in outline, and in certain lights resembled strange, weird, oriental masses. . . . At twilight when the coming shadow of light throws its enchantment over the land, they seem transformed into exquisite poems of black and gray. . . ." One of his best colliery paintings hung in the Central High School library, and a Raught landscape adorned the school's main corridor. At the Technical High School, students could see Raught's 1930 oil portrait of its first principal, Ronald P. Gleason, high up on the main entrance wall. Several of his paintings—breakers and landscapes—found a permanent home at the Century Club after his exhibition there. Thus Raught's visual and written work pervaded the lives of Jane and many other Scrantonians.³⁰

Given the high and often literary quality of the writing in *The Scranton Republican*, the sophisticated, erudite observations and critiques by the young Jane Butzner fit right in and were much appreciated by the editors, staff, and, apparently, the readers. As reflected in the breadth of the topics she took on, Jane's interests ranged far and wide. She produced insightful book reviews, such as a bylined analysis of a new book by San Diego journalist Max Miller, who had recently authored a best-selling account of his reportage, *I Cover the Waterfront*. Jane summarized Miller's latest book, *The Beginning of a Mortal*, as a "series of episodes in the life of a boy, each complete in itself but each aiding to build one of the of the most revealing and distinctive pictures of childhood since Barrie's *Sentimental Tommy.*" Pronouncing Miller "unquestionably successful in making the reader thoroughly acquainted with his characters," she discerned, "We are not sensible that we are reading character studies, but there is a sudden realization that we know these individuals better than we know our friends. Not the least artful method of achieving this is a trick of having the boy fail to understand conversations and events and yet sense significances deeper than the words." On the other hand, bizarre medical phenomena also fascinated Jane. Perhaps having heard this news from her brothers—both ardent Boy Scouts—Jane proposed to her editor an article whose headline would read "Stomach Wall of Ariel Man Leather Lined." Apparently, a caretaker at the Boy Scout camp had been bitten by a mad horse, and his physician "chose the abdominal muscles as the most convenient place" to inject the remedial shots. "After the third needle had been broken in a vain attempt to puncture the skin," the man revealed "he had worked in the Ledgedale tanneries, and the tannic acid dripping from hides as he carried them against his body had been absorbed into the skin of his stomach and arms, tanning them like leather. The injections were administered via other body parts, and he recovered."[31]

Curious about how everything worked at the newspaper, Jane tried her hand at laying out the women's page, usually the responsibility of the composing room foreman and executed "without any editorial supervision and frequently with haphazard results." Working with the foreman, Jane set a precedent that produced such well-laid-out pages that other departments followed suit. She enjoyed this task, and, at the same time, it allowed her to explore all three floors of the newspaper's operations. Leaving her usual haunts, isolated and crammed in the corner of the second floor, where she and Miss Weichel—who seemed to be the only female members of the reporting staff—carried out their duties, Jane walked by the male world of the city newsroom with its myriad logjammed desks, tobacco smoke, and constant commotion. She peeked in the sporting and telegraph editors' room, where men received the latest news and sports information from all around the world at sixty words per minute over the wires of the Associated Press. On the ground level below, in the large central space surrounded by enclosed cubicles for the paper's executives, sat a phalanx of employees—some of whom were female—in neat rows of separated desks, each with a phone, all facing the switchboard toward the front entrance. Home to the newspaper's business, advertising, and auditing offices, and the reference department, the first floor was where almost all women employees of the Republican Publishing Company worked. Anyone toiling here late into the night could hear the rumbling of the mammoth printing operation from the basement. With her layout, Jane ventured down to the lowest level, originally built as a garage, with a solid concrete floor that could support the weight of a superduty "modern high speed press," paper-roll storage, barrels of ink, and the mailing room. Not far from the printing presses was the composing room, with "fourteen of the very latest linotype machines for setting type," each operated by a skilled man. What a thrill for this female cub reporter to see her written words turned into hot-metal type and reproduced at breakneck speed.[32]

While studying the workings of the newspaper and the city, Jane was turning out articles every day. Through daily contact and a shared passion for their work, she naturally became friends with some of the reporters in the city newsroom. Jane palled around with her father's friend Joe Polakoff, who became her friend, too, and other male correspondents in their twenties. Like Polakoff and B.B. and Edwin Powell, many had started at the newspaper in their teens as low-paid copy- or errand boys and worked their way up to staff correspondents or editorial positions. Perhaps it was easier for them than it was for Jane to get a foot in the door at the paper because, when they began, times were less lean or because they were entering the traditionally male vocation of city reporter. But Jane was undaunted by either of these hurdles, and she formed fast friendships with the male reporters. Decades later, Jane and her brother Jim—who shared her fondness for the *Republican* and maintained the closest ties among the Butzner siblings to Scranton because he married a Scranton girl—reminisced about its staff journalists. In a 1969 letter to Robert J. Arthur, who had ascended to the position of editor in chief in the mid-1940s, Jim Butzner wrote, "When I mentioned to [my sister Jane] about writing to you, she asked to be remembered. She often talks about her associations with you and Gordon Williams and the others [including Jimmy Calpin] that worked on the paper about 35 years ago."[33]

A dozen years Jane's senior, Bob Arthur, whose mother was Irish-born, had served as correspondence editor in 1928. By 1933, he was a full-fledged *Republican* staff reporter as well as president and toastmaster of the Scranton Newswriters' Union No. 3. In the baseball match between the amicable rival papers, Bob Arthur also made a name for himself. "Manager E. J. Hart, of the Times' alleged ball club," the *Republican* taunted its scribe competitors, "became alarmed after watching Bob Arthur, Washington avenue hurler, twist benders with the ease of Dazzy Vance, across the home plate." Both only five years older than Jane, Gordon Williams, Jr., and Jimmy Calpin—along with "Joe Polley"—were three of the fun-loving, "nimble [score] board operators" during the 1933 baseball World Series. After cutting his teeth as a clerk at the *Republican*, Jimmy—orphaned and from a working-class Irish background—was promoted to reporting the scholastic sports news. Gordon, having come to the paper only a couple years before Jane, lived with his family in East Scranton and was assigned his neighborhood's beat. He soon covered Green Ridge, too, and wrote an occasional bylined drama review. Son of a stock and bond salesman and coal broker, he had attended the Princeton-feeding boarding school Mercersburg Academy. Altogether, reflecting the city's makeup, *The Scranton Republican*'s newswriters were a motley crew, with a hefty element of working-class boys on their way up the ladder, some of them Irish and not necessarily Republicans at the avowed Republican paper.[34]

As a respected reporter, Bob Arthur was assigned the responsibility of conveying news about negotiations between the United Mine Workers and the anthracite operators. In February 1926, young staff correspondent Arthur had covered the calamitous strike and scooped the settlement announcement before anyone else. The next day, the morning paper crowed about their scoop in a full-page advertisement. In April 1933, he produced a series of bylined articles over the dire issue of "wage revisions," in which the operators wanted to reduce workers' pay by 35 percent. Ultimately, Labor Secretary Frances Perkins intervened, and the operators expressed "'utter disgust' with the developments." Growing up in a city that had erected an imposing statue of UMW head John Mitchell in Courthouse Square in 1924, just five years after he died, Jane understood what organized labor could do to protect workers and took pride in employees at Scranton's major newspapers for having formed a historically early union. Her job at the *Republican* provided firsthand exposure to a "newspaper guild," as she called it. The Scranton Newswriters' Union, organized in 1907 under a charter from the International Typographical Union, was only the second American newspaper guild local in the country for reporters, city editors, copy editors, and telegraph and correspondence editors who worked on the city's main papers. The Scranton Newswriters' Union successfully bargained with the local publishers and set minimum wages and top salaries for members, and negotiated paid vacations and overtime. Besides representing its members, including women, the union sponsored festivities such as an annual dinner with big-name journalists from New York and Washington, D.C., drawing large audiences and prominent union members—like Edward Lynett, B. B. Powell, and Bob Arthur, its president—from the city's press. Since the speaker was an "internationally known journalist" and Jane's buddies Joe Polakoff and Gordon Williams were involved in arranging the event, Jane probably attended, too. Less than a decade later, she would attempt to unionize clerical workers at her workplace, *The Iron Age* magazine, with a primary goal of bringing women's wages into line with men's, calling for equal pay for equal work.[35]

Like her fellow paid reporters (although women's page editors were typically paid less) at *The Scranton Republican* and elsewhere, Jane worked late hours—although not late enough to hear the din of the presses rolling in the basement—and so did Dr. Butzner. "Fortunately [the paper] was right across the street from [my father's] office

Medical Arts Building, built 1929;
Dr. Butzner's office was on the ninth floor, photo 2008. Author's photo.

downtown," Jane recalled in 2002. "It was a morning newspaper, so my hours were from early afternoon until as late as need be. I liked that, working in the evening and at night and sleeping late in the morning. When I finished, I would go across the street to his office. Sometimes there were still a few people in the waiting room. Sometimes he would be reading his medical journals because everybody had left. Then, we would talk, and I would go home with him. If he was seeing any patients, he would tell me about that. I would tell him about what had happened at the newspaper. Or we would talk about things in general."[36]

While Jane was in the middle of her apprenticeship as a reporter, in February 1934 *The Scranton Republican* unexpectedly changed ownership. This announcement reverberated in cities beyond Scranton. *The New York Times* disseminated the news that Frank D. Schroth had bought the newspaper, which "for twenty years [had] been under the ownership of Colonel L. A. Watres, former Lieutenant Governor [of Pennsylvania], and members of his family. . . . Colonel Laurence H. Watres, a son, president and editor in chief, will continue as a director of the new organization." In 1856, the year Scranton became a borough, but not yet a city, "Scranton's Oldest Daily"—as the slogan on its masthead proclaimed—had commenced as a weekly. In September 1867, Joseph H. Scranton, one of the city's original founders, purchased the paper, appointed his son Joseph A. Scranton editor, and turned it into a daily morning newspaper.[37]

For the next forty-five years, Scranton's founding family was at the daily's helm. When Joseph H. Scranton died, his son Joseph became proprietor and, in the 1880s, invited his son Robert M. Scranton to join in a partnership. In 1907, Robert M. Scranton took over and, two years later, merged the *Republican* with *The Scranton Tribune*, to form the *Tribune-Republican*. In 1912, he sold the paper to Col. Louis A. Watres, owner of *The Scranton Truth*, who combined the two newspapers and retained the *Republican*'s original name. Although L. A. Watres was not related to the family for whom the city was named, he belonged to the city's elite. His family had roots reaching back to the *Mayflower* and a comparable standing in the region. His father, Lewis S. Watres, had been a pioneer settler in northeastern Pennsylvania, even preceding the Scrantons. He had opened two of the earliest anthracite mines and built sawmills in the Lackawanna Valley. The Watres (pronounced, and originally spelled, *Watrous*) family were Republicans, Presbyterians, and politicians. Like his father, L. A. Watres, Laurence H. Watres ran for office and won a seat in the U.S. House of Representatives from 1922 to 1930. Col. Louis A. Watres and his family took up residence in a twenty-three-room stone mansion on eighty acres on East Mountain, overlooking Scranton. The estate, named Pen-Y-Bryn, meaning "top of the hill" in Welsh, was completed in 1902. For many years, the Watres family opened the house and manicured grounds to civic organizations and events—such as Boy Scout rallies and an annual picnic for the blind—and to the public for picnicking and hiking.[38]

When Schroth took over "Scranton's Oldest Daily" in 1934, he and his wife and their six children moved into a demure house, compared to Pen-Y-Bryn, across from the Century Club at the foot of the city's Hill Section. Born in 1884 in Trenton, New Jersey, Schroth came from a middle-class Democratic German Catholic family. He had begun his career as a reporter on the Trenton *True American* and *Trenton Times*, and was "ambitious and liked to be a mover and shaker," said his nephew Father Raymond Schroth. In 1924, Frank Schroth, with the help of financial backers, bought the morning *State Gazette*, which later that year merged with the *Trenton Times* and *Sunday Times Advertiser* as the *Trenton Times*. When *The Scranton Republican* came up for sale, Schroth took the leap and sold his interest in the *Trenton Times*. On Monday, February 19, 1934, his first day as new editor and publisher of the *Republican*, Schroth addressed his readers in "A Personal Word" on the front page of the paper. He asked "humbly" for "the friendship and confidence of the people of the community" and expressed "the greatest faith in Scranton and in the Lackawanna Valley." Schroth sized up the city and summed up his goal in guiding the newspaper: "The industries are varied and important; the merchants progressive and the people alert. We realize fully the responsibility resting upon us and our obligation to conduct an honest and useful paper." In his letter, Schroth made sure to extend his "compliments" to his confreres, *The Scranton Times* and the Sunday *Scrantonian*.[39]

After Christmas in 1936, Schroth changed the newspaper's name to *The Scranton Tribune* to emphasize its political independence. "He said he was a Democrat and prided himself on being fair with labor," his nephew wrote, but he was a friend and supporter of Republican president Herbert Hoover and did not vote for Franklin Roosevelt until 1944. Although Jane had lived in New York for two years by then, she kept track of her alma mater newspaper. In June 1990, upon receiving a recent *Scranton Times* clipping from her brother Jim about *The Scranton Tribune*'s demise, Jane conveyed her thanks, saying, "What you sent added a great deal, especially about the history of the paper, which was fascinating to me. I was there during the Col. Watrous [*sic*] ownership and the beginning of the Schroth [*c* crossed out] ownership. We never saw hide nor hair of any owner! At least, I didn't." Frank Schroth would remain with his Scranton morning daily until 1938, when he took over the venerable *Brooklyn Eagle*, which he operated until it folded in 1955.[40]

The history of *The Scranton Times* paralleled that of the *Republican* in some respects. Both of the papers were printed as broadsheets, not tabloids, had stayed in one family for a long period of time, and each held on to its party affiliation. From its debut in 1870 as a Democratic daily, the *Times* tried to get its footing under six consecutive owners until the mid-1890s, when it switched from a morning to an evening paper and Edward J. Lynett—having worked his way up from reporter to editor and business manager of the *Free Press*—purchased

Members of the *Scranton Times* family: Elizabeth Lynett with brother Edward junior and father, E. J. Lynett, 1930s or early 1940s. Courtesy of (Scranton) *Times-Tribune* archives.

it. During the coal strike of 1900, the *Times* persisted in "calling the coal operators names and getting the [larger] circulation" and support of the miners, putting the *Times* in the lead in paid circulation among the city's newspapers. Born in Dunmore in 1856 of Irish Catholic immigrant parents and one of seven children, Lynett had experienced the mines as a breaker boy. "E. J. Lynett . . . has made the *Times* at this date a power in the city and county," Hitchcock commented in his 1914 Scranton history, "and made its owner . . . a wealthy man." The Lynett family has owned the *Times* (in 2005 renamed the *Times-Tribune*) until the present day, columnist Chris Kelly commented in the spring of 2016.[41]

With the intensification of the women's suffrage movement in the early twentieth century and the desire to report news about it came a spike in the number of female news correspondents. By 1910, four thousand American women worked as full-time reporters, and by 1930, there were twelve thousand. While Jane was writing for the *Republican*, E.J.'s daughter, Elizabeth R. Lynett, worked as a full-time staff correspondent at the *Times*. Elizabeth Lynett's articles elicited gratitude from female laborers, and her method surely inspired journalists of both genders. In May 1933, thirty-year-old Elizabeth posed as an unskilled female employee in Scranton's garment industry to learn firsthand about the appalling working conditions, long hours, and miserable wages. Her resulting series of exposés, from May 21 through 29, published nationwide, spurred the government to probe the local sweatshops and tackle some of the problems they engendered. Her embedded reportage also earned her a position with the AP's bureau in Philadelphia. In 1946, she returned to her home city to join her brother as copublisher of the *Times*. Like most women journalists of her time, she remained single until she died, in 1959.[42]

Prior to Elizabeth Lynett, in 1919, *The Scranton Times* had hired Emily Wilcox, a rare woman reporter, age thirty, who would stay with the city's evening paper until 1949, when she retired, upon the advice of her physician. Referred to variously as a "member of the news staff," "club editor," and "women's-page editor," Wilcox came from a prominent family in Wyoming County and never married. She participated in the Century Club and the DAR, both organizations where she would have known Bess Butzner and most likely have met both of Bess's daughters. A professional woman ahead of her time, Wilcox was elected financial secretary of the Scranton Newswriters' Union and was active in the Business and Professional Women's Club. Local organizations frequently engaged her as a lecturer on such topics as "Reporting."[43]

Scranton's two daily papers were not complacent about keeping up their readership, and to some degree they competed against each other. Since the two-cent price of the newspaper in no way covered expenses, they relied on revenue from advertising for financial survival. The more readers they could claim they had, the more advertisers were willing to pay. Certain segments of the population mattered, too. Even prior to 1900, big-city newspapers established women's pages to encourage women to shop at local department stores, which were some of their biggest advertisers. Regulations required that newspapers declare annually on their front page on specified dates their "average paid circulation figures" for the previous year (excluding copies given gratis, which boosted numbers for advertisers). On October 4, 1933, with an average paid circulation of 29,000, the *Republican* had notably fewer readers than the *Times*, with its average paid circulation of almost 50,000. Although from 1899 to 1946, the city of Scranton—with its majority of voters registered as Republicans—elected only one Democrat as mayor, its afternoon Democratic paper maintained the larger circulation. Given the public's penchant for checking the news first thing in the morning, American morning dailies tended to have a larger circulation than their afternoon counterparts. To woo advertisers during the Depression, the *Republican*, above its masthead, billed itself as having the "Largest Morning Daily Circulation in Pennsylvania Outside Philadelphia."[44]

When Schroth took charge of one of the state's largest-circulation morning papers, *The Scranton Republican*, to keep its circulation healthy, turned to Jane, a young female reporter, like Elizabeth Lynett and Emily Wilcox. Jane must have been tickled when she received an unusual assignment that afforded her creative writing talents an opportunity and tapped into her resourcefulness. For at least six months—during Jane's internship at the *Republican* and some months before her arrival—the newspaper had received very few letters to the editor and certainly none that would encourage subscribers to read them with any regularity. All but three of the letters expressed pro forma thanks for the paper's publicity afforded to their worthy organization—such as the Sloan Comets Club or the Ladies' Auxiliary to the Scranton Liederkranz—and were diligently signed with the writers' proper names. The sporadic and unexciting letters seldom, if ever, appeared on the editorial page, but were scattered among funeral notices, classified ads, and short news items on the back pages. On January 31, 1934, however, a man composed an impassioned letter regarding politics. The next day, someone else wrote a letter complaining about dogs that "trespass upon your property, and injure your plants, kill your other pets, such as chickens, kittens, pigeons, pup, etc." Most likely acting on the wishes conveyed from the new editor in chief, Frank Schroth himself, B. B. Powell assigned Jane the task of reviving and enlivening the "Letters to the Editor" department, which he had overseen in his early days at the paper. Powell instructed her to do whatever she saw fit to get letters coming in and readers engaged. Jane mentioned the assignment to her father over dinner. Remembering the antidog letter, Dr. Butzner suggested that Jane create some provocative letters from fictitious people to stir up interest and elicit responses. Her father's idea appealed to her, and she promptly sat down at her typewriter.[45]

Beginning on March 9, 1934, the "Letters to the Editor" column moved to the editorial page, where Jane announced the revamped, distinctively titled feature with an introduction explicitly offering the public a voice: "This column belongs to the readers. . . . In it they will be free to express themselves on questions of public interest." Given that she had taken her father's advice and authored the letters herself, the rest of her paragraph might seem ironic: "Letters . . . should bear the signature and address of the writer as an evidence of good faith." Jane composed a deliberate but restrained letter entitled "Asks Full Publicity," casually proposing disclosure of names of landlords who profited from "disorderly houses." Ostensibly still unaware of the request that writers henceforth identify themselves, she signed it dispassionately, "INTERESTED." Scranton's mayor [Davis] had ordered a survey of ownership and rentals of houses of vice. The letter writer called for the survey results to be made public. "It is not difficult for vice to flourish when some of our citizens . . . get handsome returns in rentals from buildings on which they pay little or no taxes because the properties are worthless for other purposes. They cannot deny that they know of the use . . . of their buildings, and they are therefore part and parcel of the underworld system." Having hooked her readers with the first letter, which she must have thought outrageously funny, Jane outdid herself with the second. She named it innocuously "Bells for Cats" and signed it "WEST SIDE RESIDENT." After establishing her sympathies with birds "as being of recreational and aesthetic [and insect-controlling] value," she crescendoed in her conclusion: "Dogs without licenses

Subsidence of residence and store at Birney Avenue and Campbell Street, South Side, Aug. 2, 1919. Courtesy of (Scranton) *Times-Tribune* archives.

are taken to the pound; why not cats [without bells]? The thousands of unwanted, disease-carrying stray cats in our city could thus be humanely destroyed, and innumerable squirrels and birds saved." Jane's last letter that day—ostensibly from "B.J.I." (a scrambling of her own initials)—addressed the lack of street signs "at central city corners and in the majority of those in residential sections." This time, Jane was proposing a solution the city government might actually enact. Jane's handcrafted letters got the response she had hoped for. Irate letters—particularly from animal lovers—flooded the newspaper's mailbox, and others on sundry subjects ensued, heartily resuscitating the "Letters to the Editor" feature.[46]

Galvanized by Jane's concoctions, one reader penned a letter to the *Republican* editors, directing attention to a public issue of paramount importance, subsidence of land due to mining underneath. The letter stated that other countries where mining was taking place had experienced the sudden and dramatic sinking of the surface, but this had occurred only in remote and unpopulated places. An atypical and unimaginable syndrome—therefore, "unaverage," as Jane termed it, and likely a key to understanding—in any other city its size, subsidence was all too familiar to Scrantonians. John Brown of Dunmore exhorted the Dunmore Council to "look into this most outrageous, ruthless and deplorable mining and caving of homes," which he referred to as the "mine cave situation." Because the largest and richest vein of anthracite in the Lackawanna Valley underlay the Electric City, coal companies had bought up large tracts of empty land before the city was developed. Retaining ownership of the coal beneath the surface, the companies gradually sold off subdivided plots, sometimes for housing their employees but mainly to profit from real estate sales in the growing city. Beginning in the nineteenth century, the sellers inserted into the deeds of these sales what came to be known as the "cut-throat waiver." This absolved the coal companies of any responsibility for damage sustained by surface property due to insufficient support in mines below. Home buyers—like the Butzners on Electric Street—and even coal operators signed these deeds, feeling that the day when the vast amount of coal would be removed, thus making the surface precarious, was too far in the future to worry about.[47]

By the time Dr. Butzner arrived in Scranton in the early 1900s, the "first mining" operation was finished, and a network of coal pillars bore the weight of the densely built-up city above. With increasing frequency, schools, churches, homes, businesses, roads, and even part of Nay Aug Park began sinking into the ground. The papers relentlessly ran stories and photographs of these disturbing incidents. To deal with this threat to the public, Scranton formed, in 1915, a Mine Cave Bureau as part of their municipal government, and appointed an engineer to head it. The smaller Lackawanna Valley town of Pittston, also plagued by subsidence, established a similar agency. In 1916, the year Jane was born, William Walker Scranton, son of the early *Republican* owner Joseph H. Scranton, declared that "no company has the right to sell a man a piece of property and then cause its destruction." Furthermore, he offered ten thousand dollars to help find a solution to Scranton's pervasive mine cave problem. By 1927, subsidence had touched the lives of Jane's friends and neighbors. Her Central schoolmate Carl Marzani woke up one morning, looked out from his bed on the *second floor* of his house, and saw an automobile, "the top showing just above the [window]sill!" His family's home had sunk fifteen feet as they slept. Kay Butzner's cousin and other Scrantonians worried because they could hear miners' voices when they went to their basements. While Jane's brothers were still attending the George Washington School #3 in Dunmore, cracks appeared and widened in the school's basement. Typical of other coal companies, Green Ridge Coal—responsible for the mining taking place below—proposed that the Dunmore school district buy the underlying coal pillars to forestall further mining, but the school board refused. After much resistance, the coal company finally granted school board engineers the right to inspect the mines. The engineers were temporarily satisfied that the schoolchildren were safe. The Washington School building did remain intact, but one block away, George Brooks's lavish house subsided and had to be demolished. The editors of *The Scranton Republican* pleaded for mining in places other than "under schools, homes, and other valuable buildings."[48]

During the Depression, whiskey bootleggers lost much of their market following the passage of the Twenty-first Amendment to the U.S. Constitution, on December 5, 1933, ending Prohibition. Yet *coal* bootleggers persisted and provided the necessary fuel to many. Mining illegally, the men derived their product in large part from pillars in mines that had closed. The majority of bootleggers were unemployed miners and members of the United Mine Workers, and many others came from mining families. As a *Republican* editorial bemoaned, "with a reduced market for coal . . . a number of mines have been closed, [and] thousands of workers have lost their jobs. . . ." The coal bootleggers had access to mining tools, timbers for support, and the know-how to use them. They risked not only serious injuries to themselves but also being buried alive when they extracted too much coal from the pillars or when their makeshift wooden ceilings gave way. Desperate to heat their own homes and sustain their families by selling coal to customers at cut-rate prices, these men were willing to throw caution to the wind. Often, city officials looked the other way as "coalleggers" worked in full view. For ten days, "following the discovery that a vein lay only a few feet below the surface," "hundreds of men" removed hundreds of tons of coal from the Eureka baseball field in North Scranton. City police held off halting the bootleg operations and allowing the Glen Alden Coal company to put up a fence around its property, ostensibly because "the fuel for the most part [was] being stored by those digging it out . . . as supply for the winter months." The attitude of the authorities would change by 1936, as coal bootlegging became an industry employing fifteen thousand men, stealing already mined coal from the property of coal companies, using fleets of trucks to transport it, and setting up sales agencies. This industry produced and sold five million tons of anthracite annually.[49]

As a keen observer and ardent newspaper reader, Jane knew well the saga of the conflict between the public and the coal industry.

Bootleg Coal Miner, etching, by Nicholas Bervinchak,
a Ukrainian American artist who had labored in
the coal mines in northeastern Pennsylvania, 1937.
Courtesy of Pennsylvania Anthracite Heritage
Museum and Marion Bervinchak Leschey.

Philip Van Cleef Mattes, father of her Girl Scout buddy Gertrude
Mattes, had served as solicitor for the city and the county for many
years. When studying for the bar in 1912, Philip Mattes—a Central
High and Cornell graduate, whose grandfather Charles F. Mattes
was one of the founders of Scranton—"made it [his] business to read,
digest and brief every Pennsylvania court decision dealing with surface support, mine caves and cut throat waivers." He helped to draw
up the Kohler and Fowler Acts of 1921, whose passage made subsidence caused by mining a crime and punishable by law. The next
year, fearing damage to their home from mining below, Harold and
Margaret Mahon challenged the Pennsylvania Coal Company in the

most famous case of its kind. Even though the deed to their property contained the "cut-throat waiver," they sued on the grounds that the Kohler and Fowler Acts overrode this. The case made its way to the U.S. Supreme Court, where Attorney Mattes represented the plaintiffs in front of a bench on which sat Justices Oliver Wendell Holmes, Jr., and Louis Brandeis. Ruling 5–4 in favor of the coal company, the Court invalidated the Kohler and Fowler Acts on the grounds that "where the surface owner had waived the right of support, the mine owner had the constitutional right to cave him in," Mattes explained. Surprisingly, the liberal Holmes wrote the majority decision, while Brandeis wrote the dissenting opinion. Following this ruling, for the next twenty-five years, anti-mine-cave activists relied heavily on public sentiment and newspapers to make strides against the scourge of subsidence. During the proceedings of *Pennsylvania Coal Co. v. Mahon*, anonymous citizens mailed Scranton newspaper accounts and pictures to members of the Court. The chief justice protested that these clippings were influential and therefore people should cease sending them. Mattes replied that he "had no power to censor the conduct of men and women who had been aroused by what was happening to them." In his 1973 memoir, Mattes reflected that "the elections of public officials, the delegations to Harrisburg, the editorials in the press, all played a part in convincing management . . . to forego [*sic*] reaping the last gleanings from the rich fields that had paid them so handsomely in the past."[50]

For decades, the mine-cave problem colored the lives of everyone in the region. It shed light on the city's economy, on how the government worked, and how a community responded. While Jane worked at the *Republican*, it ran almost one hundred stories on subsidence. Recalling her earliest childhood memories of Scranton, Jane spoke of the "caved-in houses": "The worst danger about them was that sometimes the gas pipes broke and then people would be asphyxiated, or else there would be an explosion. Who needs terrorists if you've got robber barons?"[51]

One of Jane's "creative" letters to the editor had achieved its goal with its humorous yet pointed proposal regarding another unique aspect of the city, the notorious red-light district. While introducing and describing Scranton in a nutshell, Carl Marzani blithely noted that Scranton "was reputed to have the largest spread of bordellos in the East." By the early 1880s, the city's papers were documenting arrests tied to brothels. For the first forty years of the twentieth century and especially during the 1930s, the city had gained a far-reaching reputation for its disorderly houses, bawdy houses, or houses of vice, ill-fame, or prostitution, as they were variously called. They attracted male clients from New York, Philadelphia, and hundreds of miles away, as well as their share of locals. Out-of-town railroad workers with a layover and big-band musicians in the area for a gig were frequent customers. "When we traveled to another city," Marie Van Bergen Mansuy confided, "young ladies were told, 'Whatever you do, don't say you're from Scranton,' because that's how outsiders thought of the place." In the late 1930s, Scranton's public safety director identified forty-six disorderly houses, primarily concentrated in the downtown alleys between Penn and Franklin Avenues and near Center Street. The two-story frame houses were often brightly painted. The public safety director found that, on average, three female workers lived and plied their trade in each house. In addition, itinerant prostitutes walked the streets and frequented bars. After Marie graduated from high school and worked in the Paramount Shoe Store, near the epicenter of the city, she became familiar with some of these women. "The girls came to the store to buy shoes with their madams," she said. "I recognized them because they would pay in one-dollar bills—which was what they were paid in." Marie sympathized with the young women. "The girls were poor and desperate, and couldn't get jobs. They were local, but not anyone I had known." Observing this exploitive business up close afforded Jane an opportunity to study and learn from it.[52]

The prostitution industry carried on in full view, but officials turned a blind eye to it because it brought in so much money. Many people profited—not only the working girls and their procurers but also landlords of the buildings used in the trade (as Jane artfully pointed out) and the municipality itself. Police regularly arrested

Bawdy house at 228 Raymond Court, allegedly bombed
by Mafia, which the owner had not paid off, Apr. 2,
1928. Courtesy (Scranton) *Times-Tribune* archives.

prostitutes and madams, fining "management" one hundred dollars
and "labor" twenty-five dollars for each offense, before dismissing
them. Arrests, however, rarely took place right before city elections,
lest politicians lose any votes. These fines put $19,500 in the city
coffers in 1939, constituting three-quarters of all fines collected that
year. Madams could avoid some of these arrests by paying off police
and politicians, or they could pay protection money to the Mafia, the
most infamous element of the "underworld system," in Jane's words.[53]

While the Depression led some poor females to turn to the world's
oldest profession, it also propelled a segment of unemployed Sicilian
male immigrants to turn to traditional forms of crime and reap profits
from not only "gambling emporiums" and speakeasies but also bawdy
houses, especially as Prohibition came to an end. The first Sicilians

had come to the Lackawanna Valley in the mid-1870s. Escaping the starvation wages and inhumane working conditions of the Sicilian sulfur mines—where the heat was so intense that they slaved away naked—Sicilian miners headed directly and hopefully to the anthracite mines. At the time, Sicily produced 90 percent of the world's sulfur and had originated the Mafia—"an unspecified number of centuries ago . . . as a grass-roots defense against alien conquerors," one of Jane's characters proffered in her Platonic dialogue on morals, *Systems of Survival.* "Scranton's mine managers, when the mines opened, were from Wales," Jane's son recalled his mother telling him. "When the owners got fed up with demands for better conditions, they replaced the Welsh miners with Sicilians. Sicilian miners with no interest in Mafia work became foremen. When Jane was in grade school, mine owners replaced Sicilian managers with Ukrainians and Poles. When the mines closed and legitimate jobs grew even scarcer, some miners fell back on what they knew. If they had come from Sicily, they knew how the mob ran."[54]

At his inauguration on New Year's Day, 1934, Mayor Stanley J. Davis announced that Scranton's unemployment rate had reached almost 20 percent. Scranton and its environs' economic decline led to the rampancy of the Mafia in the area. As early as the nineteen-aughts, however, the Scranton newspapers were running frequent stories on the mob in Pittston, Carbondale, Wilkes-Barre, and Wyoming—as well as Scranton—which had become American bastions of Mafia activity. From increasingly plentiful newspaper accounts while she was growing up, Jane knew not only about local Mafia activity—such as that of the Black Handers in Carbondale and South Scranton—but also about members of Palermo's mob in Sicily "charged with virtually every crime associated with racketeering—extortion, murder, blackmail, arson, assault and robbery," which they also reported. A year before she joined the staff of the *Republican,* the paper had run a splashy, in-depth five-part series on organized crime because of attention focused on it "through the daring capture of the Lindbergh baby," in which the Mafia was suspected. Editorials during Jane's *Republican* tenure conflated the Mafia, prostitution, and other forms of "vice," and enjoined the "public conscience" to support "the present city administration," under Mayor Davis, which was "making a more earnest, sincere, and powerful effort to maintain average decency in Scranton than has been made before" and to pressure "police authorities" not to "deviate from their strict and simple duty." Despite the editorial pleas and the letters to the editor commending the paper's "fine stand," illicit activities prevailed.[55]

The underworld lurked all around Scranton and Dunmore and throughout the valley, and at times Jane came within one degree of separation from it. She not only followed the criminal world in the press but she also knew about it through her own observations. Thomas L. Coyne, the father of Kathryn Coyne—the treasurer of Jane's eighth-grade class—made a living during the Depression as the proprietor of the Hotel Vine, which apparently served as a speakeasy, with connections to gambling and prostitution. Kathryn went on to Scranton's prestigious Central High along with Jane. Dr. Butzner was intrigued by and fond of the Sicilian families he ministered to in the borough of Wyoming, fifteen miles down the valley from Scranton. He came back with their homemade wine and stories with which to captivate his children. Jane's observation and contemplation of the Mafia, begun in her youth, would fuel her longtime curiosity about the "moral foundations of commerce and politics," culminating in her *Systems of Survival*. She postulated two opposing moral syndromes: the commercial, found in trading, business, and science; and the guardian, prevalent in government, religion, and the arts. If the two syndromes are confused or combined, she concluded, they produce "monstrous hybrids" and lead to social problems. She offered the Mafia as a prime example, because it "practices commerce in accord with guardian precepts. . . ." Although the Mafia provided its members—from whom it demanded absolute loyalty—an opportunity for economic advancement, it resorted to intimidation and violence in conducting business. Dynamite, a workaday tool for any miner, was often the Mafia's weapon of choice, as well as a calling card left at the crime site. Bombings of disorderly houses whose inhabitants were behind in their protection payments were not uncommon. On April

2, 1928, *The Scranton Times* featured an article with a photograph of a disorderly house at 228 Raymond Court, whose front porch had been dynamited while no one was inside, the fourth such incident since the first of the year, it reported. It seemed in these incidents that the Mafia intended to make a statement, not to maim or kill. The newspaper identified the building's owner as J. E. Burke, a local butcher with shops nearby on Penn and Lackawanna Avenues. Joseph E. and Mary M. Burke, who worked as a housekeeper, lived above their store with their three young daughters. This story demonstrated that this otherwise ordinary citizen-cum-landlord was indirectly complicit in and profiting from vice, as Jane had astutely made clear in her pseudonymous letter to the editor.[56]

When Jane was growing up, newspapers were still *the* source of public communication. Although its impact was not yet clear, a competitor to newspapers loomed on the horizon. From 1922 to 1929, sales of radios skyrocketed by 1,400 percent. Suspecting that this revolutionary technology might lead to enormous changes in the spread of information in various arenas, the U.S. Census sought to gauge radio's potential impact and added a new query to the 1930 census taker's interview: Is there a radio in the home? The census tabulated the number of households owning a radio set, which came to more than 40 percent nationally, with the larger proportion in urban areas.[57]

During Jane's stint at *The Scranton Republican*, when radio news was still in its infancy and television was yet to be born, the public continued to rely primarily on the papers for news and information. Many Scrantonians read both the morning and evening dailies to keep abreast of the news cycle throughout the day—and to follow different columnists and comic strips. Sometimes one newspaper would update a story the other had begun. For rapidly unfolding stories or critical news, the *Republican* and the *Times* printed multiple editions each day, known as "extras." Smaller weeklies, like the *Catholic Light*, and foreign-language papers, such as the Ukrainian *Naroda Wola* or the Polish *Republika Gornik*, still existed and served specific communities, but for news of the city, the nation, and the world, readers turned to the large-circulation dailies. Even though these dailies were usually affiliated with a political party and endorsed that party's candidates, they strove, as Frank Schroth articulated, to present the news of the day "objectively and . . . attempt[ed] to interpret it realistically. Newspapers should furnish a check on the government when politicians are crooked or stupid. Therefore we shall encourage unselfishness and high-minded effort in public office." The publisher's note reflected his mission of responsibility and commitment to the community that his paper served.[58]

Like other big-city newspapers, the Scranton papers offered young men and, increasingly, women, like Jane, a chance to begin a career as a writer and, for some, a way out of the working class. Before Carl Marzani took off on his cross-country road trip prior to entering Williams College in the fall of 1931, he arranged to report on his adventures for the Sunday *Scrantonian.* The editor supplied him with a letter of introduction on the newspaper's letterhead for whatever opportunity might present itself, stating that Carl "was doing a reportage on sectional problems in the United States." Shortly after Carl's return, the *Republican* published his jaunty literary account of hitchhiking and hopping freight trains, and the people and places along the way. They headlined it "Covers 9,000 Miles on Less Than a Dollar." The editors added a laudatory introduction about the writer, who only seven years earlier had emigrated from Italy without knowing a word of English. While Jane made the daring move—as had Edwin Powell and other young men—of forgoing college and, instead, working her way up at a newspaper, three of her school friends would write as college graduates for the *Republican* (by then renamed *The Scranton Tribune*). Both June Carter and Florence Osterland attended Marywood College, the well-respected local Catholic women's college. Florence finished her degree at Oberlin College, where she had followed and married her schoolmate, *Impressions* editor John F. Kane. John had also started college locally, but at the men-only St. Thomas College. In the later 1930s, having witnessed Jane's reportorial prowess, perhaps the *Republican* was more inclined to hiring

Interior of the *Scranton Times* newsroom, 1926.
Courtesy of (Scranton) *Times-Tribune* archives.

other young women. After graduation, Florence and John returned to Scranton and worked as news correspondents. John went on to write "many magazine articles, short stories and plays." After he and Florence divorced, Florence remained in Scranton with their children, and John had a distinguished career in the U.S. Department of the Treasury. June bought and—with the help of her lifelong friends Carol and Virginia MacAskie, from Elmhurst—ran, wrote, and physically produced the weekly *Villager*, with its offices in nearby Moscow, Pennsylvania.[59]

By the late spring of 1934, Jane felt she had completed her journalistic apprenticeship. She had watched Prohibition come to an end and the city cope with the height of the Depression—from those hit hardest to those trying to help. She learned about Scranton's institutions, including its press, and the artistic and literary culture connected with the city, yet she had reflected on the city's disreputable underside, as well. And she had honed her writing and contemplative abilities. Jane was ready to proceed to the next step in her life and career plan. She arranged to move in with her sister, Betty, across the Brooklyn Bridge from Manhattan. After graduating in June 1933 from the Pennsylvania Museum School of Industrial Art in Philadelphia as an interior designer, Betty had to settle for a job as a saleswoman at a department store in Depression-era New York. (Later, she would become vice president of Elisabeth Draper, Inc., the New York interior-decorating firm.) Jane, with her stenographer's and typist's skills, decided to find office work to support herself while she wrote articles to submit to New York newspapers and magazines for actual pay and establish herself as a writer. But first she took a detour—an entirely contrasting and eye-opening experience of living in an isolated five-hundred-person community. Betty had spent a week there the previous summer, and now Jane would stay six months with her Presbyterian missionary aunt, Martha Robison, in the Appalachian hills of northwestern North Carolina.[60]

In an unusual gesture, the editors of *The Scranton Republican* printed an appreciative farewell to the young female reporter. On May 1, 1934, three days before her eighteenth birthday, in their recurring "Things We're Told" short-takes feature on the editorial page—a potpourri of musings by the staff, frequently about other newspaper journalists or their industry—they focused on the departure of Jane Butzner, "who ably assisted in the social news department of the Republican since last fall." Jane must have piqued their interest regarding her next move, because they added several paragraphs on the history of the tiny village of Higgins. It had been founded in the early eighteenth century, readers of the *Republican* learned, by three Higgins brothers, from whom all the residents descended. Having arrived on muleback in 1922, before any roads reached the settlement, Martha Robison saw to the construction of several stone buildings and reintroduced forgotten skills and crafts to the people. "Pride of the village is the Markle Crafts school," funded by Martha's coal-baron cousin, John Markle, in response to her entreaties. In the rural subsistence economy of this bypassed place, Jane saw that the practice of trade had virtually ground to a halt, and she became aware of how knowledge and skills—from spinning yarn to masonry—could be lost. Over generations, even the memory of those things disappeared, until people lost the belief in those possibilities. Perhaps during her half year in Higgins, Jane looked back on her *Scranton Republican* days and thought of the newspaper as one of the crucial repositories of memory—its collection of verbal and pictorial snapshots frozen in time—without which even the memory of what has been lost would be lost. Fifty years hence, Jane would devote a chapter in her *Cities and the Wealth of Nations* to the cautionary tale of bypassed Higgins, disguised with respect and humor as the village of "Henry," the forename of George Bernard Shaw's professor character in *Pygmalion*.[61]

In November 1934, Jane had returned home to Scranton from Higgins and then departed again, this time for good, to settle in New York City. Scranton's population had plateaued in 1930 at upward of 143,400 and was soon to start on its steady downward trajectory as the local economy sputtered and sank. An unprecedented number of citizens were unemployed, mines continued to shrink or close, and new businesses failed to replace those that had been shuttered. Alongside Aunt Martha in the tiny hamlet, Jane had gained life-changing insights into what makes and breaks a community and its economy. She was champing at the bit to get to New York—the five-borough metropolis with a population of almost seven million and seemingly endless opportunities—to realize her ambition of being a writer. Young Jane Butzner joined a growing exodus from the once important and prosperous medium-size city of Scranton. As one of Kay Schoen Butzner's teachers at Central High School used to lament to his classes while one graduate after another left town to seek a living, "Scranton's greatest export these days is its young people."

Greater Scranton Foundation Fund, donors card, seeking
"Scranton Boosters," 1941. Author's collection.

• • •

CHAPTER II

Ex-Scranton Girl
and Her Home City

AS A MEMBER OF "Scranton's greatest export," otherwise known as its young people, Jane steeped herself in the great city of New York, yet she maintained an intense attachment to her previous city. She reveled in observing and investigating how neighborhoods in the nation's largest metropolis worked, while supporting herself with secretarial jobs as she submitted—with increasing success—freelance articles for publication in magazines and newspapers. After discovering the charming bohemian neighborhood of Greenwich Village, Jane convinced her sister that they should move there. Yet with parents and brothers in the big brick house in Scranton, the sisters had compelling reasons to visit their home city. Occasionally, they rode the train home to Scranton for weekend visits, and they rarely missed the holidays. In December 1937, however, Jane and Betty rushed back to see their father. They arrived in time to see him as he lay dying because a botched childhood appendectomy finally got the better of him at age fifty-nine. Dr. Butzner's death was a terrible blow for twenty-one-year-old Jane, but she would carry forward her father's zest for life, his intellectual curiosity, and his strong sense of civic commitment. Scranton remained the family home. Bess Butzner continued to live in their Dunmore house after Jane's brothers had finished high school and John went to St. Thomas College down the hill.[1]

In the summer of 1940, Jane stayed longer than usual at the house. She had spent two years at Columbia University's extension school and was inspired, in part by a course on constitutional law, to think through and compose her first book. After what she called "a morning's work" on the book that Columbia University Press would publish as *Constitutional Chaff*, Jane took to playing checkers with her brother Jim, home on vacation from the University of Virginia. Decades later, she reminisced to him about their time together on their Monroe Avenue porch: "I never think about that book without simultaneously thinking about those checker games. I sure did feel triumphant whenever I beat you, which was not often. Once I triple-jumped you. Wow! But you never let that happen again!" In January 1941, while *Constitutional Chaff* was in production, Jane landed her first salaried job as a writer at *The Iron Age*, a national weekly trade magazine for the metals industry with a sizable and broad readership.[2]

Since settling in in New York in late 1934, Jane had savored the metropolis's variety of districts and small businesses. Nonetheless, all the while, Jane was keeping an eye on Scranton not only through clippings from its local papers sent by family members but also via the national press and facts gleaned from her visits to Washington, D.C., and other cities for *Iron Age* articles. After the bombing of Pearl Harbor on December 7, 1941, the country had joined the Allies in World War II. With the United States fighting in the war, the need for and interest in metals intensified. Jane had risen to associate editor at the magazine, although the publishing company officials considered her a troublemaker who advocated, as a representative of the union, for equal pay for equal work by women. She received half the pay of her male predecessor.[3]

As spring was breaking in 1943, Jane threw herself into an all-out campaign to save her home city. She used the greater freedom of her new position to call attention to the depressed municipality's predicament, a cause taken up by *The Scranton Tribune* in cooperation with the Greater Scranton Chamber of Commerce. Twenty-five thousand miners' jobs and thousands more jobs dependent on mining had vanished in the last decade. Having witnessed the decline of Scranton's anthracite industry—once the bedrock of the regional economy—Jane watched the city's attempts to revive its manufacturing. Gradually, the plants turning out silk and rayon goods had begun to replace coal mining, but now "the war emergency" was dealing these predominant factories "a crippling blow." Jane's investigations revealed that government agencies were helping to transform other locations into war boomtowns by sending them new industry and opportunities to employ their citizens. But they had overlooked Scranton.[4]

In her thoroughly researched and pointedly argued exposé for *The Iron Age*, March 25, 1943, Jane fueled the fire kindled by her Scranton compatriots. The article's headline called Scranton a "neglected city." Scranton was one of "eighty-two paradoxical industrial areas of unemployment and empty houses," Jane wrote, but it was "atypical in that it [has] made the hardest fight to channel its idle labor into war production." She reeled off the staggering figures: With a population of 300,000 in the greater Scranton area, 30,000 people were unemployed and 7,000 houses stood empty. More than twenty thousand men were serving in the armed forces, one of the nation's highest per capita rates, and twenty thousand people had left the area for now overcrowded war-industry boomtowns like Bridgeport and Baltimore. The War Department had shown it was well aware of the Lackawanna and Wyoming Valley region's advantages for war production when it awarded one-quarter of all contracts for camouflage nets to Scranton's existing factories, such as the Scranton Lace Company, which could easily repurpose its looms and facilities to manufacture them. Moreover, the Federal Anthracite Coal Commission, appointed by President Franklin D. Roosevelt to assess the region's potential for industrial expansion for war plants, had concluded, almost a year earlier, in April 1942, that "it is in the national interest that the industrial resources of the anthracite area be utilized." FDR twice sent letters to the War Production Board (WPB) and other government decision-making bodies urging action, but "[t]o date,"

Jane stated, "the only concrete result has been the location of a piston ring factory."[5]

Jane had endeavored to bring war-industry opportunities to her hometown for more than a year and, apparently, had approached quite a number of journalists and people at Scranton's Chamber of Commerce, although she downplayed her own role when she penned her article. She had remained in touch with some of her newspaper colleagues from her days as a reporter at *The Scranton Republican*, now renamed *The Scranton Tribune*, and she joined forces with them in this campaign. Most active and visible among them was Tom Connor, a highly engaged member of Scranton's Newswriters' Union, who in 1931 wrote for *The Scranton Sun* and by 1938 was associate editor of the *Tribune* and its Sunday *Scrantonian*. He was a contemporary and longtime buddy of her friends Joe Polakoff and Bob Arthur. In her *Iron Age* piece, Jane's name did not appear in a byline, nor did she mention Connor's. "The [morning] newspaper editor and the Chamber of Commerce have made weekly trips to Washington for the past fifteen months in an effort to get war plants for the city," Jane noted in *Iron Age*. In the spring of 1941, when, as Jane wrote, "Scranton looked hopeless," Tom Connor had initiated the Greater Scranton Foundation Fund, seeking cash donations to rehabilitate the area through "an 'all-out' industrial program to create more jobs." The fund was "made up in large part," Jane continued, "of dollar contributions from working people" and allowed the municipality to hire "a permanent Washington representative for the city." Jane did not disclose the name of the representative. He was E. M. Elliott, a business and industrial consultant, from his eponymous Washington, D.C., firm, who lobbied government officials on behalf of Scranton's advantages for wartime manufacturing. He traveled back and forth between the capital and Scranton, where he kept an office at the Chamber of Commerce. Originally from Missouri, Elliott was well connected and known to be a personal friend of Missouri senator Harry S. Truman, who would become FDR's vice president in 1944 and, upon the president's untimely death, his successor in 1945.

Jane went on to describe a letter-writing campaign of the past three months to "400 officials . . . setting forth what Scranton has in surplus electric power, labor, sites, transportation, etc. More than 300 answers have been received and have been examined by a member of The Iron Age staff." There followed her punch line: "They provide a post-graduate course in the run-around."[6]

In preparing for her March 1943 article, this thinly veiled "member of The Iron Age staff" had also interviewed political figures, including Richard H. Bailey, Jr., secretary to U.S. senator Joseph F. Guffey from Pennsylvania. When Jane tried to pin Bailey down as to why the federal commission's recommendations had not been instituted, he dodged the facts and grasped at straws for answers. Finally, he blurted out that the Scranton area had slid so far down economically that war plants would not help anyway. Jane skewered her target: "It was pointed out to [Bailey] that his viewpoint was at odds with the one expressed in the report of the Federal Anthracite Coal Commission, which Senator Guffey had signed. Mr. Bailey's reply to this was a query as to whether his questioner wanted information or an argument." Thus Jane rested her case for Scranton's desirability and readiness for wartime industry.[7]

Although the author of this strategic journalism was not identified, the "neglected city" piece sparked a relentless series of news reports and editorials by Scranton's morning and evening dailies, and the Sunday paper. On Saturday, March 27, 1943, a couple of days after the *Iron Age* article appeared, both the morning *Scranton Tribune* and afternoon *Times* ran editorials praising the piece and reiterating Scranton's situation. The papers repeatedly echoed Jane's term "the run-around." In addition, the *Times* published a story underscoring the article's effective venue in a "trade paper highly regarded by business and industry and circulated among executives with authority to select [war-industry] plant locations. . . ." The afternoon article puzzled over how the *Iron Age* story had come about. The reporter concluded that "[f]igures issued last January [of the high number of unused homes and idle workers] by the . . . Scranton Chamber of Commerce . . . are believed to have furnished" the basis of the magazine piece. The next day, the Sunday *Scrantonian* carried three upbeat pieces on Jane's article. They disclosed that *The Iron Age* had sent out "substantial excerpts" to two hundred newspapers "throughout the Associated Press" across the country, and the story was broadcast via Arthur Hale's popular, wide-reaching radio program, "Confidentially Yours." But none of these three papers seemed to have any idea—or at least they did not let on that they did—as to who the author (and further disseminator of the piece) might be. Only once during this ten-day spate of the newspapers' reactions to the magazine's story did they leave a clue about the identity of the reporter at *The Iron Age*. In his statement, Mr. Bailey let on that his questioner had been female, when both dailies quoted him as back-pedaling: "In effect, all I said to the representative of The Iron Age when she called me on the phone was that . . . we had not been successful as yet in having [the commission's] recommendation carried out."[8]

As March segued into April, the *Tribune* stepped up its actions by sending telegrams to President Roosevelt, WPB head Donald Nelson, and members of the federal commission, which included Senators Joseph F. Guffey and James J. Davis, Democrat and Republican, respectively, from Pennsylvania, urging them to investigate the lack of promised aid to the city. The wire to the president—which they printed in full in the paper and signed "The Scranton Tribune"— asked him "to reconvene the Federal Anthracite Commission and to inquire" why their recommendations to put to work the economic assets of the area, laid out almost exactly one year ago, had not been followed. The *Tribune* also published in entirety its wire to Nelson. They closed their plea by emphasizing their strong sentiments on the matter: "There comes a time when patience ceases to be a virtue." Meanwhile, a *Scranton Times* editorial reminded citizens that twenty-five years ago "agitation" for mine-cave relief had netted favorable results. They advised their readers that, in a similar manner, "[w]e must tell the world about our situation and in particular emphasize how the community is being neglected by those in Washington."[9]

Organized labor played a major role in the campaign to implement the Federal Anthracite Coal Commission's recommendations. The unions, too, had sent members to Washington to plead the case for wartime manufacturing in the Electric City. At the beginning of April 1943, a day after the one-year anniversary of the commission's report, Scranton's Central Labor Union (CLU) staged a formal rally at Casino Hall, in the midst of downtown, to protest the WPB's failure to act on bringing new industries to the area. "The entire history of the drive will be given consideration at the meeting," and they would plan further protests and "additional treks" to Washington. "All walks of life have joined in a united front . . . ," they declared. The rally targeted Richard Bailey, who in addition to his much-publicized derogatory remark about Scranton had told the union secretary the previous August, "We got into the movement for war industries too late." Crossing over from journalism to activism—not for the last time—Jane traveled to Scranton to be a key speaker at the rally.[10]

The combined individual and organizational efforts to bring new industry to Scranton had begun gradually in 1941 but accelerated

Inside the Murray Corporation of America's bomber wing plant, 501 South Washington Avenue, 1943. Courtesy of Lackawanna Historical Society.

once Jane's article came out in March 1943. The resulting new industries included not only smaller and short-lived businesses but also substantial plants with staying power. On March 28, 1943, *The Scrantonian* quoted a letter that E. M. Elliott—who had been working for Scranton for "some time"—had received regarding the president of the National Bag Corporation, based in New York, coming to Scranton to purchase a building to move his plant into. This was not wartime industry, the editorial noted, but it was even better, as it "likely will be here permanently." On April 3, 1943, a *Scranton Tribune* editorial trumpeted, "Some twenty-nine new industries have been obtained during the past year by telling the Scranton Story and more can be had the same way." Because of the *Iron Age* article, the Scranton office of the U.S. Employment Service reported that "numerous out-of-town employers" had contacted them regarding employment, housing, and factory site conditions in Scranton and environs. Some employers were looking to hire for places other than Scranton. But the office was especially interested in those employers who would adapt buildings and sites in Scranton and employ local workers.[11]

Then, in mid-April, the Electric City reaped a long-awaited economic boost. The Murray Corporation of America committed to building a huge war-related manufacturing plant that would, when fully up and running, provide seven thousand jobs, according to a high-spirited letter of thanks from Elliott to the editors of *The Iron Age*. The *Times Leader* (Wilkes-Barre), the evening paper of Scranton's regional competitor city nineteen miles down the adjoined valleys, confirmed this news and quoted a letter from President Roosevelt to Senator Guffey: ". . . the War Production board approved an Army Air Force project which involves the construction of a new 500,000-square-foot one-story building in the city of Scranton for the manufacture of outer wing panels for airplanes by Murray Corp. of America. This project will employ about 2500 people by August of this year, and more people when production is stepped up." This was not, however, exactly the news Wilkes-Barre hoped to hear. The Wyoming Valley Chamber of Commerce, which included

Wilkes-Barre and Pittston, had simultaneously engaged Elliott to represent them and work together with Scranton and the Lackawanna Valley to attract the war industry to all three cities. Although Elliott argued the plant's South Scranton location was an easy commute for Wyoming Valley workers, benefiting Wilkes-Barre and Pittston as well, the Wyoming Valley Chamber of Commerce "decided to dispense with [his] services."[12]

Buoyed by Scranton's coup with the Murray plant, Jane—writing anonymously in this "Special to the Herald Tribune"—landed a freelance article in the prominent New York newspaper on May 2, 1943, headlined "Scranton Shifts from Mining to Manufacturing." Those who had worked with the author were delighted by the ongoing, nationwide publicity for the struggling former anthracite capital. While a mere fifteen years prior, in 1928, fifty thousand miners had toiled in Scranton, she wrote, "That number . . . has now dwindled to about 8,000." Jane recounted the odyssey of Scranton's success in acquiring new industry. During the past year, thirty firms—among them large clothing, tobacco, and radio-parts companies—had set up factories in the city, and construction of the largest was about to begin. Pointing out the symbolism of its location, Jane noted the Murray Corporation was to build its facility "on the site of the old Lackawanna Iron & Steel Company, which forty years ago moved to Lackawanna, N.Y., to be closer to the source of ore, and since has become part of Bethlehem Steel Company." She spoke of the two-year effort spearheaded by Thomas Connor, whom she named for the first time, and praised him for his paper's incessant articles on frustrations and accomplishments in the process. In conclusion, Jane articulated both her passion for her home city and her wisdom about the economic future of all cities: ". . . only by making the transition from mining to manufacturing will the city escape a disastrous decline and possible oblivion."[13]

In a September 4, 1943, article in *Editor & Publisher*—the newspaper industry's magazine—Jane Butzner, in her first bylined piece about the campaign to attract war industry to Scranton, applauded *The*

Scranton Tribune and *The Scrantonian* for their leadership and "almost entirely" engineering the effort to save Scranton from becoming a "ghost town." "Wherever possible," she explained—without mentioning her own contributions—the paper had worked with "the Chamber of Commerce, labor, and other civic organizations." And she complimented the *Tribune*, a Republican paper, on its bipartisanship: "It has worked largely with and through Democrats, and has had the cooperation of all types of civic organizations."[14]

At the end of September 1943, *The Scranton Tribune*, the Sunday *Scrantonian*, and the Scranton Chamber of Commerce acknowledged Jane's role in reigniting the campaign to bring war-era jobs to Scranton. The Sunday *Scrantonian*, proclaiming "Ex-Scranton Girl Helps Home City," divulged the identity of the author of the *Iron Age* game changer and commended "Miss Butzner" for "help[ing] materially . . . to bring about a favorable decision in the Murray Corporation locating here." As a gesture of gratitude, the city's Chamber of Commerce compiled for Jane a pressboard binder of more than two dozen neatly pasted and labeled articles, published from late March through early April 1943, that had reported on and cited the *Iron Age* piece and amplified its impact. In her family archives, Jane preserved this memento of her home city's struggle and the action she had taken. In her *Editor & Publisher* article, Jane had spotlighted the *Tribune* for saving "a mining town whose veins of mineral wealth have been worked out" from a "ghost town fate." She called their efforts "a tribute to the potency of the printed word," but she, too had, honed the power of "perfect word[s] to clothe the perfect thought" in print for a cause about which she cared deeply.[15]

While continuing as a freelance writer—landing more than twenty articles for the *New York Herald Tribune* alone—Jane left her job at *The Iron Age* in November 1943. She went on to work as a salaried writer for the U.S. government, first for the Office of War Information through 1945 and later for *Amerika* magazine at the State Department. Meanwhile, Jane and Betty had returned to their home city for the first of their siblings' weddings. In April 1942, when

Kay Schoen Butzner (leftmost) with other women chemists
at her next workplace, Socony-Vacuum Oil in Fallsburg, NY, 1945.
Courtesy of Kay Butzner.

Jim broke the news of his engagement to Mary Catharine "Kay" Schoen, both Jane and Betty wrote ebullient, affectionate letters to Kay, welcoming her into the family as "another sister." "It sure would be nice to have three girls in the family, especially since the third one is you," Jane told Kay. Jim and Kay married on September 5, 1942, after Kay's graduation that June from Hood College, in Maryland. Because of subsidence problems at the West Side's Plymouth Congregational Church, to which her mother belonged, the wedding took place at the downtown Elm Park Methodist Episcopal Church, with the Plymouth Congregational pastor performing the service. Having majored in chemistry, Kay got her first job in Wilmington, Delaware, at the Hercules Powder Company, which was manufacturing explosives and munitions for World War II, while Jim was able to secure a considerably higher-paying job at a Mobil Oil research lab, which hired only men.[16]

A couple of years later, Jane and Betty rode the train back to Scranton for another family wedding, but this time Jane was the bride.

In March 1944, while working at the Office of War Information, Jane met Robert Hyde Jacobs, Jr., an architect employed in wartime industry at Grumman Aircraft Engineering Corporation on Long Island, where Betty worked. Bob and Jane were smitten immediately and soon displayed the independent streaks for which they were known. "At that time people didn't live together before they were married," Kay reflected. "Bob and Jane did. Jane's mother didn't know, but I think she would have objected." It couldn't have been for long, because on May 27, 1944, the family gathered at the Monroe Avenue house to witness Jane and Bob tie the knot. "Getting married at home in the backyard was unusual," Kay commented, "but that was the kind of wedding she wanted." Jane's cousin Elizabeth Butzner, Nancy's

Norma Schoen (Kay Butzner's mother), Bess Butzner, and Bess's aunt Dora Kesty (Hannah Breece's youngest sister), outside Bess's house in Fredericksburg, VA, 1947. Courtesy of Kay Butzner.

younger sister, was the only Butzner from Virginia present at this wedding. Elizabeth later recalled for her niece Lucie the remarkable image of the newlyweds leaving the wedding by riding off on their bicycles for their honeymoon.[17]

For practical reasons, on August 23, 1946, Bess Robison Butzner sold the much-loved Dunmore house to Franklin and Juanita Gelder, neighbors on the next block over. Bess, then in her late sixties, had been widowed for almost nine years, and her children had settled away from Scranton. Her son John had recently married Viola "Pete" Peterson, who had worked at Grumman with Bob Jacobs. John and Pete moved to Fredericksburg, Virginia, to join John's uncle William Butzner's law practice. Bess's daughter Betty was soon to wed, in a civil ceremony, Julius Manson, a lawyer, of Eastern European Jewish descent. Like Jane and Bob, Betty and Juli would remain in New York. Bess chose to move to Fredericksburg to be close to John because she thought he would be the most likely to stay in the same place. Ironically, he was the first to relocate. In 1962, John and his family, and Bess, moved about fifty miles to Richmond, the state capital, when President Kennedy appointed him to the United States District Court for the Eastern District of Virginia.[18]

Although all the Butzners had departed Scranton, Jane—through friends, colleagues, and her brother Jim's in-laws—kept up with how her home city was faring. The Murray Corporation had ended up employing "only 3,000 people at its peak between its opening in February 1944 and the end of the war" in 1945, but these jobs boosted the city's economy, at least temporarily. After the war, the company turned to manufacturing bathtubs, sinks, and washing machines. In an effort to keep this industry in the city, the Greater Scranton Chamber of Commerce raised money to buy the Murray Corporation's building from the federal government and lease it back to the government. To attract other "responsible industry," they used leftover capital and, by 1950, acquired fifteen more community-financed factory buildings to rent or sell. Private investors added to this by constructing sixteen more plants. Citizens came together to do this in what was called the Scranton Plan, aided by the Greater Scranton Foundation Fund's selling of bonds.[19]

Despite post–World War II optimism and the 1950s community effort in the Electric City, Scranton's industry was not diversifying quickly enough to achieve or maintain a healthy economy. In the 1960s, the Tobyhanna Army Depot in the nearby Poconos hired thousands of workers, making it the largest employer in northeastern Pennsylvania. A substantial number of people working at the base spilled into Scranton as they looked for places for their families to live, and the city grew concerned about providing enough housing, especially for those of lesser means. This was an issue with a long history in her city, as Jane knew well.[20]

Since at least 1925, when Jane was only nine, as coal strikes began to threaten the city's prosperity, community leaders—including African American Dr. J. E. Foster—met to discuss the need to improve Scranton's housing for low-income residents. In 1939, Scranton's Republican mayor created the Scranton Housing Authority, with approval for one million dollars to build affordable housing. In the spirit of cooperation—not unusual then—between parties, he appointed former Democratic mayor John Durkan to the agency. Durkan was subsequently elected its first vice president. He would remain there for the next quarter century. In the years immediately following World War II, Scranton fell prey to the common wisdom, especially prevalent among urban planners and city officials at the time, that urban neighborhoods appearing to be run-down were a blight and should be torn down and replaced with modern buildings, which were generally drab and monotonous. As a writer and editor at *Architectural Forum*, America's foremost magazine on architecture, in New York in the early 1950s, Jane Butzner Jacobs came to disagree with this perception of long-established aging neighborhoods and the customary remedy for dealing with them. In the late 1950s, she would set to work on her *Death and Life of Great American Cities*, which attacked and eventually helped to halt "urban renewal." Meanwhile, Jane was disturbed to learn that the powers that be in her own city had embarked on a plan to systematically obliterate tightly knit neighborhoods whose healthy attributes she appreciated.[21]

In the mid 1950s, like planning agencies across America enticed by munificent federal funds set aside for urban renewal, Scranton's City Planning Commission engaged "expert" consultants to inventory the Electric City's housing stock. As in many other cities, an outside firm—in this case from Newark, New Jersey—unfamiliar with Scranton, conducted "a comprehensive study . . . of existing housing which will serve as an analytic base for . . . new and modern housing in line with our city's resources." The study, laden with statistics to make its case, identified eighteen areas "of concentrated substandard housing and major neighborhood deficiencies." It noted that 41 percent of housing was fifty-five or more years old, only 5.8 percent of all housing had been built since 1930, and 20 percent of all housing had no central heating—while some lacked flush toilets, private baths, or hot water. Eleven thousand people, the report said, resided in these eighteen "blighted" areas, or about one-tenth of the city's population. They recommended massive improvements that would take fifteen years and require relocating 3,400 families in the process.[22]

Among the areas chosen for "redevelopment," as planners termed the process, was the dense and vibrant neighborhood between Scranton's two public high schools, where some of Jane's friends and classmates had or still lived. City planners referred to this area as Central-Tech, which a *Scranton Times* reporter characterized in 1956 as "a mixed [neighborhood] of Negro and white families," just as it had been when Jane was a schoolgirl. By September that year, plans were already in place to demolish thirty-four properties there. Scranton city councilors voiced their fear that those whose homes were destroyed would not be able to move into the yet-to-be-constructed public housing. As it turned out, only a fraction of the displaced families were accepted into the new housing, and often these placements were in far-flung parts of the city.[23]

In *The Death and Life of Great American Cities*, Jane made a case for preserving neighborhoods like Central-Tech and cautioned against disrupting them. In October 1961, when her book was hot off the press, the *Scranton Times* laid claim to the author and pointed out her Scranton roots. With her friend Bob Arthur still editor of the morning *Scranton Tribune* and possibly other of Jane's journalistic compatriots at *The Scranton Times*, the afternoon paper ran a highly laudatory article, "Ex-Area Woman Writes Book Attacking City Revamping," about her acclaimed book. Jane Butzner Jacobs "began tapping a typewriter in Scranton," the reporter crowed, "and dedicated her first published book to her childhood home." Despite some Scrantonians' awareness of Jane's self-proclaimed "attack on current city planning and rebuilding," city officials proceeded with the demolition of homes and revered buildings and moved ahead with their large-scale plans for urban renewal and public housing.[24]

During the 1960s and 1970s, Scranton implemented much of the 1956 plan and succeeded in wiping out the lively old Central-Tech neighborhood with its courts and modest houses clustered among businesses and light industry. In her seminal book, Jane Jacobs had argued for keeping these kinds of communities, but, apparently, planners in Scranton had not read it, or they disagreed with her conclusions. Central-Tech's redevelopment would displace and therefore necessitate the relocation of 365 of 401 families as a result of urban renewal. Sixty-eight of these families were nonwhite, and 297 were white. "The mayor recently released results of an informal survey," *The Scranton Times* reported in June 1965, "which showed many residents of the sector do not favor the 'regimented' life of a public housing project." By the early 1970s, the first of the replacement projects was completed. Alongside Central High School, a seven-story, half-block-wide high-rise apartment building, blithely named Washington West Apartments, opened for the elderly.[25]

To clear the land for the high-rise, the Scranton Redevelopment Authority invoked the right of eminent domain to evacuate families from the 500 and 600 blocks of North Washington, where George Munchak had lived with his family during his eighth-grade and high school years with Jane. The government's power of eminent domain,

Nira Blue Madison felt the loss of community with the
demolition of the Central-Tech neighborhood,
photo c. 2011. Courtesy of Dorothy Walker Smith.

theoretically for the public good, also enabled the city to take and demolish many other houses, among them Nira Blue Madison's family
home of many decades. Shortly afterward, in December 1972, her
father, Paul Blue, died. Nira, her husband, and children were able
to move to an existing two-family house not far away, on the 800
block of Adams Avenue. In 1972, Midtown Apartments, a maze of
two-story redbrick structures, went up, occupying the largest area
between the high schools. "Some people moved back into" the new
buildings where the courts used to be, "and others went in different
directions," Nira observed. "But it was no longer the community it
once was," although "some people did come back to go to church."
Nira remained in Scranton until 1999, when she left her home city
to be near her children, including her daughter, who had become a
doctor.[26]

Cathy Ann Strader Hardaway vividly remembered losing her
cherished childhood home, as a young adolescent, to urban renewal.
She recalled its fireplace, their own yard, and the front porch, where

Gwen Strader and her daughter Cathy Ann Strader Hardaway
lost their house to urban renewal, photo 2009.
Courtesy of Dorothy Walker Smith and Cathy Ann Strader Hardaway.

they'd sat, greeting neighbors. On the heels of her father John Strader's tragic death at age fifty-one, she said, the city "came to us and said we had to move and paid us for our house," whose mortgage was paid off. Her bereaved mother, now a widow with five children, was emotionally in no condition to buy another house. Gwen Strader had no choice but to become a renter. She was the first person to move into the Midtown Apartments—coincidentally, at almost the same time as Jane's former eighth-grade classmate, Cidonia Mitchell [now Ratchford] and her two adopted children. The apartments, which everyone referred to derogatorily as "the projects," were "cheaply built" and had small rooms, and there were "not that many kids around." Cathy spoke forthrightly, echoing the sentiment of other community members: "The pride of home ownership was taken away from us. They robbed us of our community and our churches in the old neighborhood. It had been a mix of poor and more well-off, and you could connect with all levels of society." With all the other ethnic areas in Scranton, "why did they 'redevelop' the African American community?"[27]

Granville C. Smith, like Dr. J. E. Foster and other African Americans, had become a community leader, organizing and conducting community meetings to mitigate the city's seemingly inevitable dissolution of the Central-Tech neighborhood in Scranton. In 1972, however, when the A&P grocery chain set up its own trucking department and put Granville's trucking company out of business, he and his wife, Dottie, reluctantly pulled up stakes and moved to the greater New York area, where he had accepted a job in the financial department of the Presbyterian Church's headquarters. By May 1975, 4,409 people, constituting 4 percent of the city's population, resided in public housing run by the Scranton Housing Authority, distributed among ten low-rent developments. All but the Midtown Apartments were scattered about in nooks and crannies throughout the city. The urban renewal of the Central-Tech neighborhood ultimately ripped

Scranton Lackawanna Trust Building, built in 1898, an architectural casualty of the 1970s. Scan obtained from Scranton Public Library.

out an integral piece of the heart of downtown, the same sorry situation that Jane had observed in New York and other American cities.[28]

From sometime in the 1930s on, Scranton consistently lost population, with its greatest exodus in the 1970s, when urban renewal was supposed to be reviving the city. Municipal officials exhibited a parallel decline in appreciation for many of Scranton's central-city architectural treasures, which had become underutilized and, too often, shuttered. The 1970s saw the wrecking ball claim such gems as the YMCA, home to Dr. Kay's luxurious rented quarters, and the Renaissance Revival Scranton Lackawanna Trust Company Building, opposite the south side of Courthouse Square. The demolitions left central city gap-toothed with empty lots. "They just tore the buildings down. Period. They didn't build anything new," Nira Madison observed with exasperation. Jane's Washington School #3, in its glorious building in Dunmore, closed in 1972 and was subsequently torn down because of school district consolidation, another trend of which Jane disapproved. All Dunmore's public schools, including middle school and high school, were grouped together along the borough's northern edge, necessitating school buses for the children who no longer lived close enough to walk to school. "It divided us," Dunmore native Maria Pane MacDonald, professor of architecture at what is now Marywood University, recalled. "Some students were called the "walkers" and others were the "busers.""[29]

Simultaneously, since so many mines had been abandoned, the city set about removing the coal breakers and related surface buildings, and filling the underground shafts and tunnels with slag from the culm dumps. By doing this, they hoped to stave off further subsidence. Much of this culm-filled land, however, remains unbuildable and has been paved for parking or used as parkland. Portions of these large open spaces once occupied by coal companies, although unstable, can support low buildings without basements. Like forests after wildfires, these lands have sprouted a second growth of athletic fields, mini–strip malls, industrial parks, and salvage lots. "You can follow the river and the [generally abandoned] railroad tracks today and find the flat, sprawling spaces where the mines and breakers were," Maria MacDonald pointed out. A few small outbuildings and gentle rises of what neighborhood children once called "black sands" persist as remnants of the former flourishing coal industry. They are the lone testaments to and "tangible reminders" of a bygone era. The haunting breakers that John Willard Raught immortalized in his paintings have all disappeared.[30]

Today, the expansive site of the Green Ridge Coal Company, once served by the Erie and Wyoming Valley Railroad, displays little evidence of the massive breaker and industrial compound that lay in the short stretch between Jane's home and Central High School. Maps from 1920 through 1939 document the imposing Green Ridge Breaker and its virtual mountain of culm—rising from an area equivalent to two city blocks—and the adjacent Scranton Electric Company. Sometime in the 1940s, the breaker was removed, but the electric company endured and expanded and impenetrably fenced off the entire site, along with portions of the streets that ran through it. No one seems to know what happened to the enormous culm pile. Was it pumped into the tunnels below to shore up the city? "Note that the Scranton Electric Company used culm to generate steam to run the electric turbines," Rudy Kunz, of the Dunmore Historical Society, commented. "Maybe Pennsylvania Power & Light [which took over] used it for that purpose, too?" Beginning in the 1950s, just south of the land vacated by the breaker, on North Washington Avenue, Maria's father, Frank Pane, ran a used-car dealership. After several other individuals started dealerships farther up the avenue, Pane—a resourceful entrepreneur of Italian background who had begun as a mechanic—decided to start his own company and purchased extra land to rent out for parking on the unbuildable former breaker site up the street.[31]

Ex-Scrantonian Jane admired the resilience and ingenuity of people in her home city, and some members of Scranton's press kept tabs on her and applauded her work, as well. As she was "working on another book, also about cities" but "more on the economies of cities,"

The Scranton Times, in 1964, proudly reported on Jane Butzner Jacobs's national recognition as exemplified by her upcoming engagement as a featured guest and speaker at a White House "women-doers" luncheon with the First Lady, "Mrs. Lyndon Johnson." Mrs. Johnson had taken up the cause of city beautification. Jane told the reporter what she intended to say in her address: "Appearance and attractiveness in cities are very much involved in the substance of cities and I don't think you can promote the visual appearance of cities without thinking of their content and how the city works. . . . I like cities, and I don't think any city is hopeless. They get awful mistreatment, but they have a great deal of vitality."[32]

In May 1969, when *The Economy of Cities*, Jane's first "outgrowth" of *Death and Life*, was about to be released, an astute reporter under Bob Arthur's editorial direction at *The Scranton Tribune* informed the paper's readership of the ex-Scrantonian's latest accomplishment. In *Economy of Cities*, the "sequel to her award-winning book," the article stated, "Mrs. Jacobs took issue with Adam Smith and Karl Marx. 'Ideology is narrowing and limiting,'" it quoted Jane as saying, "'Cities are chaotic. They have an order of economic development, but they work without ideology.'" Jane's old friends who had remained in their home city followed her work and cheered her on.[33]

During Scranton's demoralized and difficult decades of the 1960s and 1970s, when Jane was immersed in writing, speaking, and taking action in defense of cities, she received sporadic news of her former hometown, but no evidence exists of Jane's visiting her old haunts during these decades. In 1968, Jane, her husband, and their three children permanently emigrated from New York to Toronto, so that her sons, Jim and Ned, would not be drafted into the Vietnam War. They all, in due course, became Canadian citizens. When Bess Robison Butzner passed away in 1981, at the age of 101, Jane and a number of relatives gathered for her funeral in Bloomsburg, Pennsylvania, and burial in the family plot in Creveling Cemetery near Espy. Afterward, Jane suggested that, on their drive back to Toronto, they stop by Scranton to see her old house.[34]

Perhaps with her curiosity piqued from her trip a couple of years earlier, Jane returned to Scranton, in May 1983, for the fiftieth reunion of her January 1933 graduating class at Central High School and thoroughly enjoyed it. The event was held at the tony all-male Scranton Club, a venue that in flush times would have been out of reach for all but a scant few of her schoolmates' families. Since it had been some years since Jane had had more than a passing glimpse of her home city, she was intrigued to see "what her classmates looked like now." Her fellow alum J. Milton Swartz had helped organize the reunion and hoped Jane would come. She arrived with her husband, Bob. Milton and his wife, Arlene, "talked with them at length." Milton had grown up in north Dunmore, near Marywood College, and his father owned and ran the Royal Crown Bottling Company. Milton eventually took over his father's company and stayed in Scranton, where he also became president of the Jewish Home in northeast Pennsylvania. Jane's father had been the doctor for Milton's family. Milton and Arlene had read Jane's books, and Milton told his wife that he was "proud of Jane." Arlene, also a Scranton native, remarked that she got a kick out of seeing that "Jane's husband always wore sneakers."[35]

Although more than a third of the class had passed away or were not locatable, sixty-two alums and spouses posed for the photograph memorializing the occasion. Jane was delighted to find her old friend Jeanne Madden, who performed the class song at the reunion. In 1938, Jeanne had forsaken Hollywood and Broadway to marry Keith Martin. After they divorced, in 1954, and her mother died the next year, she ran the family's Hotel Holland in Scranton for several years before it was turned into public housing for the elderly. She had stayed in the region ever since. Jane exchanged addresses with her fellow Girl Scout Jean Patterson Nisbet, who had traveled the world. Alums who had been Jane's eighth-grade classmates as well and still resided in the Electric City also showed up: Florence Osterland Kane, who described herself in the reunion booklet as widowed, having "worked for a while as a correspondent at the Tribune," and "still working as a

Awaiting restoration, these Lackawanna Avenue historic buildings escaped demolition, photo 2008. Author's photo.

secretary" at an insurance company; and Kathryn Coyne Lynch, who listed only her widowhood and two children and grandchildren.[36]

From 1984 on, Jane had a loyal fan in Joseph X. Flannery, a regular *Scranton Times* (later *Times-Tribune*) columnist, who made her the focus of at least several of his pieces. He lauded her books, which he deemed "important," and conversed with her on the phone to learn more. "While living here," Flannery reported, "Mrs. Jacobs spent much time pondering how Scranton, the only city she then knew, worked. She wondered: What kept it functioning? What made it vibrant? How did its economy work?" While she lacked a college degree, "she has a mind that produces common sense answers to very complex questions." He liked her championing of "old neighborhoods with their haphazard mix of apartment houses, warehouses, single homes, factories, duplexes, schools, churches, and other structures," which reflected Scranton's makeup. Flannery noted in his first column about Jane, "[She], in her writings, says what is on her mind in her books. As a result, her native city does not get the treatment the Greater Chamber of Commerce would prefer."[37]

Indeed, by the mid-1980s, Jane was in conflict with the Scranton Chamber of Commerce, with which she had once collaborated. With central city largely abandoned, the charming Victorian buildings lining Lackawanna Avenue had fallen into disrepair, and their street-level facades were shabby and disfigured. Scranton faced the dilemma of how to deal with what many regarded as a civic disgrace. Galvanized by the loss of the YMCA to the wrecking ball, a group of a dozen or so architects and civic activists in Scranton—young and old, male and female, from all walks of life—had formed the Architectural Heritage Association (AHA) of northeastern Pennsylvania in 1978. This diverse group—including psychiatrist Peter Cupple and artist Hope Horn—opposed demolishing Lackawanna Avenue's historic structures, which accommodated numerous small businesses owned by local proprietors. The Chamber and the majority of citizens, however, were eager to rid the city of what they considered an eyesore. An architect originally from Argentina and member of AHA, Nelida Amador, who had read Jacobs's books and discovered her Scranton roots, suggested AHA president Nancy Bisgnani—who otherwise worked as an office manager and U.S. Census enumerator—write to Jane and ask for her help. Jane did not hesitate to lend her support to her home city.[38]

Nancy Bisgnani apprised Jane that the situation was further complicated by a scheme to replace the razed buildings with a suburban-type mall. For some time, Albert R. Boscov, a department store developer based in Reading, Pennsylvania, had wanted to build a store in Scranton. It would be another link in his eponymous chain, but he was thwarted in his attempts until the political forces aligned—surprisingly, in a bipartisan team. In October 1986, U.S. congressman Joseph M. McDade, a Republican from Pennsylvania and member of the House Appropriations Committee, managed to get funding to establish the Steamtown National Historic Site (NHS) by tacking it onto the Department of the Interior's budget. As part of the National Park Service, this museum-park in the old Delaware, Lackawanna & Western Railroad yard at the edge of downtown's commercial district would consist mostly of trains purchased from Vermont and not authentic to Pennsylvania. Despite the Smithsonian's transportation curator's calling it a "second-class collection," Congress appropriated many millions to build the site, making it "one of the most expensive new national parks." A *Washington Post* writer commented, "McDade brought home the bacon" for Scranton in "one of the finest pork barrel boondoggles of all time."[39]

Then, in the late 1980s, Pennsylvania governor Robert P. Casey, a Democrat, joined McDade in nailing down more millions in federal funds (including thirteen million dollars in an Urban Development Action Grant) plus state aid "for a massive new downtown shopping mall." They also "coaxed loans from the state teachers pension fund and the International Brotherhood of Electrical Workers pension fund." Most Scrantonians, along with the City Council, two consecutive mayors, the city's two newspapers, and many local businesspeople, supported Steamtown NHS and the mall. They were desperate to rescue the old mining and industrial area from its long depression and to jump-start its economy, *and* they were willing to sacrifice a sizable stretch of the Lackawanna Avenue historic district in the process. AHA, other preservationists, a small number of local businesses—such as Ufberg's Home Furniture, Harding's Restaurant, and Starr Uniforms—and a few members of Congress took a stand against the project, vehemently opposing "ripping down buildings that are part of [Scranton's] historic soul."[40]

Decades later, Dr. Peter Cupple, a former president of AHA, remembered Jane's "beautiful three-page letter" written on New Year's Eve, 1987, in response to Nancy Bisgnani's request. Addressing Tim McDowell, director of Scranton's Office of Economic and Community Development, Jane launched her strategically conceived and impassioned appeal. She described her most recent visit to Scranton (to attend her fiftieth high school reunion) and why she was struck by "how unusually attractive its downtown had become" with its "visible signs of vitality and prosperity" and "many handsome and varied old buildings . . . well-tended." With these fine attributes, Jane declared, Scranton had shown itself to be "a downtown with pride and high

morale"—enviable qualities—and "has become a national treasure."
She took what some people might think of as negative components
of a city and showed their strengths: "[Scranton's] old buildings and
intact streets . . . had now become unusual and valuable assets and a
source of economic growth."[41]

Then Jane changed her tone: "I am appalled to hear that there is
a proposal to level an appreciable section of Lackawanna Avenue and
to erect, of all things, a suburban-type shopping mall . . . guaranteed
to be destructive economically, visually and socially." She vividly specified the ways. Malls "touted [before they were built] as downtown
saviors" were likely to economically deaden and victimize the central
city. Visually the mall would "stick out like a sore thumb . . . [and]
look like a gimcracky excrescence on the downtown"—a description
sounding humorously vulgar and sending readers to the dictionary.
Socially, the mall would undercut the downtown's morale, causing
"discouragement, loss of faith in the . . . downtown's future, and a
loss of care for downtown."[42]

Formerly Oppenheim's department store, known as
Scranton Dry Goods, built 1897, building rehabbed 1994, photo 2006.
Courtesy of hemmler + camayd architects.

"Why," Jane asked, "is an outsider like me being so officious as to send you advice you haven't solicited?" Answering her own question, she proceeded: "First, I hate to see gratuitous destruction visited on any city, and the more so when the city . . . is beautiful, admirable, and promising. Second, I am not entirely an outsider." She explained her connection to Scranton, Dunmore, Central High, and *The Scranton Tribune*. She "[had] felt sad when Scranton fell on hard times" and "rejoiced to see it prospering and turning weakness to strength." Jane spoke sincerely, from her heart: "I only hope that you respect what Scranton is, has been, and can be."[43]

Although the *Scrantonian Tribune* printed many pithy excerpts from Jane's critical letter and extolled her qualifications as "a foremost planning theorist" who had received "international recognition for her views on urban survival," officials ignored her admonition. The controversy over the demolition, the mall, and Steamtown NHS received broad coverage in the national press, including the *Washington Post*, as a major scandal. Other ex-Scrantonians, like Jane's brother Jim and his wife, Kay, followed "the Scranton fight," as Jane referred to it when writing to them not long after her letter to McDowell. "From what I gather, the [mall opponents] have a hard battle. It sounds to me like one of those cases," she wrote, speaking bluntly and less diplomatically to Jim and Kay, "where nobody with power is really concerned at all about what is best for the city, its businesses and so on, but rather about the money to be made from the land sales, construction, all the consulting fees and so on. When they make theirs, what do they care about how it turns out?"[44]

Soon after its founding, AHA had hired the prestigious firm of Venturi and Rauch, which helped put all of Lackawanna Avenue's blocks on the National Register of Historic Places as worthy of pres- ervation. National Register status would not ensure that the buildings would be preserved, but it would make the process of obtaining per- mission to demolish them more formidable and could lead to miti- gating actions. Spearheaded by Nancy Bisignani, AHA kept up the fight, bringing two cases against the Scranton Mall Association, in 1989 and 1991, to block the demolition of the historic buildings and the construction of the mall. AHA used Jane's letter to McDowell in the court proceedings. In early May 1989, while the fate of Scranton's downtown hung in the balance, Jane and Bob, along with their daughter, Burgin, and Burgin's husband, took a car trip purely for pleasure to see Jane's old haunts in Pennsylvania. Before Jane departed from her home city, wearing her big Latin American wool poncho, she posed, smiling, on the sidewalk in front of 1712 Monroe Avenue, while Bob photographed her. (See photo on page 128.)[45]

Although AHA did not succeed in stopping the mall, they won some mitigations. Among them, Oppenheim's department store and the Samter's building were spared destruction to be rehabbed and re-purposed, and the city of Scranton established the Historical Architectural Review Board. The day before the scheduled implosion, Joseph Flannery reported in his column, "When told that the razing had begun, Jane said: 'That's too bad. It's a bad scheme that won't work in the long term.'"[46]

On Sunday morning, April 5, 1992, the city of Scranton imploded three blocks at the epicenter of its downtown, on the south side of Lackawanna Avenue. A crowd of between twelve and fifteen thousand citizens had gathered to witness the event, broadcast live by local television stations and aired internationally on CNN. In the heart of Lackawanna Avenue's historic district, roughly twenty buildings of assorted size, age, and condition were, in a matter of minutes, reduced to rubble to make way for the shopping mall.[47]

The mall opened in the fall of 1993. Within three months, across the street and connected by a second-floor pedestrian bridge, the already floundering Globe department store suffered a steep decline in its business and closed its doors. Steamtown NHS welcomed its first visitors on July 4, 1995. Yet more neighboring businesses continued to sputter and give up. In 2001, columnist Joe Flannery reflected, "Given all the empty buildings now in the downtown, Mrs. Jacobs' 1988 warning was eerily prophetic."[48]

In September 1996, on her way back to Toronto after her husband's funeral near Bloomsburg, Jane—with a group of family members in tow—stopped, after an hour's pastoral drive, in Scranton, still her touchstone in difficult times. She wanted to show them where she grew up and the city that figured so large in her life. This time, her granddaughter Larissa Code took photographs of the Butzner family home and other favorite sites that Jane pointed out. They must have passed the incongruous mall at the crossroads of downtown, but Larissa did not snap a picture of it. It appears that this was Jane's last visit to her first city. Almost ten years later, in 2006, with her ninetieth birthday a week away and two new books in the works, Jane died. She was buried alongside Bob, close to her ancestral home in Espy, Pennsylvania, in the family plot where her baby brother, sister, parents, and grandparents had also been laid to rest.[49]

In the wake of the September 11, 2001, terrorist attack, Lackawanna County officials had secured funds from the Department of Homeland Security to build a protective stone barrier that would buffer the magnificent courthouse against vehicular assaults and, simultaneously, serve a commemorative purpose. So much of the building's surrounding open space was already devoted to memorializing na-

Granite block honoring Jane Jacobs, in the "Piazza dell'Arte," Courthouse Square, photo 2011. Courtesy of John Cowder.

tional figures, local ethnic groups, and veterans that they wanted to take a new approach by recognizing Scrantonians who had achieved national and international success in the arts and humanities. They would name this section of Courthouse Square Piazza dell'Arte. A committee of about a dozen people associated with the arts—including architecture, music, theater, literature, and the visual arts—would select the honorees. Individuals chosen had to be born in or associated with Scranton, and each had to have returned or brought something back to Scranton. Everyone came up with names to be voted on. Richard Leonori, the committee's only architect, was one of the people who nominated Jane Jacobs, and, he reported, in their discussion there was "no question about committee members choosing her."[50]

In 2007, the year following Jane's death and a decade and a half after the mall opened, a solid arc of granite blocks was unveiled to pay tribute to eight Scrantonians in diverse artistic arenas. There, citizens of Jane's first city proclaimed, as the inscription reads, that she had "inspired generations of city planners and preservationists and transformed public policy regarding cities." And they noted that in her 1969 book, *The Economy of Cities*, she had "cited Scranton as vibrant and livable." On the grounds of the city's architectural crown, facing the sidewalk along a street she had walked countless times, the name Jane Butzner Jacobs was officially carved in stone.

Today, atop the 1896 Board of Trade building, Scranton's 1926 sign, with its historic slogan, still shines its lights over the city each night. Courtesy of the Lackawanna County Visitors Bureau.

CHAPTER 12

· · ·

Learning from Scranton

WHEN RICHARD LEONORI, a native Scrantonian, architect, and
preservation activist, first read Jane Jacobs's *Death and Life of Great
American Cities* in architecture school in the early 1970s, he said he
"knew that it had to have been written by someone from Scranton."
He came upon passages that sounded as if the author were describing the "organic, gritty city" of Scranton with a deep understanding
of the value of these "livelier, dirtier, real places." Writing from New
York and Toronto, Jane transformed the attitudes of people across
America and around the globe about the importance of cities and
what makes them thrive or deteriorate. Her ideas, however, germi-
nated in the dynamic and livable Scranton of her youth, in the 1920s
and 1930s, as the city reached its economic and demographic zenith
before embarking on a steady descent. This once thriving, then tot-
tering medium-size city served as Jane Jacobs's initial observational
laboratory.[1]

Jane watched the way her city grew incrementally as individuals
extended and filled in the urban fabric. She read and thought about
its first enterprising innovators, a few daring men from the East, who
manipulated technology and succeeded in launching a boomtown
on an unremarkable site, alongside a barely Roaring Brook. As she
navigated the slate sidewalks from an early age, she saw the towering

coal breakers in the distance and walked to the small businesses dotted among the residences in her naturally mixed-use neighborhood. Along her own blocks lived people from various countries engaged in all sorts of ways of making a living. She walked or took the streetcar to school alongside fellow students and her teachers, and—just steps from her front door—first discovered the usefulness of short blocks and alleys in enlivening urban forays. Trips to the burgeoning downtown, crammed with assorted vernacular and glorious architecture, were a source of endless fascination. At school and in her neighborhood, Jane studied the characters who comprised each of her milieus and enjoyed their commonalities and their differences. She participated enthusiastically in Girl Scouts and drew lessons from nature. And from her perch as a cub reporter for the city's morning newspaper, she examined Scranton's myriad aspects and became well acquainted with the other men and a few women who threw themselves into taking the pulse of the city and took seriously the responsibility of informing the public.

Ultimately, Scranton gave Jane a lens through which to view all urban places. As a city whose population in its heyday stopped short of 150,000, Scranton was large enough to have a wide array of industry and opportunities but small enough that she could discern how its urban components affected one another. By examining her first city's moving parts—its institutions, informal organizations, built environment, its diversity of people and their occupations—she gained an appreciation for and moved toward an understanding of the messy but organized complexity of a city.

Jane's comprehension that cities contained "a sizable number of factors which are interrelated into an organic whole" was rooted in her first city. This complex system of dynamic interrelationships functioned well and, for the most part, led to social cohesion and a feeling of community. During Jane's Scranton years, people from all lines of work and cultures enjoyed coming together for a common purpose and endeavored to achieve collective goals. There was a widespread commitment to the civic good, an accepted responsibility to help those less fortunate—as exemplified by virtually the entire city's participation in the Community Chest—and, when needed, collaboration of opposing political parties to help the city and its citizens. Frequently championing bipartisanship and idealism, the city's daily newspapers reflected this sense of civic commitment. When Scranton faced hard times after America entered World War II, newspapers, trade unions, the Chamber of Commerce, citizens buying bonds, and Jane herself collaborated in an effort to bring war industry to the city. Compared to great cities, the medium-size city, with its more manageable scale, made problems easier to solve and government more accessible and less unwieldy.[2]

Late in her life, Jane's thoughts would return to her initial observations of her medium-size city and its advantages. She realized that this scale for an urban place was livable and practicable, and could breed tolerance through close contact and familiarity among a diverse population. Living in a well-populated area with a wide variety of people fostered a sense of community. In a city this size, just two public high schools could accommodate all students seeking this level of education. Thus, these institutions brought together children citywide from a multitude of backgrounds and neighborhoods. Not only African Americans but other ethnic groups mingled more easily and harmoniously than in great cities because of their proximity to one another and their attending not only the same schools but also Scout troops and a host of other organizations. The moderate size of the city allowed worlds to intersect easily through chance encounters, a phenomenon Jane pointed out in *Death and Life*. Scranton's residential streets were typically lined with houses with broad front porches, where people sat taking in the passing scene and conversing with neighbors. In a column musing about her Scranton childhood, Jane's former schoolmate June Carter Davies reminisced about the casual but recurring presence of hucksters, the ragman, gypsies, and the tramps who rode the tops of freight trains and wandered into her mainly middle-class neighborhood. Her grandmother, she said, "always gave [the tramps] a sandwich and coffee or whatever. . . ."[3]

With a smaller number of people in Scranton than in metropolises like New York or Philadelphia, citizens felt a connection to, rather than alienation from, their municipal government. In *Death and Life*, Jane cited New Haven as an example of a "small city" (what we now call a medium-size one) of 165,000. She deemed a city of that size, slightly more populated than Scranton in its prime, "understandable," and she noted that "as an administrative structure, [a city that size] has a relative coherence built right into it." In her youth, Scranton's city officials had welcomed high school students as executives for a day during the annual Boys' Week and Girls' Week, to demonstrate to young residents how the local government operated. When polio broke out in 1917, the city government invited all doctors in the community to confer with them on how best to prevent an epidemic. Many became involved, including Jane's father. The chances were likely that a large proportion of the population would know or meet municipal officials or candidates running for office, such as Harry Madden—the father of Jane's classmate Jeanne—who was elected as Register of Wills. Trying to win over a broad base and reel in his fellow musicians, Madden, in 1921, advertised his candidacy in a Polish-language souvenir concert program as the "Republikanski Kandydat."[4]

Although Jane's seminal book concentrated on great cities, she also recognized the importance of not-quite-so-great cities and took issue with the notion that bigger was better for a city or a larger administrative entity. She believed that New York City's incorporation of Brooklyn, Queens, the Bronx, and Staten Island benefited only Manhattan, while the outer boroughs lost their individual personalities. In her 1980 book, *The Question of Separatism: Quebec and the Struggle over Sovereignty*, she argued in support of the province's secession because smaller jurisdictions made more sense. Jane vehemently opposed the annexation of five outlying districts into the city of Toronto, but her warnings went unheeded. Toronto carried out its proposed merger on January 1, 1998, and became the fourth-largest North American metropolis. An antiamalgamation movement to return to Toronto's "Metro" system, away from the megacity, began almost immediately. Twenty years later, Torontonians still struggle with the problem of resolving the divergent interests of downtown and suburban municipalities within a centralized government, and they bemoan the loss of local accessibility to individual mayors and councils.[5]

Everything that Jane learned from Scranton was valuable, but not all of what she observed was to be emulated. Although Scranton nurtured inclusion, prejudice against African Americans, Jews, and working-class ethnics could, and did at times, raise its ugly head. This outraged Jane and her siblings, and they worked throughout their lives, both personally and politically, to fight discrimination. Growing up in Scranton also afforded Jane a close-up perspective of the economic pitfalls a city faced. Since at least the mid-1880s, civic leaders had sporadically warned against the economic peril of having "one main industry which provides most of the jobs and most of the money." As Jane told *Boston Globe* reporter Mark Feeney in 1993, Scranton offered her "a template of how a city stagnates and declines, and may be part of the reason why that subject interested me so much, because I came from a city where that happened."[6]

Born during the Electric City's glory days and its peak production of anthracite coal, Jane watched her city falter economically less than a century after its spectacular rise. Too dependent on the coal industry, from the mid-1920s forward, its economy followed a downward trajectory. Jane concluded that a healthy, sustainable city must have diverse economic activities that interact spontaneously and result in new forms of work. In her *Economy of Cities*, she invented the term *import replacement*, the need for a city to replace products previously imported with those manufactured within the city to maintain and grow its economy. Furthermore, Jane said, "It means nothing if there are not entirely new things being introduced into the economy by people who have been excluded in the past."[7]

Jane Jacobs had grown up amid a lively mosaic of people in Scranton, and she set great store in the many forms of diversity—in addition to economic activities—that a city should have. "In our American cities, we need all kinds of diversity intricately mingled in mutual support," she stated unequivocally in *Death and Life*. "Most city diversity is the creation of incredible numbers of different people and different private organizations, with vastly different ideas and purposes. . . ."

In Jane's day, Girls Scouts embraced girls from all backgrounds and from around the globe, and they took great interest in the culture and traditions of other countries. Jane had seen German immigrant Werner Rosteck rise to the top of their eighth-grade class. In high school, she befriended the Italian immigrant Carl Marzani and would stay in touch with him in later years after he became a successful writer of books, some of which described his immigrant experience. Enterprising Polish immigrants came to Jane's urban neighborhood as hucksters selling fresh food from their farms. Teachers such as Stella Kinback, Michael H. Jordan, and Louise Howitz went to extraordinary lengths to aid the immigrant schoolchildren so they could climb the ladder to citizenship and fulfilling lives. But Jane also understood new immigrants played important roles even before they assimilated. Speaking of people who had not yet attained certain skills, she asserted that they were "valuable and worth retaining, right where they are, before they become middle class." From her Scranton days through her last Toronto years, Jane championed the indispensable element of diversity that immigrants contributed to the life of the city. "These newcomers are enlivening the dull and dreary streets [of America]," Jane told an audience in Washington, D.C., in 2002, "with tiny grocery and clothing stores, second-hand shops, little importing and craft enterprises, skimpy offices, and modest but exotic restaurants." Immigrants who established continuous neighborhoods "become civic assets in every respect: social, physical, and economic." She recommended that cities support these neighborhoods with good municipal services and amenities, such as allowing them to organize open-air markets or jitneys. Even with Scranton's heavily diverse population, its ethnic communities were unified by shared core values and a sense of what Martin Luther King, Jr., called the "inescapable network of mutuality" among the city's populace.[8]

Community, institutional, and family ties bound together the city's great mosaic. In an era when reading books and periodicals played an integral part in the culture, parents and children from all social, economic, and ethnic backgrounds placed an exceptionally high value on education. Reflecting the public's strong commitment to

Marie Van Bergen
(later Mansuy), 1941.
Courtesy of Christopher Mansuy.

Dorothy "Dottie" Walker Smith,
2014. Author's photo.

education, the municipal government generously funneled resources into a range of public schools accommodating classical, technical, and even working children's and adult education especially aimed at immigrants. The satisfying careers and achievements of so many of Jane's schoolmates and peers attest to the quality of their education and the environment in which they grew up. Some of her friends ventured beyond Scranton for their livelihood, like Murrel Levy, who became an aerospace engineer for TRW Inc., or Kay Schoen Butzner, who followed in her father's footsteps as a chemist and high school chemistry teacher. Others led interesting lives in their home city. Don Nicholas, owner of an auto-parts store, traveled to the UK with his British wife and was arrested in the Soviet Union in 1971. Besides her longtime job in the credit office of the Paramount Shoe Store in Scranton, Marie Van Bergen Mansuy was an avid follower of the poetry of the Scranton-connected W. S. Merwin and a founding member of the Dunmore Historical Society. Many shared Jane's attachment and loyalty to Scranton even after they left. As Dottie Walker Smith, at age ninety-four, stated unequivocally, "I've lived here in Teaneck, New Jersey, for forty years, but Scranton is my home."[9]

Today, Scranton appears to be embarking on a resurgence of its vitality. Since its all-time high tally in 1930 in the decennial census, Scranton's number of residents decreased each decade through 2010. In 2016, for the first time, the number of residents actually increased to roughly 77,000, just a little more than half the people it had when the Butzners lived there. Scranton's economy is turning toward its own version of "eds and meds" with its numerous medical facilities, although geared to care and treatment rather than research and development, and the recent expansion of its medium-size educational institutions: the Jesuit-affiliated University of Scranton (St. Thomas College until 1938), Marywood University (with its school of architecture), Lackawanna College (located in Central High School's former building), and the Geisinger Commonwealth School of Medicine (one of four campuses in the region). Yet it also generates a large proportion of jobs as a regional distributor of goods and provider of government and social services. In another promising shift, Scranton has increasingly found new uses for old buildings, a process Jane Jacobs saw as essential to a healthy economy and city. Plagued by subsidence, the once magnificent North Scranton Junior High has been resuscitated and converted into fifty-eight apartments for the elderly and a splendid auditorium for community events, concerts, and theatrical productions. Suffering from a decline in the student population, the James Madison School, on the National Register of Historic Places, was transformed into an early learning center, plus graduate-student apartments for the University of Scranton. Once a beehive for doctors, dentists, lawyers, and other office occupants, the eight-story downtown Connell Building—familiar to Jane and her city-explorer friends—has been redeveloped as a mixed-use project, with retail on the ground floor and offices and some ninety units of residential space above. The giant-footprint Murray Corporation of America's industrial building, which Jane and city leaders had fought to attract, has gone through a series of uses and owners since it was vacated by the war industry. It served as a food-distribution center, where the inte-

Cherry Street side of the former Scranton Button Company
complex, awaiting redevelopment, 2018. Author's photo.

rior space was divided into several sections, a beer wholesaler, and, in
2018, a trucking company and Northeast Veal. Initiated in 1885, the
Scranton Button Company in South Side, the erstwhile largest button
manufacturer in the nation, produced millions of rubber-composite
and shellac-based buttons until the 1920s when it found it could adapt
the shellac-based material for pressing sound-recording disks. The
company became a division of Capitol Records in 1946. Today, this
enormous but empty complex of building types and styles is in the
process of redevelopment, with state and city funds, which will provide a new location for the Scranton Counseling Center.[10]

Helping to sustain a sense of community and civic pride and
contributing to Scranton's vitality is its enduring daily newspaper.
This medium-size gritty city managed to maintain both a morning
and evening newspaper until 2005, when *The Scranton Times* and *The
Scranton Tribune* combined to form the *Times-Tribune*. Along with its
Sunday Times, the seven-day-a-week paper is still partially owned by
descendants of Edward J. Lynett through the parent company, Times-
Shamrock Communications. Residents have continued to support the

city's daily broadsheet print edition, with a circulation approaching fifty thousand. Keeping up with current trends, an online version exists, as well. With its hefty serving of local news mixed with national reportage, the paper persists in covering high school sports, regional culture, and personal life events, knitting together the polyglot city. As in decades past, Scranton also has foreign-language papers. Since 2003, *La Voz Latina* has printed a monthly for the Spanish-speaking community, and the Albright Library stocks a Gujarati-language paper, produced out of town, for the Indian community. Until fall 2019, June Carter Davies's *The Villager*, under new leadership, carried on as one of many weekly regional community chroniclers before it merged with three other local papers to become the *Tri-County Independent*.[11]

Although the recreational and social service Progressive Center has a new iteration, its building on Olive Street, near central city, still stands and continues as a neighborhood organization. Its nonprofit successor, dedicated to helping low-income families and individuals, uses the facility as a child-care center. In 1969, the original organization, established in 1923, merged with another neighborhood house on Scranton's West Side. With its gradual expansion and the addition of child-care and senior programs, it was renamed the United Neighborhood Centers of Lackawanna County, and when extending its reach in 2007 to five other counties, it became the United Neighborhood Centers of Northeastern Pennsylvania. It has a number of centers sprinkled in various Scranton neighborhoods whose residents it serves. Its education and revitalization department—in a handsomely rehabbed, multi-family, mixed-use structure on Cedar Avenue—graces South Side, which remains the city's neighborhood with the largest immigrant population.[12]

UNC offers opportunities and a helping hand to Scranton's latest arrivals. Once again, a substantial number of immigrants are flocking to Scranton as their first stop in America, although others come after trying out New York, Ohio, or elsewhere. Some choose Scranton because they have family in the Electric City already, but, for all, the relatively cheap cost of living helps to lure them. UNC's Cedar Avenue center now draws participants from more than fifty countries,

United Neighborhood Centers of Northeastern Pennsylvania,
Cedar Avenue, South Side, Scranton, 2018. Author's photo.

with the largest portions from the Dominican Republic, Mexico, Ecuador, and Brazil, and many refugees from the Democratic Republic of the Congo and Nepal. In 2017, this center counted seventeen languages spoken by attendees at its language-partnership program, where residents enjoyed teaching one another their respective native tongues—Spanish, Arabic, Portuguese, Russian, French, Nepalese, and Swahili, among others. Michael Hanley, the UNC's executive director, who began working there thirty years ago as director of youth programs, quoted many of the center's newly arrived members as remarking, "Scranton has the nicest people." During the winter holidays, UNC has held an ethnic carol sing, with a spectrum of traditional music performed by neighborhood residents—from deep-rooted Polish old-timers to fresh-off-the-boat Hispanics. Because of Scranton's medium size, UNC is able to deal holistically with a range of issues, from health, housing, and food assistance to English as a Second Language and citizenship classes, which fold in a host of practical and occupational life skills. In a larger, less cohesive city, these various services would probably be relegated to separate agencies.

"When someone walks through our doors," said Terilynn Brechtel, director of community education, "even if they just came for an English-language class, we make sure to address all their needs."[13]

Jane would be pleased to know of the influx of recent immigrants to Scranton and the many new ethnic businesses and churches that have subsequently sprouted. On Cedar Avenue, the South Side's main commercial drag, can be found Florita's Mexican bakery, the Nepali Family Food Mart, and the immensely popular International Deli & Grocers, owned and run by a Dominican proprietor but serving foods from other countries, too. Restaurants and a lively mix of commercial ventures started by foreign newcomers have popped up throughout South Side and the rest of the city. In contrast to Scranton's first hundred years, new arrivals no longer seek out Scranton for its dangerous and debilitating work in the coal mines. Instead, they find employment at nearby distribution centers, hospitals, colleges, and hotels, and in the construction, installation, repair, and maintenance industries. Jane would be equally delighted to know that, in 2015, two of Scranton's long-standing homegrown businesses were among the county's fifty largest employers. Penn Foster, Inc., founded in the late nineteenth century as the International Correspondence Schools and recently rebranded to incorporate the founder's name, now offers online diploma and degree programs for high school and college students and those seeking to further their careers. Gertrude Hawk Chocolates, Inc., started in 1936 by a housewife making candy to benefit her church in the kitchen of her family's small home, more than eighty years later employs 550 people.[14]

Scranton's long-established churches are welcoming and absorbing immigrants. On Sundays, Congolese and Sudanese emigrés living on Capouse Avenue in central Scranton walked a couple of miles to attend services at St. Paul's United Methodist Church in South Side, before the church started providing a bus for them. They were warmly received into the predominantly Caucasian congregation, whose church arose in 1884 "from cottage prayer meetings held on what was known as Slocum's Flats, in South Scranton, by the First Methodist Episcopal Church." Also in South Side is Scranton's oldest

Catholic church, organized in the 1840s, now called Saint John Neumann Parish, though the imposing 1904 building with its sumptuous stained glass is known as Nativity of Our Lord. Currently, it serves a Roman Catholic community with a broad diversity of backgrounds, and conducts both English- and Spanish-language Masses to include nearby residents.[15]

Immigrants are inadvertently resuscitating churches whose congregations have dwindled with the city's loss of population and the natural aging of generations. Without the newer congregants, these institutions might have been abandoned. The Green Ridge Presbyterian Church, once frequented by the Butzners and later by Dottie and Granville Smith, held its final service of worship on May 31, 1981. Today the lovely building stands unoccupied and forlorn, used only for storage.[16]

While newcomers inject fresh life into a city, residents who are loyal and committed to staying are also essential to its overall health. In her groundbreaking book, Jane Jacobs described the need for "a continuity of people who have forged neighborhood networks. These networks are a city's irreplaceable social capital." The networks of people who have lived in a city for a good portion of their lives or are part of a succession of generations produce not only stability but also trust and support, which encourage a commitment to community and working toward the common good. These people with ties and allegiance to the city create a solid foundation for the vitality of a city, and they help ensure that a city's crucial requirement of all types of diversity is maintained. In Jane's words, "Planning for vitality must . . . [create] conditions aimed at persuading a high proportion of the indigenous residents, whoever they may be, to stay put by choice over time, so there will be a steadily growing diversity among people and a continuity of community both for old residents and for newcomers who assimilate into it."[17]

These continuous residents together with gradually assimilated outsiders can help counteract the threat of what Jane called "cataclysmic money," the overwhelming injection of capital for outsize projects and the rapid turnover of an area to a single, usually privileged, class, thus squelching diversity. "Cataclysmic money pours into an area in concentrated form, producing drastic changes," Jane wrote. She recognized and considered ways to prevent the destruction of neighborhoods and cities due to what we have since come to identify as "gentrification."[18]

Contemporary Scranton has a continuity of people devoted to protecting and improving their home city. Michael Hanley, of the United Neighborhood Centers, and Maria Pane MacDonald, of Marywood University, are two such Scranton natives who, after venturing out of the city to attend college, made a conscious decision to return to the Electric City. Maria teaches an adaptive reuse seminar for college seniors majoring in architecture. Recently, her students proposed new uses for the nine majestic stone edifices of the old Scranton State School for the Deaf, founded in 1880 and purchased by Marywood in 2011. The eager and engaged young women and men presented their plans to the neighbors and to a potential developer. They studied Jane's ideas and put together a "Jane's Walk" for the surrounding community to explore Jane's childhood neighborhood, where her family's big brick house now bears a modest plaque apprising passersby of the influential writer who made some of her earliest observations there. Jane's ideas have come full circle and are being broadcast back whence they came.[19]

In 1978, when American cities had yet to bounce back from their downward spiral, Mary Procter and Bill Matuszeski wrote a book, *Gritty Cities*, based on their personal observations of Allentown, Bridgeport, Trenton, and nine other down-at-the-heels medium-size cities. These writer-photographers were prescient in pondering the future of gritty cities similar to Scranton. "If these cities make it into an era of renewed value and purpose," they concluded, "they offer much. They are powerful visual reminders of our history, its exuberance, and its struggles. They offer human-scale opportunities for urban living, and they house treasures—ornate courthouses, grand movie houses, broad Victorian avenues, rows of stained glass windows—that enrich the lives of all who pass by."[20]

Forty years later, their words ring true. Many medium-size old industrial cities—such as Nashville and Raleigh—are growing at a faster rate than larger cities. People who have been priced out of our great cities are looking toward these cities of a moderate size as places of affordability and possibilities, places conducive to pluralism rather than tribalism. Urbanists and the urban-interested, of which there seems to be an ever-growing number, are taking notice of this phenomenon.

What will become of the medium-size city of Scranton? Will it retain enough of its longtime residents to pass on continuity of culture through word of mouth and example? Does it possess good-enough morale to appreciate and preserve documents and buildings from the past? Will the building of new university and medical buildings encroach too heavily on and overtake the central city? Will Scrantonians have the patience to listen to its citizens' ideas and implement small-scale plans, avoiding the "big fix?" Will there be enough continuity to resist the cataclysmic money of well-to-do Manhattanites and prevent the working and middle classes from being displaced?[21]

At the end of her life, Jane often mulled over these kinds of questions. She thought about Scranton and what she had learned from her home city in northeastern Pennsylvania. In her tenth and final book, *Dark Age Ahead*, published when she was eighty-eight, two years before her death, Jane cautioned that our culture was on the verge of collapse, that the very pillars of this culture were in jeopardy. The first pillar upon which we depend, said Jane, is that of family and community. She saw these as "so tightly connected that they cannot be considered separately"— after all, it takes a community to raise children. "A community is a complex organism," Jane wrote, that requires "complicated resources" to survive. In giving examples of resources for this pillar, she could have been characterizing Scranton. In the first group, resources were tangible and included affordable housing, publicly funded transportation, schools, libraries, large-scale public recreation facilities, and parks. The second group was comprised of tangible resources provided in more informal ways, such as

Interior of recently renovated Albright Library,
first floor, 2018. Author's photo.

"convenient and responsive commercial establishments," nonprofit
services run by volunteers, and publicly provided resources like homes
for the elderly, community centers, concerts, sports tournaments,
language classes, and job training centers. The third group, Jane felt,
was most important. It provided intangible and informal resources:
speaking relationships among neighbors in addition to friends, and diverse people who share the neighborhood and its needs. Jane sounded
as if she were speaking of her experience and observations of Scranton
in the 1920s and 1930s. She had found community within New York
City and, in her last several decades, in Toronto, yet her thoughts
kept bringing her back to the comprehensible, embraceable, heterogeneous, and largely cohesive city of her youth, which, in essence, had
provided the basis of her education and many of her ideas.[22]

In her last book, Jane warned that "[d]uring a Dark Age, the
mass amnesia of survivors becomes permanent and profound. The
previous way of life slides into an abyss of forgetfulness, almost as
decisively as if it had not existed." Jane would be reassured to know
that the keepers of the flame are busy in Scranton—at the bustling

Albright Library, the *Times-Tribune* archives, the Forest Hill Cemetery's archives, the Lackawanna and Dunmore Historical Societies,
the Architectural Heritage Association, the Pennsylvania Anthracite
Heritage Museum, the Greater Scranton Chamber of Commerce,
and the United Neighborhood Centers, to name but a few. College
students, neighbors of all ages, old-timers, and recent arrivals continue to forge community. Together, they are preserving and passing
on the history. They are rehabilitating the existing and adding new
increments. They are keeping alive and sustaining the great mosaic.
Its destiny is uncertain, but Scranton—like lively, diverse, intense
cities everywhere—contains the seeds of its own regeneration.[23]

• • •

Acknowledgments

I AM INDEBTED TO the many people without whom this book would never have come to be. First, I wish to thank a proactive Dunmorean for jump-starting this project. In 2008, a research trip to Scranton for my young-adult book about Jane Jacobs sparked my interest in her hometown. Three years later, I was delighted when architect John Cowder contacted me about an opportunity to return. From an article in the local newspaper about *Genius of Common Sense: Jane Jacobs and the Story of "The Death and Life of Great American Cities,"* he had discovered that Jane had grown up three blocks from his house. He planned to unveil a plaque at her childhood home and invited me to speak to American Institute of Architects members and the Dunmore Middle School. At the time, few Scrantonians knew much about the influential writer or her roots. How could I resist? The *Times-Tribune* announced and covered the event. Marie Mansuy, age ninety-five, called John Cowder to say she had been Jane's childhood friend and wanted to talk to us. I was off and running—back and forth to the Electric City for years.

I am grateful to Scranton's institutions and its people. The Albright Memorial Library was indispensable throughout this project, with the endlessly helpful reference librarians Judi Keller and Martina Soden. Judi made sure to introduce me to regular library volunteer Norma Reese, one of the library's most valuable resources. Huge thanks also to Brian Fulton at the *Times-Tribune* archives. He suggested pertinent articles and images, wrote an excellent "Pages from the Past" blog, and was an invaluable source of information. Besides wonderful exhibitions at the Pennsylvania Anthracite History Museum (PAHM), its staff—including Chester Kulesa, Richard

Stanislaus, and John Fielding—provided information about the city and its industries. Many thanks also to Virginia "Ginger" Goodrich, whom I met early on at the Greater Scranton Chamber of Commerce—vastly knowledgeable about the city, on the board of the PAHM, and an avid Girl Scout, who opened their door for me. Thanks to the Everhart Museum and its curators Nezka Pfeifer and Francesca Saldan, and preparator Michael Wisneski, for documents and permission to reproduce paintings; to the Lackawanna Historical Society and director Mary Ann Moran-Savakinus and assistant director Sarah Piccini for being so accommodating through the years; to the Dunmore Historical Society and Phil Sardo, Salvatore Mecca, Rudy Kunz, and T. C. Connolly for their meticulous help; Dr. Gerald Tracy, Lisa Brister, and Iris Johnston at the Lackawanna County Medical Society, and Tonyehn Verkitus at the Luzerne County Medical Society, for preserving and searching through their precious historic medical journals; the Columbia County Historical and Genealogical Society in Bloomsburg, PA; and Susan Pieroth for the wealth of Scranton maps and primary sources on her website www.lackawannapagenweb.com.

Heartfelt thanks to those who shared extraordinary verbal accounts of their knowledge and recollections of Scranton and life in the earlier decades of the last century. Marie van Bergen Mansuy, with her crystal clear memory, astute observations, and love of history, cited names, addresses, and dates in tales of her experiences. In our numerous conversations, Kay Schoen Butzner, in her nineties and the last living family member of Jane Jacobs's generation, enjoyed digging back into her memories and offering the careful observations of a scientific reporter, keeping to facts yet inserting strong commentary. Dorothy "Dottie" Walker Smith, in her ninety-seventh year, still offers powerful insights and continues to be an inspiration. I am grateful to her for introducing me to Scranton's African American community. Norma Reese, officially the caretaker of Forest Hill Cemetery but de facto archivist of its residents, has aided me and so many others looking into the region's history. Donna Zaleski, devoted librarian at Scranton High School, helped find and comb through old high school records and magazines, an unsurpassable treasure. I value the trust and, ultimately, the friendship of all these remarkable women.

Sincere thanks to other Scrantonians who spoke with me about Jane and their city: Architectural Heritage Association crusaders Dr. Peter Cupple, Richard Leonori, Nancy Bisignani, and Wayne Evans; civic and cultural leaders Sondra and Morey Myers; former mayor David J. Wenzel; Arlene Swartz, whose husband, Milton, was Jane's high school classmate, as was Don Nicholas. For insight into the African American community: Marcella Martin for laying the foundation with her remarkable research and written history; Nira Blue Madison and Cathy Ann Strader Hardaway for many great interviews; Parran Foster III; Valerie Jackson; Precious Flowers; Gail Waters; Evelyn Franklin; Sandra Burgett-Miller; Donald Thompson; and Angi Goodall Johnston. Michael Hanley and Terilynn Brechtel at United Neighborhood Centers of Northeastern Pennsylvania; Joe Brazil for his tour of the School Administration Building; Natalie Gelb and Dan Perry at the Lackawanna Heritage Valley Association; Louise Finetti and Geraldine Salico at the Century Club; Nikki Keller at the United Way; and Diane Walls for her reminiscences of her mother, June Carter Davies. For material on the Girl Scouts, thanks to Yevgeniya Gribov, associate collection manager at Girl Scouts of the USA, New York City; Mary Winslow, volunteer archivist at Girl Scouts in the Heart of Pennsylvania, for saving records from destruction and sharing them with me; and Jeanne Marian Gordon, former director of Girl Scouts Scranton Pocono Council. Thanks to Christian Dupont at Boston College's John J. Burns Library; to Bill Walczak for his tapes of his coal-mining family audio recordings and to his cousin John Bogdanovicz for helping us to explore Dickson City and Olyphant.

In neighboring Dunmore, thanks to educators Albert P. O'Donnell, Jr. and James Ferguson; Evelyn "Evie" Barrett Brower; Florence Gillespie Brown; Bob Everly; Barbara O'Malley, daughter of Ruth McDonough; Barbara Gelder Kelley and Margaret Gelder Reese, sisters who grew up in the Butzner House after 1946; Christopher and Merrily Mansuy, and Mary Jo Wynne, Marie Mansuy's relatives; Dr. Dennis Kapp and Susan Kapp, current occupants of Jane's childhood home, who invited us in; and Sue Cantarella at the Dunmore Presbyterian Church.

Thanks to friends: for historic medical information, Drs. Perri Klass and Marta Herschkopf; for design ideas and photo retouching, Carol Goldenberg and Shellburne Thurber. Thanks to Robert J. Walker, Michael Buryk at his Red Patch Gallery, and Margo Azzarelli for photos and permissions.

Thanks to historians Peter Laurence, James O'Gorman, Robert Fishman, Michael Lewis, David Charles Sloane, and Mark Hirsch for close reading and advice. Thanks to Father Ray Schroth and to Frank Schroth III of Milton, Massachusetts, for speaking with me about his grandfather *Scranton Tribune* publisher Frank Schroth, and to Betty Houchin Winfield for historical information about journalism.

Jane's relatives could not have been more helpful. My deepest gratitude to Jane's son Jim Jacobs, Pat Broms, and their daughter Caitlin Broms-Jacobs for all our conversations, their guidance, help in identifying photographs, and the phenomenal exhibit they orchestrated in Toronto in honor of Jane's centennial birthday in 2016. I cherish the memory of Jane Butzner Henderson and our trip together to Scranton, Camp Archbald, which she had attended, and LeRayesville to meet her mother Kay's family. Special thanks also to Carol Bier, Betty Butzner's daughter, for so much, and to Ann Butzner for elucidating Jane Jacobs's Higgins, North Carolina, experience. Thanks also for various pieces of the puzzle to Ned Jacobs and Mary Ann Code, Larissa Code-Landry, Burgin Jacobs, Dr. J. Decker Jacobs III, Nancy McBride, Lucie Vogel, and Jim and Betsy Greene.

In the fall of 2017, I had the pleasure of visiting Marywood University's recently minted School of Architecture. I spent time with Maria MacDonald and the students of her adaptive reuse studio class, based on the principles of Jane Jacobs. Besides Maria's tireless enthusiasm for Jane's ideas and unabating help, I am forever beholden to her and Josh Berman for digging through file boxes in storage—while I gave suggestions via phone—and unearthing Jane's long-lost letter imploring Scranton to preserve its downtown. We all cried at that eureka moment.

Ongoing and deepest thanks for the support of the members of the board of the Center for the Living City, Roberta Brandes Gratz and Mary Newsom among them, and my never-ending appreciation for longtime director Stephen A. Goldsmith's belief in and exceptional efforts on behalf of this book. Without the generosity of Martha Shuttleworth and the Northeastern Pennsylvania Chapter of the American Institute of Architects, and the donations made in honor of Anthony (A. J.) Rinaldi, Jr. and Francis (Frank) Pane, this book would not have come to fruition in all its glory. Lynne Elizabeth, director extraordinaire of New Village Press, and her amazing team shepherded it across the finish line.

To my father, Kurt Lang, for describing details of his immigrant experience as a German refugee in 1936, and to my mother, Gladys Engel Lang, whose childhood in Atlantic City bore many similarities to that of Jane's schoolmates. To Alex and Esmé von Hoffman, husband and daughter, for supporting my passion throughout this journey.

Finally, thanks above all to Jane Butzner Jacobs for her observations and ruminations and to the city that nurtured her and her ideas.

Abbreviations, Sources, & Notes

PLEASE NOTE that the author made extensive use of information garnered from the U.S. Census, sundry vital records, city directories, and nineteenth- and twentieth-century historical maps of Scranton and vicinity—especially Sanborn Fire Insurance Maps and street atlases—but refrained from including references to them in citations where the use of these documents would be obvious.

A great deal of information derived from multiple interviews by the author of many individuals between 2011 and 2020 in person, via telephone, and email. Therefore, citations of interviews by the author include only the name of the interviewee but omit the type of interview and specific dates. All interviews are by the author unless otherwise specified.

Abbreviations for Recurring Sources

AHA	Architectural Heritage Association (Scranton, PA)
DHS	Dunmore Historical Society
FBI	Federal Bureau of Investigation archives
Gen Chart	Genealogical chart of Robison and Butzner families, compiled by Bess Robison Butzner, John J. Burns Library, Boston College, Boston, MA
GRPC	Green Ridge Presbyterian Church
GRPC Records	The Session Minutes of the Green Ridge Presbyterian Church, Scranton, PA
GSUSA	Girl Scouts of the USA
Hitchcock	Frederick Lyman Hitchcock, *History of Scranton and Its People*, vol.1 (New York: Lewis Historical Publishing Co., 1914)
Hollister	Horace Hollister, M.D. *History of the Lackawanna Valley*, 5th ed. (Philadelphia: Lippincott, 1885)

ITM	Max Allen, ed., *Ideas That Matter: The Worlds of Jane Jacobs.* (Ontario: Ginger Press, 1997)
Jacobs Papers	Jane Jacobs Papers, John J. Burns Library, Boston College, Boston, MA
J. I. & K. Butzner Papers	James I. and Kay S. Butzner family papers
LCMS	Lackawanna County Medical Society
LHS	Lackawanna Historical Society
NY Times	*New York Times*
Scouting for Girls	Girl Scout Handbook, 1927
Scr Rep	*Scranton Republican*
Scr Times	*Scranton Times*
(Scr) *Times-Trib*	(Scranton) *Times-Tribune*
Scr Trib	*Scranton Tribune*
(Scr) *Trib-Rep*	(Scranton) *Tribune-Republican*
Scr Truth	*Scranton Truth*
Scrantonian	*The Scrantonian*
Wachtel interview	Jane Jacobs, interview by Eleanor Wachtel, 2002: "A Conversation with Jane Jacobs," from *Original Minds: Conversations with CBC's Eleanor Wachtel* (Toronto: HarperCollins, 2003). Originally in *Brick* 70 (Winter 2002). Author's transcription combines the taped and printed versions of the interview.

Abbreviations for Books by Jane Jacobs

CC	*Constitutional Chaff*, 1941
CWN	*Cities and the Wealth of Nations*, 1984
DAA	*Dark Age Ahead*, 2004
D&L	*The Death and Life of Great American Cities*, 1961; Modern Library edition, 2011
EOC	*The Economy of Cities*, 1969
NOE	*The Nature of Economies*, 2000
QOS	*The Question of Separatism*, 1980
SOA	*A Schoolteacher in Old Alaska: The Story of Hannah Breece*, 1995
SOS	*Systems of Survival: A Dialogue on the Moral Foundations of Commerce and Politics*, 1992

• • •

Notes

INTRODUCTION *"My Own City"*

1. Peter Laurence, *Becoming Jane Jacobs* (Philadelphia: University of Pennsylvania Press, 2016).

2. Erin L Nissley, "Local History: After 'The Office' Put Scranton on Map, First-Ever Convention Showed Off City," (Scr) *Times-Trib*, Oct. 22, 2017; Thomas Dublin and Walter Licht, *The Face of Decline: The Pennsylvania Anthracite Region in the Twentieth Century* (Ithaca, NY: Cornell University Press, 2005).

3. Mark Feeney, "City Sage," *Boston Globe*, Nov. 14, 1993; *ITM*, 10–13.

4. Jane Jacobs, letter to Tim McDowell, Dec. 31, 1987, courtesy of AHA and Marywood University School of Architecture, Scranton, PA.

5. *D&L*, 187; Robert Fulford, "Radical Dreamer: Jane Jacobs on the Streets of Toronto," *Azure*, Oct.–Nov. 1997.

6. See www.woolworthsmuseum.co.uk/1800s-biogcsw.htm.

7. *D&L*, 94.

8. Carl Marzani, *The Education of a Reluctant Radical*, vol. 2, *Growing Up American* (New York: Topical Books, 1993).

9. Frederick Lewis Allen, *Only Yesterday* (New York: Harper & Brothers, 1931), 73–92.

10. Richard B. Woodward, "Vincent Scully, Influential Historian at Yale, Dies at 97," *NY Times*, Dec. 2, 2017.

11. Robin Roger, "The Jane Jacobs of the Arctic: Robin Roger Speaks with Jacobs About Her Frontier Forerunner," *Books in Canada*, November 1995.

12. *CWN*, 124–26.

13. Transcript of interview of Jane Jacobs, October 1997, "Jane Jacobs: A Biographical Menu," Jacobs Papers; Mark Feeney, "City Sage"; *SOS*, subtitle.

14. Jane Jacobs, "Downtown Is for People," *Fortune*, Apr. 1958.

15. Larissa Code-Landry, Jane's granddaughter, interviews by the author; Wachtel interview; James Howard Kunstler, theamericanconservative.com/blog and interviews by the author.

CHAPTER 1 *Betting on Scranton*

1. James "Jim" K. Jacobs, Jane Jacobs's son, interviews by the author; Kay Schoen Butzner and other relatives interviewed believed this, but Jane did not.

2. Gen Chart; Wachtel interview.

3. Dr. Marta Herschkopf, interviews by the author; "State Boards of Registration," *Journal of the American Medical Association*, volume 55, no. 15 (Oct. 8, 1910): 1314–15.

4. Dr. Marta Herschkopf, interviews.

5. Mark Feeney, "City Sage"; "Medical News," *Journal of the American Medical Association*, volume 42, no. 22 (May 28, 1904): 1428; Penn University Archives & Records Center: Philadelphia Polyclinic and College for Graduates in Medicine, available at www.archives.upenn.edu/histy/features/medical/merged.html.

6. Jane Jacobs, note to granddaughter on back of photo of the house at 2719 Old Berwick Road, Espy, PA, 1990 or later.

7. Jane Butzner Henderson, Jane Jacobs's niece, interviews by the author; "John Markle, Philanthropist, Coal Man, Dies," *New York Herald Tribune*, July 11, 1933.

8. Kay Schoen Butzner, interviews by the author; Wachtel interview.

9. Joseph Curtis Platt, *Reminiscences of the Early History of Dark Hollow, Slocum Hollow, Harrison Lackawanna Iron Works, Scrantonia and Scranton, Pa.* (Scranton: Republican Press, 1889); David Craft et al., *History of Scranton, Pennsylvania* (Dayton, OH: Published for H. W. Crew by the United Brethren Publishing House, 1891); Dr. Horace Hollister, *History of the Lackawanna Valley*, 5th ed. (Philadelphia: Lippincott, 1885).

10. David Craft et al., 508; Hollister, 454–55.

11. Dr. J. Decker Butzner III, son of Jane's brother John, interviews by the author.

12. "Investigating Death of Battle; Dying Man Told His Brother He Was Victim of Foul Play," Charles "Susky" Battles's obituary, *Scr Truth*, Jan. 8, 1912.

13. Daniel K. Perry, *Pennsylvania's Northeast Treasures: A Visitor's Guide to Scranton, the Lackawanna Valley, and Beyond* (Scranton: Heritage Valley Press, 2007), 14–15; "The City's Semi-Centennial: The Story of Scranton," *Scr Rep*, Sept. 30, 1916, special magazine supplement, 1; "Wonderful Story of Development of the City," *Scr Rep*, Nov. 1, 1917; map in Hitchcock, xiii.

14. Hitchcock, 17; Cheryl A. Kashuba, Darlene Miller-Lanning, and Alan Sweeney, *Scranton* (Charleston, SC: Arcadia Publishing, 2005), 16; Cheryl A. Kashuba, *A Brief History of Scranton, Pennsylvania* (Charleston, SC: History Press, 2009), 27.

15. Kashuba, *Brief History*, 28, 30; Kashuba et al., *Scranton*, 16; John Beck, *Never Before in History: The Story of Scranton* (Northridge, CA: Windsor Publications, 1986), 36.

16. Hitchcock, 1, 17–19; Perry, *Pennsylvania's Northeast Treasures*, 18–19.

17. Hitchcock, vi; Beck, *Never Before in History*, 34–35, 40–41; "Wonderful Story of Development of the City," *Scr Rep*, Nov. 1, 1917; David Craft et al., *History of Scranton*, 250.

18. explorepahistory.com/hmarker.php?markerId=1-A-2BC; Hitchcock, 1.

19. www.data-wales.co.uk/ivanhild.htm; Connell info in Hitchcock, 92–93.

20. *EOC*, 159–60; "The Silk Industry in Scranton," *Scr Rep*, Dec. 8, 1891.

21. Hitchcock, 25–31; explorepahistory.com/hmarker.php?markerId=1-A-2BC.

22. David Craft et al., *History of Scranton*, 243–84; *CWN*, 39.

23. Kashuba, *Brief History*, 30; *Amsden map*, 1857, at LHS; Hitchcock, 97.

24. Hitchcock, 44–46; Kashuba et al., *Scranton*, 14–15; Nicolai Cikovsky, Jr., "George Inness and the Hudson River School: 'The Lackawanna Valley,'" *American Art Journal* 2, no. 2 (Autumn 1970): 36–57.

25. Amsden map, 1857; Patrick Brown, *Industrial Pioneers: Scranton, Pennsylvania and the Transformation of America, 1840–1920* (Archbald, PA: Tribute Books, 2010); "The City's Semi-Centennial," *Scr Rep*, Sept. 30, 1916.

26. Hitchcock, 363–367, which reprints Edward Merrifield's account of the "organization of the county."

27. Hitchcock, 100, 368; George E. Thomas et al., *Buildings of Pennsylvania: Philadelphia and Eastern Pennsylvania* (Charlottesville: University of Virginia Press, 2010), 482; "Wonderful Story of Development of the City," *Scr Rep*, Nov. 1, 1917.

28. Hitchcock, x; Hollister, 512–14, 518.

29. "The City's Semi-Centennial," *Scr Rep*, Sept. 30, 1916; Hitchcock, 101.

30. Hollister, 454.

31. Hollister, 529.

32. Beck, *Never Before in History*, 88; Hitchcock, 17; "Gigantic Steel Plant," *Scr Rep*, Apr. 25, 1899; Patrick Brown; "Blast Furnace Closed Down," *Scr Trib*, Jan. 30, 1902 *(closing of North Works)*; "South Steel Mill Closed Suddenly," *Scr Rep*, Feb. 27, 1902.

33. Hitchcock, iv; "Millions of Capital for Great Enterprise," *Scr Trib*, Oct 19, 1901.

34. *EOC*, 123–25.

35. *EOC*, 127–28, including footnote; 262.

CHAPTER 2 *Many Small Decisions*

1. Many historic maps studied for much information in this chapter, most of them courtesy of Norma Reese; Philip van Cleef Mattes, *Tales of Scranton* (privately printed, 1973), x; "Scranton's New Y.M.C.A. Building," *New-York Daily Tribune*, Mar. 22, 1903. In 1906, Dr. Butzner lived at 407 Wyoming Avenue and worked at the hospital at 345 Wyoming, both within two blocks of Dr. Kay at the YMCA.

2. Hollister, 3; for date on LCMS shield, see www.lackmedsoc.org/contact-us; James K. Jacobs, interviews.

3. Information from NY Passenger List: Dr. Kay was born in Brandywine, VA, Sept. 22, 1858; "Southern Banquet: Society and Guests Enjoyed Excellent Menu and Brilliant Addresses at Annual Event," *Scr Rep*, Feb. 23, 1905.

4. F. P. Hollister, J. D. Butzner, and E. L. Kiesel, "In Memoriam: Thomas W. Kay," *The Medical Society Reporter* 19, no. 1 (Jan. 1925): 11, courtesy of LCMS; Sargent's portrait of Pozzi now hangs in the Armand Hammer Collection in the Hammer Museum, Los Angeles.

5. Hollister, Butzner, and Kiesel, "In Memoriam: Thomas W. Kay."

6. "Southern Banquet: Society and Guests Enjoyed Excellent Menu and Brilliant Addresses at Annual Event," *Scr Rep*, Feb. 23, 1905.

7. Hitchcock, 320; "Dr. John Decker Butzner," obituary, (Scr) *Times-Trib*, Dec. 24, 1937; "Brevities," *Scr Rep*, Mar. 1, 1908; "Evening Social Chat," *Scr Truth*, June 25, 1908.

8. "County Bar Association Paid Tribute of Respect," *The Columbian* (Bloomsburg, PA), c. Mar. 8, 1909, clipping in Scrapbook #27, Columbia County Historical & Genealogical Society, Bloomsburg, PA; "Evening Social Chat," *Scr Truth*, Mar. 24, 1909; *The Columbian*, Mar. 25, 1909, reported the wedding, which took place at home in Espy; "James Boyd Robison" (full obituary), *The Columbian*, Mar. 4, 1909, mentions he was a member of Presbyterian church; the Butzners' apartment was at 733 Taylor Avenue, between Pine and Gibson Streets, in the "Lower Hill" section.

9. Jane Butzner Henderson, interviews; John MacWhirter (1839–1911) was a British painter of "sylvan subjects" and often painted birch trees.

10. One such journal was the Charlotte (NC) *Medical Journal*, 1906; "Automobile News and Gossip," *Scr Truth*, Mar. 15, 1910; Scranton City Directory, 1910: Geo S. Wrightnour, automobile agent, Real Estate Exchange building (126–128 N. Washington); he lived at 927 Green Ridge; *ITM*, 133; photos of cars that year all showed windscreens. It was probably a Runabout, which sold for about nine hundred dollars; Jane Butzner Henderson, interviews.

11. James K. Jacobs, interviews; *EOC*, 159–60.

12. Hollister, 486–87; Scranton Dunmore map 1874, Sanborn maps (1884, 1888), Scranton street atlases (1898, 1877) of Green Ridge.

13. All quotes from "Hon. George Sanderson," obituary, *Scr Rep*, Apr. 2, 1886, courtesy of Norma Reese; Cheryl A. Kashuba, "Sanderson Lent Intelligence, Integrity to City," (Scr) *Times-Trib*, Jan. 29, 2012; Norma Reese, interviews by the author.

14. "Hon. George Sanderson," obituary; Hitchcock, 254.

15. Margo L. Azzarelli, *Green Ridge* (Charleston, SC: Arcadia Publishing, 2012), 7, 9, 55, 84; Scranton City Directory, 1867, from Susan Pieroth, lists only his bank address and Geo. S. in Germantown.

16. Azzarelli, *Green Ridge*, 7–9, 84.

17. "Business Notice," *Scr Morning Rep*, Apr. 28, 1868; "Hon. George Sanderson," obituary; Hitchcock, 117, 254; Azzarelli, *Green Ridge*, 85.

18. Frederick L. Hitchcock, *Prominent Men of Scranton and Vicinity* (Scranton, PA: Press of the Tribune Publishing Co, 1906); Azzarelli, *Green Ridge*, 10; Edward D. Sturges, obituary, *Scr Times*, Apr. 8, 1919.

19. Lackawanna County Registry of Deeds, Deed for 815 Electric Street, Scranton, PA, conveyed from Joseph S. Judicki et ux. to F. J. Olver, recorded Dec. 10, 1909, DBK nbr. 248, p. 38.

20. Hitchcock, 118, 122, 125; Joseph X. Flannery, "Museum Must Honor Pioneer Who Put Graft, Vice on a Rail," *Scr Times* (n.d., c. 1999), courtesy of Norma Reese; Cheryl A. Kashuba, "Local History: How Scranton Became Electric," (Scr) *Times-Trib*, May 5, 2013.

21. Cheryl A. Kashuba, "Scranton Gained Fame as the Electric City" (Scr) *Times-Trib*, Aug. 22, 2010; "Hey There! What Is This?" *Scr Rep*, July 30, 1889.

22. Azzarelli, *Green Ridge*, 91.

23. "The News in Brief," *Scr Truth*, Sept. 29, 1904; "J. S. Judicki," *Scr Truth*, Sept. 25, 1905; Joseph S. Judicki et ux. to F. J. Olver, same deed as above.

24. Same deed as above; "Green Ridge," *Scr Rep*, Sept. 18, 1901; "October Movings Keep Transfer Men on Jump," *Scr Rep*, Oct. 26, 1910), with incorrect name of seller; gravestones in Forest Hill Cemetery.

25. Azzarelli, *Green Ridge*, 37, 40, 42, 43; Kashuba, *Brief History*, 35.

26. Hollister, 486–87; Sanborn 1988 Atlas shows both companies next to each other on Green Ridge Street between Von Storch (Fifth Street) and Albright (Third Street); Hitchcock, 254; *D&L*, 95.

CHAPTER 3 *Ties That Bind in the Great Mosaic*

1. GRPC Records, Apr. 3, 1912.

2. Dime Bank Building (completed in 1891), National Register of Historic Places Inventory Nomination Form, by Peter Cupple, Mar. 16, 1978, available at www.dot7.state.pa.us/CRGIS_Attachments/SiteResource/H001110 _01H.pdf; first of untitled ads for two weeks: *Scr Rep*, Apr. 30, 1912; "Social and Personal," *Scr Trib-Rep*, Apr. 1, 1912; "Tenyo's Passengers," *San Francisco Chronicle*, Mar. 21, 1916.

3. Allen, *Only Yesterday*, 95, says 8.8 percent rate of divorce in 1910; "Evening Chat," *Scr Truth*, Oct. 18, 1912; "Marriages," *Scr Truth*, Oct. 21, 1912.

4. "Evening Chat," *Scr Truth*, Sept. 29, 1911.

5. "Doctors Argue Inspection Fee," *Scr Rep*, Mar. 13, 1912.

6. "The Playground Fund," *Scr Truth*, May 23, 1908; "Big Benefit at Poli's Tonight," (Scr) *Trib-Rep*, Nov. 24, 1913; "Board of Trade Members Give Subscriptions to Fund for the Relief of the Belgians," *Scr Rep*, Nov. 16, 1914.

7. "Observance of Birthday by Trust Company," *Scr Rep*, May 10, 1915; "Stockholders of Anthracite Dine," *Scr Rep*, May 8, 1916; *United States Investor* 31, no. 2 (1921): 2782.

8. Gen Chart.

9. *Medical Record* 83 (1913): 485. "Large Attendance at Funeral of Dr. Edith Barton," *Scr Rep*, Feb. 22, 1913.

10. Ibid.

11. James K. Jacobs, interviews; "Local Doctors Attend Congress of Medicine," *Scr Rep*, July 4, 1913; "Stroller's Notebook," *Scr Rep*, Aug. 28, 1913.

12. "Stroller's Notebook," *Scr Rep*, Aug. 28, 1913; "Medical Society Meeting," *Scr Rep*, Nov. 4, 1913; New York, Passenger Lists, vol. 4901, spreads 365–83; the ship *President Lincoln* stopped at Hamburg 8/14, Boulogne 8/15, and Southampton 8/15, and arrived in NYC 8/26/1913.

13. "Suburban Notes," *Scr Rep*, Mar. 26, 1915; "Evening Chat," *Scr Truth*, May 12, 1910; "Personals," *Scr Rep*, Apr. 13, 1915.

14. James K. Jacobs, interviews; certificate of death for William B. Butzner, Aug. 5, 1915, with cause of death as "acute nephritis"; Dr. Perri Klass, interview by the author to interpret cause of death; Carol Manson Bier, Betty Butzner's daughter, interviews by the author; "William Boyd Butzner," *Scr Rep*, Aug. 6, 1915; "Obituary [William Boyd Butzner]," *Scr Times*, Aug. 6, 1915.

15. Gen Chart.

16. "The City's Semi-Centennial" *Scr Rep*, Sept. 30, 1916.

17. "One Death an Hour, Toll of N.Y. Plague," *Scr Rep*, July 6, 1916.

18. "Director Derby Calls Conference of Doctors," *Scr Rep*, July 12, 1916; "Doctors Consider Paralysis Case," *Scr Rep*, July 13, 1916.

19. "Child Dies of Paralysis; Is Only Case," *Scr Rep*, July 13, 1916; the Carlucci building was at the rear of 925 Scranton Street.

20. "Dunmore Now Has Case of Paralysis," *Scr Rep*, July 31, 1916; "One More Case of Paralysis Found in City," *Scr Rep*, Aug. 10, 1916.

21. "Schools of State Must Stay Closed on Dixon's Order," *Scr Rep*, Aug. 25, 1916.

22. Wachtel interview.

23. "Evening Chat," *Scr Truth*, Mar. 11, 1912; "Entertained for Son," *Scr Rep*, Apr. 15, 1913; "Arrange Meeting for Carbondale," *Scr Rep*, Feb. 4, 1921.

24. Nicholas E Petula and Thomas W. Morgan, Sr., *The History of the Public Schools of Scranton, Pennsylvania* (privately published, 2008), Albright Memorial Library, Scranton, PA.

25. "College Men Work to Elect Hughes," *Scr Rep*, Oct. 17, 1916.

26. "Contingent Members Leaving Central Rail Road of New Jersey Station, 1917, World War I," *The Medical Society Reporter* 37, no. 8 (Oct. 1943): 9, courtesy of LCMS.

27. "Dr. J. D. Butzner," *Scr Times*, Dec. 23, 1937, courtesy of Norma Reese; Gen Chart; James K. Jacobs thought the name was originally Butzler, despite what his grandmother entered on the genealogical chart she made.

28. "Captain Butzner Home on Leave," *Scr Times*, Aug. 8, 1918, courtesy of Norma Reese; David J. Wenzel, *Scranton's Mayors* (Eynon, PA: Tribute Books, 2006), 53–54; Oscar Jewell Harvey, *The Spanish Influenza Pandemic of 1918* (Wilkes-Barre, PA: n.p., 1920); Carol R. Byerly, "The U.S. Military and the Influenza Pandemic of 1918–1919," *Public Health Reports* 125, suppl. 3 (2010): 82–91; GRPC Records.

29. Caitlin Broms-Jacobs, notes from her conversations with her grandmother Jane Jacobs regarding items in Jane's "museum"; "Red Cross News," *Scr Rep*, Mar. 11, 1918.

30. Erin L. Nissley, "Local History: Casualties at Victory Parade," (Scr) *Times-Trib*, Nov. 10, 2013; "Green Ridge," *Scr Rep*, Nov. 19, 1918.

31. "Discharged from Army," *Scr Rep*, Jan. 21, 1919; "Dr. T. W. Kay Is Host at Dinner," *Scr Rep*, Jan. 23, 1919; Dr. Kay's investment in liberty bonds in "Mrs. Olivette Kay Gets $33,863.56," *Scr Rep*, Nov. 26, 1925.

32. F. P. Hollister, J. D. Butzner, and E. L. Kiesel, "In Memoriam: Thomas W. Kay," *The Medical Society Reporter* 19, no. 1 (Jan. 1925):11, courtesy of LCMS; "Letters from the People," *Scr Rep*, Apr. 24, 1920.

33. "Physicians Form Post of American Legion," *Scr Rep*, Aug. 1, 1919; "Legion Post to Honor Memory of Dr. Davis," *Scr Rep*, Apr. 3, 1924; GRPC Records, Sept. 17, 1919; "Society News," *Scr Rep*, Apr. 28, 1920; *GRPC Fiftieth Anniversary of the Building*, brochure at LHS.

34. John La Gorce, "The Industrial Titan of America," *National Geographic Magazine* 35, no. 5 (May 1919): 399.

35. "Green Ridge: Weber's [*sic*] Theater," *Scr Rep*, Oct. 26, 1915; Jane Jacobs, speech to the Green Building Council in Washington, D.C., Nov. 11, 2000, at the National Building Museum, upon receiving the Vincent Scully Prize, transcribed by Chris Bradshaw from a video recording by John Wetmore.

36. [Irvin] Andrew Robison, letter to his first cousin Jane Jacobs, Oct. 21, 2003, J. I. & K. Butzner Papers.

37. Wachtel interview.

38. Jane Jacobs, letter to her brother Jim Butzner, Mar. 20, 1984, J. I. & K. Butzner Papers.

39. Wachtel interview. Jane said she was four years old but had to have been five, since she mentions in the anecdote her brother Jim, who was born in Nov. 1920.

40. Kay Schoen Butzner, interviews.

41. Ibid.

42. Wachtel interview; Jane Butzner Henderson, interviews.

43. Wachtel interview; speech by Jane Jacobs, Amsterdam, 1984, Jacobs Papers.

44. Wachtel interview.

45. Lackawanna County Registry of Deeds, Deed for 815 Electric Street, Scranton, PA, conveyed from Francis J. Olver et ux. to J. D. Butzner, recorded Oct. 28, 1910, DBK nbr. 248, p. 39.

46. "Physician in Narrow Escape in Accident," *Scr Rep*, Jan. 24, 1921; "Dr. Butzner Improved," *Scr Rep*, Jan. 25, 1921; "Driver Jumps When Truck Goes Over Bank into River," *Scr Rep*, Dec. 28, 1923.

47. James K. Jacobs, interviews.

CHAPTER 4 *Crossing the Line into Dunmore and at School*

1. Hitchcock, 92.

2. Beginning with the 1934 Scranton City Directory, the house's address would change to 1712 Monroe.

3. First used in "Houses for Sale," *Scr Rep*, Mar. 29, 1924; another example in "Houses for Sale," *Scr Rep*, Apr. 19, 1924; Evelyn Franklin (married name withheld upon request), interview by the author.

4. *Dunmore 1862–1962: Commemoration of Incorporation of Dunmore as a Borough . . . April* 10, 1862 (Dunmore Centennial Committee, Inc., Aug. 29, 1962), unpaged; 1860 U.S. Census information, courtesy of Rudy Kunz; Hollister, 211.

5. Stephanie Longo, *Dunmore* (Charleston, SC: Arcadia Publishing, 2012), 67, 94; "Dunmore Schools," by Rudy Kunz, Dunmore Historical Society website; Alice Schoonover, "The Dunmore Book—1915," handwritten manuscript, Dunmore Presbyterian Church archives.

6. Lackawanna County Registry of Deeds, Deed for 1728 Monroe Avenue, Dunmore, PA, conveyed from George and Margaret Jiencke to Bess Robison Butzner, recorded Feb. 25, 1921, DBK nbr. 306, p. 71.

7. "F. E. Sykes & Co.," *Scr Truth*, Dec. 15, 1909; Scranton City Directory 1906, advertising sheet bound between pp. 678 and 679.

8. Kurt Lang, a German immigrant in 1936, recognized the name Jiencke as southern German; Lackawanna Paint & Color Works was on Capouse Avenue, near the Lackawanna River, between the central city and Green Ridge; Margaret McKee Jiencke's funeral record and other documents from Forest Hill Cemetery.

9. "[Carl] Jiencke Tells of Being Held as German Spy," *Scr Rep*, Dec. 23, 1914; Barbara Gelder Kelley, interviews by the author; Max Allen, interviews by the author, and photograph in *ITM*, 33.

10. "Board Is Assured of School Safety," *Scr Rep*, Nov. 23, 1931; the George Washington School #3 was not on the 1877 and 1888 maps but is on the 1898 map; by 1898, Dunmore schools had not yet appeared in the Scranton city directories, although the Dunmore School Board is listed in 1898; Albert P. O'Donnell, Jr., interviews by the author.

11. Albert P. O'Donnell, Jr., interviews.

12. Marie Van Bergen Mansuy, interviews by the author.

13. "Business Notice," *Scr Rep*, Sept. 23, 1887, courtesy of Norma Reese; Marie Van Bergen Mansuy, interviews.

14. Advertisement for H. C. Van Bergen, *Scr Truth*, Dec. 20, 1909; Marie Van Bergen Mansuy, interviews.

15. William Warren Scranton, born in 1917, was Pennsylvania's governor from 1963 to 1967; Marie Van Bergen Mansuy, interviews; Marie Van Bergen's fifth-grade report card from the George Washington School #3 in Dunmore, PA, courtesy of the DHS; Barbara Gelder Kelley and Margaret Gelder Reese, interviews by the author.

16. Marie Van Bergen Mansuy, interviews; "Over 150 in Attendance at Meeting of P.T.A.," *Scr Rep*, Jan. 31, 1936; Barbara Gelder Kelley and Margaret Gelder Reese, interviews.

17. James K. Jacobs, interviews; Kay Schoen Butzner, interviews.

18. "Teachers Do Not Have to Resign If Married," *Scr Times*, May 4, 1937, courtesy of Norma Reese; In their laws and contracts with teachers, some

municipalities required teachers who married during the term to resign. Pennsylvania state senator Leo Mundy introduced a new teacher tenure law that excluded this stipulation, and he was quoted as saying that any clause in a contract requiring instructors to resign if they married was illegal; Kay Schoen Butzner, interviews.

19. All of these teachers are listed in the *Report of the Proceedings of the Pennsylvania State Educational Association* (Lancaster, PA: Pennsylvania School Journal, 1919); Barbara Gelder Kelley and Margaret Gelder Reese, interviews.

20. Barbara Gelder Kelley, although born in 1934, felt in certain ways she had followed Jane's trajectory: She and her family belonged to the GRPC; she and her sister Margaret were ardent Girl Scouts and went to Camp Archbald; they attended the same grammar and high schools; they knew many of the same neighbors; and Barbara and Jane had used the same bedroom in the Monroe Avenue house.

21. Marie Van Bergen report cards, courtesy of the DHS; Barbara Gelder Kelley, interviews; Mildred F. Gallagher, Jane's autograph book, courtesy of the Estate of Jane Jacobs; Evelyn "Evie" Barrett Brower, interviews by the author; Albert P. O'Donnell, Jr., interviews.

22. Albert P. O'Donnell, Jr., interviews; Evelyn "Evie" Barrett Brower, interviews; Marie Van Bergen Mansuy, interviews; Barbara Gelder Kelley, interviews.

23. James K. Jacobs, interviews; Marie Van Bergen Mansuy, interviews; Barbara Gelder Kelley, interviews; Jane's autograph book, courtesy of the Estate of Jane Jacobs; Mark Feeney, "City Sage."

24. James K. Jacobs, interviews; Marie Van Bergen Mansuy, interviews; Judi Keller, reference librarian, Albright Memorial Library, Scranton, PA, interviews by the author.

25. Jane Jacobs, "Autobiography," *ITM*, 3; Barbara Gelder Kelley and Margaret Gelder Reese, interviews.

26. Marie Van Bergen Mansuy, interviews; James K. Jacobs, interviews; *ITM*, 3, 16, 17; Wachtel interview.

27. Marie Van Bergen's tenth-grade report card, 1930, from the Dunmore Senior High School in Dunmore, PA, on South Apple Street, east of Dunmore's Corners, identifies the school with this official name, courtesy of the DHS; "Dunmore School District History," available at www.dunmoreschooldistrict. net; Marie Van Bergen's report cards from the George Washington School #3 in fourth and fifth grades, 1923–1924 and 1925–1926, show that her teachers were Anna L. McGuire and May Mongan, respectively, courtesy of the DHS; Marie Van Bergen Mansuy, interviews; Barbara Gelder Kelley and Margaret Gelder Reese, interviews; Adele Freedman, "Jane Jacobs," *The Globe and Mail*, June 9, 1984, in *ITM*, 26; "Jane Jacobs: A Biographical Menu," interview in Sept. 1997, Jacobs Papers.

28. Marie Van Bergen Mansuy, interviews; Barbara Gelder Kelley, interviews.

29. Marie Van Bergen Mansuy, interviews; gravestone of Simon Ward (Jan. 5, 1800–Mar. 27, 1894), Forest Hill Cemetery; Marie's great-great-grandfather

Simon Ward was an original builder of and intricately involved in the city. He arrived in Scranton in 1840.

30. Marie Van Bergen Mansuy, interviews; "Students Are Advanced by Stanford Tests," *Scr Rep*, Feb. 7, 1925; the last class to graduate in January in Dunmore was in 1945; "Dunmore Schools," by Rudy Kunz, Dunmore Historical Society website.

31. Florence Gillespie Brown, interviews by the author; Jessup, eight miles northeast of Scranton, is an example of a town built largely as a patch by coal companies; Marie Van Bergen Mansuy, interviews; Marzani, *The Education of a Reluctant Radical*, vol. 2, *Growing Up American*, 3; Green Ridge Coal Company remained active until the early 1940s, Longo, *Dunmore*, 50.

32. James K. Jacobs, interviews; Marie Van Bergen Mansuy, interviews.

33. Marie Van Bergen Mansuy, interviews; Kay Schoen Butzner, interviews; Charles Trueheart, "In Cold Toronto, 'Cities' Critic Is Hot Again,'" *Washington Post*, Apr.19, 1993. Jane speaks of pre-K children in Toronto introducing themselves as being from another country, unlike American children, who seemed ashamed of their immigrant parents.

34. Marie Van Bergen Mansuy, interviews; Gladys Engel Lang, interviews by the author. Born in 1919 and having grown up in Atlantic City, NJ, she spoke of the ubiquitousness of these clubs; "Banks Distribute Christmas money," *Scr Rep*, Dec. 8, 1921; ad by First National Bank, Dunmore, *Scr Rep*, Jan. 1, 1930; ad by Peoples-Savings and Dime Bank and Trust Company, *Scr Rep*, Dec. 12, 1923.

35. James K. Jacobs, interviews; Barbara Gelder Kelley, interviews; Wachtel interview; www.mininghalloffame.org/inductee/mitchell. Led by UMWA president John Mitchell, victorious striking anthracite miners returned to work on Oct. 29, 1900, which from then on was celebrated as John Mitchell Day. Although originally from Illinois, Mitchell is buried in Cathedral Cemetery, Scranton.

36. "Efficiency and the Commons," a conversation between Jane Jacobs and Janice Gross Stein, Nov. 15, 2001, *Ideas That Matter: A Quarterly Digest 2*, no. 2 (2002), J. I. & K. Butzner Papers; Kay Schoen Butzner, interviews.

37. "Death Summons R. A. Zimmerman," *Scr Rep*, Feb. 16, 1923; James K. Jacobs, interviews.

38. Marie Van Bergen Mansuy, interviews.

39. Barbara O'Malley, interviews by the author; Jane Jacobs, *SOA*, vii; Marie Van Bergen Mansuy, interviews.

40. Marie Van Bergen Mansuy, interviews.

41. "Class Will Hold Debate at Washington School," *Scr Rep*, Apr. 19, 1930.

42. Caitlin Broms-Jacobs, notes from her conversations with her grandmother Jane Jacobs regarding items in Jane's "museum"; Thomas Lomax Hunter, *The Free Lance-Star* (Fredericksburg, VA), Oct. 14 and 28, 1927.

43. Marie Van Bergen Mansuy, interviews.

CHAPTER 5 *Eyes on Monroe Avenue*

1. Wachtel interview.
2. Barbara Gelder Kelley, interviews; June Carter Davies, "Jade Writes Potpourri," *The Villager* (Moscow, PA), May 5, 1993.
3. Marie Van Bergen Mansuy, interviews; Barbara Gelder Kelley, interviews; Kay Schoen Butzner, interviews.
4. Barbara Gelder Kelley, interviews; Kay Schoen Butzner, interviews; Marie Van Bergen Mansuy, interviews.
5. Barbara Gelder Kelley, interviews; Carol Manson Bier thinks that the Fashion Institute of Technology library might have a copy of Betty Butzner's rose patterns; Marie Van Bergen Mansuy, interviews.
6. Evelyn "Evie" Barrett Brower, interviews; Marie Van Bergen Mansuy, interviews; Kay Schoen Butzner, interviews; Jane's autograph book, courtesy of the Estate of Jane Jacobs.
7. Barbara Gelder Kelley and Margaret Gelder Reese, interviews.
8. Kay Schoen Butzner, interviews; crossword puzzles, although around since at least 1913, became all the rage with the publication of the first crossword puzzle book, with a pencil attached, a runaway bestseller in 1924—see Allen, *Only Yesterday*, 159; Lisa McGirr, *The War on Alcohol: Prohibition and the Rise of the American State*, (New York: W. W. Norton, 2016), 161–63.
9. Marie van Bergen Mansuy, interviews; Barbara Gelder Kelley, interviews; Kay Schoen Butzner, interviews; Margaret Gelder Reese, interviews.
10. Evelyn "Evie" Barrett Brower, interviews; *SOA*, xi; Jane Jacobs, "Reading, Writing, and Love-Apples," in *At Grandmother's Table: Women Write About Food, Life, and the Enduring Bond Between Grandmothers and Granddaughters*, ed. Ellen Perry Berkeley (Minneapolis: Fairview Press, 2000), 1, and an earlier draft entitled "Fried Tomatoes with Gravy," Jacobs Papers; a collection of these Jay E. House columns was published as *On Second Thought* (Philadelphia: Westbrook Publishing Co., 1937). All but two pieces in this volume first appeared in his column in the *Public Ledger* (Philadelphia) and *Philadelphia Inquirer*; Wachtel interview; Marie Van Bergen Mansuy, interviews.
11. Wachtel interview; "Institute Head to Talk Before Medical Society," *Scr Rep*, Mar. 21, 1922; "Local Doctors Taking Post-Graduate Courses," *Scr Rep*, Oct. 22, 1922; "Physician's Post to Attend Ryan Funeral," *Scr Rep*, Dec. 18, 1923).
12. James K. Jacobs, interviews.
13. Caitlin Broms-Jacobs, notes from her conversations with her grandmother Jane Jacobs regarding items in her "museum"; Jane Jacobs, letter to her mother, Jan. 25 (no year), Jacobs Papers.
14. Caitlin Broms-Jacobs, notes from her conversations . . . ; "Dr. Kay Dead," *Evening News* (Wilkes-Barre), Oct. 4, 1924; "Dr. Kay Left Estate Amounting to $25,000," *Scr Rep*, Oct. 7, 1924; "Waverly," *Scr Rep*, Aug. 3, 1925.
15. "Dr. Kay Victim of Heart Attack," *Scr Rep*, Oct. 4, 1924; "Stroller's Note Book," *Scr Rep*, Oct. 6, 1924 (editorial page); F. P. Hollister, J. D. Butzner,

and E. L. Kiesel, "In Memoriam: Thomas W. Kay," *The Medical Society Reporter* 19, no. 1 (Jan. 1925): 11, courtesy of LCMS; "Mrs. Olivette Kay Gets $33, 863.56," *Scr Rep*, Nov. 26, 1925; "Dr. Kay Left Estate Amounting to $25,000," *Scr Rep*, Oct. 7, 1924.

16. Jane Jacobs, letter (summarizing what Mary Robison told her) to Jim and Kay Butzner, July 25, 1996, J. I. & K. Butzner Papers; Martha Robison Fawcett, letter to Jane Jacobs, c. late Sept. 1996, J. I. & K. Butzner Papers; [Irvin] Andrew Robison, letter to Jane Jacobs, Oct. 21, 2003, J. I. & K. Butzner Papers.

17. Carol Manson Bier, interviews; *Free Lance-Star* (Fredericksburg, VA), June 2, 1930; Lucie Vogel, Nancy Butzner's daughter, email to the author, Mar. 28, 2016.

18. Jane Jacobs, letter to Jim Butzner, Aug. 16, 1973, J. I. & K. Butzner Papers.

19. Jane Jacobs, "Reading, Writing, and Love-Apples," in *At Grandmother's Table*, 2; Mary Jane "Jennie" Breece Robison's dates corrected according to her death certificate and gravestone (1848–1930); [Irvin] Andrew Robison, letter to Jane Jacobs, Oct. 21, 2003, J. I. & K. Butzner Papers; Jane Butzner Henderson, interviews.

20. Bob Everly, interview by the author.

21. Marie Van Bergen Mansuy, interviews; Margaret Gelder Reese, interviews.

22. James K. Jacobs, interviews; Evelyn "Evie" Barrett Brower, interviews; "M'Clintock funeral Will Be Held Today," *Scr Rep*, Dec. 6, 1927; both florists were still there in 2016; Rudy Kunz of the DHS, email to the author, Mar. 5, 2011.

23. Marie Van Bergen Mansuy, interviews.

24. Barbara Gelder Kelley, interviews; Barbara O'Malley, interviews.

25. Ibid.

26. Marie Van Bergen Mansuy, interviews; James K. Jacobs, interviews; *EOC*, 159–60; ad for Wickham Brothers' products at the Industrial Exposition: "Scranton Made Pure Food Products," *Scr Rep*, Oct. 12, 1921.

27. Harmony Court was on the 1300 block of Adams, between New York and Larch Streets; Marie Van Bergen Mansuy, interviews.

28. Leo Walczak, interview on tape by his nephew Bill Walczak, 1977, courtesy of Bill Walczak; Vetz was Bill Walczak's father, whose real name was Vincente H. Walczak, although he later changed it to William H(enry).

29. Barbara Gelder Kelley, interviews.

30. Philip Swartz bought a house at 1760 Monroe Avenue and worked downtown at 332 (rear) Lackawanna Avenue. His parents lived at 733 Jefferson Avenue; Arnine Cumsky Weiss and Darlene Miller-Lanning, *Jews of Scranton* (Charleston, SC: Arcadia Publishing, 2005), 19; "Social News," *Scr Rep*, Apr. 15, 1926; Evelyn "Evie" Barrett Brower, interviews; "Marriages," *Journal of the American Medical Association* 79, no. 27 (1922): 2245; Barbara O'Malley, interviews.

31. 150th Anniversary Committee, "The Presbyterian Church of Dunmore, PA, 1854–2004" (booklet), 15, 38, Dunmore Presbyterian Church archives; Longo, *Dunmore*, 54, 61, 62, 64; *Dunmore 1862–1962: Commemoration of*

Incorporation of Dunmore as a Borough . . . April 10, 1862 (Dunmore Centennial Committee, Inc., Aug. 29, 1962), unpaged.

32. *Dunmore* 1862–1962, unpaged; Cheryl Kashuba, "Italian Stoneworker's Scranton Work Includes Courthouse Statue," *Scr Times*, Oct. 4, 2009; James K. Jacobs, interviews; Allen, *Only Yesterday*, 40; Richard Stanislaus, curator at the Pennsylvania Anthracite Heritage Museum, interviews by the author.

33. Commonwealth of Pennsylvania, *Report of the Department of Mines of Pennsylvania: Part 1—Anthracite,* 1929–1930 (Harrisburg, PA: Department of Mines, 1931); Benedict "Benny" Holeva, interview on tape by his nephew Bill Walczak, 1977, courtesy of Bill Walczak.

34. Marie Van Bergen Mansuy, interviews.

35. Richard Stanislaus, interviews; Robert H. Zieger, "Pennsylvania Coal & Politics: The Anthracite Strike of 1925–1926," *Pennsylvania Magazine of History and Biography* 92, (April 1969): 244-62.

36. Robert H. Zieger, "Senator George Wharton Pepper and Labor Issues in the 1920s," *Labor History* 9, no. 2 (1968): 163–83; Richard Stanislaus, interviews; "Anthracite Strike Settled," *Scr Rep*, Sept. 4, 1922.

37. *Scr Times*, Feb. 12, 1926, clipping from (Scr) *Times-Trib* archives; "Scranton Republican Scoops the Country," ad displaying headlines from New York, Philadelphia, and Buffalo papers regarding the strike's end, *Scr Rep*, Feb. 13, 1926; *DAA*, 54; Zieger, "Pennsylvania Coal & Politics"; Marie Van Bergen Mansuy, interviews; Stefania "Stephie" Holeva, interview on tape by her nephew Bill Walczak, 1977, courtesy of Bill Walczak.

38. Richard Stanislaus, interviews; Jane Jacobs, letter to her mother, Dec. 30, 1974, Jacobs Papers; Marie Van Bergen Mansuy, interviews.

39. "Jane Jacobs: A Biographical Menu," interview in Oct. 1997, Jacobs Papers; Leticia Kent, "More Babies Needed, Not Fewer: An Interview with Jane Jacobs," *Vogue*, Aug.15, 1970, J. I. & K. Butzner Papers.

40. "Jane Jacobs: A Biographical Menu."

CHAPTER 6 *The Liberating Ideology of the Girl Scouts*

1. *Lackawanna County Medical Society Pennsylvania 1926*, print of 208 individual photographic portraits of physicians as well as a list of names of 18 physicians "In Memoriam" (Photocraft Press, Bound Book, N.J. Publishers, photography by F. W. Hornbaker and Bachrach, Inc.). Portraits include Helen Houser, a physician with an office in Suite 202 of the Bowman Building, who graduated from Woman's Medical College of Pennsylvania in 1915, and Anna M. Levy, a physician with an office in Suite 422–3 of the Real Estate Building, who graduated from the University of Pennsylvania in 1922. This print hung in Mansour's Market Café, Scranton, PA, as of 2018.

2. Katherine O. Wright, *Twenty-Five Years of Girl Scouting* (New York: Girls Scouts, Inc., 1937); FBI, "Jane Butzner Jacobs, Special Inquiry—State

Department," Mar. 22, 1948. The other organization Jacobs mentioned was a labor union.

3. "First Honors Went to Miss Butzner," *Scr Rep*, Aug. 28, 1922; Jane Butzner, "Scout Writes Interestingly About Life at Camp Archbald," *Scr Times*, Oct. 24, 1928, courtesy of Mary Winslow, volunteer archivist at Girl Scouts in the Heart of Pennsylvania.

4. The Session Minutes of the Green Ridge Presbyterian Church, Scranton Church Records, 1873–1944 (Green Ridge Avenue Presbyterian Church [Scranton, Pennsylvania]), Family History Library, available at www.family search.org/search/catalog/787274; Marie Van Bergen Mansuy, interviews; Nicole Hlavacek Keller and Nicole A. Barber, eds., *For the Girls: A History of Girl Scouting in the Scranton Pocono Council* (Scranton, PA: Girl Scouts, Scranton Pocono Council), 2003.

5. "Present Awards to Girl Scouts at Xmas Rally Here," *Scr Rep*, Dec. 11, 1926; GRPC Records. Betty was confirmed in April 1922, John and Jane in 1930; Jane Jacobs, letter to John Butzner, c. May 27, 1993, J. I. & K. Butzner Papers; "Girl Scouts Enjoy Reunion at Simpson," *Scr Rep*, Apr. 9, 1927.

6. en.wikipedia.org/wiki/Scouting_for_Boys; www.history.com/this-day-in -history/boy-scouts-movement-begins; David Smith, "Scouts Uncool," *The Guardian*, Apr. 21, 2007.

7. Tammy M. Proctor, *Scouting for Girls: A Century of Girl Guides and Girl Scouts* (Santa Barbara: ABC-CLIO, 2009); Hlavack and Barber, eds., *For the Girls*, 1–2.

8. *The Scranton Republican* in the 1920s and 1930s reported regularly on Girl Scout troops in small towns surrounding Scranton; Scranton Council Girl Scouts, Inc., "Heritage Girl Scout Hikes," 1962, mimeographed fiftieth anniversary booklet, courtesy of Ginger Goodrich; GRPC, *50th Anniversary of the Present Church Building*:1893–1943 (Scranton, PA: Allied Printing, 1943), LHS; GRPC Records.

9. www.girlscouts.org/en/about-girl-scouts/our-history/timeline.html; "Girl Scout Director Is Guest at Luncheon Here" *Scr Times*, May 11, 1920; Mary Levey and Mary Degenhardt, *Highlights in Girl Scouting*, 1912–2001 (New York: Girl Scouts of the USA, 2002).

10. GRPC, *100th Anniversary*, 1875–1975 (Scranton, PA, 1975), LHS; "Weston Field and New House Are Dedicated," *Scr Rep*, Feb. 23, 1917. Weston Field and the field house were a 1915 gift of Mr. C. S. Weston and his sister Mrs. Frank Bird; Hitchcock, 274; the original GRPC was on Monsey Avenue at Green Ridge Street near Green Ridge Corners; Marie Van Bergen Mansuy, interviews; no evidence in GRPC records or *Scr Rep* of Bess Butzner's involvement with the Girl Scouts.

11. "Our City's New Parks," *Scr Rep*, June 16, 1894.

12. Bill Steinke, *Steinke's Story of Scranton with Who's Who and Why in Cartoons* (Scranton, PA: Scranton Publishing Co., 1914), 77; Cheryl Kashuba, "Italian

Stoneworker's Scranton Work Includes Courthouse Statue," *Scr Times*, Oct. 4, 2009; "Churches and Pastors," *Scr Rep*, Aug. 16, 1892.

13. GRPC Records.

14. Levey and Degenhardt, *Highlights in Girl Scouting, 1912–2001;* www.wagggs .org/en/about/about/History; the original WAGGGS member countries consisted of Australia, Belgium, Canada, Czechoslovakia, Denmark, Estonia, Finland, France, Hungary, Iceland, India, Japan, Latvia, Liberia, Lithuania, Luxembourg, Netherlands, New Zealand, Norway, Poland, South Africa, Sweden, Switzerland, United Kingdom, United States, and Yugoslavia.

15. "Women's Activities," *Scr Rep*, Sept. 17, 1927; Marie Van Bergen Mansuy, interviews; Gene Brislin, "Friendship House to Honor Miss Briggs," *Scrantonian*, Nov. 15, 1987, courtesy of Norma Reese.

16. Brislin, "Friendship House to Honor Miss Briggs"; Marie Van Bergen Mansuy, interviews; Vita Barba, message in Jane Butzner's autograph book, Jan. 9, 1927, courtesy of the Estate of Jane Jacobs; nepagrantmakers.org/profiles /margaret-briggs-foundation; Margaret Briggs obituary, *Scr Trib*, July 16, 1992, courtesy of Norma Reese.

17. Girl Scouts of the United States of America, *Scouting for Girls: Official Handbook of the Girl Scouts*, abr. ed. (New York: Girl Scouts, Inc., 1927), 32.

18. Girl Scouts of the United States of America, *Scouting for Girls*, 87–90; James K. Jacobs, interviews.

19. Levey and Degenhardt, *Highlights in Girl Scouting, 1912–2001*; Hlavack and Barber, eds., *For the Girls*, 36.

20. Girl Scouts of the United States of America, *Scouting for Girls*, 30–31, 413; Glenna Lang and Marjory Wunsch, *Genius of Common Sense: Jane Jacobs and the Death and Life of Great American Cities* (Boston: David R. Godine, 2009), 11.

21. "Girl Scout News," *Scr Rep*, Jan. 15, 1927; "Women's Activities," *Scr Rep*, Oct. 26, 1929.

22. Girl Scouts of the United States of America, *Scouting for Girls*, 413–14; "Honors Are Awarded at Girl Scout Rally," *Scr Times*, May 21, 1927, courtesy of Mary Winslow.

23. Girl Scouts of the United States of America, *Scouting for Girls*, 33; "Girl Scout Notes," *Scr Times* (?), Jan. 1929, courtesy of Mary Winslow; "Honors Are Awarded At Girl Scout Rally"; "Girl Scout News," *Scr Rep*, Jan. 15, 1927; "Girl Scout News," *Scr Rep*, Feb. 7, 1929.

24. Girl Scouts of the United States of America, *Scouting for Girls*, 455; *The American Girl* magazines, June 1926 –Dec. 1931.

25. *The American Girl* magazines, June 1926–Dec. 1931.

26. Oleda Schrottky (1894–1969), *A Pot of Red Geraniums* (New York: Girl Scouts, Inc., 1924); "Girl Scout News," *Scr Rep*, Nov. 26, 1926, and Dec. 13, 1926; Mount Holyoke College Annual Report, Nov. 1920.

27. Scranton Girl Scouts Council History Summary, July 31, 1936, GSUSA archives; "Girl Scouts Enjoy Reunion at Simpson," *Scr Rep*, Apr. 9, 1927; "Halloween," in Sabilla Bodine, *Verses*, J. I. & K. Butzner Papers; Oleda Schrottky,

letter to Jane Butzner, Jan. 5, 1927, and Helen Ferris, letter to Jane Butzner, Jan.18, 1927, Jacobs Papers; Helen Ferris obituary, *NY Times*, Sept. 29, 1969. Today, Camp Archbald is the second-oldest Girl Scout camp in the nation; see www.gshpa.org/en/camp/archbald.html.

28. Jane Butzner, "Girl Scout Writes Interestingly About Life at Camp Archbald," *Scr Times*, Oct. 24, 1928, courtesy of Mary Winslow.

29. Girl Scouts of the United States of America, *Scouting for Girls*, 111; Clarence S. Day, Jr., comp., *Decennial Record of the Class of 1896, Yale College* (New York: De Vinne Press, 1907), 183; Hlavack and Barber, eds., *For the Girls*, 11.

30. Jane Butzner, "Nature Notebook," 1928, unpublished, "Jane at Home" exhibit, Urbanspace Gallery, Toronto, 2016.

31. Jane Butzner, "Scout Writes Interestingly About Life at Camp Archbald," *Scr Times*, Oct. 24, 1928, courtesy of Mary Winslow; Carol Manson Bier, interviews; poems from Sabilla Bodine, *Verses*, J. I. & K. Butzner Papers; *D&L*, xxvi.

32. Jane Butzner, "Scout Writes Interestingly About Life at Camp Archbald," *Scr Times*, Oct. 24, 1928, courtesy of Mary Winslow.

33. Jane Butzner, "Scout Writes Interestingly About Life at Camp Archbald," *Scr Times*, Oct. 24, 1928; Hlavacek and Barber, eds., *For the Girls*, 11; *Scr Rep*, Apr. 9, 1927; "Flying Squadron to Stage Drive at Outdoor Pools," *Scr Rep*, Aug. 20, 1927.

34. Scranton Girl Scouts, "Camp Archbald, June 29–August 24, 1936," booklet, courtesy of Mary Winslow; "Girl Scout Camp Filled to Capacity," *Scr Rep*, Aug. 11, 1930; "Scout Camp Activities Attractive," *Scrantonian (?)*, Aug. 9, 1931, courtesy of Mary Winslow; "Higgins," *Burnsville (NC) Eagle*, c. Aug. 25, 1932, courtesy of Ann Butzner; Marie Van Bergen Mansuy, interviews.

35. Girl Scouts of the United States of America, *Scouting for Girls*, 34–35; www.nccgscf.org/about/history, History of the National Catholic Committee for Girl Scouts USA and Campfire USA by Virginia Reed, Diocese of Galveston-Houston; www.girlscouts.org/en/about-girl-scouts/our-history/timeline.html.

36. U.S. Censuses; Scranton city directories; Marie Van Bergen Mansuy, interviews.

37. Lucie Vogel, Nancy Butzner's daughter, interviews by the author; Charlotte Campbull, Jane's autograph book, courtesy of the Estate of Jane Jacobs; Scranton Girl Scouts Council History; Weiss and Miller-Lanning, *Jews of Scranton*, 9.

38. Scranton Girl Scouts Council History; "Girl Scout News," *Scr Rep*, Nov. 18, 1927.

39. Gladys Engel Lang, interviews.

40. Hlavack and Barber, eds., *For the Girls*, 37; *Seventh Annual Report of the Community Chest, Scranton, Pa.*, Jan. 1928, United Way of Lackawanna County archives.

41. Scranton Girl Scouts Council History; ads in *The American Girl*, June 1926–Dec. 1931; "Officials of Scouts to Leave for Camp," *Scr Rep*, Sept. 21, 1933; "Many Doughnuts Sold by Scouts," *Scr Rep*, Dec. 12, 1933; www.girlscouts.org/en/about-girl-scouts/our-history/timeline.html; "First Brownie Revel Held in Scranton," *Scr Times* or *Scr Rep* (?), May 24, 1932, courtesy of Mary Winslow.

42. Hlavacek and Barber, eds., *For the Girls*, 35, 37; "Girl Scouts," *Scr Rep*, Nov. 13, 1933; Scranton Girl Scouts Council History.

43. "Women's Activities," *Scr Rep*, Nov. 2, 1929; "Girl Scout News," *Scr Rep*, Feb. 21, 1928; "Society," *Scr Rep*, Dec. 19, 1917; "Girl Scouts," *Scr Rep*, Dec. 20, 1933.

44. Proctor, *Scouting for Girls*, 172; Girl Scouts of the United States of America, *Scouting for Girls*, 13–17.

45. Barbara Gelder Kelley, interviews by the author; Hlavacek and Barber, eds., *For the Girls*, 14, 21; JamesK. Jacobs, interviews by the author.

46. Wachtel interview.

CHAPTER 7 *Eighth Grade at the "Model School of the City"*

1. Hitchcock, 343; kindergartens were part of the Scranton school system by at least 1912, and newspapers reported some schools with kindergartens by 1890; "Junior High to Open Tomorrow," *Scr Rep*, Sept. 1, 1924; Florence Gillespie Brown, interviews.

2. Longo, *Dunmore*, 67, 69, Dunmore High had been erected in 1891 just south of Dunmore Corners and rebuilt after a fire in 1908; Marie Van Bergen Mansuy, interviews; Kay Schoen Butzner, interviews; "Dunmore Seniors Present Drama," *Scr Rep*, June 18, 1926; "Local Aquatic Stars in Meet Tomorrow Night," *Scr Rep*, Mar. 25, 1927.

3. Marie Van Bergen Mansuy, interviews; Florence Gillespie Brown, interviews.

4. Beck, *Never Before in History*, 50; David J. Wenzel, *Scranton's Mayors* (Eynon, PA: Tribute Books, 2006), 28, 71; "Plan to Annex Dunmore to This City Is Rejected," *Scr Rep*, Jan. 27, 1923; Florence Gillespie Brown, interviews; Kay Schoen Butzner, interviews.

5. June Carter Davies, "Jade Writes Potpourri," *The Villager* (Moscow PA), March 22, 1995; "Class Conducts Final Program," *Scr Rep*, Feb. 2, 1929; Davies, "Jade Writes Potpourri," *The Villager*, Nov. 10 and 24, 1993.

6. Natalie Gelb (daughter of Miriam Parker), interviews by the author. Parker's Deli was at 314 Linden Street.

7. Kurt Lang, interviews by the author; Marzani, *The Education of a Reluctant Radical*, vol. 2, *Growing Up American*, 8–9.

8. "Many Present at Conservatory Recital," *Scr Rep*, Feb. 8, 1928; "Conservatory Recital," *Scr Rep*, Mar. 28, 1928; "Interesting Program at Conservatory Hall," *Scr Rep*, Mar. 15, 1929; "Will Present Comedy at Bethel Church," *Scr Rep*,

Feb. 29, 1932); "Events at Progressive Recreation Center," *Scr Rep*, Apr. 22, 1932.

9. Information about Murrel Levy came from the Penn State 1936 yearbook; "50th Reunion, Central High School, Scranton, Penna., Class of January 1933, The Scranton Club, May 14, 1983," booklet, Jacobs Papers; "Scout Troop Holds Parents' Night Program," *Scr Rep*, June 21, 1930; "Arrange Program for Y.M.H.A. Camp," *Scr Rep*, July 22, 1932.

10. Weiss and Miller-Lanning, *Jews of Scranton*, 8, 58, 59, 62; Hollister, 267; Cheryl A. Kashuba, "Globe, Dry Goods Anchored City Shopping," (Scr) *Times-Trib*, Nov. 22, 2009; Jack Shean, *Scranton's Hill Section* (Charleston, SC: Arcadia Publishing, 2015), 57.

11. Weiss and Miller-Lanning, *Jews of Scranton*, 8–10.

12. "Social News," *Scr Rep*, Mar. 31, 1928.

13. Hitchcock, 152; the *Scranton Republican* ran many stories from April 1925 through February 1933 concerning complaints about and raids on the Hotel Vine.

14. "Realtor [George Munchak, Sr.] Is Dead After an Illness," *Scr Times*, Dec. 5, 1955; *Thomas Capek, The Czechs and Slovaks in American Banking* (New York: Fleming H. Revell Co., 1920); "Polonia Building to Be Remodeled," *Scr Rep*, June 17, 1924; "New Munchak Building Under Construction" (at 643 North Washington Avenue), *Scr Rep*, Mar. 4, 1924; "Chest Pleas in Schools Were Given by Students," *Scr Rep*, Nov. 15, 1928; "Club to Reorganize," *Scr Rep*, Dec. 6, 1930.

15. Albert P. O'Donnell, Jr., interviews; Kurt Lang, interviews; "Alderman Kinback Dead," *Scr Rep*, Oct. 22, 1891; "Ah There, Mr. Burns," *Scr Rep*, Aug. 14, 1889; "Henry Kinback Dead," *Scr Rep*, Nov. 25, 1901. The Kinback family's modest residence was at 740 McKenna Court.

16. "The Pupils Who Were Successful," *Scr Rep*, June 29, 1898; "Those Who Were Given Citizen Certificates," *Scr Rep*, Mar. 18, 1922; "All Have Passed," *Scr Rep*, May 17, 1905; "Graduation of Training School," *Scr Truth*, June 21, 1905.

17. "School Officials Are in New Home," *Scr Trib-Rep*, Oct. 4, 1911; "Schools of the City Will Open Today," *Scr Trib-Rep*, Sept. 4, 1911; "Fine Showing of Students' Work," *Scr Rep*, Mar. 27, 1915.

18. "School Officials Are in New Home," *Scr Trib-Rep*, Oct. 4, 1911; Nicholas E Petula and Thomas W. Morgan, Sr., *The History of the Public Schools of Scranton, Pennsylvania* (privately published, 2008), Albright Memorial Library, Scranton, PA.

19. "Those Who Were Given Citizen Certificates," *Scr Rep*, Mar. 18, 1922; "Women's Activities," *Scr Rep*, Mar. 18, 1931; Kurt Lang, interviews.

20. There were many accounts of the naturalization courts. One of the best is "Many New Citizens," *Scr Rep*, Oct. 3, 1891; David J. Wenzel, Scranton mayor 1986–1990, interview by the author; Allen, *Only Yesterday*, 108; Kurt Lang, interviews.

21. *Report of the Board of School Directors of the City of Scranton, PA*, 1918; "Fatal Fall Shatters Plans of Ex-Educator to Wed," *Scr Times*, Oct. 28, 1950; beginning in fall 1932, Stella Kinback served as principal of the William Prescott and the Muhlenberg public schools in Scranton.

22. "To Revise Course of School Studies," *Scr Rep*, Oct. 4, 1919; while Stella Kinback was principal, the *Scranton Republican* covered Scranton's George Washington School's class 8A graduation in 1923, 1925, 1928, 1929, and 1930.

23. The Florence Apartments still stand at 643 North Adams Avenue, designed in 1908 by New York architect Edwin Kaufmann, who graduated in 1897 from Columbia University's School of Architecture. Now subsidized housing, the building has been restored and is on the National Register of Historic Buildings.

24. "School Exams for Two Grades," *Scr Rep*, Jan. 25, 1929; Davies, "Jade Writes Potpourri," *The Villager*, Mar. 22, 1995 and Apr. 27, 1994.

25. Davies, "Jade Writes Potpourri," *The Villager*, Mar. 22, 1995; Barbara Lidstone, June Carter's cousin, lived with her family at 1707 Monroe Avenue from at least 1921 and for many years thereafter; "Business Notice," *Scr Rep*, July 6, 1889; Megan Diskin, "Elmhurst Still Lumbering Along," (Scranton) *Sunday Times*, Apr. 8, 2001, courtesy of Norma Reese; Davies, "Jade Writes Potpourri," *The Villager*, June 23, 1993.

26. "Begin Operation Here Monday for Beautiful New Masonic Temple," *Scr Rep*, Apr. 1, 1927; "Corner Stone of New Temple Laid in Storm," *Scr Rep*, June 11, 1928; "Thomas Building, Fine New Structure . . ." *Scr Rep*, Apr. 16, 1924; prolific local architect Edward Langley designed the Thomas Building, New York architect Lansing C. Holden designed the Lackawanna County Courthouse in 1896, and James Hamilton Windrim, a Philadelphia architect who specialized in public buildings, designed the old Post Office. Chris Kelly, "150 People Who Made Scranton Great—Lansing C. Holden," (Scr) *Times-Trib*, Feb. 13, 2016; George E. Thomas et al., *Buildings of Pennsylvania: Philadelphia and Eastern Pennsylvania* (Charlottesville: University of Virginia Press, 2010), 486.

27. Hitchcock, 94. The Connell Building is at 129 North Washington Avenue; Lackawanna Heritage Valley Association and the Lackawanna Historical Society, "History Set in Stone: A Guide to Downtown Scranton Architecture," booklet, 2009; Jane Jacobs, letter to Tim McDowell, Office of Economic and Community Development, Scranton, Dec. 31, 1987, courtesy of AHA and Marywood University School of Architecture.

28. Kashuba, "Globe, Dry Goods Anchored City Shopping," (Scr) *Times-Trib*, Nov. 22, 2009; Davies, "Jade Writes Potpourri," *The Villager*, Mar. 22, 1995. Jane possessed a tightly cropped clipping of this article, which she donated along with her papers to the Burns Library at Boston College, indicating that she must have gotten a kick out of it. Much of the article is reprinted in *Ideas That Matter*, page 17, with the source cited erroneously as the *Scranton Times*

and no identification of "Jade." The author is indebted to Norma Reese for recognizing its provenance.

29. Architect John A. Duckworth opened his practice in Scranton in 1883 and had an office in the Coal Exchange Building until he died, in 1912. The building was demolished in 1963; "John A. Duckworth," *Scr Rep*, July 22, 1908; Mary Therese Biebel, "Behold the Hill: Scranton's Historic Houses . . ." *Times Leader* (Wilkes-Barre, PA), June 1, 2002.

30. Thomas et al., *Buildings of Pennsylvania: Philadelphia and Eastern Pennsylvania*, 491; James D. Watkinson, "Education for Success: The International Correspondence Schools of Scranton, Pennsylvania," *The Pennsylvania Magazine of History and Biography* 120, no. 4, (Oct. 1996), 349–52.

31. Watkinson, "Education for Success"; "Officers Re-elected by Board of Trade," *Scr Rep*, Jan. 18, 1921; "State and Nation Join in Tribute," *Scr Rep*, Sept. 30, 1921; *Steinke's Story of Scranton*, 159–60.

32. Jane Butzner Henderson, interviews.

33. Marie Van Bergen Mansuy, interviews; the DL&W station was renovated and opened in 1983 as the Radisson Lackawanna Station Hotel, with the waiting room and tiles still intact; Jane Jacobs, interview by James Howard Kunstler, 2000, in *Metropolis Magazine*, Mar. 2001; Kenneth Murchison, "Station at Scranton, Pa. for the Delaware, Lackawanna and Western Railway," *The American Architect and Building News* 94 (Dec. 30, 1908): 217–18.

34. Kay Schoen Butzner, interviews.

35. "Class Conducts Final Program," *Scr Rep*, Feb. 2, 1929.

36. "Diplomas Awarded at Grade Schools," *Scr Rep*, Jan. 27, 1923.

37. "170 Pupils to Be Graduated at Tech," *Scr Rep*, June 12, 1931; "Three Are Arrested in Burglary Attempt," *Scr Rep*, June 1, 1931.

38. "June Carter Davies," obituary, *Scr Trib*, Jan. 25, 2005.

39. *DAA*, 44, 63, 64.

CHAPTER 8 *The African American
Community in the Heart of the City*

1. David Craft et al., *History of Scranton*, 553; Hollister, 486–87; David Charles Sloane, *The Last Great Necessity: Cemeteries in American History* (Baltimore: Johns Hopkins University Press, 1991), 15, 83, 187, 188; Norma Reese, interviews.

2. *D&L*, 89: "A public character is anyone who is in frequent contact with a wide circle and who is sufficiently interested to make himself a *public character*"; Dorothy Walker Smith, "Bits and Pieces from My Life," videotaped interview, 2000, and typed speech script delivered at the Prudential Financial Celebration of African-American Culture, Masonic Temple, Feb. 23, 2003, courtesy of Dorothy Walker Smith; Jane Butzner Henderson, interviews.

3. Marie Van Bergen Mansuy, interviews.

4. Emerson I. Moss, *African-Americans in the Wyoming Valley*, 1778–1990 (Wilkes-Barre, PA: Wyoming Historical and Geological Society and the Wilkes University Press, 1992), 17–19.

5. Moss, *African-Americans in the Wyoming Valley*, 34; Mildred Mumford, *This Is Waverly* (Waverly, PA: Waverly Woman's Club, 1954), 107–21; The AME church was at 129 Carbondale Road; Marcella Martin, "The History of the Negro in Scranton," unpublished paper, 1966, courtesy of Michael Hanley, United Neighborhood Centers of Northeastern Pennsylvania, Scranton, PA. This unpublished forty-page paper was written when Marcella Martin worked as a research assistant in 1966 for John Baldi, professor of sociology at the University of Scranton, during the summer between her freshman and sophomore years at Penn State University. Well researched and thorough in scope, this appears to be the only written work on the subject to date.

6. Mumford, *This Is Waverly*, 107–21; "Colored Waiters," (Scranton) *Republican Weekly*, Mar. 3, 1874, courtesy of Norma Reese; Martin, "The History of the Negro in Scranton."

7. "Death of John Lilly," *Scr Rep*, Apr. 10, 1893; "John Lilly on Trial," *Scr Rep*, July 7, 1891; "John Lilly Acquitted," *Scr Rep*, July 8, 1891; "License Decisions," *Scr Rep*, Mar. 22, 1892; John Lilly's death certificate, signed by G. W. Brown, at Forest Hill Cemetery, courtesy of Norma Reese.

8. Dorothy Walker Smith, interviews by the author; Martin, "The History of the Negro in Scranton."

9. "Let Me Tell You," a memoir by Matilda (Simms) Kearney, 2009, courtesy of Norma Reese; the Simmses lived at 618 Forest Court.

10. Nira Blue Madison, interviews by the author; the Blues lived at 612 Lee Court for many years.

11. *Pennsylvania Negro Business Directory*, 1910 (Harrisburg, PA: Jas. W. H. Howard & Son, 1910), 14, 19, 20; George W. Brown, funeral pamphlet, courtesy of Dorothy Walker Smith; Ethel A. Miller, "A Successful Woman in a Man's Game," *Opportunity: Journal of Negro Life*, July 1930, 214–15.

12. In "The History of the Negro in Scranton," Martin wrote that were almost 1,000 Negroes in Scranton in 1925 and that 281 members belonged to the Baptist church in 1930. If I could ascertain how many members the AME church had then, this might tell us which figure is correct.

13. The spelling of the surname Burkett/Burgett evolved and was supposedly taken from the town of Burkittsville, Maryland, located along the journey to freedom; Cathy Ann Strader Hardaway, interviews by the author; Hitchcock, 309; "Colored Y.M.C.A. Plan Gets $4,413," *Scr Rep*, Jan. 29, 1912.

14. "Prohibition Scores Another Victory Here," *Scr Rep*, Jan. 2, 1924; the Newport Hotel was located at 307 Center Street. After it closed, it became a storeroom for the Cleland-Simpson Co.; "Investigating Death of Battle . . . ," *Scr Truth*, Jan. 8, 1912.

15. "Investigating Death of Battle . . . ," *Scr Truth*, Jan. 8, 1912; "Watching for Jack Johnson," *Scr Truth*, Nov. 18, 1909; "Johnson Mad Because Color Line

Is Drawn," *Scr Truth*, Oct. 13, 1910; Ken Burns, *Unforgivable Blackness*, documentary film, 2004.

16. Martin, "The History of the Negro in Scranton"; "Entertainment Given for Benefit of Playground," *Scr Rep*, July 13, 1923; Hitchcock, 309; "Open Playgrounds for Summer Work," *Scr Rep*, July 2, 1924; "Meeting to Discuss City Housing Problem," *Scr Rep*, Jan. 19, 1925.

17. By 1936, both the Girl Scout reports and the *Scranton Republican* fairly consistently referred to the organization with its shortened named, as the "Progressive Center," which was located at 614 Pine Street; "Interest in Recreation Center Is Growing Here," *Scr Rep*, Mar. 16, 1929.

18. Dorothy Tucker, "Association Meeting Needs of Community," *Scr Rep*, Oct. 30, 1929.

19. Ibid.

20. Joe Polakoff, "Ex-Scranton Girl Spanish Olympian," *Scr Rep*, July 9, 1936.

21. "Scranton," *The Afro-American* (Baltimore), May 3, 1930. In its roundup of events and news stories from around the country, this newspaper covered Scranton and events in its African American churches and the Progressive Center; "Notice," *Scr Rep*, Oct. 11, 1928; Nira Blue Madison, interviews; Dorothy Walker Smith, interviews; Elvira and John King lived at 1312 Linden Street; Martin, "The History of the Negro in Scranton."

22. "Recreation Center Will Open Today," *Scr Rep*, May 26, 1930; "New Recreation Center Is Opened," *Scr Rep*, May 27, 1930; Dorothy Tucker, "Association Meeting Needs of Community," *Scr Rep*, Oct. 30, 1929.

23. "E. R. Johnson Elected Association President," *Scr Rep*, May 8, 1934; "Those Who Passed the Civil Service Exams," *Scr Rep*, Feb. 5, 1907; "Afro-American Realty Company Gets Charter," *Scr Rep*, June 8, 1912; Hitchcock, 309; "Boy Struck by Auto," *Scr Rep*, June 19, 1913; "Lincoln Club to Round Up Colored Voters," *Scr Rep*, Sept. 30, 1913.

24. Dorothy Walker Smith, interviews; "Progressive Recreation Activities Scheduled," *Scr Rep*, June 7, 1932; "Forthcoming Activities at Progressive Center," *Scr Rep*, Dec. 10, 1932; Lackawanna County marriage records and "Lilly-Myers Nuptials," *Scr Rep*, June 6, 1900; *Pennsylvania Negro Business Directory*, 1910, 111; "Social News," *Scr Rep*, Oct. 28, 1929.

25. Reid Coploff, "Masons Secure in Their History," (Scr) *Times-Trib*, Mar. 20, 2005, courtesy of Norma Reese.

26. "Lodge of Elks," *Scr Rep*, July 7, 1905; " The Black Elks: A Home Away from Home," available at www.aaregistry.org/historic_events/view/black-elks-home-away-home/.

27. Untitled paragraph, *Republican Weekly* (?), Aug. 2, 1876, courtesy of Norma Reese; untitled paragraph, *Scr Rep*, Sept. 7, 1878, courtesy of Norma Reese; "An Organization of Colored Republicans," *Scr Rep*, Aug. 24, 1905; "Colored Voters Form Republican Club," *Scr Rep*, Jan. 29, 1926; the Keystone Republican Club had its headquarters at the Odd Fellows Hall, 513 Pine Street, while

the Lackawanna County Colored Democratic Club convened at 236 Penn Avenue; Martin, "The History of the Negro in Scranton."

28. Martin, "The History of the Negro in Scranton"; "Colored Association [NAACP] Will Conduct Meet Tomorrow," *Scr Times*, Feb.17, 1934, courtesy of Norma Reese.

29. "Fewer Lynchings," *Scr Rep*, Apr. 18, 1929; "Faulty Suspenders Help Cops Catch Negro and Stolen Fowl," *Scr Rep*, Apr. 9, 1934.

30. "Ex-Slave at 93 Sews Quilts and Reads Her Bible: Aunt Fannie, Born on a Virginia Plantation, Speaks with Charm Typical of Southern Gentlefolk of Civil War Days; Recalls Girlhood," *Scr Rep*, Feb. 21, 1934; "Social," *Scr Rep*, June 11, 1932; Dorothy Walker Smith, interviews; www.studythepast.com /weekly/pacrow.html: By 1911, Pennsylvania statutes barred public carrier, school, and public accommodations segregation.

31. Marie Van Bergen Mansuy, interviews; Brian Fulton, "Pages from the Past" blog, on Helen Louise Mitchell Brown, in *Scr Times* Aug. 7, 1953, (Scr) *Times-Trib*, blog c. 2011.

32. "Bureau Report for February," *Scr Rep*, Mar. 18, 1926; "Mrs. King Reports on Colored Center," *Scr Rep*, Dec. 16, 1931; "Girl Scout News," *Scr Rep*, Mar. 7, 1932; Scranton Girl Scouts Council History Summary, July 31,1936, GSUSA archives.

33. Francis X. Burke and family resided at 1222 Marion Street, Dunmore; Dorothy Walker Smith, interviews; Marie Van Bergen Mansuy, interviews; Marcella Martin, interview by the author.

34. Nira Blue Madison interviews; Kay Schoen Butzner, interviews.

35. Nira Blue Madison interviews; Kay Schoen Butzner interviews; [Scranton, PA] Central High School's Commencement program, class of June 1938, J. I. & K. Butzner Papers; Dorothy Walker Smith, interviews; the Franklins lived at 617 Lee Court; "Let Me Tell You," Matilda (Simms) Kearney memoir; during her high school years, Alice Porter lived with her family at 1335 Sanderson Avenue; Alice Porter Foster's funeral program, courtesy of Dorothy Walker Smith.

36. Evelyn Franklin (married name withheld upon request), interview; Nira Blue Madison, interviews.

37. *Pennsylvania Negro Business Directory*, 1910, 81; Dorothy Walker Smith, interviews; "Meeting to Discuss City Housing Problem," *Scr Rep*, Jan. 19, 1925.

38. "Social," *Scr Rep*, Sept. 16, 1933.

39. Careful combing through Lackawanna County Medical Society publications and photographs as well as other records has, so far, turned up no evidence of African American members through the 1930s.

40. *Lackawanna County Medical Society Pennsylvania* 1926, print of 208 individual photographic portraits of physicians and a list of names of 18 physicians "In Memoriam," (Photocraft Press, Bound Book, N.J. Publishers, photography by F. W. Hornbaker and Bachrach, Inc.), in Mansour's Market Café, Scran-

ton, PA. Neither Dr. Foster nor Dr. Davis is among the physicians in this print, although Dr. Foster is listed in the 1926 Scranton City Directory; "E. N. Goodall, Waiter, Dies at Age 77," *Scr Times*, Apr. 15, 1957, courtesy of Norma Reese. "Conservatory Recital," *Scr Rep*, Nov. 10, 1913; Angi Goodall Johnston, interview by the author; *Pennsylvania Negro Business Directory*, 1910, 139.

41. Ethel A. Miller, "A Successful Woman in a Man's Game," *Opportunity: Journal of Negro Life*, July 1930, 214–15; ad for "G. W. Brown, Drayman," *Scr Rep*, June 16, 1931; Cheryl Kashuba, "Immigrants Found Opportunity in Scranton" (Scr) *Times-Trib*, Mar. 17, 2013; Dorothy Walker Smith, interviews; Margo Azzarelli, "A Woman Doing a Man's Job," *Our Town, Lackawanna County*, c. Mar. 2013; Elizabeth Lindsay Davis, *Lifting as They Climb* (Washington, D.C.: National Association of Colored Women, 1933), 389.

42. Louise Tanner Brown lived at 532 Prescott Avenue; Dorothy Walker Smith, interviews.

43. Dorothy Walker Smith, interviews; Granville and Dottie Smith lived at 921 Pine Street, now demolished.

44. "Colored Voters Form Republican Club," *Scr Rep*, Jan. 29, 1926; Cathy Ann Strader Hardaway, interviews; "Celebrating the Life of Gwendolyn Jones Strader Douglas," memorial brochure, Shiloh Baptist Church, June 3, 2013, courtesy of Dorothy Walker Smith, whose husband, Granville, had stood at the wedding of Gwen and John Strader; Marcella Martin, interview.

45. Marcella Martin, interview.

46. Dorothy Walker Smith, interviews; Nira Blue Madison, interviews.

47. *EOC*, 22; Garrett Epps, "The Fourth Circuit Court of Appeals Is Losing a Star," *Style Weekly* (Richmond, VA), Jan. 1, 1980.

CHAPTER 9 *The City's "Best Investment"*

1. June Carter Davies, "Jade Writes Potpourri," *The Villager* (Moscow, PA), Mar. 2, 1994; "The Weather," *Scr Rep*, Feb. 6, 1929; "Registration in Schools," *Scr Times*, Feb. 7, 1929.

2. *Impressions* 37, no. 2 (Dec. 1932): 10–11; "A New Era in the City's History," *Scr Rep*, Sept. 25, 1896.

3. Arlene Swartz (wife of Jane's high school classmate J. Milton Swartz), interviews by the author; *Impressions* 36, no. 1 (Nov. 1931): 18–19; Kay Schoen Butzner, interviews.

4. Marzani, *The Education of a Reluctant Radical*, vol. 2, *Growing Up American*, 16; "Central High School, 1929–1933 [and other years] Quarterly Reports, Girls/Boys," handwritten record books, in Scranton High School library; Kay Schoen Butzner, interviews; "Jones Reveals Central Class Honor Pupils," *Scr Rep*, Nov. 25, 1930.

5. Kay Schoen Butzner, interviews.

6. Kay Schoen Butzner, interviews; "Class Entering [Central High School]," books for various years; Hitchcock, 343; "83 Students Make Tech Honor Roll," *Scr Rep*, Apr. 9, 1929; *Impressions* 38, no. 3 (Apr. 1934): 17.

7. Marzani, *The Education of a Reluctant Radical*, vol. 2, *Growing Up American*, 3, 9; North Scranton Junior High was designed in 1924 by Gilbert Edson, with Sinclair & Grigg, contractors; "Edson Services Monday Morning," *Scr Rep*, July 30, 1927.

8. Information about Willard Parker Little, courtesy of Christine Sala, Avery Architectural and Fine Arts Library, Columbia University; "A New Era in the City's History," *Scr Rep*, Sept. 25, 1896.

9. "A New Era in the City's History," *Scr Rep*, Sept. 25, 1896; Hitchcock, 341–43; Nicholas E Petula and Thomas W. Morgan, Sr., *The History of the Public Schools of Scranton, Pennsylvania* (privately published, 2008), Albright Memorial Library, Scranton, PA; George E. Thomas et al., *Buildings of Pennsylvania: Philadelphia and Eastern Pennsylvania* (Charlottesville: University of Virginia Press, 2010), 487; "Outlines Plans for a New Addition," *Scr Rep*, Jan. 24, 1922.

10. "Register and Directory of the Public Schools and Teachers, 1931–1932," city of Scranton, Pennsylvania, in the archives at the School Administration Building; Dorothy Burkhouse's pay stub found in the archives at the School Administration Building; Kay Schoen Butzner, interviews; Barbara Gelder Kelley, interviews; the swim team started at the end of 1931 or the beginning 1932; *Impressions* 36, no. 1 (Nov. 1931): 31.

11. Kay Schoen Butzner, interviews; Barbara Gelder Kelley, interviews; "Register and Directory of the Public Schools and Teachers, 1931–1932"; Hitchcock, 343.

12. Kay Schoen Butzner, interviews.

13. Ibid.

14. Ibid.

15. Kay Schoen Butzner, interviews; Marzani, *The Education of a Reluctant Radical*, vol. 2, *Growing Up American*, 7, 46, 58–59.

16. "Tailor Whose Son Won Oxford Scholarship Is 'Not Surprised,'" *Scr Rep*, Feb. 29, 1936; Marzani, *The Education of a Reluctant Radical*, vol. 2, *Growing Up American*, 8–9, 58–59, 62.

17. Marzani, *The Education of a Reluctant Radical*, vol. 2, *Growing Up American*, 22, 77; Marie Van Bergen Mansuy, interviews; Hitchcock, 342, 344; Tech charged nonresidents $75 tuition, payable in two installments at the start of each term, so Central probably charged more or less the same amount.

18. Marzani, *The Education of a Reluctant Radical*, vol. 2, *Growing Up American*, 47, 87.

19. "Register and Directory of the Public Schools and Teachers, 1931–1932"; Barbara Gelder Kelley, interviews.

20. Marzani, *The Education of a Reluctant Radical*, vol. 2, *Growing Up American*, 4, 87; "In School Play," *Scr Rep*, Dec. 4, 1930; "Central High School Students to Give Play," *Scr Rep*, Dec. 12, 1930.

21. "Register and Directory of the Public Schools and Teachers, 1931–1932"; Marzani, *The Education of a Reluctant Radical*, vol. 2, *Growing Up American*, 78, 81–82; "Death Claims M. H. Jordan," *Scr Trib*, May 26, 1953; "Teachers Must Walk," *Scr Rep*, June 26, 1906; "Lively Fight on for School Job," *Scr Rep*, Apr. 11, 1908.

22. Marzani, *The Education of a Reluctant Radical*, vol. 2, *Growing Up American*, 81–82; "Register and Directory of Public Schools and Teachers, 1931–1932"; Michael H. Jordan lived two blocks south of Forest Hill Cemetery, at 1621 Jefferson (now 1609); "Summer Sessions for Delinquents Begin on Monday," *Scr Rep*, July 6, 1932; "Seven Veteran Instructors Retired Here," *Scr Rep*, June 20, 1936.

23. Marzani, *The Education of a Reluctant Radical*, vol. 2, *Growing Up American*, 78–81; *Impressions* 3, no. 3 (Nov. 1927): on page with masthead; among Eugene Morley's black-and-white lithographs in the Smithsonian Museum are *Exodus from the Coal Fields*, n.d., *Mine Rescue*, 1938, and *Two Miners with Cart*, 1936.

24. Marzani, *The Education of a Reluctant Radical*, vol. 2, *Growing Up American*, 88.

25. Ibid., 88–89, 91.

26. Ibid., 11–12, 37, 40–43, 51, 76.

27. "Class Entering [Central High School] February 1929"; James K. Jacobs, interviews; Arlene Swartz, interviews; Natalie Gelb, interviews; Nancy McBride (Jane's niece), interviews by the author.

28. James K. Jacobs, interviews; Kay Schoen Butzner, interviews.

29. "50 Years Later: An Interview with Jason Epstein," Greenwich Village Society for Historic Preservation, October 2011; Mark Feeney, "City Sage."

30. Kay Schoen Butzner, interviews; "Class Entering [Central High School] February 1929"; *Impressions* 37, no. 2 (Dec. 1932): 40–41.

31. *Impressions* 37, no. 2 (Dec. 1932): 12; Kay Schoen Butzner, interviews; Marie Van Bergen Mansuy, interviews.

32. "Central Book Club to Have Anniversary," *Scr Rep*, Nov. 21, 1931; "Wooster Addresses Central High Club," *Scr Rep*, Feb. 27, 1934; "Central High Book Club Elects Officers," *Scr Rep*, Sept. 22, 1936; *Impressions* 36, no. 2 (Dec. 1931): 25–26; Kay Schoen Butzner, interviews.

33. "Neal Moylan Is Member of the Cast," *Scr Rep*, Dec. 3, 1932; "Name Committees for Central High School Production," *Scr Rep*, Nov. 24, 1932; "High School Club to Present 'Devil's Disciple,'" *Scr Rep*, Dec. 9, 1932; for *Impressions*, Jane interviewed the actor Clayton Hamilton, whom she had seen in a fine production of *Cyrano de Bergerac* at the Century Club.

34. *Impressions* 38, no. 3 (Apr. 1934): 17; "Program Is Given by Writing Club," *Scr Rep*, May 14, 1932; "Play Given by Pupils at Central High School," *Scr Rep*, Nov. 20, 1931.

35. "Things We're Told," *Scr Rep*, Dec. 21, 1931; "May 'Impressions' Issued to Students," *Scr Rep*, May 27, 1932; *Impressions* 36, no. 2 (Dec. 1931): on page with masthead; *Impressions Supplement* 1, no. 1 (Nov. 20, 1931): 1; *Impressions* 37, no. 4 (June 1933): 25.

36. Marzani, *The Education of a Reluctant Radical*, vol. 2, *Growing Up American*, 16; "Things We're Told," *Scr Rep*, Dec. 21, 1931; "Plans Are Discussed to Improve Magazine," *Scr Rep*, Apr. 21, 1932; *Impressions* 37, no. 1 (Nov. 1932): on page with masthead; *Impressions Supplement* 1, no. 1 (Nov. 20, 1931): 1.

37. *Impressions* 36, no. 1 (Nov. 1931): 12; *The American Girl*, June 1931, 20–21, and Nov. 1931, 21.

38. "Social," *Scr Rep*, Feb. 22, 1932; Nellie B. Sergent, ed., *Younger Poets: An Anthology of American Secondary School Verse* (New York: D. Appleton and Co., 1932), vii, 196, 377.

39. *The American Girl*, June 1931, 20–21; *Impressions* 36, no. 2 (Dec. 1931): 18.

40. *Impressions* 37, no. 1 (Nov. 1932): 16–17; issues of *Impressions* for several years prior to this did not list a position for a poetry editor among the board of editors or staff.

41. *Impressions* 37, no. 2 (Dec. 1932): 14, 18.

42. *Impressions* 36, no. 5 (May 1932): 29; *Impressions* 37, no. 1 (Nov. 1932): 17; *Impressions* 37, no. 2 (Dec. 1932): 18; Janny Scott, "Gershon Legman, Anthologist of Erotic Humor, Is Dead at 81," *NY Times*, March 14, 1999.

43. "Class Entering [Central High School] September 1928"; upon their arrival, the Toatleys resided at 308 Kressler Court; "Lecture Course Begins Tonight," *Scr Rep*, Jan. 10, 1936; "Pastor Says Public's Attitude Toward Critics of Vice 'Silly,'" *Scr Rep*, Jan. 11, 1936.

44. Kay Schoen Butzner, interviews; Marzani, *The Education of a Reluctant Radical*, vol. 2, *Growing Up American*, 83, 84, with photo in tennis clothes with racket in hand.

45. Kay Schoen Butzner, interviews; "Central Swimmers Down Junior High," *Scr Rep*, Jan. 7, 1933; *Impressions* 36, no. 1 (Nov. 1931): 31.

46. James K. Jacobs, interviews; Scranton Girl Scouts Council History Summary, July 31, 1936, GSUSA archives; Barbara Gelder Kelley, interviews; "Girl Scout Notes by Local Scribes," *Scr Rep*, Feb. 15, 1932; "Girl Scout Notes," *Scr Rep*, Mar. 22, 1932; Girl Scout, Inc., *Girl Scout Handbook*, rev. ed. (New York: Girl Scouts, Inc., 1930), 437, courtesy of Mary Winslow, volunteer archivist at Girl Scouts in the Heart of Pennsylvania.

47. Sergent, ed., *Younger Poets*, 377; "Girl Scout News," *Scr Rep*, Jan. 27, 1927; "Scouts Appoint Field Captains," *Scr Rep*, Oct. 14, 1929; "Scout Camp Activities Attractive," *Scrantonian*, Aug. 9, 1931, courtesy of Mary Winslow; Mary Levey and Mary Degenhardt, *Highlights in Girl Scouting*, 1912–2001 (New York: Girls Scouts of the USA, 2002); Jane Jacobs, letter to her mother, Bess Robison Butzner, Sept. 26, 1972, Jacobs Papers; "Miriam Camps, 78, a Writer on Europe," *NY Times*, Jan. 2, 1995.

48. "Golden Eaglet Award Made at Troop Meet," *Scr Rep*, Apr. 12, 1934; "Three Scouts Will Be Awarded Eaglets," *Scr Rep*, Aug. 17, 1933.

49. "Boys' Week Proclamation," *Scr Rep*, Apr. 26, 1930; Marzani, *The Education of a Reluctant Radical*, vol. 2, *Growing Up American*, 87; *Impressions* 36, no. 5 (May 1932): masthead/editorial page; "Expect 15,000 Boys Will Participate in Parade," *Scr Rep*, Apr. 28, 1932; "Will Take Part in Girls' Week Pageant at Central High Tonight," *Scr Rep*, Oct. 14, 1933.

50. Nikki Keller and Nicki Hlavacek, "The United Way of Lackawanna County," *United Way Supplement*, Oct. 8, 1995; *Impressions Supplement* 1, no. 1 (Nov. 20, 1931): 1; Community Chest sixteen-page pamphlet, 1922, United Way of Lackawanna County archives; *Seventh Annual Report of the Community Chest, Scranton, Pa., January* 1928, United Way of Lackawanna County archives.

51. "Students to Write Stories on Community Chest Drive," *Scr Rep*, Oct. 3, 1931.

52. "Civil War Veterans Visit Many Schools," *Scr Rep*, May 22, 1929; "High School Club Will Give Concert," *Scr Rep*, May 17, 1932; "Capacity Audience at Spring Concert," *Scr Rep*, May 21, 1932; "Central Musicians to Give Concert," *Scr Rep*, May 1, 1931; "World Premiere of Jeanne Madden Film Here Friday; Star Will Appear in Person at Gala Opening at Strand," *Scr Rep*, Aug. 26, 1936.

53. Joseph Polakoff, "Most Beautiful Building in City," *Scr Rep*, May 28, 1927; "The Medical Arts Building," *Scr Rep*, Apr. 6, 1929; Kay Schoen Butzner, like other high school students, often ushered at the Community Concerts, and her mother sometimes played piano in them.

54. "Will You Help?" *Scr Rep*, June 30, 1927.

55. "Begin Operation Here Monday for Beautiful New Masonic Temple," *Scr Rep*, Apr. 1, 1927; "Two Sections of the New Masonic Temple," *Scr Rep*, May 14, 1927; "Temple Theater to Have Opening," *Scr Rep*, Feb. 15, 1930.

56. Kay Schoen Butzner, interviews.

57. "Technical Teachers Purchase Clothes for Needy Graduates," *Scr Rep*, Jan. 30, 1936; *DAA*, 53–54; "Wins Scholarship," *Scr Rep*, Sept. 14, 1933; *Impressions* 37, no. 1 (Nov. 1932): 11.

58. "Diplomas Given to 198 Seniors at Central High," *Scr Rep*, Jan. 28, 1933; "Class Entering [Central High School] February 1929," handwritten record book, in Scranton High School library. "Nearly 600 Will Enter High Schools," *Scr Rep*, Feb. 3, 1930; the addition of students from North Scranton Junior High entering Central High in sophomore year accounts for the increase in the number of students in this class as of Feb. 1930.

59. "Central High to Graduate Class of 198 Tonight," *Scr Times*, Jan. 26, 1933, courtesy of Norma Reese; "50th Reunion, Central High School, Class of January 1933"; Jane Jacobs, "Autobiography," *ITM*, 3.

60. "Marie Mansuy, Obituary," *Scr Rep*, Apr. 3, 2012.

CHAPTER 10 *"First to Be a Newspaper Reporter*

1. "50 Years Later: An Interview with Jason Epstein," Greenwich Village Society for Historic Preservation, October 2011; Nellie B. Sergent, ed., *Younger Poets: An Anthology of American Secondary School Verse* (New York: D. Appleton and Co., 1932), 377.

2. *D&L*, 577–78.

3. *ITM*, 3.

4. "Stroller's Notebook," *Scr Rep*, Apr. 29, 1925; "Charles Powell, Head of School, Dies Suddenly," *Scr Times*, Feb. 17, 1938, courtesy of Norma Reese.

5. Ad for the Powell School, *Scr Rep*, July 26, 1919; "Stroller's Notebook," *Scr Rep*, Apr. 29, 1925; "Powell School Is Rapidly Growing," *Scr Rep*, Aug. 20, 1924; ad for the Powell School of Business, *Scr Rep*, Aug. 31, 1932.

6. "15th Graduation of Powell School on Friday Night," *Scr Rep*, June 20, 1933; untitled ads, *Scr Rep*, Aug. 31, 1933, and Aug. 30, 1933.

7. Century Club, Scranton, printed membership booklets for various years, in the club's archives; *EOC*, 159–60; "Large Audience Hears America's Foremost Poet," *Scr Rep*, Feb. 10, 1933; Elinor Frost, letters to Jessie M. Wainwright, Aug. 1, 1932, Jan. 19, 1933, and Jan. 30, 1933, Dartmouth College Library.

8. James K. Jacobs, interviews; Robert Frost, *Selected Poems*, new ed. (New York: Henry Holt and Company, 1928), courtesy of the Estate of Jane Jacobs.

9. "Jane Butzner Wins Prize in Nation Wide Contest," *Impressions* 37, no. 4 (June 1933): 41.

10. "Statement of the Ownership, Management, Circulation, Etc. . . . of The Scranton Republican," *Scr Rep*, Oct. 4, 1933; printed above the *Scr Rep* masthead was "Largest Morning Daily Circulation in Pennsylvania Outside Philadelphia and Pittsburgh," January–April 1929; ad for "The Powell School of Business," *Scr Rep*, Aug. 20, 1924; "The Scranton Republican's New Home," *Scr Rep*, Apr. 12, 1928; its new home was at 309–11 N. Washington Ave.

11. "New Structure Being Occupied by Its Tenants," *Scr Rep*, Mar. 28, 1929; "Medical Arts Building," *Scr Rep*, Apr. 6, 1929; "These Physicians and Dentists Now Located in New Medical Arts Building . . . ," *Scr Rep*, Apr. 5, 1929.

12. James I. Butzner, letter to Robert J. Arthur, editor, *Scr Trib*, June 3, 1969, in which Jane Jacobs's brother Jim Butzner furnished almost all the material printed verbatim in "Widow of City Physician, Bess Butzner, Ex-Teacher-Nurse, Celebrates 90th Birthday Saturday," *Scrantonian*, June 15, 1969, J. I. & K. Butzner Papers; "Class Entering [Central High School], February 1929"; "Personalities," *Scr Rep*, Jan. 21, 1929; "Two St. Thomas Students Receive Literary Awards," *Scr Rep*, June 6, 1929; "Most Beautiful Building in City," *Scr Rep*, May 28, 1927; "Biography of Joseph Polakoff," part of index to the Joseph Polakoff Collection in the University of Scranton archives, available at digitalservices.scranton.edu/cdm/biography/collection/polakoff; Polakoff's first "Polley's Chatter" column appeared in the *Scr Rep*, Aug. 24, 1934,

although when the paper's name was changed to the *Scr Trib*, they spelled it "Polly's Chatter."

13. Joseph Polakoff, "Polly's Chatter," *Scr Trib*, Dec. 24, 1937, Jacobs Papers; "Widow of City Physician, Bess Butzner, Ex-Teacher-Nurse, Celebrates 90th Birthday Saturday"; Jane Jacobs, letter to her brother Jim Butzner, June 18, 1990, J. I. & K. Butzner Papers; "Huge Crowd Watches Play by Play Reproduced on Republican Scoreboard," *Scr Rep*, Oct 4, 1933.

14. *DAA*, 53.

15. Civilian Personnel Records and FBI file, 7, 15, courtesy of Peter Laurence; Jane Jacobs, "Autobiography," written for *Architect's Journal*, Nov. 22, 1961, in *ITM*, 3; Jane Jacobs, "Biographical information," c. 2000, sent to Ellen Perry Berkeley for *At Grandmother's Table*, Jacobs Papers; "Where the Social News Is Prepared," *Scr Rep*, Sept. 28, 1928; "New Social Editor," *Scr Rep*, June 16, 1930; "Mrs. E. C. Weichel Dies in Hospital After Brief Illness," *Scr Rep*, Feb. 17, 1932; "Editor's Playlet Wins First Prize," *Scr Rep*, Apr. 15, 1933; "Flow of Beer Begins Through Unregulated Channels Here Today," *Scr Rep*, Apr. 7, 1933.

16. "Social," *Scr Rep*, Mar. 24, 1934, in Jane's clipping scrapbook, courtesy of the Estate of Jane Jacobs; "Committee on Camp to Report Thursday," *Scr Rep*, Sept. 11, 1933; "Girl Scout News," *Scr Rep*, Sept. 29, 1933.

17. Ad for the Scranton Republican Annual Republican Cooking School, *Scr Rep*, Sept. 29, 1933; "Republican Cooking School Breaks Attendance Records," *Scr Rep*, Oct. 7, 1933; the "Homemakers Page" debut, *Scr Rep*, Oct. 13, 1933; ad for the "Homemakers Page," Oct. 31, 1933; Louise Bennett Weaver, "Helping the Homemaker," *Scr Rep*, Aug. 13, 1928.

18. James K. Jacobs, interviews; "Housewives Here Submit Recipes," *Scr Rep*, Nov. 3, 1933; "Apple Cake," recipe, *Scr Rep*, Dec. 29, 1933; "B. B. Powell, Retired S-T Official, Dies," *Scrantonian*, Feb. 20, 1983.

19. Jane called B. B. Powell her boss, FBI file, 6, courtesy of Peter Laurence; "B. B. Powell, Retired S-T Official, Dies"; "B. B. Powell," *Scr Trib*, Feb. 23, 1983, courtesy of Norma Reese.

20. "Ex-Managing Editor Succumbs at Age 86," *Scr Times*, Feb. 21, 1983, courtesy of Norma Reese; "Stroller's Notebook," *Scr Rep*, Nov. 25, 1916; "Twenty Men in Casualty Lists," *Scr Rep*, Nov. 27, 1918.

21. "Society News," *Scr Rep*, July 18, 1921; "West Side Training Ground for Successful Journalists," *Scr Rep*, July 25, 1924.

22. "Republican Has Been Leader in This Territory for Many Years," *Scr Rep*, Sept. 28, 1928; Margaret A. Blanchard, ed., *History of the Mass Media in the United States: An Encyclopedia* (Chicago: Fitzroy Dearborn Publishers, 1998), 37; "Scribes Enjoy Annual Outing at Thompson's," *Scr Rep*, Sept. 3, 1928.

23. "Municipal Primaries Hold Public Interest," *Scr Rep*, Sept. 19, 1933; David J. Wenzel, *Scranton's Mayors* (Eynon, PA: Tribute Books, 2006), 75; "Election Night Service," *Scr Rep*, Sept. 19, 1933; "Davis Captures Mayor Fight;

Democrats Winners in County," *Scr Rep*, Nov. 8, 1933; James I. Butzner, letter to Robert J. Arthur, editor, *Scr Trib*, June 3, 1969.

24. "Routine of Municipal Affairs Fades as Girls Run Offices," *Scr Rep*, Oct. 14, 1933, in Jane's clipping scrapbook, courtesy of the Estate of Jane Jacobs; "Plans Are Being Perfected for Girls' Week in Scranton," *Scr Rep*, Sept. 30, 1933.

25. "Davis Captures Mayor Fight," *Scr Rep*, Nov. 8, 1933.

26. In this note and in subsequent notes in this chapter, if the citation includes Jane's name as author of an article, her name was bylined in the newspaper. If the citation does not include Jane's name as author, this book's author (and sometimes Jim Jacobs) deemed the article Jane's writing. Articles from Jane's clipping scrapbook are indicated as such, and dates—handwritten by Jane— often indicate only month and year. Clipping scrapbook, courtesy of the Estate of Jane Jacobs; Jane Butzner, "Fine Performance Presented by Guild," *Scrantonian*, Oct. 1933, in Jane's clipping scrapbook; Jane Butzner, "Comedy Presented by Catholic Group," *Scrantonian*, Nov. 1933, in Jane's clipping scrapbook; Jane Butzner, "Muse and Masque Club Scores Hit," *Scr Rep*, Nov. 27, 1933, in Jane's clipping scrapbook; "University Training Stressed by Ziegler," *Scr Rep*, Nov. 10, 1933; "Prominent Critic Will Speak Here," *Scr Rep*, Nov. 16, 1933; "Miss Dorothy Sands Scores with Her Performance Here," *Scr Rep*, Nov. 17, 1933.

27. "Dorothy Hausser in Central Play," *Scr Rep*, Nov. 10, 1933; "[Selma Bloch] In Central Play," *Scr Rep*, Nov. 15, 1933; "[Eugene McAndrew] In Central Play," *Scr Rep*, Nov. 28, 1933; Jane Butzner, "'The Perfect Alibi' Presented by Club," *Scr Rep*, Dec. 11, 1933.

28. *EOC*, 159–60; Kay Schoen Butzner, interviews; R. N. Davis, "Museum Musings," *Scr Rep*, Aug. 14, 1933; "Art at the Everhart Museum," *Scr Rep*, Sept. 23, 1933; R. N. Davis, "Museum Musings," *Scr Rep*, Mar. 11, 1932.

29. Richard Stanislaus, "Industrial Landscapes: The Anthracite Coal Breaker Paintings of John Willard Raught," excerpted in the *Lackawanna Historical Society Journal* (Spring 1992): 4; "John Raught, Noted Artist, Dies Suddenly," *Scr Rep*, Jan. 6, 1931; Chris Kelly, "150 People Who Made Scranton Great," (Scr) *Times-Trib*, Feb. 12, 2016; Brian Fulton, "Pages from the Past" blog, on John Willard Raught in 1915, (Scr) *Times-Trib*, Apr. 25, 2010; "Exhibition of Paintings by John Willard Raught [at the Real Estate Building, Scranton]," pamphlet with price list, April 23–28, 1928, Everhart Museum, Scranton, PA.

30. John Willard Raught, "The Tragedy of Coal Mining," *Scr Rep*, Feb. 6, 1928; Richard Stanislaus, interviews.

31. Jane Butzner, "Miller's New Book Series of Episodes" *Scr Rep*, Dec. 9, 1933, in Jane's clipping scrapbook; "Stomach Wall of Ariel Man Leather Lined," *Scr Rep*, Dec. 8, 1933, in Jane's clipping scrapbook.

32. Peter Laurence, *Becoming Jane Jacobs* (Philadelphia: University of Pennsylvania Press, 2016), 20; FBI file, 15, courtesy of Peter Laurence; "Where the News of The Daily Republican Is Prepared," *Scr Rep*, Sept. 28, 1928.

33. James K. Jacobs, interviews; James I. Butzner, letter to Robert J. Arthur, editor, *Scr Trib*, June 3, 1969, J. I. & K. Butzner Papers.

34. "Scribes Enjoy Annual Outing at Thompson's," *Scr Rep*, Sept. 3, 1928; "Skillful Operators Bring World Series Plays to Local Fans," *Scr Rep*, Oct. 5, 1933; "Scoreboard Operators in Action," *Scr Rep*, Oct. 6, 1933; "East End," *Scr Rep*, Apr. 27, 1931; Gordon Williams, Jr., "'Coquette' Given by Drama League," *Scr Rep*, Feb. 18, 1932; Williams started covering Green Ridge on a regular basis in August 1933.

35. Robert J. Arthur, "Settlement of Strike to Be Clinched Today," *Scr Rep*, Feb. 12, 1926; "Scranton Republican Scoops the Country," ad, *Scr Rep*, Feb. 13, 1926; Robert J. Arthur, "Operators Renew Request for 35 Per Cent Wage Slash," *Scr Rep*, Apr. 20, 1933; Robert J. Arthur, "Hard Coal Operators May Effect Drastic Retrenchment Plans," *Scr Rep*, Apr. 28, 1933; *DAA*, 53; Betty Houchin Winfield, ed., *Journalism, 1908: Birth of a Profession* (Columbia: University of Missouri Press, 2008); "Local Scribes to Have Noted Writer as Guest," *Scr Rep*, Feb. 14, 1933; Laurence, *Becoming Jane Jacobs*, 65.

36. Blanchard, *History of the Mass Media in the United States*, 699–702; Wachtel interview.

37. "Change of Ownership," *Scr Rep*, Feb. 17, 1934; "Scranton Republican Is Sold," *NY Times*, Feb. 18, 1934; Hitchcock, 527–28.

38. "Republican Has Been Leader in This Territory for Many Years," *Scr Rep*, Sept. 28, 1928; *American Biography: A New Cyclopedia*, vol. 10 (New York: American Historical Society, 1922), 3–6; "Laurence H. Watres, Ex-Congressman, 81," *NY Times*, Feb. 9, 1964; "Blind Enjoy Annual Picnic at Pen-y-Bryn," *Scr Rep*, June 15, 1933; Sandra Skies Ludwig, "This Home Was Really a Castle: Scranton Estate Was Beloved Residence of Watres Family," *Times Leader* (Wilkes-Barre, PA), Sept. 23, 2001.

39. "Republican Oldest Newspaper in the City; Established 1856," *Scr Rep*, Feb. 17, 1934; the Schroth family lived at 621 Jefferson Avenue; Father Raymond Schroth, interviews by the author; Raymond A. Schroth, S.J., *The Eagle and Brooklyn: A Community Newspaper, 1841–1955* (Westport, CT: Greenwood Press, 1974), 186; Frank Schroth, "A Personal Word," *Scr Rep*, Feb. 19, 1934.

40. Jane Jacobs, letter to Jim Butzner, June 18, 1990, J. I. & K. Butzner Papers; "Scrantonian Tribune Had Colorful History," *Scr Times*, May 21, 1990, courtesy of Brian Fulton; Schroth, *The Eagle and Brooklyn*, 185–86, 239–41.

41. E. J. Lynett, death certificate, Jan. 1, 1943; "E. J. Lynett, 86, Dies; Published Scranton Paper," *New York Herald Tribune*, Jan. 2, 1943; Hitchcock, 529–31; Chris Kelly, "150 People Who Made Scranton Great: E. J. Lynett," (Scr) *Times-Trib*, Apr. 6, 2016.

42. Blanchard, *History of the Mass Media in the United States*, 699–702; Chris Kelly, "150 People Who Made Scranton Great: Elizabeth Lynett" (Scr) *Times-Trib*, Mar. 20, 2016; Josephine M. Dunn and Cheryl A. Kashuba, *The Women of Scranton, 1880–1935* (Charleston, SC: Arcadia Publishing, 2007), 43.

43. "Emily Wilcox Quits," *Wilkes-Barre Record*, Feb. 5, 1949; "Newspaper Women Meet in Scranton," *Times Leader* (Wilkes-Barre, PA), May 10, 1947; "Emily Wilcox, Editor and Parliamentarian," obituary, *Philadelphia Inquirer*, Mar. 25, 1968; Emily Wilcox died at 79 in Bucks County, PA.

44. Blanchard, *History of the Mass Media in the United States*, 699–702; "Statement of the Ownership, Management, Circulation, Etc. . . . of The Scranton Republican," *Scr Rep*, Oct. 4, 1933; "Semi-Annual Statement of the Ownership, Management, Circulation, Etc. . . . of The Scranton Times," *Scr Times*, Oct. 4, 1933; Wenzel, *Scranton's Mayors*; John F. Durkan was the Democratic mayor from 1922–1926; Betty Houchin Winfield, interviews by the author; "Largest Morning Daily Circulation in Pennsylvania Outside Philadelphia and Pittsburgh," *Scr Rep*, 1925–1929.

45. James K. Jacobs, interviews; "Letters to the Editor," *Scr Rep*, Jan. 31, 1934.

46. "Letters to the Editor," *Scr Rep*, Mar. 9, 1934.

47. Ellis W. Roberts, *The Breaker Whistle Blows: Mining Disasters and Labor Leaders in the Anthracite Region* (Scranton, PA: Anthracite Museum Press, 1984), 133; "Letters to the Editor," *Scr Rep*, Mar. 23, 1934; Philip Van Cleef Mattes, *Tales of Scranton* (privately printed, 1973), 16, Scranton High School library.

48. "City Without Right to Stop Coal Removal," *Scr Rep*, Aug. 3, 1933; "Mine Cave Bureau," *Scr Truth*, Jan. 4, 1915; "W. W. Scranton Offers $10,000 to Help in Finding Solution of Cave Problem," *Scr Times*, Aug. 5, 1916, courtesy of Norma Reese; Marzani, *The Education of a Reluctant Radical*, vol. 2, *Growing Up American*, 62–63; Kay Schoen Butzner, interviews; "Mining in Sanderson Tract Which Underlies Disturbed Area Started Back in 1875," *Scr Times*, Nov. 24, 1931, courtesy of Norma Reese; Marie Van Bergen Mansuy, interviews; "Why More Mine Caves?" editorial, *Scr Rep*, Mar. 14, 1934.

49. "Why More Mine Caves?"; "No Move Made to Halt Mining on Ball Field," *Scr Rep*, Oct. 10, 1933; "'Bootleg' Miners Busy on North End Baseball Field," *Scr Rep*, Oct. 11, 1933; "Police Reserves Enforce Coal Ban," *Scr Rep*, Oct. 13, 1933; "15,000 Employed in Bootlegging Anthracite Coal," *Scr Times*, Jan. 1, 1936, courtesy of Brian Fulton.

50. Philip Van Cleef Mattes, *Tales of Scranton*, 9, 13, 17, 21–28; Hitchcock, 180; Roberts, *The Breaker Whistle Blows*.

51. Wachtel interview.

52. Marzani, *The Education of a Reluctant Radical*, vol. 2, *Growing Up American*, 3; Marie Van Bergen Mansuy, interviews; Patrick McKenna, "Scranton Was Once the Friendly City for Prostitutes," *Scr Times*, Dec. 23, 1989, courtesy of Brian Fulton; Ira L. Reiss, *An Insider's View of Sexual Science Since Kinsey* (Lanham, MD: Rowman & Littlefield, 2006), 2–3; Joseph X. Flannery, "Sleuths Couldn't Find City Tourist Attraction," *Scr Times*, Jan. 13, 1980, courtesy of Brian Fulton; Brian Fulton, "Pages from the Past" blog, on bawdy houses, (Scr) *Times-Trib*, June 12, 2012.

53. Flannery, "Sleuths Couldn't Find City Tourist Attraction"; McKenna, "Scranton Was Once the Friendly City for Prostitutes."

54. *SOS*, 93–94; "The Mafia Originated in Sicily in the Middle Ages," *Scr Rep*, Jan. 27, 1921; James K. Jacobs, interviews.

55. "243 Men Accused as Mafia Members," *Scr Rep*, Oct. 13, 1931; Alexander Jamie, "Lifting the Curtain on the Crime Trust," *Scr Rep*, Mar. 21, 1932; "Public Conscience," editorial, *Scr Rep*, Apr. 5, 1934; "Social Righteousness," letter to the editor, *Scr Rep*, Apr. 7, 1934.

56. James K. Jacobs, interviews; Jane Jacobs quoted in Christopher Lehmann-Haupt, "Books of the Times: An Imaginary Round Table on Social Concerns," *NY Times*, Feb. 18, 1993; Feeney, "City Sage"; Brian Fulton, "Pages from the Past" blog, on bawdy house bombing on Apr. 2, 1928, (Scr) *Times-Trib*, Aug. 20, 2013.

57. Allen, *Only Yesterday*, 137; Stephen Smith, "Radio: The Internet of the 1930s," American RadioWorks, Nov. 10, 2014, available at www.americanradioworks .org/segments/radio-the-internet-of-the-1930s.

58. Jill Lepore, "The Party Crashers," *The New Yorker*, Feb. 22, 2016, 25; Frank Schroth, "A Personal Word," *Scr Rep*, Feb. 19, 1934.

59. Marzani, *The Education of a Reluctant Radical*, vol. 2, *Growing Up American*, 23–24, 32; "Covers 9,000 Miles on Less Than a Dollar," *Scr Rep*, Sept. 16, 1931; some information on Florence Osterland from "50th Reunion, Central High School, Class of January 1933"; "John F. Kane Succumbs: Ex-C of C Attache Here," *Scr Times*, Apr. 23, 1973, courtesy of Norma Reese.

60. Today the Pennsylvania Museum School of Industrial Art is known as University of the Arts, and the museum is known as the Philadelphia Museum of Art; "Betty Butzner Weds Veteran in New York: Ex-Scrantonian Becomes Bride of J. J. Manson," undated Scranton newspaper (the couple was married at New York's City Hall on March 3, 1947, so the article appeared shortly after), J. I. & K. Butzner Papers; collection of news clippings and documents about Martha Robison in Higgins, NC, courtesy of Ann Butzner, Jane's niece.

61. "Things We're Told," *Scr Rep*, May 1, 1934; Ann Butzner, interviews by the author; *CWN*, 124–29.

CHAPTER 11 *Ex-Scranton Girl and Her Home City*

1. James K. Jacobs, interviews.

2. Jane Jacobs, letter to Jim Butzner, Nov. 17, 1975, J. I. & K. Butzner Papers; Laurence, *Becoming Jane Jacobs*, 62–63.

3. "Chilton Boss Says He Won't Do It Again," undated, unidentified newspaper, Jacobs Papers.

4. Jane Butzner, "Daily's Effort Saves City from 'Ghost Town' Fate," *Editor & Publisher*, Sept. 4, 1943, Jacobs Papers; "Tribune Asks F.D.R. to Investigate Failure of Promised Aid Here," *Scr Trib*, Mar. 31, 1943, in Jane's clippings scrapbook, entitled "Newspaper Clippings, Scranton, Pa., Prepared by Scranton Chamber of Commerce," courtesy of the Estate of Jane Jacobs; Jane Butzner (but no byline), "30,000 Unemployed and 7000 Empty Houses in Scranton, Neglected City," *The Iron Age*, Mar. 25, 1943, 93–95.

5. Butzner, "30,000 Unemployed . . . Neglected City"; Norma Reese, interviews about working at the Scranton Lace Company in the 1950s and 1960s and speaking with "old-timers"; "1942–April 2, 1943," editorial, *Scr Trib*, Apr. 2, 1943, in Jane's clippings scrapbook by C of C.

6. "Scribes Make Ready for Dinner," *Scr Rep*, Feb. 3, 1931; Butzner, "30,000 Unemployed . . . Neglected City," 94; Butzner, "Daily's Effort Saves City from 'Ghost Town' Fate"; "E. M. Elliott," obituary, *Wilkes-Barre Record*, Sept. 1, 1945; "Greater Scranton Foundation Fund," Scranton Boosters Donors Card, 1941, property of the author.

7. Butzner, "30,000 Unemployed . . . Neglected City," 93–95.

8. "The Iron Age Scranton Article," editorial, *Scr Trib*, Mar. 27, 1943, in Jane's clippings scrapbook by C of C; "Figures Announced by C. of C. Believed Basis for Article in Iron Age," *Scr Times*, Mar. 27, 1943, in Jane's clippings scrapbook by C of C.; "Reveals Brush-off Given Statesman; Murphy Says He's Ready to Fight," *Scrantonian*, Mar. 28, 1943, in Jane's clippings scrapbook by C of C; identical paragraphs in "Secretary to Senator Says Iron Age Remark on Scranton Incorrect," *Scr Times*, Apr. 1, 1943, and "Guffey's Secretary Denies Stating Area Has Been Going Back," *Scr Trib*, Apr. 2, 1943, in Jane's clippings scrapbook by C of C.

9. "Tribune Asks F.D.R. to Investigate Failure of Promised Aid Here," *Scr Trib*, Mar. 31, 1943, in Jane's clippings scrapbook by C of C; "Tribune Asks WPB Chief for Plant Action," *Scr Trib*, Apr. 1, 1943, in Jane's clippings scrapbook by C of C; "No Time to Hush Up," *Scr Times*, Mar. 30, 1943, in Jane's clippings scrapbook by C of C.

10. "C.L.U. Will Challenge Senator's Secretary," *Scr Trib*, Apr. 3, 1943, and "Labor to Start Isolationism Scrap Tonight," *Scr Trib*, Apr. 5, 1943, in Jane's clippings scrapbook by C of C; "Ex-Scranton Girl Helps Home City," *Scrantonian*, Sept. 26, 1943, Jacobs Papers.

11. "Getting Results," editorial, *Scrantonian*, Mar. 28, 1943, in Jane's clippings scrapbook by C of C; "Magazine Article Brings Response," editorial, *Scr Trib*, Apr. 3, 1943, in Jane's clippings scrapbook by C of C; "Concerns Reported as Making Inquiries Here," *Scr Times*, Apr. 2, 1943, in Jane's clippings scrapbook by C of C.

12. E. M. Elliott, letter to the editors, *The Iron Age*, Apr. 17, 1943, in "Look What Happened to Scranton," advertising flyer for and by *The Iron Age*, Jacobs Papers; "Scranton Fears 'Sabotage by Sister City' in Plans to Get New Industries," *Times Leader; the Evening News* (Wilkes-Barre, PA), Apr. 29, 1943; "C. of C. Terminates Service of Agent in Washington," *Times Leader; the Evening News* (Wilkes-Barre, PA), Jan. 31, 1944.

13. "Scranton Shifts from Mining to Manufacturing," *New York Herald Tribune*, May 2, 1943; the Murray Corp. building was located at 501 South Washington Avenue; Jon O'Connell, "Scranton Firm Buys Former Giant Supermarket Warehouse," (Scr) *Times-Trib*, Jan. 27, 2017.

14. Butzner, "Daily's Effort Saves City from 'Ghost Town' Fate."

15. "Ex-Scranton Girl Helps Home City," *Scrantonian*, Sept. 26, 1943, Jacobs Papers; Butzner, "Daily's Effort Saves City from 'Ghost Town' Fate"; the line "perfect word[s] to clothe the perfect thought" comes from Jane's own poem. See Jane Butzner, "While Arranging Verses for a Book," sonnet in a column called "The Corning Tower," *New York Herald Tribune*, Jan. 22, 1935, Jacobs Papers.

16. Laurence, *Becoming Jane Jacobs*, 66–67, 70–71; Jane Butzner, letter to Catharine [Kay] Schoen at Hood College, Frederick, MD, Apr. 29, 1942, in Jim Butzner Family Album, J. I. & K. Butzner Papers; Kay Schoen Butzner, interviews.

17. Laurence, *Becoming Jane Jacobs*, 74; Kay Schoen Butzner, interviews; Jane and Bob Jacobs wedding announcement, Saturday, May 27, 1944, Scranton, PA, Jacobs Papers; Lucie Vogel, Elizabeth Butzner Tankard's niece, interviews.

18. "John Decker Butzner, Jr.," obituary, *Daily Progress* (Charlotesville, VA), Jan. 24, 2006; "Betty Butzner Weds Veteran in New York," from a Scranton newspaper, c. Mar. 3, 1947, Jim Butzner Family Album, J. I. & K. Butzner Papers.

19. Thomas Dublin and Walter Licht, *The Face of Decline: The Pennsylvania Anthracite Region in the Twentieth Century* (Ithaca, NY: Cornell University Press, 2005), 115; "Scranton Saves Its Life," *The Kiplinger Magazine*, Mar. 1950, 30.

20. Dorothy Walker Smith, interviews; "Fact Box: A History of Tobyhanna Army Depot," *Pocono Record* (Stroudsburg, PA), June 19, 2012.

21. "Meeting to Discuss City Housing Problem," *Scr Rep*, Jan. 19, 1925; Wenzel, *Scranton's Mayors*, 71, 83; for an examination of the development of Jacobs's thought about urban planning, see Laurence, *Becoming Jane Jacobs*, 122–31.

22. "Areas Marked for Redevelopment by City Planning Commission," *Scr Times*, Feb. 14, 1956, courtesy of Brian Fulton.

23. "Public Housing Topic of Parley," *Scr Times*, Sept. 8 (?), 1956; "Cusik Denies Binik Charges," *Scr Times*, Dec. 8, 1971, courtesy of Brian Fulton.

24. "Ex-Area Woman Writes Book Attacking City Revamping," *Scr Times*, Oct. 26, 1961, courtesy of Brian Fulton; *D&L*, 5.

25. "No SHA Plans for Public Housing in Tech-Central Present Site: Noto," *Scr Times*, June 30, 1965, courtesy of Brian Fulton; "Personal/Pertinent," *Scr Times*, May 6, 1971, courtesy of Brian Fulton.

26. "Housing Plans Promising," *Scr Times*, Jan. 11, 1968, courtesy of Brian Fulton; Nira Blue Madison, interviews.

27. Cathy Ann Strader Hardaway, interviews.

28. "Notice" of meeting of "the entire Negro community of Scranton" with representatives of state Human Relations Commission at Bethel AME Church, Mar. 21, 1965, typewritten flyer, courtesy of Dorothy Walker Smith; Dorothy Walker Smith, interviews; "Personal/Pertinent," *Scr Times*, May 24, 1975, courtesy of Brian Fulton.

29. Richard Leonori, interviews by the author; Albert P. O'Donnell, Jr., interviews; Maria Pane MacDonald, interviews by the author.

30. Maria Pane MacDonald, interviews; *SOA*, 252.

31. Rudy Kunz, DHS, interviews by the author; Maria Pane MacDonald, interviews.

32. "Former City Writer Featured Guest of First Lady at White House Fete," *Scr Times*, June 16, 1964, courtesy of Brian Fulton.

33. "Jane Butzner Jacobs Writes About Status of Cities: Ex-Tribune Writer Authors Second Book," *Scr Trib*, May 5, 1969, J. I. & Kay Butzner Papers.

34. "Bess R. Butzner, Richmond, Va.," obituary, *Morning Press* (Bloomsburg, PA), Mar. 30, 1981, J. I. & Kay Butzner Papers.

35. Dr. John Decker Butzner III, Jane's nephew, interviews by the author; "50th Reunion, Central High School, Class of January 1933"; James K. Jacobs, interviews; Arlene Swartz, interviews.

36. Group photo of fiftieth reunion attendees and spouses, Jacobs Papers; "Jeanne Madden Martin, Former Film Star, Dies," *Scr Times*, Jan. 16, 1989, courtesy of Norma Reese; Jean Patterson Nesbit's address on back of envelope, Jacobs Papers; "Florence C. Kane," obituary, *Scr Trib*, Mar. 23, 2000, courtesy of Norma Reese; "50th Reunion, Central High School, Class of January 1933."

37. Joseph X. Flannery, "Ex-Resident's Book Lumps City with Wales, Sicily and Spain," *Scr Times*, Aug. 12, 1984, courtesy of Brian Fulton; Joseph X. Flannery, "Books Can Have Impact of Bomb," *Scr Times*, Apr. 4, 1992, J. I. & K. Butzner Papers; Joseph X. Flannery, "Jane Jacobs, 81, Still Fights City Bigness, Urban Renewal," *Scr Times*, Jan. 18, 1998, courtesy of Brian Fulton; Joseph X. Flannery, "She Wrote the Book on City Planning," (Scr) *Times-Trib*, Feb. 17, 2001, courtesy of Brian Fulton.

38. Richard Leonori, interviews; City of Scranton Historical Architectural Review Board, "Downtown Scranton Landmarks and Historic Buildings," May 2016; Dr. Peter Cupple, interviews by the author.

39. Richard Leonori, interviews; Don Phillips, "Dispute Over Costly Railroad Park, Mall in Scranton Builds Steam," *Washington Post*, Nov. 24, 1991, courtesy of Nancy Bisignani; Guy Gugliotta, "Congressman Brings Home the Bacon with Steamtown," *Citizens' Voice* (Wilkes-Barre, PA), Dec. 8, 1993, courtesy of Nancy Bisignani.

40. Roberta Brandes Gratz and Norman Mintz, *Cities Back from the Edge: New Life for Downtown* (New York: John Wiley & Sons, 1998), 199–203; Jim Collins, "Do You Want a Mall? Let the Opponents Know," *Scr Times*, Jan. 18, 1987, courtesy of Nancy Bisignani; Phillips, "Dispute Over Costly Railroad Park, Mall in Scranton Builds Steam."

41. Dr. Peter Cupple, interviews; Jane Jacobs, letter to Tim McDowell, Office of Economic and Community Development, Scranton, Dec. 31, 1987, courtesy of AHA and Marywood University School of Architecture.

42. Jane Jacobs, letter to Tim McDowell, Dec. 31, 1987.

43. Ibid.

44. Mitch Grochowski, "Scranton-Bred Urban Theorist Denounces Concept Behind Lackawanna Ave. Mall," *Scrantonian Tribune*, Jan. 10, 1988, courtesy

of Nancy Bisignani; Jane Jacobs, letter to Jim Butzner, Mar. 9, [1988], J. I. & K. Butzner Papers.

45. Dr. Peter Cupple, interviews; Richard Leonori, interviews; Burgin Jacobs, interviews by the author.

46. "Historic Scranton-Downtown Scranton Landmark Buildings and Historic Districts," 2, available at www.scrantonpa.gov/HARB/Historic%20Scranton-Downtown%20Scranton%20Landmark%20Buildings%20and%20Historic%20Districts.pdf; Flannery, "Books Can Have Impact of Bomb."

47. Wenzel, *Scranton's Mayors*, 147–49, 160; Richard Leonori, interviews.

48. Gratz and Mintz, *Cities Back from the Edge*, 202; Wenzel, *Scranton's Mayors*, 162; Flannery, "She Wrote the Book on City Planning."

49. Larissa Code-Landry, interviews; Jane Jacobs, letter to Jim, Kay, and Ann Butzner, undated but shortly after Sept. 16, 1996, J. I. & K. Butzner Papers; Robert Kanigel, *Eyes on the Street* (New York: Knopf, 2016), 386–387.

50. Richard Leonori, interviews.

CONCLUSION *Learning from Scranton*

1. Richard Leonori, interviews.

2. *D&L*, 563.

3. June Carter Davies, "Jade Writes Potpourri," *The Villager* (Moscow, PA), May 11, 1994.

4. *D&L*, 535, 536; Harry T. Madden's 1921 campaign ad for Register of Wills in a Polish music program from Susan Pieroth's website: lackawannapagenweb.com.

5. Joseph X. Flannery, "She Wrote the Book on City Planning," (Scr) *Times-Trib*, Feb. 17, 2001, courtesy of Brian Fulton; Joseph X. Flannery, "Jane Jacobs, 81, Still Fights City Bigness, Urban Renewal," *Scr Times*, Jan. 18, 1998, courtesy of Brian Fulton; David Rider, "The Case for Ending the Toronto Megacity," *Toronto Star*, Jan. 15, 2015; Shawn Micallef, "Looking Back on the Birth of a Megacity—20 Years Later," May 6, 2017, www.thestar.com/news/gta/2017/05/06/looking-back-on-the-birth-of-a-megacity-20-years-later-micallef.html.

6. "Scranton Saves Its Life," *The Kiplinger Magazine*, Mar. 1950, 30; Mark Feeney, "City Sage."

7. Christopher Lehmann-Haupt, "The Death and Life of Economies" (review of *Economy of Cities*), *NY Times*, May 19, 1969, J. I. & K. Butzner Papers.

8. *D&L*, 315; *D&L*, 369; Jane Jacobs's Talk to the Green Building Council in Washington, D.C., Nov. 11, 2000, at the National Building Museum, upon receiving the Vincent Scully Prize (transcribed and titled by Chris Bradshaw, pednet discussion list, from a video recording by John Wetmore); Martin Luther King Jr., "Letter from a Birmingham Jail," Apr. 16, 1963.

9. "50th Reunion, Central High School, Class of January 1933"; "Murrel Loring," obituary, (Scr) *Times-Trib*, Dec. 14, 2008; "Marie Mansuy," obituary, (Scr) *Times-Trib*, Apr. 4, 2012.

10. Pennsylvania Department of Labor and Industry, "Top 50 Employers," 4th Quarter, 2017, available at www.workstats.dli.pa.gov/Documents/Top%2050/Lackawanna_County_Top_50.pdf; "Goodwill to Break Ground at North Scranton Junior High Next Week," (Scr) *Times-Trib*, Oct. 24, 2014; Norma Reese, interviews; Kathleen Bolus, "Historic Scranton School Transformed into Early Learning Center, College Apartments," (Scr) *Times-Trib*, Nov. 20, 2015; James Haggerty, "$23 Million Connell Building Downtown Project Back on Track," (Scr) *Times-Trib*, Apr. 14, 2010; Jim Lockwood, "Plan Calls for Remake of Old Button Factory in Scranton into Counseling Center," (Scr) *Times-Trib*, Jan. 27, 2018.

11. thetimes-tribune.com, May 29, 2020; *La Voz Latina* began in 2003 on N. Rebecca Ave in West Side, Scranton, and is a monthly with a Dunmore P.O. box; "Newspapers Merging in Wayne, Lackawanna, Pike Counties," www.wnep.com, Sept. 10, 2019.

12. Michael Hanley and Terilynn Brechtel, interviews by the author.

13. Michael Hanley and Terilynn Brechtel, interviews; Norma Reese, interviews; Boris Krawczeniuk, "Hanley Retiring as United Neighborhood Centers Leader," (Scr) *Times-Trib*, Apr. 10, 2018.

14. Pennsylvania Department of Labor and Industry, "Top 50 Employers," 3rd Quarter, 2015, available at www.workstats.dli.pa.gov/Documents/Top%2050%20Employers/lack_t50.pdf; Norma Reese, interviews.

15. Hitchcock, 288; Erin L. Nissley, "Local History: South Scranton Church Has Deep Community Roots," (Scr) *Times-Trib*, Dec. 4, 2016.

16. Covenant Presbyterian Church, "A Celebration of 150 Years of Presbyterian Presence in Scranton," c. 1998, courtesy of the LHS.

17. *D&L*, 180, 532.

18. *D&L*, 383.

19. Jane's Walk is a locally organized "walking conversation" by groups of neighbors in the tradition of Jane Jacobs that takes place around the world on the first weekend in May each year to celebrate Jane's birthday. In 2011, after learning that Jane Jacobs had grown up in a house a few blocks from his in Dunmore, architect John Cowder initiated and oversaw the placing of a plaque in Jane's honor on a brick pillar in front of 1712 Monroe Avenue; Maria Pane MacDonald and her Marywood University students, interviews by the author.

20. Mary Procter and Bill Matuszeski, *Gritty Cities* (Philadelphia: Temple University Press, 1978), 31.

21. *DAA*, 5.

22. *DAA*, 24–25, 34–37.

23. *DAA*, 7; this last sentence is an adaptation of Jane Jacobs's hopeful message ending her seminal masterpiece, *D&L*, 585: "But lively, diverse, intense cities contain the seeds of their own regeneration, with energy enough to carry over for problems and needs outside themselves."

Index